Deep History

The publisher gratefully acknowledges the generous support of the Ahmanson Foundation Humanities Endowment Fund of the University of California Press Foundation. The publisher also gratefully acknowledges the support of the Harvard Historical Series.

Deep History

The Architecture of Past and Present

Andrew Shryock
and Daniel Lord Smail

WITH

Timothy Earle

Gillian Feeley-Harnik

Felipe Fernández-Armesto

Clive Gamble

April McMahon

John C. Mitani

Hendrik Poinar

Mary C. Stiner

Thomas R. Trautmann

UNIVERSITY OF CALIFORNIA PRESS

Berkeley · Los Angeles · London

University of California Press, one of the most distinguished
university presses in the United States, enriches lives around
the world by advancing scholarship in the humanities, social
sciences, and natural sciences. Its activities are supported by
the UC Press Foundation and by philanthropic contributions
from individuals and institutions. For more information, visit
www.ucpress.edu.

University of California Press
Berkeley and Los Angeles, California

University of California Press, Ltd.
London, England

Library of Congress Cataloging-in-Publication Data

Shryock, Andrew.
  Deep history : the architecture of past and present /
Andrew Shryock and Daniel Lord Smail ; with Timothy
Earle . . . [et. al.].
      p. cm.
  Includes bibliographical references and index.
  ISBN 978-0-520-27028-2 (cloth : alk. paper)
    1. Human evolution.   2. Social evolution.
3. Anthropology, Prehistoric.   4. World history.
I. Smail, Daniel Lord.   II. Earle, Timothy K.   III. Title.
  GN281.S457   2011
  599.93'8—dc22   2011017773

Manufactured in the United States of America

20 19 18 17 16 15 14 13 12 11
10 9 8 7 6 5 4 3 2 1

In keeping with a commitment to support environmentally
responsible and sustainable printing practices, UC Press
has printed this book on Rolland Enviro100, a 100% post-
consumer fiber paper that is FSC certified, deinked, processed
chlorine-free, and manufactured with renewable biogas
energy. It is acid-free and EcoLogo certified.

Contents

Figures

Preface

All arguments about the past are shaped by rhetorical and narrative devices. It is not just an assessment of "the facts" that helps us decide whether a historical account is convincing: facts emerge as such, and acquire their power as evidence, within narrative structures. The story of an empire's rise or a nation's collapse may be filled with dates and textual sources, which can be right or wrong, reliable or dubious; but the story's integrity as history also depends on a deeper architecture of likenesses. Empires and nations, though they consist of millions of individuals who do not know each other, are often treated as if they were physical bodies. They are born, mature, and die in history books. They have (or appear to have) character traits; they make decisions, acquire friends and enemies, form and dissolve unions. They are compared, in countless ways, to persons, families, and bodies. At a certain level we know these likenesses are metaphorical, but doing without them is difficult. When the metaphors seep into everyday usage among historical actors, we can even say that they shape the evidence and events that historians choose to write about. Metaphors determine what goes into a historical argument, what is left out, and how new forms of historical argumentation can be developed. What matters to good history writing is to develop a knowing relationship with the narrative motifs and metaphors that we employ.

This is a book about the deep history of humankind, a domain of inquiry that extends millions of years into the past. Although it might seem the perfect subject matter for historians, this vast time-space was left out of most historical writing almost as soon as it was discovered. Humans have always been interested in their origins, but the deep past, as typically understood by modern historians, is never deeper than antiquity and is sometimes positioned in an even more recent era. Awareness of a time before antiquity became acute only in the nineteenth century, as the Darwinian revolution displaced the widely shared belief that the world was only 6,000 years old. The new age that suddenly opened up before Eden, dividing the human past into long and short chronologies, soon became the object of systematic study. Yet deep time seemed impervious to the methods of conventional historical writing, a state of affairs captured in the word coined to describe this newly remote past: *prehistory.*

As this volume demonstrates, the assumptions that initially conspired to mark off prehistory as a time before history are still very much with us. At stake is a methodology based on written evidence, along with a commitment to a powerful set of narrative motifs, most of them grounded in notions of progress and human mastery over nature. Together these commitments have made the deep past an unsettling place for academic historians. Thanks to the industrious work habits of archaeologists and paleoanthropologists, prehistory today is carefully mapped, meticulously dated, and creatively analyzed. In recent decades, discoveries about the evolution of humans and related hominid species have been accumulating thick and fast. But for all that, the deep human past remains curiously off limits to many anthropologists and historians, even to those interested in the big questions of what it means to be human. In fact, the chronological domain of the research explicitly described as historical has narrowed dramatically in scope over the past century, even as our knowledge of human prehistory has expanded. Most historical research is now concentrated in the centuries that followed the global expansion of the European powers, in times vaguely described as "modern," in societies described as colonial and postcolonial.

This volume grows out of our discomfort with this trend and our desire not only to explain it but also to create alternatives to it. We do not think that the systematic neglect of deep history among historians and anthropologists—two fields that make the human past their business—is a product of ignorance or disdain. Nor is it a simple byproduct of specialization. It arises instead from the architecture of historical arguments, from the narrative motifs and analogies preferred by the writers of history. A century ago, the simplistic notions of progress and the misapplications of Darwinian evolutionary theory that dominated history and anthropology conspired to make all premodern civilizations inconsequential except, perhaps, as living evidence of Europe's primitive past and a way of understanding its rise to global superiority. All that has changed. Historians and anthropologists today routinely invoke a new set of patterns, such as diaspora, subalternity, hegemony, resistance, commodification, and agency, to characterize the intricate feedback patterns that accompanied the emergence of the modern world system. The triumph of the global perspective shows how, through concentrated effort, the very patterns of historical writing can be transformed. In this transformation, the formerly irrelevant is made intensely relevant not through a new set of facts but through a new set of intellectual devices for describing the arc of change. Yet the very success of the global paradigm has revealed the continuing absence of the patterns and forms that might allow us to recuperate the deep human past.

The goal of this book is to offer a set of tools—patterns, frames, metaphors—for the telling of deep histories. These include kinshipping, fractal replication, exchange, hospitality, networks, trees, extensions, scalar integration, and the spiraling patterns of feedback intrinsic to all coevolutionary processes. Skillfully deployed, these frames and the narratives and evidence they create offer a dynamic of connectedness that can render deep time accessible to modern scholarship, thereby bringing the long ages of human history together in a single story. In offering these analytical innovations, we do not insist on the jettisoning of narrative patterns that describe histories of origin, birth, or decline. Instead, we want to call attention to how these narrative devices, sometimes unwittingly, evoke transitions from nature to civilization, from biology to culture, from traditional society to modernity. These devices may work in a limited array of circumstances. As general means for the relating of deep history, however, they are highly problematic. They tend to postulate an age-old, unchanging, or primal humanity that is awakened from its slumbers by a stimulus external to this "state of nature." The external force might be culture, language, civilization, or even climate, but the creationist roots of this imagery are not hard to discern. The move from nature to culture, from prehistory to history, brings to mind the clay that is given life by the breath of God. In almost all cases, this is bad science, and it is equally bad history. There are better ways to account for change.

The editors of this volume, Andrew Shryock and Daniel Lord Smail, belong by disciplinary training to the tribe of humanists and social scientists. Even so, we share the fascination for the deep past that animates our colleagues in archaeology, human evolutionary biology, historical linguistics, genomics, and primatology. Concerned by an apparent erosion of historical interest in eras predating the modern, and inspired by a belief that history could be written on much larger scales, we invited a number of colleagues to join us in January 2008 for a workshop at the Radcliffe Institute in Cambridge, Massachusetts, to begin discussions of how we might develop a new architecture for human history. In May 2009 a nucleus of authors returned to the Radcliffe Institute for another workshop to sketch out the chapters that appear in this volume. We decided early on not to produce single-authored chapters. Though this approach would have been more efficient and certainly less time-consuming, it would not have allowed us to achieve our aim of transcending specialization. Instead, we grouped ourselves by theme and tackled our subjects collectively, generating chapters that are genuinely transdisciplinary. By dissolving the monographic voice and developing a collaborative one in its place, we sought to escape the untidy polyphony that can mar collections of this kind. We very much hope that readers will hear unexpected intellectual harmonies in this volume. This effect is the result of many conversations, robust editing, and tremendous goodwill on the part of all involved in this project.

Our debts of gratitude go, first and foremost, to the Radcliffe Institute for hosting two wonderfully productive seminars, and especially to Phyllis Strimling and Allyson Black-Foley, who handled all the arrangements for the workshops with impeccable attention and efficiency. The participants at the first workshop included Ann Gibbons, Sarah Blaffer Hrdy, Christopher Loveluck, Michael McCormick, Gitanjali Surendran, Christina Warinner, and David Sloan Wilson; their enduring influence has shaped the volume in many important ways. Colleagues and students too numerous to name here have read proposals or chapters and helped with conceptual issues and references; we thank all of them for their enthusiasm as well as their words of advice, caution, and correction. Jennifer Gordon helped us put the illustrations in order, and Mary Birkett designed several of the book's figures. Niels Hooper, Eric Schmidt, and Erika Büky offered wise editorial counsel. Finally, we are deeply appreciative of our entire author team, whose patience, thoughtfulness, and dedication have been exemplary. Our labors have been shared in the most profound way.

We gratefully acknowledge a publication subvention provided by the Department of History at Harvard University, as well as financial contributions provided by the Arthur F. Thurnau Charitable Trust at the University of Michigan.

A Note on Dates

One of the obstacles to bringing the deep past into human history lies in the diversity of customs for reckoning time and the precision that we can bring to the task. European historians have been using calendrical dating at least sporadically since Bede (d. 735) wrote his treatises on the reckoning of time, and they have used dates consistently from the twelfth or thirteenth century onward. The time revolution of the 1860s, which decisively broke the grip of the short chronology of the Judeo-Christian calendar, made deep human time a historical reality. Even so, it was a reality that remained undatable for at least a century. Instead, archaeologists and paleoanthropologists sorted early human sites, civilizations, fossils, and artifacts into chronological bins based on practices of relative or period dating that did not require absolute time scales. The edges of the bins were defined either by geological horizons (Miocene, Pleistocene, Holocene) or changes in the dominant technologies (Paleolithic, Neolithic, metal). The latter were further subdivided into coarse gradations (Lower, Middle, and Upper Paleolithic in the case of chipped-stone technologies) and even finer gradations within them (e.g. Acheulean, Magdalenian), in much the way that social scientists might speak of the interwar period (1918–40) as a subdivision of the modern era.

Nowadays, the edges of the bins are also defined using absolute dates. The dates may change either because of improvements in estimating ages by scientific means or because the contents of a chronological period are no longer compatible with models of change and development. Similar things happen when European historians stretch the edges of the nineteenth century so as to make "the long nineteenth century," a terminology that has allowed them to conveniently bracket a historical era running from 1789 to 1914.

The use of the word *Paleolithic*, by convention, has been largely confined to European contexts. With reference to other sites, notably in Africa, archaeologists have continued to use plain English (Early Stone Age, Middle Stone Age, Late Stone Age) rather than Latin neologisms. Because the tools and technological systems on different continents do not necessarily overlap in time, and certainly did not develop in lockstep, it is particularly difficult to correlate evolutionary developments across continents. Finally, the chronology of human speciation, which has become increasingly precise thanks to better dating techniques and to genetic modeling, does not coincide neatly with dates associated with tool types and technological transitions. This is because human physiology and behavior can evolve more or less independently of one another.

When absolute time scales are used for dates, some people specify years "BP," or "before the present," the technical expression developed for radiometric dating. Others use the more casual initials "ya," for "years ago," which is consistent with the concept of BP. Because it is tedious to write out "million years" and "thousand years," these expressions are commonly abbreviated using "M" or "k" (for example, the earliest stone tools currently known date to around 2.6 Ma). Absolute dating, because it is calendrical, bears some similarity to the Common Era (or Anno Domini) system used by historians of the past two thousand years. An obvious difference between CE (Common Era) and BP is that the former counts up toward the present, whereas the latter counts down. In addition, dating systems in the archaeological literature covering the past ten thousand years or so often alternate between BCE and BP. The existence of a two-thousand-year gap between BCE and BP dates—an event that took place 10,000 BP is dated 8,000 BCE—requires a certain agility on the part of readers, somewhat like converting between the metric and Anglo-American systems of measurement.

The chronology employed by students of deep human time depends on where they work and the intellectual tribe to which they belong. Like any speakers of dialect, paleoanthropologists can easily move in and out of different conversations. To historians and some anthropologists who are used to dealing with calendrical dating, however, it can seem odd that earlier fields do not use the apparent convenience of absolute dating more often. The reason for this is that the fields of paleontology, paleoanthropology, and archaeology developed their chronological systems long before the many innovations in radiometric dating in the 1950s that made absolute dating possible. Period dating, in point of fact, is quite useful. European historians have never ceased using words like *ancient, medieval,* and *modern,* let alone phrases like *the long nineteenth century,* to bracket interesting cultural units. In considering the structure of historical arguments, some readers might find it convenient to assume that the designations of the Lower, Middle, and Upper Paleolithic are roughly analogous with the terms *ancient, medieval,* and *modern.* Translating the terms in this way gives practitioners in one field a rough sense of how to navigate the other.

Period dating remains essential, moreover, because no paleoanthropological dating technique is ever wholly secure, even when its physical or sample requirements are met. Dates derived from the analysis of tree rings soon showed that early radiocarbon dating for some periods was consistently biased. Analysis of trapped gases in fine annual layers in ice cores from Greenland has shown us that the ratios of the different isotopes of atmospheric carbon, ratios that are so essential to radiocarbon dating, are not constant but vary in different periods. Humans' greater fuel use over time is partly to blame, but natural variations in atmospheric carbon occurred even in remote periods. Calibration curves, which are being constantly updated, allow labs to generate ever more accurate dates. Even so, radiocarbon dating does not offer the literal precision provided either by human calendars or by the natural calendars embedded in the growth rings of trees, in coral, or in the very fine layers that may form at regular intervals at the bottom of lakes or oceanic basins. Radiocarbon dating describes a *probable* date, expressed in intervals of centuries or millennia and hedged about with a margin of error. What is more, the technique is accurate only within the last 50,000 years. Advances in optically stimulated luminescence (OSL) have extended dating on sediments that contain artifacts back to 120,000 years, but the age estimates have large error margins, as do those produced by electronic spin resonance, another form of radiometric dating that can be used on dental enamel dating from as far back as 2 Ma. The techniques for dating necessarily vary as we look further back in time, and the error margins and chronological intervals typically grow larger.

In this book, we have followed the custom of using geological periods (e.g., Pleistocene) when referring to climate, geology, or environ-

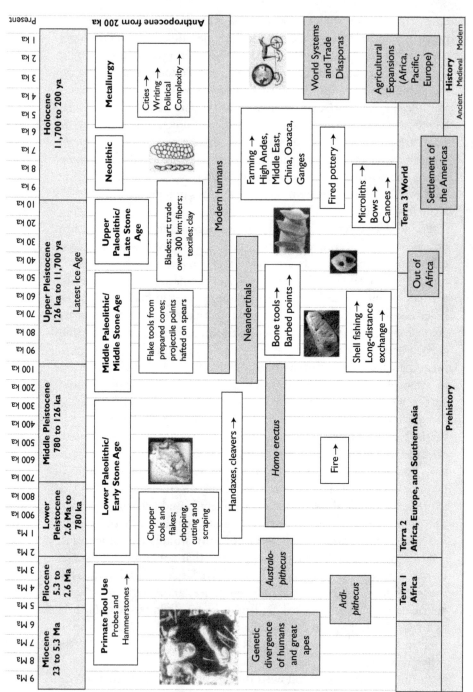

FIGURE I. Dates in deep time.

ment, and archaeological periods (e.g., Paleolithic) when referring to human societies. Figure 1 presents a concordance of dates following different disciplinary styles, referring to periods mentioned in this book. Representing human time, of course, is a bit like representing the solar system: the spans are so vast that absolute scales cannot hope to represent the information in a readable way. For this reason, the figure adopts a log scale to represent time; that is to say, the time intervals represented on the X axis grow progressively larger the further back in time you go. Where the information itself is concerned, there is still much room for disagreement. Every new discovery is capable of pushing the known boundaries of important evolutionary developments to the more recent or the more ancient end of several time scales. Researchers at work on questions of human evolution must conceive of time and temporal boundaries with a pencil in one hand and an eraser in the other, constantly refining their assessments according to new technologies of measurement as well as new data. This is not to say that we know nothing about when things actually happened in the distant past, only that we are talking about events and processes that transpired in very deep time, for which crisp dating is seldom reasonable or even possible to expect.

PART ONE

Problems and Orientations

CHAPTER I

Introduction

ANDREW SHRYOCK AND DANIEL LORD SMAIL

History is a curiously fragmented subject. In the conventional disciplinary structure of academia, the study of the human past is scattered across a number of fields, notably history and anthropology but also folklore, museum studies, philology, and area-studies programs. Together, these fields constitute a dense layer cake of time. The bottom layer, by far the thickest, is grounded in deep time. The deep time of a discipline is not a specific date range or era: it is simply the earliest period to which the discipline pays attention. Among archaeologists and human evolutionary biologists, deep time is represented by the paleoanthropology of the simple societies of the Paleolithic, from the earliest known stone tools (dated to 2.6 Ma) to the origins of agriculture. Among historians, the deep time of the discipline is located in Greco-Roman antiquity. Though the Paleolithic and the ancient world are dramatically offset in absolute time, each provides the bedrock that supports disciplinary narratives. The middle layers of the cake are given over to the archaeology of complex societies and, among historians, to the study of "early modern" societies. On the very top is a veneer of modern frosting. Seldom more than a few centuries deep, this upper layer is what attracts the interest of most fields of contemporary historical research and almost all fields of cultural anthropology.

The entire span of time may come together in teaching: in the grand sweep of general anthropology, say, or in survey courses of world history. In their own research, however, most scholars limit their work to a single chronological layer and feel ill-equipped to move beyond this layer. In the great age of historico-anthropological writing of the nineteenth century, authors like Auguste Comte, Karl Marx, Herbert Spencer, Lewis Henry Morgan, and Edward Tylor ranged across vast reaches of human history, producing conjectural arguments characterized by spectacular vision and very little in the way of hard evidence. Today, the pattern is reversed. As methods of analysis improve and knowledge of the recent and deep past rapidly accumulates, the division of intellectual labor has become exceedingly precise. Conjecture and grand vision have given way to hyperspecialization, an intensified focus on ever-smaller units of time and space, and a pervasive reluctance to build analytical frames that can articulate deep history and the recent past.

A century ago, modern historiography was built on the scaffolding of progress, a story line rooted in the rise of civilization and the break with nature that supposedly took place some five thousand to six thousand years ago. This narrative enshrined a triumphalist account of human achievement. In the words of an observer from the 1920s, history describes "the processes by which the chaotic chatter of anthropoid apes has been organized in the wonderful fabric of human speech." It offers a panoramic vision of man "in every stage of his long climb up from his feeble and brutish beginnings."[1] The imagination of the age was suffused with sentiments that today seem almost unbearably trite. Cringing at such naiveté, we congratulate ourselves on having purged our anthropologies and histories of this exuberant evolutionism. But the congratulations are premature. The belief in human exceptionalism that drove earlier models of history still shapes narratives of progress, which are now told using the vocabulary of political modernization, economic development, and cultural emancipation from past prejudices. When telling these tales, we sometimes reverse the moral charges of the narrative of progress. We celebrate the merits of the simple and traditional and note the obvious dangers in the modern and complex. This stopgap solution does not eliminate the underlying problem. It leaves in place the idea that human evolution (or the emergence of culture, or the growth of historical consciousness) entails, for good or ill, an ever-increasing mastery of culture over nature, of cultivation over mere subsistence, of civilization over mere habitation. Seeing the humanity of others means recognizing their historical movement toward various forms of mastery, even if the movement is modest and still in its formative stages.

In the wake of the Darwinian revolution, the problem of human origins was transformed from a matter of speculative philosophy into a scientific research program. This transition, which required a radical reassessment of the older, biblical cosmology, was initially made intelligible by linking it to ideas of progress that had proliferated during the Enlightenment. Over the course of the twentieth century, which witnessed two world wars and the collapse of the European colonial order, historians and anthropologists grew increasingly skeptical of Enlightenment ideas, and Victorian-style social evolutionism was rejected as a justification for racism, class privilege, and global imperialism. In cleansing historical and cultural analysis of their nineteenth-century ideological baggage, most of the high modern (and postmodern) versions of cultural anthropology and history turned their backs on the deep human past, leaving problems of evolution to the archaeologists, paleontologists, and historical linguists.

The goal of this book is to remove the barriers that isolate deep histories from temporally shallow ones. These barriers have a complex history of their own, but they need not dominate future studies of the human past. Moving them aside solves multiple intellectual and political problems, and this renovation project is not as difficult as it might at first seem. The necessary analytical tools already exist. Some, like genetic mapping and radiocarbon dating, are recent innovations; others, like genealogies, bodily analogies, and predictive modeling, are older than written history itself. The gap between deep and shallow history, we believe, can easily be bridged; indeed, great efforts must be exerted simply to keep the gap in place. What motivates these efforts? How did they develop? And why do so many scholars think it is important to keep prehistory in its place?

TIME'S STRAITJACKET

The fragmentation of historical time is not inherent to the study of the past. It was produced by highly contingent historical trends that were triggered and amplified by the time revolution of the 1860s, when the short chronology, which envisioned a world roughly 6,000 years old, was abandoned as a geological truth, and human history began to stretch back into a limitless time before Eden.[2] Before the 1860s, the human and the natural sciences had constituted a single field of inquiry. This field was framed by religious tradition and organized in accord with the universalizing framework of the Book of Genesis, in which history and geology are coeval. Knowledge production in all the societies of the Jewish, Christian, and Muslim worlds was contained within this totalizing model of creation.

Following the time revolution in Europe, however, this unified vision of human history fell apart. The chronology of the past fractured at precisely the point where human prehistory was being grafted onto ancient and modern history, which now seemed chronologically recent. By all appearances, a history long beholden to scriptural understandings of time was incapable of absorbing the fact of deep time. It is not difficult to find nineteenth-century historians who circled the wagons around the short chronology and declared the new, bottomless time to be anathema. Because respected scientists such as Georges Cuvier and Louis Agassiz refused to accept the new timeline, it is hardly surprising that many rank-and-file historians also proved skeptical—or, in some cases, openly resistant.[3] But reaction to the time revolution was generally more complex. A short chronology is not, in fact, intrinsic to the cosmology of the religions of the Near East. The authors of Genesis measured time as a succession of life spans and genealogies; the New Testament and Qur'an are devoid of what we would now call calendar dates. The short chronology was in fact an artifice retroactively imposed upon scriptural traditions. This retroactive dating occurred as generations of Jewish, Christian, and Muslim chroniclers struggled to bring sacred texts into alignment with the solar and lunar calendars they had created to keep track of ritual obligations and to record the movement of creation through time. Ironically, it was the careful work of premodern and early modern historians, not the teachings of the prophets, that gave Abrahamic chronology its brittle precision, a level of detail that could date the first day of creation to the eve of Sunday, October 23, 4004 BC. This brittleness would cause it to snap when placed under stress by the intellectual trauma of the time revolution.

In a larger sense, however, the demise of the short chronology made no difference to practicing historians. In the decades following the Darwinian turn, there were historians who looked with curiosity at the strange new terrain on the other side of Eden, and, later, historical visionaries who advocated for a reunion of deep time with history.[4] Yet the gap grew so wide that it became nearly unbridgeable. Lacking written texts, practitioners in the emergent fields of archaeology and paleoanthropology had to develop new methods of inquiry designed to tease meaning out of scattered evidence and refractory sources. The new discipline of history, in turn, adhered to the very chronology that historians had fashioned for themselves in their vain attempts to apply a chronology to the Bible. As later chapters show, the questions that historians of the nineteenth century asked about the origins of human languages, races, agriculture, cities, and nations were often defined in specific relation to the Book of Genesis. This is hardly surprising. The European scholars best suited to become academic historians when the discipline arose in the nineteenth century were heavily invested in intellectual traditions anchored in a biblical worldview, to which a long pedagogical tradition had added Greek and Roman learning. It is hard to imagine the works of such luminaries as Leopold von Ranke or Jacob Burckhardt outside this milieu.

Yet neither inertia nor the prestige of older intellectual traditions can explain how time got bound up in the straitjacket created by disciplinary history at the beginning of the twentieth century. The decision to truncate history was a deliberate intellectual and epistemological move, bound up with the fate of the discipline itself. By the late nineteenth century, the proud new discipline of history was shouldering its way into the academy; and to justify its presence, the field adopted as its signature methodology the analysis of written documents. "No documents, no history," as Charles Langlois and Charles Seignobos declared in their 1898 manual of historical study, probably the most important of its kind.[5] The methodology they advocated sought to assess human intentions as revealed in textual evidence. Their peers used the manual to train students in the art of ferreting out the truth that lies behind the creative omissions and downright fabrications intrinsic to historical documentation. Humanity's deeper history had no documents of this kind. This critical absence of data made a deep history of humanity methodologically unthinkable.

Oddly enough, this epistemological package was also gradually accepted by cultural anthropologists, whose chronologies tend to contract whenever they attempt to historicize their discipline. The classic instance is *Europe and the People without History*, in which Eric Wolf tried to pry anthropology out of the ethnographic present in which he believed it was hopelessly stuck.[6] To bring "the people without history" into the domain of proper history, Wolf portrayed European expansion as a global interaction of human populations organized by kin-ordered, tributary, and capitalist modes of production. Wolf was not especially interested in how the kin-ordered and tributary modes had emerged in deep time; instead, he wanted to know how these modes of production were taken into a world system dominated by capitalism. As a result, although Wolf's historical analysis is based on social forms that developed sequentially over tens of thousands of years, it is limited to roughly the last five centuries. The evidence he used to historicize the world's ahistorical peoples would satisfy the criteria devised by Langlois and Seignobos, and Wolf was unapologetic about the resulting Eurocentrism of his project. What one learns from "the study of ethnohistory," he noted, "is . . . the more ethnohistory we know, the more 'their' history and 'our' history emerge as part of the same history."[7]

Wolf's intent was not to cut ethnography off from its deep historical roots but rather to open it up spatially. Yet his eager embrace of a history based on textual evidence led immediately to temporal foreshortening, and his five-hundred-year frame is in fact vast when compared to the studies his work inspired. It is now virtually axiomatic that any anthropological approach advertising itself as "historical" will focus on the recent past. Its subject matter will be modern or postmodern, colonial or postcolonial. Rarely is this focus perceived as narrow. It is seen as vital, and engagement with events and societies located before European expansion, before textual evidence, is often considered politically irrelevant unless such events and societies can be interpreted—and some poststructural theorists would argue that they can *only* be interpreted—through intellectual lenses crafted during the great shift to colonial and postcolonial modernity. Otherwise they are best left to classicists, medievalists, and Orientalists. If the past in question predates the emergence of literate state societies, it falls under the jurisdiction of archaeologists and biological anthropologists, whose methods of inquiry are scientific, not historical. This pattern is visible across the academy, and attempts to disturb it quickly generate resistance on all sides.

MAN AGAINST NATURE

Why does disciplinary history, as a set of methods and motivations, so predictably conform to this epistemological grid? The blame lies with a commitment to human exceptionalism, a sensibility that survived the Darwinian revolution largely intact. As creation gave way to nature, the assumption that humans are part of nature, and that human systems are natural systems, slowly took hold in the biological and behavioral sciences. Among historians and cultural anthropologists, however, the equation of cultural systems with natural ones has never been easy, nor has it been easily historicized. Both difficulties, we believe, are related to the lingering power of the metaphors that dominated history writing in the

19th cent

nineteenth century. The human story, in this worldview, is centered on the conquest of nature and the birth of political society. A passage from one of the works of the great French historian and archivist Jules Michelet (d. 1874) captures the logic perfectly: "When the world was born there began a war that will last until the world's end, and this is the war of man against nature, of the spirit against the flesh, of liberty against determinism. History is nothing but the story of this endless conflict."[8]

The claim made here was hardly new. The Judeo-Christian tradition has long celebrated human stewardship over nature. What gives Michelet's remark special poignancy is the fact that, even in his own day, there was a growing awareness that geological time was far older than human time and that human time itself might be deeper than hitherto imagined. A quarter of a century later, human time was known to be long indeed, and by the last quarter of the nineteenth century, the history of humanity threatened to merge insensibly with natural history. In this changing context of time, the need to mark the break between animal and human took on special urgency. Michelet, whose opinions on this matter reflected those of his day, had already divined the solution to the conundrum. Animals live in harmony with nature. Humans, by contrast, are at war with nature. In the pious bromides of early-twentieth-century science writing, evident in a 1912 work immodestly called *The Conquest of Nature,* "barbaric man is called a child of Nature with full reason. He must accept what Nature offers. But civilized man is the child grown to adult stature, and able in a manner to control, to dominate—if you please to conquer—the parent."[9] In this act of emancipation, in this shift from passivity to agency, history itself was created.

The conquest of nature, in turn, was tightly linked to the origins of political society. In the social thought of the eighteenth century, the natural unit had been the family—or, for some, the solitary individual. Everything humans had built on top of this natural substrate, and especially the newly insistent nation-states of nineteenth-century Europe, could be treated as historical artifices and therefore beyond nature. The history that came into being, and loudly proclaimed its own objectivity, was in many ways an apology for nationalism.[10] The new history was for the nation-states of late nineteenth-century Europe what the Torah was for the kingdom of David: a genealogy (fictitious or otherwise) designed to anchor the imagined community in the past, give it legitimacy, and lend weight to its grievances and aspirations. It is thanks to the nation-building enterprise, in fact, that we have medieval European history, for few nations (with tragic and bloody exceptions, including

Napoleonic France and Hitler's Germany) sought to identify explicitly with the empires or city-states of antiquity. If the task of history was to provide the ontogeny of a single nation, that is to say a description of how the nation was born and came, through many travails, to adulthood, there was little use for Greece or Rome—outside Greece and Italy, of course—except in the lingering sense that classical antiquity belonged to a privileged Western heritage that justified the superiority of Occidental empires. Even less use was there for the periods and social forms that predated the ancient world, except to provide a holding tank for all that was not civilized or part of the modern story—what Michel-Rolf Trouillot calls "the savage slot," a time and space set aside for the world's backward and non-Occidental peoples.[11] As subsequent chapters show, this worldview was heavily influenced by the ideas of Georg Wilhelm Friedrich Hegel, a philosopher of history who, like his near-contemporary, Michelet, saw the human story as one of hard-won progress, as a steady movement out of a state of nature into political agency and awareness.

In the twentieth century, disciplinary history began to roam well beyond the limits of the nation-state. Historians took up the history of ideas, civilizations, and economies. In addition, disciplinary history began to tackle subjects rigorously excluded from the history of nations: family, women, peasants, workers, and eventually the non-West, nonwhites, the alternatively sexual, and the differently abled. Yet history written in the Hegelian mode has had the last laugh. The history of the disempowered could have proceeded by denying agency to white male Western heteronormative political actors, the God-substitutes excised from history by Charles Darwin. But it did not. Instead, the new history has proceeded by attributing agency to subalterns located in every branch of the human family. The universal attribution of agency has become a recipe for historical research, as scholars, trapped in Hegelian logic, create new subjects by incorporating ever more voices.

Politically, the consequences of this trend have been enabling. Where the straitjacketing of time is concerned, however, the consequences have been otherwise. In the hopes of granting speech and agency to those on the receiving end of European history, we have transformed the world's subalterns into characters of a suspiciously uniform type. The very people whose inclusion was meant to be a triumph of diversity have been homogenized by theory. The accelerating pace of agency attribution, moreover, has led many into the mistaken belief that agency itself is a creation of modernity. Hegel had attributed agency to progressive males all the way back to the origins of the state. This was the whole point of his formulation: to replace divine providence and the guiding hand of God with the far-seeing vision of wise leaders. Hegel, in other words, never escaped the instincts of sacred history; he just knocked the agent in chief down a peg. But here is the rub: the extension of agency to modern subalterns is meaningless if modernity itself was created by the powerful men of the past. To evade this paradox, one could deny Hegel's bias and extend agency to *all* past actors. But what if this gesture is practically impossible? What can one do if the vast majority of premodern historical sources were generated by the very men whose thoughts and deeds they typically celebrate? Given this paradox—a paradox that historians generated for themselves by adopting for their discipline a *textual* methodology—it is enormously tempting to pretend that the remote past belongs to nature, to a cultural reality that cannot be fully historicized, and thereafter to ignore it.

As a result of this bind, the great questions that used to cut through the layer cake of time are not being asked. Instead, historians and cultural anthropologists turn their attention to the world around them, treating it as a secular creation even newer, empirically, than the sacred world of Genesis. In recent decades, the short chronology of disciplinary history has continued to shrink. As measured by professorships, course offerings, dissertation topics, and publications, the weight of knowledge production in cultural anthropology and history is now solidly centered in the centuries after 1750, as it is in the other human sciences.[12] One measure of the erosion of historical time can be found in the tendency among historians to add metaphors of birth, origins, or roots to book titles and arguments. Use of this metaphorical complex has accelerated in the last two decades. If we could track the average birth date proposed in this burgeoning array of titles, it would in all likelihood be moving closer and closer to the present day.

THE GROUNDS FOR MAKING A DEEP HISTORY

The prospects for a reunion of the short and long chronologies within the human sciences seem rather grim, and it would be simple enough to frame this volume as a nostalgic story of loss and what might have been. Yet now, 150 years after the time revolution, the elements and frames necessary for writing a deep history of humankind may finally be falling into place. The field of big history, led by David Christian and Fred Spier, has already shown how the wholeness of time can be woven into a compelling historical narrative.[13] Thanks in part to the biological turn, scholars in all fields are now feeling the pull of humanity's deep past. They fret about chronological constraints and issue calls for "evolutionary politics," "evolutionary economics," or evolutionary studies of the law.[14] These approaches hold promise; however, many of them have adopted a form of analysis centered on the postulate of an evolved human psychology that shapes behavior in the present day. The logic deployed is distinctly reminiscent of the logic of the orthodox, Augustinian version of Christian theology, which also proposes the existence of an abiding human psychological condition that has profound latter-day effects: original sin. Though the neo-Augustinian trajectory of evolutionary psychology evokes the past, it does not provide a history. The two are very different things. When the past is simply a repository of the "natural," it is not a historical past: it is instead a mythical or cosmological past, providing yet another mirror in which humanity can search for its own reflection. Such an understanding of the past has no room for contingency, no room for change, no way to understand the path-dependent nature of variation within systems.

It is difficult, though, to blame the purveyors of these models. Providing the missing history is the job of anthropologists and historians, not psychologists or behavioral social scientists. The chapters in this volume are designed to supply the historical frames that are, for now, absent in the new evolutionary approaches. Despite the apparent hegemony of Darwinian evolution among the educated classes, a great deal of unfinished business remains. The soft social sciences and the humanities have never really come to terms intellectually with human evolution. Early attempts to bring Darwinian models into social thought produced Victorian disasters. But the accumulation of knowledge about the human past has become so impressive that a rapprochement is needed. The natural-selection paradigm has enabled us to generate highly nuanced understandings not only of how the hominin lineage has evolved but also of how human social forms and cultural capacities have developed over long stretches of time. Many of the analytical techniques employed by archaeologists, evolutionary ecologists, and paleoanthropologists can in fact be applied to ancient and contemporary societies alike. In the anthropological sciences since the nineteenth century, the study of kinship and language has linked the short and long chronologies, and new fields, such as genomics, now allow analysts to move across great distances in time and space, following lines of genetic transmission that link living humans to ancestral populations. Absolute and relative dating techniques that first emerged in the 1950s have become increasingly precise and reliable, as have the transregional chronologies and models of long-term trends (from the development of toolkits to the transcontinental migrations of early humans) that have been worked out using these dating techniques. In short, the means to reconnect short and long histories have been in place for many years.

Meanwhile, historians have gradually abandoned the idea that the only thing to do with written sources is to sift through them in search of the motives and intentions of their authors. The skills necessary for data mining (and for reading between the lines) are now routinely taught. That unabashedly fictional sources can count as legitimate historical data is widely accepted as self-evident; few historians today find it necessary to defend the notion that literary texts serve as repositories of social logics.[15] Histories can be written from every type of trace, from the memoir to the bone fragment and the blood type. Moreover, the ongoing merger of history and social science has produced an intellectual world in which most scholars realize that intentions are social products, and the grounds for their production are largely beyond the control of individuals and their desires. In this realization, the methodological distinctions that once separated history from anthropology and archaeology all but disappear.

Yet translation problems remain. Scholars who study the deep past—let us call them *paleohistorians* for convenience—face numerous challenges when presenting their work to scholars who focus on more recent periods. These challenges include the unhelpful assumption that the deep past is best understood in relation to a fixed human nature or universal behavioral tendencies (such as "economizing," "rational choice," or "kin selection"). Also troublesome is the belief that certain cultural forms, such as "ethnicity," are quintessentially modern and that similar processes of group identification are not found in the past. Paleohistorians do daily battle with the assumption that human prehistory is marked by long periods of behavioral fixity and cultural stasis, not variety and change. In addition to these problems of misunderstanding, paleohistorians contend with difficulties inherent to their own practice. The amount of material stuff available for analysis decreases dramatically as they move back in time, a trend that generates both recognition and bafflement. Often, it is not clear what ancient human artifacts signify. Is the design scratched into a piece of bone "symbolic"? Of what? Might it be a product of boredom? Might the symbol be apparent to us, but perhaps not to the maker of this ancient object?

Also, paleohistorians must be alert to powerful notions of progress and primitivism that color their work and determine how their findings are received and put to use in wider intellectual circles. The idea that the deep human past is best treated as a variant of biological science or natural history, and that evolution describes a strictly biological process rather than a social or cultural one, is another problem that arises in the field. Yet even developments as basic as bipedalism, hairless bodies, or concealed ovulation are implicated in complex assumptions about social life. Finally, paleohistory needs narrative and reconstructive storytelling. However much we may complain about the coercive, streamlining qualities of historical narratives, they do convey information in vivid and compelling ways. Paleohistory attracts the talents of numerous science writers: this fact reflects both the mass appeal of the field and its inaccessibility and overspecialization. A judicious use of narrative is needed to bring paleohistorians into dialogue with social science and humanities scholars.

The histories we present in this volume are meant to resolve some of these translation problems. They draw on the resources of all fields of history and anthropology to present a broad-spectrum history of hominins—that is, of humans and their immediate ancestors. For reasons of convenience, this history begins about 2.6 million years ago, when our hominin ancestors began to use tools that would later enter the archaeological record; but we also situate human bodies and social forms in the larger context of primate evolution, using genetic, bone, and behavioral evidence to extend our analytical reach back 6 to 8 million years, when our ancestors diverged from the ancestors of modern-day chimps and bonobos. Despite its immense time depth, the ensuing history is surprisingly similar, in substance, form, and trajectory, to the histories framed by the short chronology, with these exceptions. First, earlier periods feel stretched out by comparison to later ones, and the study of deep history emphasizes trends and processes more than events and persons. Second, the historical processes with which we engage, often enough, are not strictly calendrical: they have a logic that transcends the time and place of concrete example. Third, the arguments presented here, although evidentiary, are seldom dependent on what historians have typically considered evidence—namely, written texts. A deep history of this kind is thick with culture and epigenesis, even as it acknowledges the crucial role of biology, which is consistently woven into our accounts of human change over time. The result is an engagement with the human past that, instead of reinstating the old Hegelian distinction between natural and cultural existence, overturns the static imagery deployed in the nineteenth and twentieth centuries to deny historicity to the deep past.

PATTERNS AND FRAMES

If this volume can lay claim to innovation, it will lie not in matters of theory or method but in the realm of imagination. What we intend to provoke in the chapters that follow is a shift in sensibilities, and our principal tool is the reframing of intellectual practices that have been prematurely sorted into separate boxes. These practices can be thoroughly reconfigured, even unified, when they are situated within much larger spatial and temporal frameworks. The novelty at stake is best expressed as one of scale, of the level at which a story can be imagined and then told using methods and assumptions already available to scholars who study the movement of humans through deep and shallow time. To create this more broadly encompassing field of analysis, we have constructed our own master narrative. It unfolds in four parts, each of which addresses, from different angles, the patterns and frames of a deep history.

The first, called "Problems and Orientations," includes the arguments developed in this introduction, which stress the importance of deep history as an intellectual project, showing how the short and long chronologies of the human past came apart and have been kept apart by disciplinary practice. After explaining the time revolution of the nineteenth century, we suggest that historians have not yet adjusted their thinking to the reality of a deep past, and we consider the effects, desirable and problematic, of making such an adjustment now. In chapter 2, "Imagining the Human in Deep Time," we attempt to reconceive the human condition as a hominin one—that is, one that includes all the species in the genus *Homo* that are ancestrally as well as collaterally related to *Homo sapiens*. The logic that makes Neanderthals and other early hominins visible to a deep history is the same logic that has made subalterns everywhere visible to modern historical praxis. We ask what new methods and intellectual habits must be developed to deal with the immense variations in time and space that form the backdrop of hominin, as opposed to strictly human, history. We develop several orientations and base metaphors that resurface throughout the book: kinshipping, exchange, extension, hospitality, and genealogy. These concepts have always been historical in orientation and application; they can be used to create links to the past and, quite literally, to travel through time.

plan

In the second part of our story, "Frames for History in Deep Time," we explore three frameworks in which new and old intellectual problems can be examined. Specifically, we show how humans use bodies, environments, and languages to situate themselves in deep and shallow time. Each frame consists of social technologies that facilitate human inhabitation of and movement through space. In chapter 3, "Body," we suggest that the human form is both an objective and subjective system, a historical trace and an ongoing historical project. The body connects us viscerally to the past; it is a living medium of ancestry and relatedness. In response to the suggestion that the ancient hominin body is a natural body, unlike the culturally constructed body of modernity—a suggestion that mirrors the narrative arc of creationism—we propose two alternative claims. First, throughout its existence, the hominin body has been shaped by tools, social relations, and other elements of something we typically call "culture." Second, the epigenetic forces characteristic of the modern world sculpt the body in unintended ways. Our phenotypes, thanks to their plasticity, are continuously molded by the environments we inhabit, even if that molding is not always expressed in the genome.

In chapter 4, "Energy and Ecosystems," we pursue the idea that ecosystems shape and constrain our histories, and that human intentions cannot fully explain, and often obscure, this process. The lines we customarily draw between natural and cultural systems prevent us from understanding how these spheres constitute each other. Although we have no interest in disputing the human impact on the environment that is so profound a feature of modernity, we do contest two closely related assumptions: first, that these ecosystemic effects are unique to humanity, reflecting its mastery over nature; and second, that significant effects emerged only in recent centuries. Reframing the terms of discussion, we show how major trends in ecosystemic change are influenced by coevolutionary spirals—feedback loops and conjoined patterns of cause and effect—that can be traced deep into the Paleolithic. We return to the spiral in later chapters (notably chapter 9), employing it as a key narrative device for the writing of deep histories.

In chapter 5, "Language," we show how the discovery of genealogical relationships between human languages, past and present, has played a central role in scientific and humanistic attempts to explain deep history in the modern era. The image of the tree was central to nineteenth-century philology, and it is endlessly recycled in genetic and historical linguistic research today. Alongside this powerful frame, we explore the metaphor of the web or net. Webs direct our attention to exchange, a process crucial to the development of human languages and to recent attempts to simulate the origins of language. Because language, the body, and ecosystems are intellectual frameworks still capable of producing and organizing vast amounts of research, the three essays in this section establish the utility of deep-time perspectives for contemporary work across the human sciences.

In our third set of essays, "Shared Substance," we explore topics that have long been treated as necessary to human survival: food and kinship. These topics are of special interest to us because, as cultural systems, they create bodies, ecosystems, and languages over time. They have also left material traces—indeed, some of the oldest available to us, namely genes and isotopic data—that enable us to reconstruct events that occurred in the remote past. In chapter 6, "Food," and chapter 7, "Deep Kinship," we show how ancient forms of shared substance, and habits of sharing generally, are in fact highly adaptable processes that reveal striking transformations in what can be understood as human. Because we share our interests in eating and relating with our primate cousins, the essays in this section allow us to situate human histories within larger taxonomic contexts. We demonstrate how humans have used food and kinship to create worlds that, by comparison with other primate standards, are highly dependent on an awareness of past and present. As social projects, these shared substances are media of "kin-shipping," a tactic for moving through time and space that requires networks of relationship and exchange. We argue that because kinship-ping allows us to communicate across distances and to reconnect after absences, it is one of our most basic tools for making history.

In our final set of essays, "Human Expansion," we deal with a complex array of problems created and solved by the rapid spread of humans into multiple physical and social environments. In chapter 8, "Migration," we chart the most literal of expansions: the movement of hominins around the globe. This process was enabled by the cultural toolkits hominins developed in response to their own mobility in and beyond Africa. Movement and innovation were interrelated. The settling of Asia, Australia, Europe, and the Americas brought the extension of social networks, changes in foodways, and adaptation to new ecosystems. These changes played out differently in different eras of hominin evolution. Among modern human populations, who colonized the Earth in less than fifty thousand years, the effects of movement varied greatly depending on whether the new terrain was empty of other humans, whether related hominin species or other humans had to be displaced, and whether human populations were dislocated, subordinated, or reconnected within expanding social systems marked by political and economic inequality. Exploring how alternative modes of dispersal, displacement, and diaspora have affected human movement across deep time, we also show the remarkable extent to which mobility has shaped the frameworks in which deep history can be imagined.

In chapter 9, "Goods," we study the expanding array of material objects used to connect distant populations and build complex interactive networks. Goods are made and circulated in human economies, but the goods themselves reshape their makers, triggering feedback patterns that resemble coevolutionary spirals. These spirals contain histories precisely because their effects on the human body, languages, and ecosystems leave multiple traces. Connecting these traces and arranging them in narratives is crucial to the work of deep history. Finally, in chapter 10, "Scale," we consider the scalar leaps that have punctuated human history, including rapid population growth and the growing size and intricacy of human social formations. Like the other chapters, "Scale" is highly integrative. Showing how deep historical analysis can effectively bridge short and long chronologies, we redirect our key arguments to the task of dissecting one of the dominant metanarratives of the modern age: the belief that human development is progressive, cumulative, and directional and leads inevitably to social hierarchy and larger political institutions. This narrative of increase is itself a product of the historical trends analyzed throughout the volume, and we conclude by subjecting it to a rigorous critique—not a rejection, but a recontextualization—based on insights that arise when critique is undertaken at levels of significance and at scales that only deep historical frameworks make possible. *in "prehistory" what creates history?*

METAPHORS FOR DEEP HISTORY

This interpretive journey entails broad syntheses of major trends in the natural and human sciences. We do not, however, intend these essays to be encyclopedic. Although our team of writers includes three historians, two cultural anthropologists, a linguist, a primatologist, a geneticist, and three archaeologists, we realize that the areas of scholarship we cover in this book are vast and constantly expanding. We cannot produce full coverage; we can only inspire curiosity. We also understand that the subjects we have chosen for scrutiny are not the only or even the best domains for illustrating the promise of a deep historical perspective. Much more could be said about climate, music and art, religion, law and violence, technology, and sex. This volume does not exhaust the possibilities: it offers some and hopes to suggest more.

The principal goal of this book, then, is not to achieve encyclopedism but to propose a new array of base metaphors for the writing of deep history. Metaphors are necessary to the making of good historical arguments. They determine the shape of historical trajectories as well as the subjects and the silences of such arguments. The strategic use of new metaphors can thus lead, as Richard Dawkins and J. R. Krebs put it, to "new and productive habits of thought about old and familiar material."[16] The writing of deep histories requires analytical frames that do not resort to narratives of ontogeny ("the birth of the modern"), genesis ("something new under the sun"), or original sin ("stone-age brains in twenty-first-century skulls").[17] These are powerful metaphors, and in the hands of skilled authors, they generate exciting perspectives on the past. But the history they lead us to imagine is often flattened and foreshortened; it is a history that cannot generate sustained interest in the deep past.

We propose a different array of governing metaphors. When skillfully deployed, analytical devices such as kinshipping, webs, trees, fractals, spirals, extensions, and scalar integration can help us better comprehend the immensity of human time and the dynamic of connectedness that both propels and constrains change. Kinshipping, for instance, offers ways to connect across time and space. It surmounts the metaphor of ontogeny, which describes the life history of an organism: that story necessarily begins at the moment of conception or birth, whether the birth of a nation or of a political idea. What comes before is analytically invisible or fundamentally different. By contrast, kinshipping is possible only if (and only because) a formative relation preexisted and continues to define the new and particular. It has no point of origin. Likewise, the coevolutionary spiral, which envisions two genealogies entwined and feeding off each other, displaces metaphors of genesis, revolution, and the biblical Fall. Notions of the latter sort predispose us to exaggerate the singularity of historical events and to downplay the many ways in which change builds on itself. The idea of the fractal, of patterns that are replicated at every level of magnification, helps us discern how dramatic changes seem unique only if we restrict ourselves to a single level of observation. The fractal, and the imagery of ever-smaller scales it evokes, suggests that leaps are always built on other leaps. Like kinshipping and spiraling, fractal patterns draw us ceaselessly into the past. They explain why changes in the things we can measure, such as gross population, population density, and energy consumption, do not have to be large to be profound. If we can generate a transdisciplinary discussion of these base metaphors and the other tactics we have proposed for reconnecting short and long chronologies, then current research will fall into place within new narrative frames. The frames themselves will help generate new research endeavors.

Our agenda is critical of well-established trends in how historians and cultural anthropologists concentrate their analytical efforts in space and time. We hope this critical stance is not interpreted as a claim for the superiority—intellectual, moral, or political—of temporally deep history over the historical study of recent times. An argument of that sort would be about as compelling, and convincing, as the claim that a history of the fifteenth century is better, and more profound, than a history of the seventeenth century because it is two hundred years older. What we insist on, by contrast, is a revamped historical imagination that sees deep and shallow history as analytical contexts that can endlessly reshape each other once they are allowed to speak to each other. If historians of the seventeenth century claimed that a history of the fifteenth century was not possible, we would suspect that something was amiss. Yet statements of this kind have come between deep and shallow history for almost two centuries now. They have produced short and long chronologies, natural and social sciences, and, in the end, an unhelpful excess of mutual incomprehension. It is time to close the gap.

CHAPTER 2

Imagining the Human in Deep Time

ANDREW SHRYOCK, THOMAS R. TRAUTMANN,
AND CLIVE GAMBLE

THE CHRONICLE'S MISSING YEARS

"All profound changes in consciousness," Benedict Anderson wrote, "by their very nature, bring characteristic amnesias. Out of such oblivions, in specific historical circumstances, spring narratives."[1] The discovery *time* of deep time in the nineteenth century was certainly a profound change *revolution* in consciousness. It altered perceptions of the natural order and triggered an explosion of new stories purporting to explain human origins. Yet for historians, the amnesia associated with an epistemological shift of this magnitude failed to materialize. The new Darwinian worldview did not cause them to forget what they already knew about the French Revolution, the spread of Islamic civilizations, or the decline of the Roman Empire. Rather, the advent of deep time made historians realize how little they knew compared to what could potentially be known and, just as important, how much they could never know using the *def.* historiographical methods they cherished. The result was *prehistory*, a conceptual innovation that functioned as a protective barrier between remote antiquity and a set of scholarly techniques that was applicable only to a recent sliver of the human past.

In the modern tradition of history writing, the author blends narrative, chronology, and textual evidence to produce an account that seems full and convincing. Without dates, storylines, and documentary evidence, today's historians cannot practice their craft; if even one of these components is missing, the historian is confronted by debilitating gaps. He or she will try valiantly to fill them or move on to more promising terrain. Of course, this tendency says more about the mechanics of modern historiography than it does about our knowledge of the past. There are many genres of history making—among them the genealogy, the chronicle, the kings list, the heroic poem, and the monument—that include no plots, no dates, and no events at all. The historical accounts that pervade the Old and New Testaments, once the quintessence of historical truth, came to us without calendar-based chronologies attached, and the larger world, before and after biblical time, is filled with oral historical traditions that make no appeal to written evidence. These diverse ways of remembering might be of occasional use to the academic historian, who may regard them as data, but they are generally considered inadequate for creating reliable accounts of the past.

Hayden White put his finger on an essential aspect of modern historiography when he noted how strange the habits of medieval chroniclers appear to us now.[2] The annalists, usually clerics, kept lists of years to which they affixed important events, but they left certain years empty, as if to say, "Nothing of importance happened in 734." The entry of a year into the chronicle without a single memorable event associated with it strikes the modern sensibility as odd, as unfinished work—as if the passage of years were the important part, not the happenings and trends that are measured in years. Of course, to the eighth- or ninth-century chronicler, the passage of years was indeed very important, as it brought humanity ever closer to Christ's promised return. What to the modern eye looks like an empty spot that necessarily contained *something* to the chronicler must have looked like an uninteresting step, dutifully recorded, in the collective, unstoppable march toward the end of time.

It is ironic that modern historians should look askance at the annalist's little gaps, given the immense holes in time we have opened up, and left unfilled, over the past two centuries. Whatever we might say about the Bible as a historical document, we can agree that it attempted to tell the whole story, from Creation to Last Judgment. This universal framework explains why Archbishop James Ussher, one of the most distinguished members of a long lineage of chronologers, thought it a worthwhile endeavor to apply calendar dates to the Book of Genesis, dating creation to 4004 BC and thereby making it the consummately historical event it had to be; it also explains why the time revolution of the nineteenth century ended the Bible's long reign as a literal account of human history. The discovery of deep time, as Benedict Anderson deftly put it,

✗ time revolution

"drove a wedge between history and cosmology."[3] In the world of history writing, prehistory became the equivalent of the medieval chronicler's empty year. But the empty space called prehistory was immeasurably large, and the modern historiographer's inability to fill it created analytical challenges that were moral (that is, cosmological) as well as technical. To the extent that humans still believe that history is about us and that our history, like the biblical one, should go back to the beginning, the discovery of deep time requires us to imagine human nature in new ways.

This change in orientation began very suddenly and is still unfolding. At the beginning of the nineteenth century, the educated classes of Europe believed the biblical story of creation to be a true historical account. By the beginning of the twentieth century, this belief system was disintegrating, and new stories of human origins were replacing it. The growing certainty that our planet and our species were here long before the date promulgated by Archbishop Ussher meant that these new stories had to be constructed on a massive time scale. Evidence that humans had evolved from prior forms—thought, in the Victorian age of progress, to be more primitive forms—meant that a greater range of physical variation had to be worked into the story of our species. A new sense of distance and differentiation was needed to provide architecture for knowledge of the remote past.

Once again, there is the semblance of a gap, of missing years. But was this opening up of space and time as revolutionary as it now seems to be? Could we perhaps understand it better, and historicize it more creatively, if we treated it as a situation we have encountered many times before? Covering vast spatial and temporal distances and making human variations part of our social lives are practical (and conceptual) activities at which humans excel. The time revolution is a very recent event, and its effects on the way we imagine the human are best appreciated if we place it first in contexts that are historically particular—where dates, narratives, and texts matter a great deal—and then in contexts that are more general, in which a different array of historiographical devices enable us to reconnect to a larger human past.

BELL, BOOK, AND BIFACE

England in 1859 was a banner year for time, and in particular deep time. Just over 150 years ago—equivalent to about seven generations for an anthropologist, a long century for a historian, and an acceptable error range in a radiocarbon date for an archaeologist—the passage of one year was marked by the events surrounding three artifacts: bell, book, and biface (a stone tool whose surface is worked on both sides). To make sense of them required an imaginary geography, a step into the dark of human prehistory.

The biface led the way. On April 27 the geologist Joseph Prestwich and the antiquarian John Evans stood in a gravel pit outside Amiens in the Somme Valley of France, watching a photographer, and his very large camera, record what they had come to find: undisputable evidence of a stone tool found in the same geological stratum as extinct animals.[4] Such a find had been anticipated but elusive. The discoveries by the Frenchman Jacques Boucher de Perthes lacked scientific supporters, whereas an earlier discovery in 1797 by a Suffolk landowner, John Frere, had been noted but forgotten. Frere's stone artifacts from Hoxne were rediscovered on Evans's return to London, when he chanced on them in a display case at the Society of Antiquaries.[5] They were Acheulean hand axes, a tool tradition that originated in the Lower Paleolithic among *Homo erectus* and survived, in roughly the same form, for more than a million years (figure 2).

Once these artifacts were accepted as human creations, they allowed Prestwich and Evans to build a reasoned, evidence-based case for the long-debated existence of pre-Adamite humans.[6] They also created a deep time that was not anchored in chronology, because they never even speculated on how many years separated the bifaces from the present. Frere's letter famously attributes them "to a very remote period indeed; even beyond that of the present world."[7] However, Prestwich thought that rather than distancing the past, their discovery could place extinct animals and humans closer to the present.[8] Charles Lyell referred to their discovery as representing "a vast lapse of ages," older than the Romans and Celts by a considerable degree and thus outside history.[9] Six years later, Sir John Lubbock, a close friend of Evans and a neighbor since boyhood of Charles Darwin at Down House, placed the Amiens biface in a Paleolithic period that, together with the later Neolithic, he labeled the "Stone Age" in his *Pre-historic Times*.[10]

Then came the bell. The Palace of Westminster had been destroyed by fire in 1834. Rebuilding was slow and over budget. Indeed, the principal designer, Augustus Pugin, died in 1852, long before the completion of the imposing clock tower, best known by the name of its great bell, Big Ben. The tower was officially opened on September 7, 1859, and its architect, Sir Charles Barry, outlived it by only a year. Ever since (more

FIGURE 2. The hand ax found at Amiens, France. (Natural History Museum, London, Prestwich Collection, accession no. E 5109; photo by Clive Gamble.)

or less), this sonorous monument of public time has struck out the hour, on the hour, at five-second intervals, like the heartbeat of the nation. Big Ben was one in a succession of public timepieces installed since the seventeenth century to establish a new urban temporality.[11] The point of Big Ben, and all his smaller brothers, was that citizens no longer had to seek very hard to know the time; it now reigned over them.

Big Ben epitomizes a concern for chronological accuracy and the proper division of time (with chimes sounding every quarter of the hour). The same concerns dominated the next century of Paleolithic research. Chronology provided a narrative focus for archaeologists by encouraging them to construct ever more accurate timelines. However, their pursuit of time contributed little to a history of the period. It yielded not a deep public sense of time but rather a succession of dates, associated with different types of stone tools.

Big Ben suggests another origin point, however, more in keeping with the public imagination of past and present. Barry and Pugin cloaked their timepiece in the style of Gothic revival. Pugin's designs for the

collective memory/ public time

Palace of Westminster reflect the contemporary obsession with chivalry and the medieval. Time, like the houses of Parliament, was wrapped in a manufactured past. As history became an integral part of government, timekeeping became a national project in service to a sense of heritage and collective memory for which the state was responsible. Under these conditions, the telling of time had to be marked culturally by embedding it in the past.

And finally we come to the book: Charles Darwin's long-awaited *On the Origin of Species by Means of Natural Selection,* published on November 24, 1859. Darwin provided a mechanism to account for evolutionary change, and he argued that the tempo of this change was gradual, requiring the passage of vast amounts of time. When combined with Evans and Prestwich's biface discovery earlier in the year, Darwin's model resulted in a new sense of history, one in which the human role in the universe was no longer seen as essential and permanent. According to biblical and classical sources, a universe of this kind was not possible. A literal reading of Genesis allowed only five days in the entire history of the universe that were devoid of human life; and in the Aristotelian tradition, humans had always been present. It was, as Martin Rudwick emphasizes, the presence of humans that gave meaning to time and created a world with history.[12] But Evans, Prestwich, and Darwin opened up a cosmos in which humans appeared very late, leaving vast stretches of time without people and, therefore, without meaning or history in either the biblical or Aristotelian sense. They were by no means the first to think in these terms, but by transferring the burden of proof away from ancient texts and onto objects, they achieved a convincing demonstration of the sheer "otherness" of the deep past. Previously, this quality had applied only to fossils; now it applied to humans as well.[13]

PRE-HISTORIC TIME(S), AND WHEN HISTORY BEGAN

These three events in 1859 point up several issues concerning history and deep time. In the first place, the representation of time we take from Evans and Prestwich is rather different from that found in Darwin's account of the mutability of species. The dominant image from the Amiens pit, nicely captured in their photograph and section drawings, is of a time neither linear nor cyclical but vertical and layered. It must be dug into rather than traced with a finger or walked as a timeline. Deep time presents itself as sequentially compressed slabs composed of different materials, both organic and inorganic; it is compacted, oppressively heavy, and impenetrable; it is hidden from public view. Prestwich, Evans, and the geologists and archaeologists who followed them were cast as expert time foragers; they imagined the deep past (as it was prior to compression) before they encountered it (as deposits and remains).

A second point builds on this necessary imaginative exercise. Because deep time could not be measured in 1859, some nontemporal device was needed in order to explore it and classify its inhabitants. One successful strategy was to equate remote times with remote places—with the uttermost ends of the Earth. This device, which substituted distance for time, was already well-used in pre-Adamite investigations.[14] An often-cited example is Joseph-Marie Degérando's memorandum to the Pacific explorer Nicolas Baudin before he set sail from France for the South Pacific, never to return. "We shall in a way be taken back to the first periods of our own history; we shall be able to set up secure experiments on the origin and generation of ideas, on the formation and development of language, and on the relations between these two processes. The philosophical traveller, sailing to the ends of the earth, is in fact travelling in time; he is exploring the past; every step he makes is the passage of an age. Those unknown islands that he reaches are for him the cradle of human society."[15]   space =time

The simple equation of geographic distance from Paris with temporal distance from the human present drew on a prior conception of who stood within world history and who did not. The asymmetry of the historical process was indicated in material and cultural ways and in the act of discovery itself. The French explorers did not need to mention the absence of written records. Peoples were also assigned to deep time on the basis of linguistic connections mapped out by philologists: their comparative methods produced genealogies of languages and nations, suggesting that peoples once thought to be separate and racially distinct actually shared ancestors in the distant past.[16] These equations, spatial and linguistic, were still drawn in relation to classical and biblical worlds. They were not designed to accommodate flint tools found in proximity to extinct animals; nor could they immediately define or encompass the vastness of time out of which these simple objects were extracted.

The vertical, impenetrable character of deep time, in which tools were the key proxy, postdates the age of exploration, when anchors were dropped by the sandy shores of a remote human history. It is therefore possible to identify two communities concerned with establishing deep time: one that encountered it at the uttermost ends of the Earth, and one that imagined its historical possibility in the uncovered depths of the Earth. Darwin belonged to both communities. During his visit to the Beagle Channel in Tierra del Fuego, he famously noted: "The astonishment which I felt on first seeing a party of Fuegians on a wild and broken shore will never be forgotten by me, for the reflection at once rushed into my mind—such were our ancestors. He who has seen a savage in his native land will not feel much shame, if forced to acknowledge that the blood of some more humble creature flows in his veins."[17]

Like so many others, Degérando and Darwin filled deep time with the primate figures that Eric Wolf would later call "the people without history."[18] For these "more humble creatures," history began as a result of their encounter with Europeans. It was conferred on them, like the name "Jemmy Button" that was given to the Fuegian returnee aboard the *Beagle*. It was not imagined, like the deep time in the gravel pit at Amiens (about which Darwin formed a favorable opinion under Lubbock's guidance, having previously dismissed Boucher de Perthes's claims for stratified stone tools as "rubbish").[19] Hence, as a member of both the community that encountered deep time directly in its supposedly primitive human form and the community that had to imagine and reconstruct it as a remote era in which modern humans were absent, Darwin was able to reject forcefully the notion of historical degeneration. "To believe that man was aboriginally civilised and then suffered utter degradation in so many regions, is to take a pitiably low view of human nature. It is apparently a truer and more cheerful view that progress has been much more general than retrogression; that man has risen, though by slow and interrupted steps, from a lowly condition to the highest standard as yet attained by him in knowledge, morals and religion."[20]

The issue of prehistoric time returns us to Big Ben. The time revolution of the nineteenth century enfolded the monuments and materials of the past into a political narrative. Self-determination, nationhood, and good government needed a well-imagined past to create a palpable sense of common history, and the allure of genuinely old histories for demonstrably new nation-states was all but irresistible. This trend is exemplified in the call to arms by Jens Worsaae in 1849, during the formation of the Danish state (an important site in the development of prehistoric archaeology):

> The remains of antiquity thus bind us more firmly to our native lands; hills and vales, fields and meadows, become connected with us, in a more intimate degree; for by the barrows [burial mounds], which rise on their surface, and

the antiquities, which they have preserved for centuries in their bosom, they constantly recall to our recollection, that our forefathers lived in this country, from time immemorial, a free and independent people, and so call on us to defend our territories with energy, that no foreigner may ever rule over that soil, which contains the bones of our ancestors, and with which our most sacred and reverential recollections are associated.[21]

Prehistoric monuments were less important for national identity in Britain, although they have shaped the practice of regional history, and the emergence of the Stonehenge brand has satisfied other demands on the past. The architecture and design of Big Ben remind us of the variety of geographical readings involved in any understanding of what constitutes deep time. But just how different are Worsaae's claims on the past from those made in July 2004 by Gordon Brown, then chancellor of the exchequer, in his much-reported speech on Britishness? "Out of [the] tidal flows of British history—2,000 years of successive waves of invasion, immigration, assimilation and trading partnerships that have created a uniquely rich and diverse culture—certain forces emerge again and again which make up a characteristically British set of values and qualities which, taken together, mean that there is indeed a strong and vibrant Britishness that underpins Britain" (*Guardian*, July 8, 2004).

Although this could be interpreted as a similar plea for nationalism, Brown's target is wider: how can national identity be turned to advantage in a global economy? But most informative is his choice of timescale for a distinctive British history. Rather than looking back as far as Stonehenge (4,000 years) or the Hoxne hand axes (400,000 years), he settles, rather predictably, on a history traced no further than the arrival in Britain of the Romans. The temporal scale of statecraft and empire (the natural preserve of clerics, court historians, and official histories— in short, the realm of the book) trumps that of hand axes and standing stones any day. If the Danes had possessed *only* the contents of their burial mounds as evidence for their national history, they would suddenly have found themselves at the ends of the Earth, in the company of Darwin's Fuegians.

OBJECTS AS AGENTS IN TIME

"Archaeology," wrote Lubbock, "forms the link between geology and history."[22] The fossilized bones of animals and the works of humans provide clues about how they lived. So much is well understood. Yet Lubbock never explained what he meant by *history*, except that it had to be written down. He compounded the problem by coining, along with David Wilson, the word *prehistory,* which appears in the title of his magnum opus, *Pre-historic Times, as Illustrated by Ancient Remains, and the Manners and Customs of Modern Savages.*[23] His opening assessment of this period, "Our pre-historic antiquities have been valued as monuments of ancient skill and perseverance, not . . . as pages of ancient history," seems unchanged by the end of his 640-page treatise.[24]

The challenge to bring deep time into the writing of history remains. Attempts to emphasize the materiality of deep time that began in the nineteenth century have not been overtly successful. The three technological ages—Stone, Bronze, and Iron—and the many global, national, and local subdivisions of material types have left earliest prehistory dehumanized, a place merely to plant an origin myth for the modern world.[25] Indeed, most archaeologists working in deep time have imagined a past that accentuates the Evans-Prestwich-Darwin model. In this view, not only did hominins appear late in the story of the evolution of life, but humans appeared late in the story of hominins.[26]

There are, however, signs of an alternative perspective emerging. Biface, book, and bell are not simply markers of time or metaphors that capture certain ways of thinking about time: they are objects actively engaged in its production—not in the way Big Ben sounds out the hour, perhaps, but through the agency of material things, such as the biface that Evans and Prestwich found in April 1859. If objects have no agency, then these men would not have been visiting a gravel pit, and we would not be scratching our heads about deep time and history. That simple biface was both the source of and the target for human agency because it stood in a network of social relationships.[27] The small community of inquiry created in the spring of 1859 was composed of materials, things, and flesh-and-blood people. It made novel connections between places as varied as muddy gravel pits and the metropolitan meeting rooms of learned societies.[28] The biface, and the networks of relationship that emanated from it, certainly affected the lives of its discoverers and all those who have subsequently come into contact with it.

Hominins have always been constituted by the agency of persons and things. Our history is a material history, not just a succession of thoughts or speech acts. If deep time is to figure in our histories, then we need narratives that can triangulate between agents and materials. This shift in focus brings into play a model of cognition that differs from the one that underpinned the deep-time revolution of 1859, which stressed a rational appreciation of the evidence rather than a relational understanding. A mind distributed in social relationships and physical materials takes cognition outside of the head, beyond skin, and into the world.[29] Such externalism means that materials and artifacts are always implicated in our cognitive architecture rather than being simply the outputs of internal cognitive processes. Thinking *through* objects rather than thinking *about* objects becomes the description of cognitive processes.[30]

KINSHIPPING

If we think about a biface, we are already locating it, and ourselves, in time. We know the Amiens biface came from a remote place. Not only had it been underground for a very long time, but the Victorians could only assume that the people who made it were of a kind distant from and inferior to themselves. Prestwich and Evans sat atop an imperial world filled with primitives, colonials, stagnant civilizations, and subject races. The idea that similar hierarchies sank down into the Earth and could be dug up was not hard to entertain. The biface, set within the evolutionary frames developing in the nineteenth century, confirmed and constituted a social relationship. The absent party to this relationship, the maker of the biface, had to be imagined. It was easy to do. As Martin Jones has argued, Victorians would have pictured any stone-tool maker as a savage, consigning him to a world populated by "Plains Indians and Inuit Eskimo in all but name"; for us, Hollywood movies and more than a century of paleoanthropology provide stock mental images.[31] But we always imagine someone who would act and interact in a certain way, and the biface is crucial to this construct. If Evans and Prestwich had found a scroll in their exposed strata, we would be compelled to imagine another kind of human and another kind of human history.

Kinship is central to these imaginative acts. The maker of the Amiens biface was long ago assimilated into the category of "ancestor," which means we are somehow part of the same "family." Over the past 150 years, we have had trouble extending our nations, languages, and civilizational complexes into deep time; there is nothing to persuade us that there is anything *prehistoric* about any of them. The idea of human kinship, by contrast, travels well through time. We no longer find it difficult, or even problematic, to assume that we are related to the human (and prehuman) occupants of deep time, that we "descend" from them and share physical substance with them. If the time revolution created

remote areas in the human past, *kinshipping* (moving through time and space by means of relationship and exchange) has proved an effective way of exploring these areas and reconnecting with them.

The perception of kinship, wherever we find it among humans, is based on ideas of similarity, mutual obligation, and sharing. Yet kinshipping plays on difference as well. Some people are closer to us than others, and kinship can wear thin over time. The opening up of deep history has reproduced, in novel forms, many of the challenges to kinship that have long been associated with distant epochs and regions. The book of Genesis tells us that, in the early generations of human history, there were "giants in the earth," the Nephilim, offspring of the "sons of God" and the "daughters of men." The ancient Greeks populated the edges of their world with monstrous creatures that were somehow related to humans.[32] European explorers, during their initial journeys to the Americas, fully expected to encounter the one-footed, dog-headed, and flesh-eating races posited in classical geography. Instead they found people like themselves, but different enough to prompt debate. Were these people descendants of Adam? Did they have souls worth saving? The answer was yes, but it came only after years of disagreement, and a papal decree was needed to settle the matter decisively.

Today, the idea that all humans belong to a single species is taken for granted, and kinshipping is still used to mark the outer boundaries of humankind. Our nearest primate relatives, the chimpanzees, have emotions and behaviors we immediately recognize, and 98 percent of the human and chimp genomes are the same. The remaining variations have accumulated over roughly 6 million years, and paleoanthropologists examine them following highly nuanced kinshipping agendas, parsing fine distinctions between several species of australopiths and several varieties of *Homo,* including our close cousins, the Neanderthals. The kinshipping done within this 2 percent margin of difference draws on a peculiar blend of hypermodern science and representational tools that are decidedly premodern in origin.

The most indispensable of these tools is the family tree. This is a genealogical construct, and a deeply historical one. Although academic historians today consider genealogy (or family history) a rather plebeian form of historical research, there was a time not so long ago when history and genealogy were inseparable genres. Modern historiography is defined by the loosening of genealogy's grip on written accounts of the past, which once fixated on topics that were best treated in the language of pedigrees. Hereditary dynasts, the nobility, clerical elites, and received

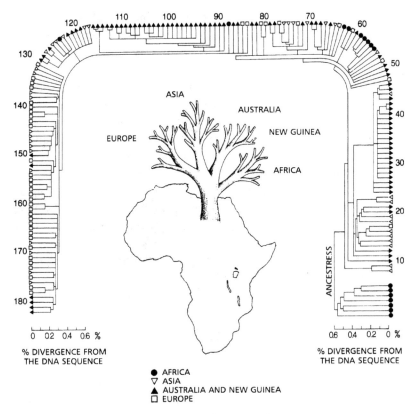

FIGURE 3. The mitochondrial Eve. Early research on mitochondrial DNA in humans, which is transmitted through the female line, produced a wealth of tree and genealogical diagrams. This one, which appears in *The Great Human Diasporas* by Luigi Cavalli-Sforza and Francesco Cavalli-Sforza, represents the findings of Rebecca Cann, Mark Stoneking, and Allan Wilson, who "discovered" the mitochondrial Eve in 1987. Starting with our female ancestor in Africa (bottom right-hand corner), the tree illustrates one line of descent that produced seven branches in Africa and a second line of descent, curving around to the left, from which sprang myriad branches and twigs in New Guinea, Australia, Asia, and Europe. Because it has been curved to conform to the geographical distribution of the descendants, the family tree depicted here does not have the usual shape of genealogical trees. (Cavalli-Sforza and Cavalli-Sforza 1995, 66; used by permission of Perseus Books Group.)

scriptural traditions all derived their historical authority in large part from pedigrees. Ironically, the rise of genomic research is based on its literal, unapologetic interest in the sort of authenticating genealogy that secured kings on their thrones and nowadays draws millions of ordinary people to public libraries or genealogy websites in search of their ancestors. Faced with traversing the great temporal and spatial distances that have opened up in human history since the nineteenth century, modern bioscience is returning to an old and sturdy way of imagining human community.

Today genomic kinshipping takes the form of *lineal* genealogy, and there is a distinctly biblical resonance to the family trees that molecular anthropologists are piecing together. Genomic maps enable us to calibrate the nearness of all humans to each other, to our hominin ancestors, and to nonhuman species. The explosion of new genetic research has yielded an expanding universe of deep histories built around family trees in the form of cladistic diagrams and tracings of human migration, beginning in Africa (the new Eden) and fanning out across Asia, Europe, and then North and South America (see chapter 8). The models are impeccably scientific, yet Adam (with his Y chromosome) and Eve (with her mitochondrial DNA) still figure as ancestral mascots for our kind. They have been crucial to the popularization of genomic research, whose first great discovery was the African Eve, mother of us all (see figure 3).

PRUNING THE FAMILY TREE

Genealogy is not kinship as we ordinarily experience it. If it were, we would not need to spend hours in archives researching it; nor would there be, even in societies without writing, people who specialize in remembering and transmitting it. Genealogy's reputation as expert knowledge has been won, oddly enough, by means of simplification, by the cutting away of certain relations from the thicket of kinship and the scrupulous tending of others. The branches of genealogy extend forward in time and are forever expanding. In early Jewish, Christian, and Muslim societies, descent was traced through male links, and the sacred texts of the Abrahamic tradition are replete with lists of men begetting and begotten. In medieval European manuscripts that represent the genealogy of the Messiah as described in the prophecy of Isaiah, the genealogy takes the form of a tree that springs from the recumbent and dreaming figure of the patriarch Jesse (figure 4).

Though less common, the tracing of descent through female links is found in a diverse range of African, Asian, and Amerindian societies. It is possible to trace descent through males and females simultaneously, or to trace it back and forth across gender lines; many human societies, including all those in which English is spoken, have kinship systems

FIGURE 4. A genealogical tree from an illuminated manuscript. Variations on the Tree of Jesse appear in numerous biblical commentaries from medieval Europe. Many versions depict a simple line of descent from one patriarch to the next, typically ending with Jesus or Mary. Others, like this one, sketch a branching tree with many limbs and twigs, representing a broader family. (Bibliothèque nationale de France, MS Français 159, Bible historiale de Jean de Berry, fol. 175.)

that are bilateral and do not produce lineages of kin related exclusively through paternal or maternal lines. In short, there is immense variation in the way humans keep track of their kin. The tight link between genomic research and one very particular way of tracing descent, the unilineal genealogy, is a fascinating pattern that needs explanation.

Charles Darwin lived in a pre-genomic society, but the genealogical tree was central to the deep history he made possible. *The Origin of Species* argued that descent reveals the hidden logic of Linnaean classifications of plants and animals, and that similarities in form are explainable as the outcome of genealogical proximity.[33] In his chapter on classification, Darwin used genealogical lines to connect scattered points of the necessarily incomplete fossil record, bridging the gaps between related species. Genealogy, in other words, brought the Linnaean species of the present into relation as codescendants of ancient species known through the fossil record. The genealogical diagram was perfectly suited to the task of synthesizing the record of deep history with the record of the present.

Since Darwin set deep history on its present course, genealogical diagramming (alongside advances in genetic analysis) has only grown in importance, partly because of a fortuitous coincidence. Current genomic research follows the unilineal pathways of the Y chromosome (which is patrilineal) and mitochondrial DNA (which is matrilineal) for tracing branching lines of descent. Genealogical diagrams are ideally suited to represent these pathways. Like the genealogical tree itself, the analysis of change in the human genome over time isolates lineal relations from other relations of descent and marriage. Our strong fondness for genealogical trees cannot, however, be fully explained by biogenetics; it predated the knowledge of genes and has figured prominently in bodies of scholarship distinct from the biological sciences.

One field in which genealogical or cladistic diagramming reigned supreme was historical linguistics (see chapter 5). Darwin himself recognized the similarity of language trees to his own "branching diagram" in the matter of biological classification:

> It may be worth while to illustrate this view of [biological] classification, by taking the case of languages. If we possessed a perfect pedigree of mankind, a genealogical arrangement of the races of man would afford the best classification of the various languages now spoken throughout the world; and if all extinct languages, and all intermediate and slowly changing dialects, had to be included, such an arrangement would, I think, be the only possible one. Yet it might be that some very ancient language had altered little, and had

given rise to few new languages, whilst others (owing to the spreading and subsequent isolation and states of civilization of the several races, descended from a common race) had altered much, and had given rise to many new languages and dialects. The various degrees of difference in the languages from the same stock, would have to be expressed by groups subordinate to groups; but the proper or even only possible arrangement would still be genealogical; and this would be strictly natural, as it would connect together all languages, extinct and modern, by the closest affinities, and would give the filiation and origin of each tongue.[34]

Historical linguistics creates genealogical trees of relationship among languages by first removing all signs of borrowing. This paring away of borrowed material is analogous to the formation of unilineal genealogies through the paring away of marriages and kinship relations conveyed through both genders. The cladistic diagrams that result are in both cases partial and reductive. Narratives of mixture are not possible in these terms and must be fashioned through analysis of a different kind. Nevertheless, the ability of historical linguistics to discern kinship across great distances revolutionized deep history in the late eighteenth century in ways that were profoundly resonant with the deep history that Darwin built.

Given the obvious importance of cladistic diagrams to the deep histories emerging from eighteenth-century linguistics and nineteenth-century biology, where did they come from? If Darwin had the example of historical linguistics before him, where did the linguists get it? The answer is surprising. The patrilineal trees connected with deep history prior to the emergence of historical linguistics and Darwinian biology were drawn from the Bible, from the book of Genesis. Following the flood of Noah, the Earth was repopulated by Noah and his three sons Shem, Ham, and Japheth, and their wives, begetting more sons and sons of sons. These descendants formed a tree of nations, or rather of patriarchs who fathered the nations, such as Javan, father of the Greeks, and Heber, father of the Hebrews. For centuries, this patrilineal tree of nations was the master image of deep history for the "peoples of the book," Jewish, Christian, and Muslim. The tree itself was extended by the addition of new patriarchs. According to Muslim accounts of India's history, for example, Hind, son of Ham, son of Noah, was the father of the Indian peoples. Turks also had to be fitted into Noah's progeny, as did the Chinese.

The outcomes of this project are the many universal histories of the past. One of the first printed books of Europe is the *Nuremberg Chronicle* of Hartmann Schedel, a magnificent compendium showing the whole of world history from Adam and Eve to the present, and the future to the second coming of Christ, represented as a great "week" of seven thousand years.[35] The sons of Noah are connected to the kings of Europe by twisty vines, prototypes of the cladistic diagrams of today's genetics. First published in 1493, this tidy narrative was about to be greatly strained by Columbus's discoveries. Its chronology of seven millennia would prove to be a relatively shallow foundation for deep history; but its basic genealogical structure has been preserved, albeit unwittingly. What molecular geneticist today would claim to labor in the tradition of Genesis, or of Hartmann Schedel?

The biblical source of the modern tree of languages is not widely acknowledged, but this point of origin is, when one ponders it, highly fitting. The comparative linguists and Darwin were pioneering a new history of the world, a new Genesis narrative. In doing so, they breathed new life into a kinship structure that has helped make our world intelligible, perpetuating its logic in self-consciously scientific forms. It is a stunning instance of the human capacity to use kinshipping to discover (and create) relations over great distances of time and space. This power must have been important to our distant ancestors as well. What were their kinship maps of deep space-time like? We have good reason to believe that long genealogies and large, cohesive descent groups were not common among humans before the domestication of plants and animals, when economic surpluses and sedentary living turned kinship into a means of limiting access to resources via categories of relatedness. If unilineal genealogy established its dominance late in the human story, what were the kinshipping tools people used to speed their geographical expansion within and beyond Africa, tens of thousands of years before agriculture? Might these structures be useful to us in thinking about deep history?

CROSSNESS AND CONNECTION

Every person is the center of a web of kinship formed by marriage and descent through persons of both genders: a *personal kindred* of immediate kin and secondary, more distant kin. These relations form kinds, with names like *father, mother, brother, sister, cousin,* and so forth. These terms are patterned by a logic we learn to apply as children: if Sarah is the mother of Jim, then Jim is the son of Sarah. These personal kindreds, made up of individuals sorted into kinship categories, form the experiential world of kinship. Unilineal structures such as lineages and clans are formed by giving special privilege to relationships defined by links to ancestral males (patrilineal) or ancestral females (matrilineal). The more basic agenda of human kinship, however, is not about modeling pedigrees but about creating new kin (offspring) and new kinship relations with people who are not kin, or with people who are related to us as kin of a specific kind: namely, the kind we can marry.

Like other primates, humans generally avoid mating with their offspring, parents, and siblings. Anthropologists were once fascinated by incest taboos, which are found in all human societies, and this fascination predated accurate knowledge of mating patterns among other primate species. When Claude Lévi-Strauss argued that the incest taboo is what makes humans human, he did not know that incest avoidance is also characteristic of other primates.[36] If we are to locate kinship structures as deep as the deepest human histories, then we should look for them not in universal genealogies, nor in the fact that we abhor incest, but in the marital strategies and mating practices that produce living arrangements unique to human societies.

For Lévi-Strauss, the most elementary structure of human kinship was the relationship between "a maternal uncle, his sister, and his nephew."[37] This "atom of kinship" has recently been tweaked by Bernard Chapais, who argues, in language slightly less sexist, that all human kinship systems are based on a relationship between "a sister (and daughter) linking her brother (and father) to her husband."[38] In both cases, incest avoidance between siblings, parents, and children requires the incorporation of outsiders who create new atoms of kinship. This incorporation is achieved through the exchange of persons and objects, and it results in the forging of kinship networks across genders, generations, and, most distinctively, space. Compared to chimps and gorillas (see chapter 7), humans have extensive regional networks of kin relations, and we build these networks by making difference (and distance) essential to the creation of sameness, of kinship itself. Among contemporary hominids, humans are the only species that maintains active kinship ties between individuals who live in separate breeding groups. We are also the only primate species in which offspring have active kin ties to their mother's male siblings.

This very human way of creating kin is based on the fundamental appeal of crossness and connection. Crossness, explained in chapter 7, is a way of arranging kin such that everyone is sorted into a checkerboard of equal and opposite classes of same (or parallel) and other (or cross).

Without resort to lengthy genealogies, these relations can be extended laterally by a recursive logic according to which the parallel kin of my cross kin are my cross kin, and the parallel kin of my parallel kin are my parallel kin. Given this pattern, a few basic questions can establish the mutual social locations of two people when they first meet. Irving Hallowell found that among Ojibwa people in Canada, opposite-sex siblings were expected to observe relations of respect and distance (it was improper for a brother and sister to be alone together in the same canoe or the same dwelling, for example). He also found that parallel cousins—that is, mother's sister's children, or father's brother's children—were considered siblings and treated with similar reserve. But cross cousins—mother's brother's children, or father's sister's children—were not classed as siblings; they were marriageable, and they were subjected to all kinds of sexual teasing. When Hallowell and Chief Berens canoed upcountry several hundred miles, it took but a few minutes to determine that Berens was in a cross relation to people they met and for the suggestive joking to begin between Chief Berens and an old married woman, to general hilarity.[39] The ability to assign people to parallel and cross categories ensures that kin, no matter how distant, are never lost through remoteness of the relation. Indeed, remoteness becomes yet another tool for the creation of familiar ties.

Humans have developed many forms of kinship that play with notions of crossness and connection. Among the Garo of Meghalaya in India, people of Marak lineages marry people of Sangma lineages and vice versa: every married couple has behind it segments of these two large matrilineal categories.[40] Many Australian peoples have kinship systems that combine the crossness of kin, the duality of gender, and the alternation of generations (my generation versus those of my parents and children) to form marriage classes of four or eight categories. Fathers in marriage class A and mothers in class B have children belonging to C, who marry people of D, and so on. The structural similarity of marriage classes, and the fact that class names often extend across vast territories, makes it possible to find or create relations between strangers. People do this by asking a series of routine questions about names, language, genealogy, and locality. Aram Yengoyan, an ethnographer who has worked among Pitjandjara aboriginal groups, reports that after a journey of several weeks with him by truck, Australians meeting strangers of other tribes and languages immediately established relations through marriage sections.[41]

However complex these systems might seem to us, they are rooted in basic dichotomies between male and female, sibling and nonsibling, parent and child. In societies that do not distinguish cross and parallel kin, a set of close relatives (parents, siblings, children) is differentiated from those who are more distant (aunts and uncles, cousins, nieces and nephews), and the kin terms used to describe relatives on the mother's side are the same as those used for relatives on the father's side. In these bilateral systems, found among Inuit whale hunters and European capitalists alike, concepts of near and far shape marriage rules, and the closest kin are, by definition, those a person cannot marry. The experts are divided over whether cross or bilateral kinship developed first.[42] Each system is demonstrably ancient, and the fact that both remain common today is a testament to the durability of human kinshipping traditions. It also suggests that kinshipping is a viable way of imagining community in deep time.

The DNA trails that connect us to our most ancient ancestors are a compelling way of pursuing this work of the imagination. But as we look to the future of studying the past, much older forms of kinshipping might help us reacquaint ourselves with our remote kin. We conclude this chapter by imagining ourselves in relation to people we have never met but know to be, at least potentially, our kin. Putting this knowledge to work requires not only that we think about kinshipping in the abstract, as a set of ideas and practices, but also that we actively engage in it by using objects (like the biface) and tactics (like the visit and the exchange) to create relationships across a gap. Humans are very good at this game, which we have always been willing to play with our dead kin, spirits, animals, material artifacts, and forces of nature. The intellectual experiment that follows, in other words, has a deep history of its own.

VISITING DISTANT KIN

We began with the idea that modern historians turn away from gaps, from problems and periods for which there are no dates, no archives, and no verifiable stories to tell. Perhaps we should continue now by inverting this idea. Modern historiography in fact depends on gaps, distances, and empty spaces. When these intervals do not exist, historians create them, thus making it possible to write infinitely many books on Elizabethan military technology, or taxation in the Xing dynasty, each one insisting that something essential has been left out of all previous accounts. R. G. Collingwood thought he was stating the obvious when he argued that thought is historical only if it involves the imagination of events and people who are absent, or "*res gestae:* actions of human beings that have been done in the past."[43] The challenge is to work around absence by means of "documents." For Collingwood, documents are residual evidence from an earlier time—not just written materials, but stone tools, skeletal remains, and burned seeds plucked from ancient hearths. An object becomes a document when we use it to figure out what the absent people who created it were doing. Asking new questions about what people did in the past, it follows, creates new gaps in the historical record, and new documents are needed to fill them.

If we take this model of history seriously—which means, first of all, not confusing it with what academics call history—it becomes possible to think of human kinship itself as a form of historical thought, perhaps the oldest and most effective we possess. Kinship links us to absent people, past and present; it enables us to figure out who they were and how they interacted; and it allows us to arrive at these conclusions properly only if we think through objects, which must be (or have been) aligned and exchanged in ways that allow us to conclude that certain people are truly "related." The objects of kinship include bodily substances, names, shared foods, physical resemblances, stereotyped behaviors, and the materials, feelings, and ideas connected to these "documents."

Human kinship is like history because it is knowable only in relation to absent parties. Humans are unique among primates for keeping up relations—interacting and visiting—with kin who no longer live with us on a daily basis. In a sense, kinship terminologies help us construct miniature historical accounts of these absent individuals, and these family histories help us remember each other and interact on familiar terms when we are reunited or meet for the first time. The benefits (and costs) of this linking behavior are distributed across several human life spans. Indeed, the most remarkable attribute of human kinship is not simply its "release from proximity," a byproduct of language that is found in several varieties of human thought; nor is it simply the development of what Clive Gamble describes as "concepts that related people when they were apart," which must originally have been very simple.[44] Rather, it is the seamless articulation of the living with the long-dead and the not-yet-born that gives human kinship its greatest connective and systematizing power. This latter capacity might be recent—Gamble, for instance, argues that it facilitated the global human diaspora that began roughly sixty thousand years ago—but it is now as much a part of the human package as bipedalism or pair bonding.[45]

Given the weight and antiquity of kinship systems, it is not hard to understand why nation-states are likened to families (and have founding fathers); why citizenship is described as *fraternité;* or why the time revolution of the nineteenth century, a moment of triumph for modernity and science, should have resulted, a century and a half later, in genomic research that tells us how we are all related, where our ancestors came from, and how and why we are different from each other. In short, we have become good at using different tools to provide the same kind of information that people used to find by opening their Bibles, and much of deep history is shaped by Abrahamic cosmology. What would happen if, in pursuit of a less recognizable deep history, we not only drew on the genealogical imagination that underlies Darwinian (and biblical) models of descent but tried as well to put the lateral affinities of Ojibwa- and Pitjandjara-style kinship to historiographic use?

EXTENSION AND COMPRESSION

When Chief Berens meets other Ojibwa for the first time and quickly ascertains that they are cross kin, this conclusion depends on articulation with, and through, abstract categories. It depends on the ability to separate kin relations from the realm of discrete individuals, to treat these relations as rules, and to apply them to strangers. There is always a gap between kinship systems and the real, living people they describe. The potential to be cross or parallel exists independently of the fact that Chief Berens is one or the other. If a set of clan names is arranged in terms of cross and parallel relations, they can be used to sort out thousands of people across a large geographical region. This process of lateral extension is ingenious for its ability to work forward and backward in time; it expands in order to collapse. Once Chief Berens is defined as a cross relative, he can be treated in a familiar way, like other cross cousins local to the village he was visiting.

The idea that kinship was designed to support individuals who travel is rooted in its capacity to extend and compress social networks. When geneticists extend lines of ancestry tens of thousands of years into the past using DNA evidence, they are creating affinities in the present; just as often, the identities and affinities of the present are transported back through time. Hence, the National Geographic Society can comfortably merge past and present in its *Book of Peoples of the World,* a compendium in which 222 ethnic, linguistic, and national categories are sorted into seven major culture areas, all of which are linked (genetically) to ancestral human populations many thousands of years old.[46] (Think of the *Nuremberg Chronicle,* updated.) Little is made of the fact that these seven culture areas would not have been recognizable as such before the age of European expansion and that each is now demographically mixed, except to imply that human diversity is somehow threatened, not enhanced, by this process. Even less is made of the fact that Masai tribesmen, German burghers, and Gypsy tinkers are historically recent human categories, each defined by principles other than biogenetic relatedness. These points of confusion are useful. They enable National Geographic to persuade thousands of American readers that the cultural and biogenetic variations found on the planet today are worth savoring, like the quirks of so many relatives; that the bewildering array of colors, languages, and cultures we see around us is nothing to be afraid of. It is the natural result of the human family's spread across the planet.

All kinship systems double as history and geography, and each predisposes us to draw peculiar conclusions. Ojibwa, for instance, would not be troubled by the fact that Chief Berens was as closely related genetically to a female parallel cousin (whom he could not marry because she belonged to his clan) as he was to a female cross cousin (whom he could marry because she belonged to another clan). In many societies, people believe that they descend originally from birds, land forms, plants, or spiritual beings (and are thus essentially unconformable to National Geographic's *Book of Peoples of the World*). What is constant in human kinship systems, however, and worth working into the way we imagine humanity in deep time, is the use of mediating objects to constitute, extend, contract, and increase the predictability of human relationships. Kinship systems and kin terms are best thought of as a particular kind of mediation. They have objective qualities in their own right, and they are expressed and experienced through objects. As tools of mediation, kinship systems figure as the third party to any exchange that brings two humans, or collective bodies of humans, into relation, literally or figuratively, as kinds. Kinship closes and creates gaps, just as historians do.

FACTORS OF THREE

The image of two parties connected by a third surfaces repeatedly in contemporary depictions of human society over time, and this tendency is strong evidence (for those who still need it) that the study of deep history is itself an exercise in kinshipping. Since the time revolution, we have witnessed a parade of three-part typologies of human development: stone, bronze, and iron; savage, barbarian, and civilized; foraging, agricultural, and industrial. These layer-cake typologies could also be projected onto spatial or temporal grids. The Polynesians who awaited French explorers like Baudin were considered savages here and now, representative of the savages Europeans must have been in the remote past; either way, they were made into kin of a distant, primitive sort.

Some tripartite sociological models seem synchronic but have strong diachronic implications. Marxian concepts of base, structure, and superstructure can be mapped onto older typologies in which "primitive" life is skewed toward infrastructural concerns (survival, reproduction, obtaining food), and "civilized" life is marked by dense elaborations of superstructure (art, literature, religion, philosophy). Likewise, Eric Wolf's discussion of modes of production, which divides human societies into kin-ordered, tributary, and capitalist economies, can be projected into deep time, despite Wolf's reluctance to do so.[47] It is perfectly sensible to conclude that kin-ordered modes of production came first (because kinship is ancient), followed by tributary modes (which require social stratification, a novelty compared to kinship systems), and then capitalist modes (which are very recent). The same implicit temporality is central to comparisons of economies based on reciprocity (which came first), redistribution (next), and market exchange (most recent), or to comparisons of political systems based on egalitarianism (bands and tribes), rank (tribes and chiefdoms), and social stratification (chiefdoms and states).

Whether these temporalities are ill-founded or empirically justifiable—they can be either, in theory and in practice—they are traveling devices akin to kinship. In almost every case, the key contrast is between the near and far ends of a spectrum, with a middle term figuring as the medium of translation, as the kinshipping device. This form of translation works to the extent that we assume the three stages belong to a progression, that they are linked through a process akin to (or, in some cases, equivalent to) descent or maturation. The Darwinian approach to deep time, with its reliance on genealogical explanations of variation, imbues these models with a sense of progress and directionality in which Darwin, the model Victorian, firmly believed; at the same time, however, Darwinian thought could, and eventually did, opt for explanatory accounts that accentuated adaptive radiations in which change was gradual and cumulative but could not be described as inherently progressive or regressive.

If we make descent and natural selection central to our theories of human variation over long periods of time, we can dispense with stages and deal instead with spectra. Some of the most influential approaches to deep history now take the latter approach. Robin Dunbar's theory of the social brain, for instance, proposes that human brains have become bigger over time because natural selection has favored individuals who live in larger social groups over those who live in smaller ones.[48] To sustain larger groups, individuals need larger brains (to accommodate language capacity, because language, in addition to grooming, is a means of creating social solidarity among humans). The model is genealogical; it transects human, nearly human, and nonhuman primate species; and the process it depicts (brains becoming bigger, smarter, and more human) is so commonsensical that there is little need for translation. To succeed at kinshipping, the advocates of this theory contend, it helps immensely to have big brains; and, not surprisingly, we do! As a translation device, the social brain stands between us and a chimp; between us and *Homo erectus;* and between us and anything with a smaller brain.

Explanations based on rigorous application of selection theory avoid translation (or make it a nonissue) by eliminating gaps in the story of human development. Instead they render it continuous in ways that are in fact averse to the logic of kinshipping, which bridges real gaps in time and space, thereby enabling humans to move away from each other and then return. Tripartite models that preserve this structure of fission and fusion, with a middle term as connector, continue to thrive in recent studies of deep history, largely because they reenact, in the present, a set of processes that we now believe developed over millennia. Tripartite models make it possible to think through objects (or, more accurately, to think our way through to objects) that belonged to active kinship networks in the remote past. Examples of this theoretical style include the following:

1. Alan Barnard's division of hominin history into phases of "proto-kinship" (marked by sharing and inclusive kinship, characteristic of australopiths and *Homo erectus*), "rudimentary kinship" (marked by us/them kinship, exchange, and incest rules, characteristic of archaic *Homo sapiens* and Neanderthals), and "true kinship" (with fully developed kinship systems, universal kin categorization, explicit rules of sharing, exchange, and kin behavior, characteristic of modern *Homo sapiens*) (figure 5).[49] Barnard sets these stages parallel to similar stages in human language development and then inserts ancestral hominins into each stage.

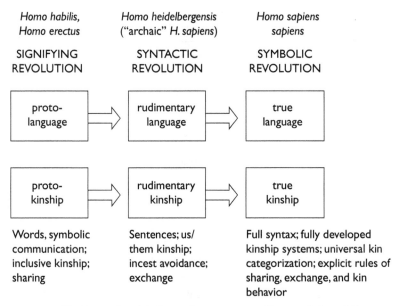

Homo habilis, Homo erectus	Homo heidelbergensis ("archaic" H. sapiens)	Homo sapiens sapiens
SIGNIFYING REVOLUTION	SYNTACTIC REVOLUTION	SYMBOLIC REVOLUTION

proto-language → rudimentary language → true language

proto-kinship → rudimentary kinship → true kinship

| Words, symbolic communication; inclusive kinship; sharing | Sentences; us/them kinship; incest avoidance; exchange | Full syntax; fully developed kinship systems; universal kin categorization; explicit rules of sharing, exchange, and kin behavior |

FIGURE 5. The Barnard model. (Barnard 2008, 235; used by permission of Alan Barnard and John Wiley & Sons Ltd.)

2. Steven Mithen's division of human development into prehistoric, evolutionary time, before roughly 50,000 years ago (which was not historical and has no history) and a more recent period, which is historical and can be so because people had developed, by this time, a "modern mind" (figure 6).[50] This historical period is divided into three stages: the prelude to history (50,000–20,000 years ago); the Neolithic revolution (20,000–5,000 years ago); and the last phase, beginning 5,000 years ago, which includes the contemporary world. The Neolithic revolution is assimilated to the modern world, and the prelude to history verges into the remote, evolutionary past.

And, finally, to make a trio of our own:

3. Clive Gamble's division of the hominin past into three periods: the long introduction (which runs from 2.6 million to 100,000 years ago), the middle ground (100,000–20,000 years ago), and the short answer (20,000–5,000 years ago) (figure 7).[51] Although Gamble's typology registers phases, and poses a zone of translation aptly

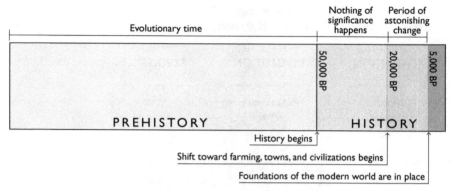

FIGURE 6. The Mithen model. (Based on Mithen 2003; adapted by Mary Birkett.)

called the "middle ground," it is designed to reflect the continuous nature of change. As humans move through the three domains, they transition, in fits and starts but cumulatively, from technologies that privilege instruments to those that privilege containers; from brico-lage and improvisation to modularity and engineering; from smaller to larger brains; from smaller, intense kin networks to larger, extended ones; from concentration in Africa to global expansion; from subsistence strategies based on models of "the giving environ-ment" to those based on "growing the body"; and from communi-cation through objects and material metaphors to communication based increasingly on linguistic metaphors.

Each of these approaches poses and solves a unique set of problems, but when the three models are superimposed, the variations that result are telling. Mithen's stark discontinuity between history and prehistory is erased in Gamble's system of gradations. Barnard's types map well onto Gamble's, but much of the progression Barnard describes belongs to a time when, according to Mithen, "little of significance happened." In all three models, the last 5,000 years belong to a different kind of history (fully modern), or represent a brief continuation of a complex jumble of trends and consequences that came to a head in the develop-ment of sedentism, domestication, social inequality, and city and state formation. The past 5,000 years constitute the realm of "shallow his-tory," where patterns and events pile up with incredible speed. Keeping abreast of them requires an almost journalistic pace of reportage, not the grand, synthetic theory appropriate to a span of 2.6 million years.

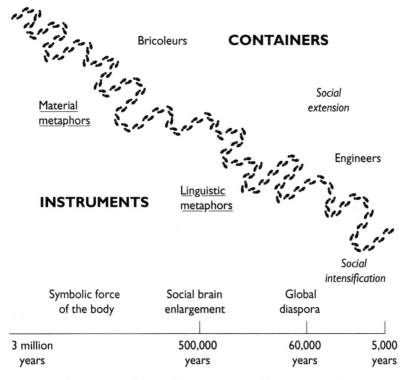

Long introduction		Common ground	Short answer

CONTAINERS

Bricoleurs

Material metaphors

Social extension

Engineers

INSTRUMENTS

Linguistic metaphors

Social intensification

Symbolic force of the body	Social brain enlargement	Global diaspora	
3 million years	500,000 years	60,000 years	5,000 years

FIGURE 7. The Gamble model. (Gamble 2007, 278; used by permission of Clive Gamble.)

The essential kinshipping function of these tripartite models of deep time can be seen if we sort them into a kindred schema that Julian Pitt-Rivers used to explain the importance of hospitality in human societies, especially those of the Mediterranean "prior to modern urban development."[52] Although it is drawn to fit entirely within the past 5,000 years, an age of houses, villages, and agriculture, Pitt-Rivers's model, like those of deep time, has a recent period—in this case, the era of the modern city—to which it apparently does not apply. The social world of the premodern Mediterranean was, according to Pitt-Rivers, divided into (1) the house, which is internally divided into a private sphere associated with women and dependents, and a more public space where guests can be received; (2) the areas outside the house, the "common meeting grounds of the whole community," which is made up of similarly structured households whose members know each other and have real, continuous relations of rivalry and alliance; and (3) the "outside world" beyond the community, "from which come strangers, that is, unknown persons who, unlike the fellow-members of the community with whom relations are habitual and clearly structured, remain mysterious, their nature and their power in doubt and who derive from their strangeness a preferential relationship to the Divine."[53]

The transposition of categories from this model onto those depicting deep time is straightforward and suggestive. The household is analogous to Gamble's "short answer," Barnard's zone of "true kinship," and Mithen's "last 5,000 years." The community is Gamble's "middle ground," Barnard's zone of "rudimentary kinship," and Mithen's "Neolithic revolution," and so on across the types. The world of strangers is the truly remote world in all these models; it is remote temporally for our paleohistorians and spatially for Pitt-Rivers. The hominin ancestors who occupy this realm are mysterious indeed. Gamble, in his account of the "long introduction," confesses to an inability to figure out what these creatures are up to: "puzzles abound," and material remains are "difficult to read."

This quality of strangeness is pervasively felt by scholars who study the deep past. Like the strangeness of the guest in Mediterranean societies, the strangeness of human ancestors is captivating. It provokes a desire to accommodate and examine their otherness (the way one stares at a stranger sipping tea in the guest room) without necessarily assimilating it (the guest is not allowed to enter all parts of the house). In his recent study of human food cultures over time, Martin Jones acts out these tendencies in written form. He begins each chapter of *Feast: Why Humans Share Food* with an imaginative narrative in which he reconstructs events at a famous archaeological site.[54] In the oldest sites, he writes strangeness into his accounts of archaic *Homo sapiens* (who mix animal butchery with sexual exchanges in ways that recall the behavior of chimpanzees collectively devouring a red colobus monkey) and Neanderthals (whom he depicts as slightly autistic, avoiding each other's stares, acting in parallel but not quite together, and not thinking thoughts but considering images that "echo in their minds").

In many ways, these storytelling gestures mark the outer limits of human kinshipping, insofar as Jones suggests that the gap cannot be closed and indeed should be left open out of respect for the differences and imponderables the archaeological record holds. Was this odd pile of mammoth jaws a shelter? Did these people exchange men and women between groups? What did they give in exchange? Did these exchanges create what we would call kinship, or marriage? Did they eat meals together, or in rank order, or did they eat randomly throughout the day, as hunger and opportunity arose? Answers to these questions must be formed carefully, just as the treatment of a stranger in the Pitt-Rivers model must proceed carefully. If the guest is to be brought into closer relations with his hosts, this transition can be accomplished only by securing a place for him, and for his apparent differences, in local society. As Pitt-Rivers put it, "the community" lies between the precincts of intimacy and those of the extraneous world, "with which contact is exceptional, sporadic, and subject to special provisions."[55]

In Mediterranean settings, these interactions between the remote and the familiar are conducted through ritualized greetings, gifts of food, access to sovereign spaces, and physical protection. The social distance between stranger and household is continually renegotiated using conventions made available to both by the larger society. Pitt-Rivers locates this social drama (which always has a stagelike quality) in a particular cultural tradition, but its key components are ethnographically widespread, and he seems to realize fully how fundamental the arrival and reception of the stranger has been to the development of human society over time. His tripartite schema is a model of spatial relations, but its grammar can be temporalized to produce a model of kinshipping that replicates not only what paleohistorians do when they create tripartite models of their own, but also what humans do, and have done, when using kinship to travel.

CONCLUSION: RETURNING HOME

The study of deep history is ultimately an encounter with strangers, but with strangers whose otherness seems potentially intelligible and with whom a relationship seems possible, if only through interaction with their objects. To the extent that material residues left by earlier hominins were shaped by object relations ancestral to our own, we can work back toward those relationships, using analogies and recurrent patterns, to arrive at relations more familiar to us. This is what historians do with their "documents." It is what humans did as they journeyed to the uttermost ends of the Earth, constantly doubling back, reestablishing ties, and coaxing others to join them.

Kinshipping, we have argued, is a social technology that enables two parties to create relationships through the mediation of abstract categories, or absent thirds, and the objects that convey them. We should end this journey, then, by insisting that kinshipping is of no value if it does not allow for infinite returns. The fascination with deep history we explore in subsequent chapters might have begun, for us, in the years surrounding 1859, when the collapse of biblical time compelled us to retell the human story on a larger temporal scale. But this new fascination with the remote past inevitably reconnects us to the past 5,000 years, the period left out of deep history (perhaps because it is the period that genuinely animates it). If this reconnection across time were not to occur, the intellectual enterprise we undertake here would not be kinshipping of the human sort.

Interacting with our stranger kin, as their imaginary hosts and guests, requires that we stretch our imagination to accommodate them, working our way back to them gradually, using all the links (and enlisting the aid of all the human intermediaries) we can discover. The moment of hospitality has been essential to human kinshipping. It enables host and guest to reinterpret the social world they inhabit through encounter and then to move on, or to establish relations of a more durable sort. As students of deep history, we will know this interpretive connection has been made—alas, for us, only in the realm of imagination—when the past 5,000 years seems as new to us, as strange and distinctive, as the oldest eras of what, since roughly 1859, we have come to know as "prehistoric times." Then, in short order, we will ask the most inevitable of human questions: "Where do we go next?"

PART TWO

Frames for History in Deep Time

CHAPTER 3

Body

DANIEL LORD SMAIL AND ANDREW SHRYOCK

The human body, in the form of skulls, teeth, and bones, has been a central figure in humanity's deep history for no more than a century. In 1859, as Prestwich and Evans were offering their demonstration of the antiquity of stone tools and Big Ben was beginning to toll the hours, the ancient body as a media figure was still over the horizon. For several decades to come, the arresting visual evidence for human antiquity would consist largely of the accumulating discoveries of flint artifacts and other stone tools. By the close of the century, however, the cold, one-dimensional proof provided by stone tools had been enriched in two spectacular ways. One was the discovery of the cave paintings at Altamira in Spain: when their authenticity was finally confirmed, they created a dizzying sensation of spiritual contact with ancient humans.[1] The immense popularity of the site was reflected in its rapid incorporation into the tourist itinerary, producing a crush of latter-day pilgrims to rival those who had begun to frequent the shrine of Notre Dame de Lourdes a few decades earlier.[2]

Even more compelling than cave paintings was the growing fossil evidence for early human existence. In conjunction with the genealogies of primate descent postulated by Sir Arthur Keith and others, the evidence provided by a growing collection of skeletal fragments created a new genealogical reality for the twentieth century.[3] Human remains, of course, predated Prestwich and Evans's 1859 demonstration of the antiquity of stone tools. The skull of the Gibraltar woman, which was

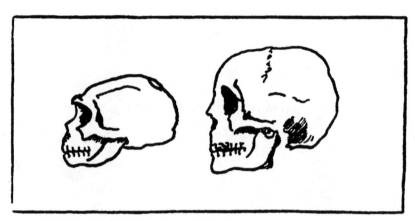

FIGURE 8. "Our First Man-like Ancestor." (Van Loon 1921, 8.)

not quite *not* human, had turned up in 1848 at the foot of the Rock of Gibraltar. She was soon upstaged by the more widely publicized discovery of remains in the Neander Valley in Germany in 1856. But these ancient remains were not incorporated into the human genealogy for decades. For much of the nineteenth century, physical anthropology was devoted to the synchronous categorization of the "races of man," and it was only by the turn of the century that the immensity of human genealogical depth became a vivid reality in the press and an object of growing paleoanthropological inquiry. We can measure this transformation in many ways. Among the evidence is the rapid emergence of cartoons and fiction featuring Stone Age humans, and of fantasies about their diet around the end of the nineteenth century.

The shock to the public imagination was profound. In his best-selling *Story of Mankind* (1921), Hendrik van Loon capitalized on the unsettling new reality by offering, near the outset, a description of the first true men.[4] "We have never seen their pictures," he writes, perhaps to explain why the image that accompanied his text could compare only two skulls (see figure 8). "In the deepest layer of clay of an ancient soil we have sometimes found pieces of their bones. ... Anthropologists (learned scientists who devote their lives to the study of man as a member of the animal kingdom) have taken these bones and they have been able to reconstruct our earliest ancestors with a fair degree of accuracy."[5] The great-great-grandfather of the human race, he goes on to say, "was a very ugly and unattractive mammal," small, dark brown, and covered with long, coarse hair, with fingers of a thinness reminiscent of a monkey's. "His forehead was low and his jaw was like the jaw of a wild ani-

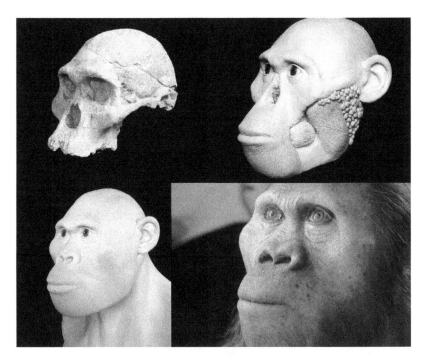

FIGURE 9. The process of scientific reconstruction. This series of images represents the principal stages of the reconstruction of the face and skull of an *Australopithecus africanus* female, known as Mrs. Ples, by the paleontological artist Elisabeth Daynès. (Top left: Photo by E. Daynès. All others: © 2007 Photos by P.Plailly/E.Daynès/Eurelios. Reconstruction: Atelier Daynès Paris.)

mal which uses its teeth both as fork and knife. He wore no clothes." But despite this rather shocking image, this man, he tells his readers, "was your first 'man-like' ancestor." This was kinshipping in practice.

Biological anthropologists have thoroughly absorbed van Loon's gift for harnessing the power of the body's genealogy, though they have learned that face and skin speak more persuasively than skull and bone. As the Soviet archaeologist Mikhail M. Gerasimov put it some years ago, we feel strongly the urge to know what early man looked like.[6] In keeping with the Gerasimov principle, paleoanthropologists routinely commission drawings, plastic models, and computer simulations to flesh out the mute fragments of human bone, for when all is said and done, such fragments are little more evocative than flints. The reconstructions are generated by highly trained artists who specialize in paleontological subjects. Starting with nothing more than the skull of *Australopithecus africanus,* Elisabeth Daynès, a specialist in this craft, adds layers of muscle, skin, and hair to transform the fossil into a face (figure 9). The coming-out party of *Ardipithecus ramidus* in the fall of 2009 would not have been complete without line drawings; three-dimensional simulations of her eyes, face, and gait; and the vivid reconstruction of her body. Deep histories are made viscerally and emotionally vivid through the genealogy of the body.

Bodies matter to history. They form a bridge between the present and deep human time. We channel kinship, lineage, and time through the bodies of those we claim as our ancestors, turning the body itself into a powerful frame in which the past can be organized and interpreted. The body evolves, at the species level, just as individual bodies grow, and these two processes—one producing, over millennia, bipedalism and large brains, the other leading to a youngster's ability to walk and talk—are woven together in stories of human evolution. Indeed, these narrative links allow parts of the body to travel through time in our eerie recognition of the hips we share with *Ardipithecus,* the nose we may have inherited from *Homo erectus,* and, for that matter, the ears that came to us from Grandma.

Bodies also extend over space. They serve as representations of the whole and as measures of the world around us. Bedouins display this synecdochal awareness when they describe their tribes in terms of thighs, bellies, and arms; this habit is amply reproduced in the language of modern statecraft, which supplies nations and government institutions with arms, heads, muscle, backbones, and other useful bits of anatomy. The political theology of medieval Europe attributed to kings both a personal body and a body politic, the latter extending well beyond the monarch's peripersonal space to the far reaches of the realm.[7] Confronting the attempts of other rulers to penetrate or dismember their realms, monarchs responded with visceral emotion. According to chroniclers, they felt the incursion as a body blow. The thirteenth-century Ebstorf *mappa mundi* took the metaphor even further, for the world it portrayed, an enormous canvas roughly twelve feet in diameter, was one vast body, Christ's body, with feet, hands, and head (figure 10). Wondrous beasts, including anthropophagi, or eaters of men, inhabit the space depicted in the Ebstorf and the still-extant Hereford *mappae mundi*. To many, the world is indeed a body.

The Ebstorf *mappa mundi,* as it happens, was made from bodies, in the form of thirty pieces of vellum produced from the skins of sheep. After surviving for seven centuries, this collection of skins was destroyed in an Allied air raid in World War II, and all we are left with is a copy. But the map itself is, or was, a marvelous statement of how the human

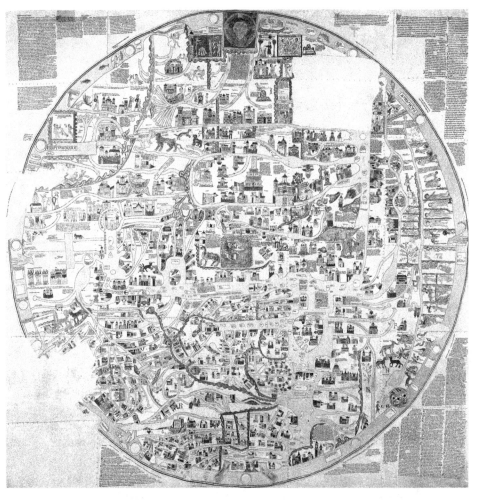

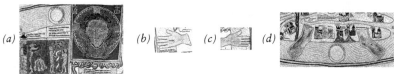

(a) (b) (c) (d)

FIGURE 10. The Ebstorf *mappa mundi*. Among the great *mappae mundi* of thirteenth-century Europe, the Ebstorf is unusual in depicting the entire world as the body of Christ. Like all medieval maps, the Ebstorf is "oriented": east, where the sun rises (*oriens*), is at the top of the map. In medieval Europe, Eden was thought to be located in the east, and indeed a picture of Adam, Eve, the tree, and the snake is placed next to the right ear of Jesus (see detail *a* above). His hands can be seen at the left and right edges of the map (details *b* and *c*), where Europe and Africa are located, with his feet planted in the Atlantic Ocean, on the lower edge of the map (detail *d*). This is an artistic reproduction of the original, which was destroyed in World War II. (Photo provided by Kloster Ebstorf, Germany; used by permission of Kloster Ebstorf.)

body has grown larger over the past several million years, encompassing entire worlds of experience and imagination. This is the insight around which a deep history of the body can coalesce.

DISTRIBUTED BODIES

One of the books of the Bible, which is not shy about the human body, tells the gruesome story of what happened to the Levite's concubine on the night that she, her husband, and their servant accepted hospitality in Gibeah. News of the arrival of a stranger had spread across the town, and as the guests were making merry with their host, a crowd of local men surrounded the house, pounded on the door, and demanded that the Levite be brought forth that they might abuse him. To preserve his male guest from shame, the host demurred and offered instead his own daughter. But because the rules of hospitality demanded as much from the Levite as from his host, the Levite, acting precipitately, offered his concubine to the villagers and closed the door behind her. In the morning, he found her ravished body on the doorstep. When she did not respond to his order to stand up, he realized she was dead. He slung her body on his donkey, took her home, and then, as the text goes, "he picked up his knife, took hold of his concubine, and limb by limb cut her into twelve pieces; he then sent her all through the land of Israel." He instructed his messengers as follows, "This is what you are to say to all the Israelites, 'Has any man seen such a thing from the day the Israelites came out of the land of Egypt, until this very day? Ponder on this, discuss it; then give your verdict'" (Judges 19: 29–30). Things went badly for the people of Gibeah after this.

Bodies, the story reminds us, do powerful things in human societies, not only when they are whole but also when they are fragmented into pieces, into stages of maturation, into memories and transferable powers. In classical Greek mythology, the Earth itself is the body of a woman, Gaia, and the sky is a man, Uranus. The world that emerges from their union is, in its first generations, a murderous scene in which offspring are repeatedly crushed or consumed—Cronus, son of Uranus, swallows his own children—and then forcibly disgorged, to murder or be murdered by their closest kin. The gods, human beings, the land and seas, the entire cosmos are the product of this violent intermingling of bodies. If the story of the Levite's concubine ends in disarticulation and communal disgrace, the chaotic struggle between the Earth, the sky, and their children ends in a stable family structure based on the patriarchal authority of Zeus, a durable separation of the bodies and powers of the Olympian gods, and their peaceful relationship with Gaia, the mother body from which they all sprang.

Tales of dismemberment and reincorporation are by no means unique to the ancient Mediterranean world. They appeal widely to humans, who are quick to assume the centrality of these processes to social life. The anonymous author of the fourteenth-century *Travels of Sir John Mandeville* told the tale of a South Asian people called the Lobassy, among whom the son mourned his dead father first by separating the head from the body and then by cutting the body in pieces for the birds of the valley to eat. His father's honor was measured by the number of birds who showed up for the pickings. The son then took the head and divided its flesh among his friends, all of whom would partake of it in the most solemn fashion.[8] In this way, the flesh of the dead was transmitted from generation to generation. Here, it matters not whether the Mandeville author was simply making up the account, for what he described was a variation of the Christian eucharist, a real and instrumentally powerful ceremony that created the *gens Christianorum,* the Christian race, through the act of consuming the distributed body of an ancestor.

Bodies like that of the Levite's concubine, the Lobassy father, and Jesus are routinely distributed across landscapes in bits and pieces, often to be reassembled in larger contexts. Comparative ethnography is replete with examples. The Yanomami of the Venezuelan rain forest drink the ashes of their dead in a funeral soup, giving their ancestors a new home in the living community. Until recent decades, the Parsis of South Asia, faint echoes of whose practices showed up in the story of the Lobassy father, allowed the bones of their dead to be picked clean by birds, a rite that returned human flesh to nature in nonpolluting forms. On the island of Madagascar, the remains of dead relatives are periodically disinterred and reburied, their disintegrating bodies wrapped in new shrouds, until their remains are reduced to dust, at which point they are wrapped with other decomposing ancestors in a collective bundle called "the great ancestor."[9]

Practices of this sort are demonstrably ancient. Archaeologists describe sites with disaggregated body parts that could only have come from exchanges in bones, anticipating the trade in saints' relics during the early Middle Ages in Europe.[10] Funerary customs from the late Neolithic onward apparently included the dispersal of ancestors' ashes and urn fragments, deliberately broken, among the members of the kin group.[11] Ceramic fragments, in this context, mimic the material goods distributed in last wills and testaments, which gain meaning as contact relics that transmit memories of the dead and create patterns of enchainment linking past and present. This is a form of kinshipping through material objects that parallels and amplifies the kinshipping of genealogical descent.

Once bodies can be reproduced in metonymic and synecdochal ways, they can be distributed on a truly massive scale. The coins of the ancient Mediterranean often displayed the heads of the kings and emperors who caused them to be minted. It is possible to find images of the head of Charlemagne in coin hoards as far away as Visby in Gotland, Sweden—heads not consumed in the way of the Lobassy father but facilitating other forms of consumption.[12] The Muslim prohibition on the depiction of the human image was easily evaded by representing instead the voice of God, whose utterances, as revealed in the Qur'an, were stamped on the 'Abbasid caliphate's gold dinars, some of which traveled from Baghdad to trading centers in China and Viking hamlets in Scandinavia. All these representations are a prelude to the technologies of print capitalism and electronic media, which allow images of sovereigns, presidents, and dictators to be distributed like icons across large spaces, thus uniting whole nations as bodies politic.

In suggesting that ancient and modern political communities are organized in relation to the human body, we have in mind something more basic than a symbolic likeness or an enduring set of metaphors. At issue is the peculiar ability of the human body to expand, to displace itself in language and experience, and to rematerialize in larger social fields that contain and create individual bodies.

THE LONG REACH OF THE NERVOUS SYSTEM

When you pick up a hammer or a hand ax and pound a nail or a nut, interesting things start to happen inside your head. Your brain is used to keeping track of the edges of your body, for the extremities are always liable to tread on thorns, get burned in fires, or knock themselves against branches or doorjambs. So when you wield a hammer of any kind, your brain is inclined to ask itself how this extra bit of body got attached. Pound some nuts or nails every day for a week or two, and new maps gradually form in the premotor cortex, so that the action becomes more precise and more automated. Over time, the hammer is incorporated into the map of the body. Like any tool or implement, it becomes a curious sort of limb, a prosthesis that can be put on and taken off at will.[13]

As far as the brain is concerned, the human body does not end at the surface of the skin. The body encompasses toes, fingers, and heads, not to mention thighs and bellies, but it can also comprise hats, canoe paddles, and tennis rackets. It includes the peripersonal penumbra described both by neuroscience and by the Himba of Namibia, who postulate a kind of bubble or "self space" that envelops the human body.[14] Some parts of the body, like the phantom limbs of amputees, need not be present to be considered integral to the body; and the edges of the body, real or imagined, extend into other bodies. Pain communicates itself readily across the space between the sufferer and the observer. So does sexual arousal. This is simple empathy; but empathy, it turns out, may be something more than an ethical desideratum. Some degree of empathy may be wired into the brain in the form of mirror neurons, neurons that fire merely at the contemplation of a motor action. It is thanks to mirror neurons, according to some, that we flinch at the sight of someone else hit suddenly by a fist or a ball and wince while reading a gruesome account of torture. Mirror neurons were discovered first in monkeys, and indirect evidence suggests the existence of a mirror neuron system in humans.[15] The neuroscientist V.S. Ramachandran has argued that culture itself would be impossible without mirror neurons.[16] Mirror neurons, in this view, allow us to emulate. They have made it possible for language to evolve and for traits to spread rapidly through human populations.[17]

Large claims have been made for the role of mirror neurons in human evolution, and they have provoked loud demurrals. Wherever the research takes us, and regardless of whether the evocation of mirror neurons spurs indignant accusations of biological essentialism, one thing is clear: the probable existence of mirror neurons hints at the long reach of the autonomic nervous system, and it reveals this reach to be social. Bodies are innately capable of being distributed, both physically and metonymically. They are not bound by the edges of their skin, and this expansive capability offers another means of constructing kinship, through likeness and interaction.

Similar observations hold for the autonomic nervous system as a whole, which operates through the transmission of electronic signals across synapses and along nerves. The system is lubricated by neurotransmitters, chemicals that are generated in synapses and, when present, speed up the rate of firing. But the reach of the system does not end here. Much as letters, sounds, and images can be transformed into analog or digital signals, sent across space, and decoded again by fax machines, radios, televisions, and computer screens, a signal can be transmitted between two or more individuals. All of us, from mates and godsibs to publicists and pornographers, have the ability to reach into the autonomic nervous system of other bodies, there to excite neurons and stimulate or shut off neurotransmitters and hormones. This capacity exists in all primate societies and is most highly developed in human societies. The Bedouin image of the tribe as a distributed body is thus much more than a metaphor: it is a neurologically accurate description of a human society bound together as a vastly interconnecting nervous system.

This insight has enormous implications for our understanding of deep human history. In the captivating argument proposed by the anthropologist Robin Dunbar, primate grooming is a practice essential to the building and maintaining of social relations.[18] Grooming generates a pleasant dose of dopamine and serotonin, along with oxytocin, the peace-and-bonding neurotransmitter. But the capacity to groom peers is limited by two factors. The first is time: an ape or a monkey can groom only so many allies in a day and still have enough time to find food. Second, because grooming is a component of a larger system of tracking alliances, the number of grooming mates is limited by the size of the neocortex, where primates keep track of their mutual obligations. Language, according to Dunbar, allowed human group sizes to grow larger, for language permits gossip, a kind of group-oriented, verbal grooming. Using gossip, greetings, and speech directed at several parties at once—in a word, conversation—humans were able to extend neurochemical bonds across a much larger network. This extension made larger, more empathetic, and better-organized groups a standard feature of human social life.

Dunbar's model has been tied tightly to a single argument: the origins of language. But it also points to something else: the emergence of human societies knit together as much by neurochemical signals as by language and culture. Gossip is one of many ways in which signals are transformed into sound waves, sent across the gap between individuals, and then turned back into electrical signals and neurotransmitters. Power is implicated in this process, for relations of power can emerge from the selective manipulation of the social ether. This possibility has long been contemplated by observers. Writing in the mid-sixteenth century, the French essayist Étienne de la Boétie (d. 1563) observed that "theatres, games, plays, spectacles, marvellous beasts, medals, *tableaux,* and other such drugs were for the people of Antiquity the allurements of serfdom, the price for their freedom, the tools of tyranny."[19] To be enticed by what Juvenal called "bread and circuses" was to submit to voluntary servitude. La Boétie's idea of voluntary servitude was an early contribution to a long intellectual thread leading through Karl Marx's *Critique of Hegel's Philosophy of Right* ("religion is the sigh of the oppressed creature"), to Antonio Gramsci's reflections on hegemony, the soma-fed inhabitants of Aldous Huxley's *Brave New World,* and the cultural critique of late capitalism found in Neil Postman's *Amusing Ourselves to Death.*[20] It may be possible some day to generate a new approach to political science in which power is interpreted as the adroit manipulation of the nervous systems of others.

What we must add to Dunbar's model, in other words, is the fact that neurochemical messaging is not only about altruism and group bonding but also about power and manipulation. The political messages conveyed are not limited to the druglike allures that target the reward system. The stress-response system, after all, is just as finely tuned as the reward system to electrochemical messages and equally susceptible to manipulation. Primatologists describe a daily dialectic between the stress-response system and the reward system. Dominant males and females visit stress on subordinates through physical attacks, threatening displays of teeth or testicles, cold shoulders, and the taking away of food and the occupation of space, all in order to maintain their own high rank.[21] Grooming and sex help rebuild and repair social bonds and alliances. Among humans, the daily dialogue between the dopamine reward system and the stress-response system can also be seen as a kind of historical dialogue.

The neuroscientist Robert Sapolsky has offered the most vivid point of departure for this argument.[22] Stress, he argues, is distributed unequally across the social spectrum, for the poorer you are—the lower you are on the totem pole—the more likely it is that you suffer from chronic stress. Transitions that have taken place in recent human history, that is to say the last ten thousand years, have created hierarchies of wealth and power that have institutionalized forms of stress. Because chronic stress is debilitating, this trend has had the effect of fixing social hierarchies in body chemistry through social imprinting.

Chronic stress can be alleviated, at least temporarily, by practices that relieve stress and provide diversions. These include spectacles and recreations, as La Boétie divined, as well as repetitive practices, like collecting baseball cards or keeping a personal journal. Almost everything we do that is mildly addictive, ranging from shopping and reading to using Facebook and text messaging, acquires its hold over us in part because of the neurochemical reward. The most addictive stimulants of all are psychoactive substances. These substances, ranging from alcohol to coca and *qat,* are old enough. Beginning in the eighteenth century, psychoactive substances were traded all over the world, uncoupled from their ritual contexts; in this way they created what David Courtwright refers to as the "psychoactive revolution."[23] The modern world system has not only harnessed itself to the task of producing mildly addictive consumer goods; it has also generated a new assemblage of addictive psychoactive substances.

We may use consumer goods and psychoactive substances to modify our own body states throughout the day.[24] Other people and other institutions are constantly modifying our bodies too: sometimes against our will, sometimes with our compliance. As La Boétie and Huxley both knew, enticements can induce a state of compliance that runs against our own interest, duping us into voluntary servitude. But if everyone's body is promiscuously available for others to meddle with, where exactly do we draw the boundaries of the nervous system? If our mirror neurons fire when we see someone else having sex, eating an ice cream cone, or kicking a soccer ball, are our brains all interconnected in some way? Words, deeds, and symbols send cognitive messages, but they also send messages to the autonomic nervous system of other bodies. As the evolution of mirror neurons suggests, the brain has become increasingly open to these messages over the span of human history, not least because communication has become ever more efficient and wide-ranging. But improved reception is not the only factor at issue. Social intelligence means, among other things, being able to manipulate the nervous systems of other people. This is learned behavior, a product of history.

Large communities may be imagined communities, as Benedict Anderson has argued of modern nations and states, but they are also very real neurological communities or networks.[25] They are the whole bodies imagined by medieval Europeans, Bedouin tribespeople, and countless other societies undeceived by the mind-body dichotomy that seemed so logical to the makers of the Enlightenment. Human communities, in other words, are not just ideas. The ties that bind communities are grounded in the capacity of brains to connect over space—a skill that, among hominins, has grown increasingly complex over time and come to form one of the essential components of our natural history.

THE PLASTIC BODY

On rare occasions, hard bits of old bodies—the bits that made it into the ground and were not scattered across the landscape like the Levite's concubine or the Lobassy father—become infused with silicates and other minerals, a process that bestows on them a longevity that is otherwise unnatural to bone or teeth. On even rarer occasions, these fossilized bits are found by archaeologists. Over the past century and a half, archaeologists have discovered several thousand fragments of bone and teeth extant from Lower and Middle Paleolithic sites as well as pre-Paleolithic sites, anywhere from 50,000 years ago to 4.4 million years ago. There is not always much evidence to go on, but from these fragments it has been possible to describe a history of a body that evolved, in fits and starts, from *Ardipithecus* to australopiths and from *Homo habilis* to modern *Homo sapiens*.

Bodies are built from within. They are made and continually remade from proteins stitched together according to instructions contained in the genome. During the execution of instructions, however, the process is open to epigenetic influences that range from chemicals in the ambient environment to parental care. Gene expression in fetuses, children, and adults can be accelerated, damped down, and turned off or on. For this reason, all bodies are reasonably plastic within limits set by the genome.

This plasticity is evident not only during development but also in the maturing and mature body. Many animals, especially males, have devices for enlarging or changing parts of their bodies at crucial moments. They puff or swell or bristle. Male gorillas and sea lions, when maturing into breeders, bulk up rapidly. Cichlid fish change color as well. Similar things happen to human bodies, both male and female, during puberty and at other stages in the life cycle. The human body, in fact, is an excellent site for the conspicuous display of rank or prestige. It can be fattened up by good eating where calories are scarce. It can be thinned by exercise where leisure time is scarce. The remarkable thing about the human body, however, lies in the way in which it has also come to serve as an all-purpose scaffolding for layers of epigenetic artifice. Across our genealogy, the bare human body, from the point of view of signaling, has become increasingly less robust. We have lost body hair, canine teeth, and brooding eyebrows. But the decorated body, a social creation, now sends a resplendent array of messages. To take in the full effect of a representation of a medieval saint with a halo, a picture of Queen Elizabeth I in full regalia, or the Hawaiian kings with their feathered mantles, one must read elaborate signs that the naked body, as a medium of display, cannot possibly transmit. A kind of inflationary spiral dressed the high-status body in ever more abundant and elaborate goods and fabrics. Eventually, the quantity of stuff became far too much to hang on the body—but that, in fact, was no difficulty, for items were simply attached to it by the concept of ownership, allowing bodies to grow as big as houses, herds of cattle, whole territories, and even the whole world, as depicted in the Ebstorf *mappa mundi*.

Cultural anthropologists, historians, and specialists in literature and cultural studies have had much to say about socially constructed bodies: bodies that are sexed or unsexed, bodies in pain, bodies enslaved, bodies perfumed and surgically altered, and some, like the body of Robert-François Damiens, who attempted to kill Louis XV of France, that are burned with molten sulfur, drawn, and quartered.[26] These bodies have been worked on by power and discipline, and it would seem that humanity, rather than nature in the broad sense, has become their principal sculpting agent. The plastic body fashioned by neck rings, shoes, and surgery, by genital cuttings both crude and refined, by exercise and dieting, stands in contrast to the supposedly natural body of the deep past, a body unshod, unclad, undiapered, and odoriferous, a body without menstrual cycles or bunions or impacted wisdom teeth.

Thanks to a kind of disciplinary handoff, a rupture between the deep time of biology and the shallow time of culture is built into the very ways we think about the body. And yet the body itself is continuous, the product of an unbroken genealogy that extends back far beyond the earliest hominins. Where, in this genealogy, is there ever a moment when we can point to the "natural" human body? Did the human body take shape with archaic *Homo sapiens,* marked by a bulging forehead and large brain? With *Homo erectus,* the species that pioneered the shrunken gut, smaller teeth, and narrower pelvis? With the upright posture of *Ardipithecus?* The bodily changes that define humanity are inconveniently stretched out over at least 4.4 million years. What is more, how could we define the natural foot when every foot is sculpted by the demands of its environment, or the natural stature when stature varies according to levels of nutrition? How can we instantiate a historical divide between biology and culture, knowing as we do that bodies have been worked on by cultural or epigenetic influences from the moment they began to stretch beyond the edges of the skin, deep in our mammalian past? And does this divide make any sense in light of accumulating evidence to the effect that changes in the human genotype have, if anything, been accelerating over the past five to ten thousand years, precisely the time frame in which human cultural developments have allowed us to dominate and destroy the "natural" world around us?

To contemplate the human body in deep history, let us begin, arbitrarily, about 2.6 million years ago with the body of the earliest species of the genus, Homo habilis. The habilines differed only in subtle ways from the gracile australopiths from whom they presumably descended. The cranial capacity of H. habilis, for example, was a bit larger, and the new species was also taller and had longer legs better suited to long-distance walking, though habilines could still climb trees better than recent humans.[27] But the bodily differences are not all that profound. The threshold at 2.6 million years, in fact, is defined by something else: the beginning of chipped stone tools, probably used largely for food preparation, though tool use likely began much earlier. Flakes chipped off from handy cobbles served to slice the hide of a scavenged corpse. Cobble hammers and anvils enabled habilines to crush seeds or break open large bones to extract the marrow. Tools, in effect, replaced the need for apelike incisors and molars, for the molar teeth of H. habilis were markedly smaller than those of the australopiths, nearly identical to those of modern humans. It is easy to appreciate how the human body has adapted itself to changing environmental demands and ecological niches. But here we encounter something that we can interpret as culture, not environment, having direct and measurable effects on anatomy and morphology. Tools are, after all, artificial extensions of the human body.

Homo habilis eventually was replaced in the fossil record by another hominin species, Homo erectus, which evolved around 1.7 million years ago and overlapped for several hundred thousand years with the robust australopiths, albeit in different areas. Erectus is spectacularly represented by the well-preserved if somewhat trampled skeleton of the Nariokotome boy from some 1.6 million years ago, whose remains were found in a mud hole west of present-day Lake Turkana. He and his relatives have been described by Richard Klein as "the first hominid species whose anatomy and behavior justify the label human."[28] The anatomical similarity is easy to measure, notably in the narrow hips and broad shoulders. The Nariokotome boy, at eleven years of age, had already reached 5 feet 3 inches in height. Had he survived, he might have grown to nearly 6 feet tall. His cranial capacity was a large 880 cubic centimeters, and other members of his species had a cranial volume of 1000 cubic centimeters, close to the low end of the modern range.

Females and males averaged 115 and 140 pounds respectively, within a few percentage points of the modern average, and at 5 feet 11 inches, the average male height actually exceeded that of modern men by 2 inches. The Nariokotome boy also possessed a small pelvis better adapted for walking than that of his forebears and an external nose, a crucial part of the breathing and cooling apparatus that enabled the species to forage effectively in the hot sun. Depending on whether the artist has chosen to add hair or not, anatomically correct pictures of an erectine like the Nariokotome boy definitely look more human than apelike.

The question of body hair is an intriguing one, as the lack of it obviously distinguishes humans from other primates. Desmond Morris once argued that nakedness was associated with human tenderness and sex, part of a complex of traits that promoted pair bonding.[29] Yet there is another way of approaching the question. *Homo erectus* was the first hominin to exploit the savanna ecosystem to its fullest and was certainly the first to live in the arid climate that set in 1.7 million years ago, during which the forest retreated to its minimum extent, reducing shade cover. The savannah heat would have been intense. Yet the large brain of *H. erectus* itself generated a lot of heat; as a result, it needed a cooling capacity greater than that required by small-brained *Ardipithecus* or the australopiths. The metabolic solution to this problem was to develop a system based on the cooling potential of sweat glands distributed over nearly the entire body.[30] Sweating, in turn, is more efficient on a hairless body, which is why *H. erectus* is considered by some to have been the first nearly hairless species of hominin. Upright posture may have augmented the cooling capacity of *H. erectus* by diminishing the body surface exposed to the midday sun and by exposing the body, especially the long limbs, to breezes.

Brain, linear body plan, hair: the anatomical similarities between *H. erectus* and modern humans are clear enough. But how is Klein able to make a claim for trends toward behavioral modernity? Some of the behavioral surmises can be read directly off the changing anatomy of *H. erectus*. For example, various clues, including the size and shape of the arms and toes, suggest that these hominins had more or less given up climbing trees. Slim hips and long legs were efficiently designed for walking, implying a completely terrestrial lifestyle. The diminishing difference in male and female body size suggests a mating pattern with less scope for a dominant male's harem than was the case with australopiths and possibly habilines.

The narrower pelvis, finally, points to a smaller gut and therefore a much richer food supply, requiring less time in the intestines to digest.[31] The smaller gut is associated with the introduction of a wider array of tools used for food preparation, including biface hand axes and choppers not found at habiline sites. But as Richard Wrangham has argued, the richer food supply was also a product of cooking with fire, a practice that, even more than pounding, allowed digestion to begin outside the body.[32] Digestion is an enormously expensive part of the primate metabolism, and the energy saved by predigesting food could be diverted to building and feeding a larger brain. The expansion of the brain, in turn, allowed the accumulation and processing of resources outside the body in the form of shared language, social thinking, cross-generational teaching, collaborative planning, and collective remembering.

Given the absence of clear evidence for the human mastery of fire before 780,000 years ago, the evidence for a cooked diet prior to this time is indirect and takes the form of a physiological signature. But if we accept, as a working hypothesis, the argument that Wrangham has proposed, the implications for the history of the body are profound. Along with stone tools, fire became a culture attribute. If we accept, moreover, the principle that changes in the environment are written on bodies by natural selection, then fire was certainly an extension of the hominin phenotype. Whereas some marine mammals shed their toes when they took to the seas, *H. erectus* developed a cooling system so as to exploit a hot ecosystem. They also experienced spectacular changes to the teeth, gut, and brain that are partly explained by the taming of fire. In this case, a cultural innovation wrote changes on the human genotype.

If culture can change the body, then we can look at the human body from at least *H. erectus* forward as increasingly sensitive to practices or selective pressures that are not just environmental but social or cultural in nature. Canines, brows, and other physical attributes of male dominance display receded in part because weapons and other elements of the extended phenotype took their place. Neanderthal peoples developed stronger front teeth because they used their teeth not only for cutting food into bite-sized chunks but also as a handy vise for gripping hide, tough meat, and possibly other things while cutting or shaving them.

This process of writing cultural change onto the human body has grown to remarkable proportions in more recent millennia. Thanks to the extraordinary selection pressures induced by agriculture and population growth, the human genotype has changed with considerable rapidity. Some of the best-known examples include lactase persistence in adults and the gene for sickle-cell hemoglobin. Lactase persistence allows adults to drink fresh milk. The trait developed, it seems, in the Linearkeramikband culture of modern-day Poland around 7,500 to 6,500 years ago and independently in Africa around the same time. The evolution of the trait was a somewhat delayed response to the rise of dairying: hitherto, milk could be consumed only in the form of predigested milk foods such as yogurt and koumiss.[33] Sickle-cell hemoglobin, in turn, confers some resistance to malaria. The trait spread in the last 7,000 to 3,200 years as human settlement and agricultural deforestation in Africa created huge, watery breeding grounds for mosquitoes.

Diseases like smallpox, which once ravaged humanity, are mutated forms of viruses that circulate among livestock; the global distribution of the human ABO blood types can be explained, in large part, by the differential resistance they confer to illnesses we acquired long ago from domesticated sheep, goats, and pigs, which are themselves elaborate cultural creations. Likewise, innovations in clothing, fire use, and food-getting technologies allowed modern humans to colonize northern climates, where lighter skin color was favored because it facilitates bodily production of vitamin D in reduced sunlight. These changes are not detectable in teeth or bones, the primary evidence of the fossil record, but they are significant nonetheless.

Culture and society have long been altering the human genome. But humans have been in the business of modifying their own bodies, or those of others, probably for as long as they have been modifying their body chemistry and neural states. This deliberate kind of sculpting takes two forms, the most vivid of which consists of the cutting, burning, filing, stretching, and scraping of various parts of the body. It is vanishingly unlikely that we will ever find direct evidence for tattooing in Paleolithic populations, but the practice is very common in recent societies and in the oldest naturally mummified humans. Archaeologists suspect that the Paleolithic body also bore tattoos, but this is difficult to prove. Certainly these early people put much stock in natural colorants such as red ocher and black manganese, which were probably used to color the bodies of both the living and the dead. Many animals use surface coloration for signaling; to this extent, tattooing and body painting pick up where involuntary responses like flushing and pallor leave off.

The range of body reshaping in recent societies, from the elongation of necks to the binding of feet, is impressive; current practices of plastic surgery, Botox injections, hair replacement, lip and penile enhancement, stomach stapling, and the like are merely the most recent instances of long-standing practices. These mutilations are intended to beautify, even if they do not appear beautiful to all. Ugly mutilations, consisting of limbing, branding, hair shearing, and eye gouging, are nearly as common: these are designed to distinguish the disgraced from the rest of society. Some mutilations are difficult to classify on this spectrum, notably the practice common in the United States during the 1960s of surgically transforming ambiguously sexed children into visibly male or female bodies. Some modifications, such as body building and compulsive dieting, shape the whole body; and secure placement within a socioeconomic class, or even a profession, can produce a distinctive body type.

A second type of body modification, which targets the extended phenotype, involves layers of artifice that are placed on the scaffolding of the body. Layers of ocher perhaps belong in this category, as they are, in a sense, very thin layers of clothing. Clothing itself is relatively old. Hide working is an ancient skill, certainly practiced among the Neanderthals. A recent discovery has identified 36,000-year-old fibers from the Upper Paleolithic, and evidence from the genome of the clothing louse, which can live only on clothed bodies, points to a branching node some 107,000 years ago, implying the existence of garments of some kind at that time.[34]

In addition to these practices, we must consider the role that goods have played in the extension of the human body. Humans are a well-wrapped species, metaphorically and literally, and the wrappings help sediment personal histories and biographies in the body. Contemplating the accumulating layers of epigenetic elaboration, we return to the stunning revelation of the new neuroscience. The human nervous system is designed not to distinguish overmuch between the genetic body and the cultural body; the brain builds any extension of the body right into the body map. As far as the nervous system is concerned, biology and culture are seamlessly integrated in the human phenotype, and attempts to distinguish these two domains, which dominated twentieth-century social science, are now giving way to new approaches that insist on the mutual constitution of culture and biology in the social life of the human body.

Just as human bodies adapt to unanticipated environmental changes, they also adapt to the unintended consequences of cultural, economic, or social transformations. As Richard Wrangham has illustrated, diet has a very powerful effect on the human body. Wrangham is primarily interested in the influence of diet on the genotype, but it has an equally profound impact on the phenotype. Consider, in this regard, some of the consequences of the transitions in the food regime at different times and places over the past ten thousand years. The milling and refining technologies that have rendered food more digestible have brought on new problems of digestion, particularly the problem of how we cope with foods rich in sugar and carbohydrates. Excessive grain consumption may also lead to debilities ranging from bladder stones to autoimmune disorders, including celiac disease.[35] The availability of cooked gruel led to earlier weaning of babies, shortening the interval between births and bringing about dramatic transformations in family forms.

The eating of highly processed foods typical of postindustrial and urban populations has had direct and measurable consequences for the anatomy of the human face. Because soft foods need less bite pressure and take fewer chews to process, postindustrial populations use their jaws and teeth less than our foraging and agricultural ancestors did. Because of the complex way in which the head is integrated, as Daniel E. Lieberman has argued, a change in how much and how hard we chew affects how many parts of the face grow and fit together as we mature. The dental problems characteristic of postindustrial populations, including crowding, over- and underbites, and impacted wisdom teeth, may be the price we pay for our highly processed diet.[36]

Our reading of the past is dogged by the instinct to moralize. Surveying the host of setbacks occasioned by agriculture, scholars have found it easy to criticize the Neolithic transition as a bad move.[37] Oddly enough, the instinct to moralize disappears when the observer is contemplating supposedly natural processes. No one calls the eruption of Mount Toba or even Krakatoa a "bad" thing, however unfortunate the immediate consequences for humanity. Instead, we lament it, accept it, and try to compensate. But once our own handiwork is invoked, our ability to detect the inexorable logic of systems flies out the door, and we fall prey to the voluntarist fallacy: the belief that all the consequences of our handiwork are planned and therefore capable of being judged on the spectrum from good to evil. The recent history of the body, and of the epigenetic influences that have created modern bodies that differ in important ways from their Paleolithic antecedents, reminds us that the forces that act on our bodies are not always our own.

Although many of the body modifications we find in recent societies are the product of changing diets, others are not. Encased in a shoe, the bone structure of the foot changes, leading to a striding gait rather than the gliding gait characteristic of the unshod, splayed foot.[38] The recent global upsurge in obesity is certainly due in part to a ready supply of processed foods saturated with fat and simple sugars, but it is also a

consequence of numerous other technological innovations, from auto-
motive transport to screen-based entertainment and work environments,
that encourage sedentary lifestyles. One of the most striking changes
in the body in recent centuries has emerged from the increased use of
psychoactive substances. We know that caffeine and alcohol consumption affect fetal development. We also know that certain psychoactive
substances cause permanent neurological modifications. Although we
do not have the scientific grounds for proving that our brains, in the
aggregate, are different from those that predate the psychoactive revolution, it is likely that brains have changed as a result of psychoactive
substance use.

The point here is not to give more weight to body modifications than
to environmentally induced changes: indeed, it is increasingly difficult
to distinguish these two domains. Rather, the point is that what happens to the body is often the unintended (or not fully anticipated) result
of changes in cultural, social, and economic substrates. Who could have
imagined that eating more starch would lead to myopia?[39] Bodies adapt
to cultural changes, in other words, in much the same way that they
adapt to environmental changes. The only difference here is that cultural influences like diet and labor do not necessarily write their effects
onto the genotype; the changes they induce are expressed directly on
the plastic phenotype. A model of history that distinguishes Paleolithic
animals, at the mercy of the environment, from modern humans, at the
mercy only of themselves, fails to account for the complex interaction of
factors that has shaped the human body over the past 2.6 million years.

CONCLUSION

Michel Foucault, channeling Wilhelm Friedrich Nietzsche, once wrote:
"We believe, in any event, that the body obeys the exclusive laws of
physiology and that it escapes the influence of history, but this too is
false. The body is molded by a great many distinct regimes; it is broken down by the rhythms of work, rest, and holidays; it is poisoned
by food or values, through eating habits or moral laws; it constructs
resistances."[40] Foucault was appropriately sensitive to the constructed
nature of the human body. But Foucault was a thinker trapped in shallow time, and for that reason he often did not understand how the creative human influence on the human body was itself part of larger evolutionary processes that, over long stretches of time, had shaped the
human body and the elaborate ways in which humans put it to work.

In developing his influential notions of biopower and biopolitics, which continue the old human trick of likening political life to the life of the body, Foucault argued that Western societies had crossed the "threshold of modernity," combining the facts of life and politics in unprecedented ways. "For the first time in history," he wrote of the emerging capitalist world, "biological existence was reflected in political existence; the fact of living was no longer an inaccessible substrate that only emerged from time to time, amid the randomness of death and its fatality; part of it passed into knowledge's field of control and power's sphere of intervention. Power would no longer be dealing simply with legal subjects over whom the ultimate dominion was death, but with living beings, and the mastery it would be able to exercise over them would have to be applied at the level of life itself; it was the taking charge of life, more than the threat of death, that gave power its access even to the body."[41]

These insights, however insightfully they describe biopower in eighteenth-century Europe, become more interesting, and less Eurocentric, when considered against the backdrop of deeper histories. Six hundred years before Foucault, Ibn Khaldun created his famous sociological model of dynastic authority, in which dynasties have "a natural lifespan like individuals"; they are biopolitical entities that show signs of health and decline based on the lived experience of royal authority, which is distributed across the lives of dynasts and their supporters as they move from a desert existence of nomadism and tribal organization to an urban existence of luxury and law.[42] Political existence, for Ibn Khaldun, reflects biological existence in very literal ways, and any sitting dynast would probably have drawn the same conclusion.

Medieval North Africa can stand in for deep history only if we take such concepts as "the threshold of modernity" seriously, which perhaps we should not. The Foucauldian process of "taking charge of life" in order to give "power its access even to the body" can be traced much, much further back in time. It is evident in circumcision rites intended to make men and women healthy and morally sound; in the arrangement of individuals into age grades that order society in accord with the logic of the maturing human body; and in the timeless art of adorning the body to make it beautiful or frightening, to suggest fertility or conceal menstruation, to convey lethal force or healing powers.

The human body has been a site of knowledge and power ever since it became human. Seen in deep time, the human body has shown a continuous tendency to enlarge and extend itself socially, both through phenotypic artifice and through the long reach of the nervous system. As it enlarges, it also comes to pieces. The pieces have meaning in their absence—a foreskin, a plucked eyebrow, the hand of a criminal, or the head of a deposed monarch. They have meaning in their presence—a relic, a sequence of ancestral DNA, a bit of memorabilia, the cranium of a Neanderthal woman discovered in 1848. And in all their forms, they connect, taking charge of life and producing, as they do so, the frames and durable forms of history.

CHAPTER 4

Energy and Ecosystems

MARY C. STINER AND GILLIAN FEELEY-HARNIK

Ecological systems are the products of the organisms that inhabit them. They adjust isostatically to the ebb and flow of their herbivore and carnivore members, their trees and grasses and beds of kelp, and their fungi and bacteria. All organisms, to greater or lesser degrees, interact continuously with the physical environment and with each other. In some cases, their impact or "footprint" in ecosystems may be disproportionate. Elephants and wildebeest, for example, have made the Serengeti plains what they are, from the characteristics of the grasses on which they tread to the chemical structure of the soil. Billions of years ago, photosynthetic bacteria created the earliest form of the atmosphere as we know it—and, not coincidentally, sparked the first Ice Age.[1] All organisms have a constant and never-ending impact on their ecosystems.

Over the past 2.6 million years and more, humans and their ancestors have also interacted technologically with the environments in which they live, beginning on the African continent, spreading to Eurasia, and eventually to all continents. The human impact on the Pleistocene ecosystems arose largely in the context of the timeless endeavor to extract calories and nutrients from the environment: in short, the need to eat. Practices such as overhunting and land clearances through burning had a direct impact on Pleistocene ecosystems only toward the end of this long geological period, whereas human foraging practices created perturbations over the full extent of their existence.

when?

The calories harvested by Pleistocene foragers were spent on production and reproduction. Historians have long been accustomed to thinking of this as the endless biological cycle of a world before history. The limits of digestion, which can process only a few thousand calories per day, would seem to have placed a cap on the amount of energy that could flow through early human populations. But long ago that cap was already being raised by means of another use of calories: fuel, fed to campfires. Other technologies also allowed for some degree of predigestion of food outside the body. The energy captured in this way, energy otherwise destined to be spent on finding, chewing, and digesting food, was essential to the growth of the brain.[2] Across the Paleolithic, changes in foraging efficiency, energy storage, and strategies of risk management continued to raise this cap.

With the onset of agriculture and the age of metals and ceramics, new sources of calories, both foods and fuels, were added to the mix. In many ancient complex societies, the need for fuels to stoke furnaces generated massive waves of deforestation, causing erosion and valley infilling, with direct consequences on the environment and even on weather patterns and local climate.[3] Metalworks, then as now, had spillover effects on the environment. On the island of Crete some 3,000 years ago, ironworking generated environmental impacts ranging from the slag heaps that still dot the island to airborne pollution that deposited lead in the Greenland ice cap. Over the past two hundred years, the graph of human environmental impact has taken a dramatic turn upward.[4] The consequences of industrialization, as in ancient Crete, have reached far beyond the local environment.

Some of the great historians of the nineteenth century, like Jules Michelet, described the onset of the war against nature as the moment when history itself began. The date of first conquest was assigned to the comfortably distant past: when forests were first cut down and turned into fields, when animals were first domesticated or driven off, when houses were first built to shelter us from wind, rain, and ice. In the new environmental history, the date assigned to this Pyrrhic victory has shifted into the very recent past. Indeed, ecologists and ecoconscious citizens now lament the grand scale of human disturbance to natural environments over the past two centuries. Humans have generated large volumes of certain gases, altered the acidity of rivers, depleted aquifers, introduced alien species, and impoverished landscapes as they extract and consume resources. Soils have been ruined over large areas by the wicking upward and crystallization of salts from irrigation. Surprising numbers of species have been driven to extinction. Yet the lachrymose school of environmental history, far from escaping the old frame, has actually replicated the arc of history's triumphalist narrative. It shares, with Michelet, the belief that human history consists of two phases: prehistory, the age when humans merely reacted passively to the environment; and history, when humans first began to transcend the environment.

If human history must be defined in terms of a *conquest* of nature, a draining of swamps, a channeling of rivers, and a taming of the landscape, then our histories will be short indeed—the gist can be covered in scarcely three centuries.[5] But the very idea of conquest is just another kind of nineteenth-century historical hubris. Humans are not unique in their power to reshape environments locally or globally. Some plants are so well adapted to cyclical range fires that they actually promote ignition, helping to keep huge areas open to their progeny and suppressing the establishment of competing plant species.[6] Burrowing rodents maintain vast grasslands rich in their favorite foods by continuously turning the soil and discouraging the growth of forests.[7] Sheep, brought to Mexico with European settlement, created their own grazing land through the action of their hooves on the soil.[8] Then there are the not-so-humble roles of microbes, worms, and other invertebrates in soil formation and rejuvenation. Some plant species have redefined the conditions of natural selection for countless living things and geological processes alike. The lesson is that humans, in their effects on the environment, are on a par with many other organisms. The effects of environmental trauma are real, but they are a product of scale, not human exceptionalism. Although the human impact on the planet today is surely the result of human agency, that agency should never be confused with intention or control. Nature, much like human society, typically declines to follow the scripts we sometimes choose to write for it.

This chapter considers how humans have long exploited ecosystems through social, technological, and physiological adaptations. The history that emerges from the deep perspective taken here helps us understand how and why human influences have grown relentlessly over time. Key to this history is an understanding of the bonds that have formed between humans and other species, for these have generated coevolutionary processes with their own logic and drive. These processes lend themselves to what Stephen Jay Gould once called "the maddening acceleration" toward the future.[9] In many ecosystems today, humans are the dominant species. But such dominance cannot exist apart from the systems and processes that sustain it.

HUMANS IN THE FOOD WEB

During most of the Pleistocene, the period of the great ice ages lasting from roughly 2.5 million to 10,000 years ago, humans trod lightly on their ecosystems—compared, at least, to elephants, insects, and microbes. The human biomass was far too small to have a significant impact. With the arrival of humans on Australia more than 50,000 years ago, we can begin to detect a measurable human impact in the form of megafaunal extinction.[10] The rippling extinctions of megafauna across the globe toward the end of the Pleistocene probably owe something to human expansion and hunting, though the matter is still debated.[11] Massive burn-offs instigated by humans to encourage new plant growth to feed herbivores reveal another way in which humans were becoming more like elephants.[12] Under pressure from human foraging, tortoises became smaller during the Upper Paleolithic in the Middle East, as the larger ones were eaten.[13] Much the same happened later to the large land mammals and fish exploited intensively by Californian Indians.[14]

Historic and archaeological evidence together show us that humans' ecological footprint has grown in fits and starts during the long span of human history. The growth of the human ecological footprint, both in recent times and in the remote past, has depended first on the growing density of human populations on the landscape and the way that the economy exploits the food web. To put this differently, if we want to track the growth of the human ecological footprint, we have to consider the energy flows that characterized early human systems. Fundamentally, we have to explore how energy from the sun—whether in the form of fossil fuels dating from hundreds of millions of years ago or a blade of grass a day before being eaten—finds its way up the trophic pyramid as it moves from the eaten and through the eaters. We also have to explore how changing social and economic structures constrain or direct energy flow in new ways.

Energy flow in biotic communities is normally modeled as a food web. There are many pathways for the transfer of energy from the base of production, at the bottom of the trophic pyramid, upward. Humans are a proverbially "K-selected" species, that is to say a species with long intervals between generations, high parental investment in offspring, and slow population turnover. The population dynamics of K-selected species emphasize stability and competitive efficiency rather than speedy growth.[15] Like elephants and whales, humans tend to occupy environments at or just below carrying capacity most of the time.

But if that is so, then why have human population densities grown nearly continuously around the world? Significant increases in human populations characterize the transitions from the Middle to the Upper Paleolithic, from the Upper to the Epipaleolithic or Mesolithic, and from the early Neolithic onward.[16] According to the hypothesis, K-selected species shouldn't operate this way. Clearly, the carrying capacity of the environment changed as humans harnessed energy in new ways. The reasons for this change do not lie (or do not lie solely) in exogenous factors like climate change. Human behavioral evolution has been paralleled by a remarkable capacity to raise the carrying capacity of the land and more recently the sea. The growing climate crisis caused by anthropogenic global warming was created by our use of fossil fuels. But if we acknowledge the equivalence between food and fuel, if we acknowledge that a calorie is just a calorie, it turns out that Pleistocene societies were already generating scalar leaps in the human ability to extract calories efficiently from the environment.

Some of the most significant transitions in the socioeconomic organization of cultures therefore relate to changes in human trophic level, or how efficiently humans capture and transform energy. As a rule of thumb, the pace at which entropy reduces available energy along these pathways determines many of the properties of biotic communities, including the overall shape of the trophic pyramid and the ratio of predators to prey. When a food item—plant, insect, arthropod, or mammal—is eaten, a great deal of its stored energy is lost in the conversion of food into the living tissues of its consumers, partly because it takes energy to pursue food items, and partly because digestion itself is costly and inefficient. Additional energy is lost each time a calorie packet makes its way up the food pyramid. Top carnivores, in every ecosystem, are vastly inefficient consumers. This fact keeps their relative population size very low.

Most organisms are easily assigned to one level in the trophic pyramid, such as a primary producer, primary consumer, or tertiary carnivore. Omnivores are an interesting exception, as they eat a much broader variety of foods and may extract energy from several levels of the trophic pyramid simultaneously. Most important for our purposes is the potential flexibility of omnivorous adaptations, which may allow some species or populations to shift up or down the food chain. Humans are a remarkable case in point. Among recent hunter-gatherers, for example, population density is determined primarily by trophic level.[17] Very carnivorous hunter-gatherer populations, at least those that get most of their meat from large terrestrial game animals, tend to be thinly distributed in landscapes. By contrast, populations that have broader, more diverse diets, especially diets that include many plant foods, tend to exist at somewhat higher densities.[18] The differences in trophic level among hunter-gatherers generally follow latitudinal variation in animal and plant diversity. Humans in the high Arctic mostly eat reindeer and seals. A richer mix of large and small animals and seasonal plants is available in the temperate zone; and small animals and fruits, seeds, and greens are abundant in many tropical regions, where large prey animals may be less common.

Farmers get most of their calories from plants. As a result, when farmers and foragers inhabit exactly the same environment, the farming populations exist at higher densities because they derive more of their energy from exceptionally productive plants and animals. The crops and herds that they tend, moreover, monopolize the calories available in the ecosystem and thereby suppress the population size of competing species. In effect, with the transition to agriculture, farmers moved down the trophic pyramid, taking up a position below carnivores, though slightly above primary consumers such as ungulates. We have, in essence, become less wolflike and more piglike in our diet: that trade-off allowed population growth. Some highly mechanized farming methods can raise the food yield much higher still, and words like *improvement* are often used to describe increases in energy off-take from ecosystems. However, the incentives for intensifying energy extraction are far from obvious, because the long-term consequences of such improvements vary from beneficial to utterly disastrous.

Why have economies changed so much, and particularly, why have some shifted so radically with respect to trophic level? There is a price to pay for diversifying diets, for example, because even in the best of circumstances, food quality is traded for greater availability. Humans and other animals are more willing to pay the price of diversification when the good stuff is hard to find. Meat from large animals yields exceptionally high quantities of energy relative to the time spent obtaining it, even if hunting success seems low or unpredictable.[19] This preference for meat in the diet helps explain why many industrialized nations have invested so heavily in meat production.

The central importance of meat in the diets of many recent humans and the perceived high value of meat in situations of food sharing naturally raise questions about earlier patterns of food consumption, including the balance between animal and plant food sources. Humans always face a trade-off between maximizing economic returns and managing future economic and social risks. The strategies for making these choices vary tremendously, but they normally include food storage, diet diversification, trade, and delayed reciprocity. Delayed reciprocity may involve alliances of individuals spread over large areas or reciprocal cooperation via division of labor. Importantly, these relations may alter the efficiency with which a resource can be exploited.

Human cultural systems can experience economies of scale in cooperative production, whereby patterns of labor allocation and exchange allow linear increases in human group size and greater-than-linear increases in production (see chapter 10). Such shifts accompanied the rise of Neolithic economies, maritime trade, and regional markets. But the evolutionary bases for these phenomena reach even deeper into the past and include the transition from the Middle to Upper Paleolithic (see below), when expanded social networks seem to have developed alongside dietary diversification. By resisting dietary specialization at the level of the population or species (but specializing as individuals), Late Pleistocene humans bypassed a common tendency among other animals to specialize in just a few foods. In effect, humans ceased to focus on large game hunting alone and instead captured energy through diverse foraging tasks and managed risk through diet expansion and reciprocity.

The fundamental achievement of the Green Revolution, the adoption of intensive agricultural methods (especially in Asia) in the late twentieth century, was to raise the carrying capacity of the land through monocropping and the use of artificial fertilizers and mechanized equipment.[20] Whether this was ingenuity or malfeasance is a question for others to decide. Despite what J.R. McNeill claimed in the title of his book, however, this accomplishment was not "something new under the sun." It occurred in the Pleistocene landscape long before the transition to agriculture.

COEVOLUTION OF HUMANS WITH OTHER SPECIES

A species is said to coevolve with another when close interactions affect the reproductive success of one or both, either positively or negatively. Coevolutionary processes can generate directionality in selection without much provocation from the environment. Humans are exceptionally likely to form coevolutionary bonds with other species.[21] Indeed, virtually every period in human evolutionary history provides examples of coevolutionary processes involving animals, plants, or fungi.

Coevolutionary bonds take many forms, from competition to mutualism. Perhaps the most influential of all coevolutionary models is Leigh van Valen's Red Queen hypothesis, which refers metaphorically to the interaction between Alice and the Red Queen on a landscape-sized chessboard in Lewis Carroll's *Through the Looking Glass*.[22] In their game, Alice and the Red Queen lock hands and run like mad. When they stop for breath, they find that they have changed their positions not at all. A coevolutionary bond may be a proverbial arms race between a predator and its prey, as each develops new ways to outwit the other, or selection for greater tolerance in a host and lowered virulence in a virus or parasite that infects it. There are also many examples of mutualism, wherein the attraction is either one-sided (as between humans and houseflies) or mutual, as was the case for humans and rock doves (pigeons) in the Middle East, where these birds willingly nested in human-made cavities in rock overhangs, providing meat, eggs, and fertilizer to early farmers.[23] As long as the behavior or properties of the one species imposes selective constraints on the other, coevolution will occur.

Such relations have greatly influenced the evolutionary history of humans and companion species, sometimes rapidly, and despite other transformations in their environment. Cut marks and fractures from hammer stones on the bones of antelopes and other big animals in early African sites testify to meat eating by hominins between 1 and 2 million years ago.[24] To get meat, whether by hunting or scavenging, these early hominins inserted themselves into the well-established guild of formidable meat eaters populated by great cats, hyenas, and members of the dog family.[25] Because meat from large prey animals is both a rich and a scarce resource, interference from competing predators can be fierce. In fact many of the bones off which hominins fed were also gnawed by large carnivores, suggesting that close shaves with competitors were regular events.[26] Hominins' membership in meat eaters' guilds in Africa and Eurasia through the rest of the Pleistocene allowed them to evolve into highly skilled hunters.[27] Several human behaviors that are not typical of primate relatives, but are important to many large carnivores, also developed among humans in this highly competitive forum, such as the tendency to move food to safer places, hoarding, and the sharing of meat at safe spots.[28] Humans also became more efficient at processing their food before eating it.

Coevolutionary processes strongly influence the structure of animal and plant communities and ecosystems. The formative interactions among species can ultimately have broader consequences, fostering common behavioral or physiological traits in a range of species. In the late nineteenth century, Fritz Müller showed how whole groups of tropical butterfly species with a similarly foul taste to predators developed convergent patterns of coloration.[29] Some of the most troublesome weeds of all time and on several continents, including the tumbleweed (*Salsola kali*), originated on the harsh Irano-Turanian steppes, where rapid colonization of disturbed ground and fast and sure reproduction were essential for survival.[30] According to Jared Diamond, Eurasian ungulate species evolved common tendencies for hierarchical herd structures and clustering (rather than flight) responses to threats long ago: these traits also happened to make many of these species especially amenable to domestication in the early Holocene. In other words, they showed a behavioral predisposition for domestication.[31] This behavior may explain why Eurasia has a near monopoly on the early domestication of hoofed animals.

COEVOLUTION WITHIN THE HUMAN SPECIES

Though coevolution is better known as a phenomenon linking the history of two or more species, coevolutionary processes can occur between populations or subpopulations within species as well. An especially significant example of coevolutionary processes within the human species concerns the division of labor and pooling of resources. These behaviors can reduce foraging and other environmental risks and arguably contributed in some periods to new economies of scale. Cooperation and division of labor have also affected humans' interactions with other species and the physical environment. In a variety of animals, differences in foraging behavior and territory use occur between the sexes and by individual size: juvenile lizards may eat smaller bugs than adults do, and female bears or macaques may eat more of some foods than adult males in the same region. But humans are distinctive in pooling resources from separate foraging and other economic activities, divided according to skill, circumstance, gender and age. These relations have undergone significant changes over hundreds of thousands of years and continue to change. The process of change is directional and has a powerful cultural (social) component. One early example comes from the Paleolithic.

The Middle Paleolithic was a watershed in hominin behavioral evolution, marking a significant increase in social and technological complexity.[32] Hominin brain size reached its maximum at the outset of the Middle Paleolithic (MP). This period is distinguished by important innovations in the techniques for working stone (see figure 11). The hominins of this period were skilled big-game hunters, and they lived in societies

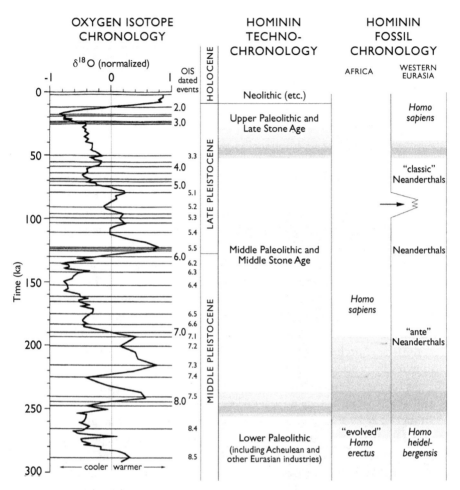

FIGURE 11. Summary of climate-driven environmental fluctuations and cultural and human fossil chronologies for Old World Paleolithic cultures in Eurasia and Northern and Eastern Africa over the past 300,000 years. This figure provides a basic timeline for dating the periods and trends discussed in this chapter. Graduated shading indicates variable timing by region, unclear dating results, or both. The arrow in the right column indicates early and apparently short-lived incursions of anatomically modern *Homo sapiens* into Western Asia from Africa; these hominins possessed Middle Paleolithic technology and therefore are considered anatomically modern-looking but not behaviorally modern. Marine oxygen isotopes (MIS) provide an independent record of past climate events and cycles based on the ratio of O^{18} and O^{16} in the shells of dead microorganisms whose remains accumulate on the sea floor. This process of deposition creates year-by-year layers that can be used to infer small changes in ocean surface temperatures, which in turn reflect shifts in world climate. The climate cycles and certain events within these cycles are assigned "stage" numbers, with odd numbers reflecting generally warmer intervals and even numbers reflecting cooler intervals. This MIS curve is based on Martinson et al. 1987. (Adapted from Stiner and Kuhn 2010, 110, fig. 1; © M.C. Stiner.)

founded on sharing and cooperation. They took considerable pains to bury members of their social group in shallow graves.[33] Sometimes they even cleaned up their residences, piling excess garbage at the edge of the habitation area inside caves.[34]

Although some of these behaviors and qualities resemble those of modern humans, others seem quite remote. In fact the hominins of the Middle Paleolithic, including the Neanderthals, pose many challenges to common notions of modern human nature. They were clever and inventive—and yet they were an evolutionary dead end.[35] There is comparatively little geographic differentiation in MP technology over vast stretches of Eurasia and few, if any, durable traces of art or symbols. MP populations in Eurasia did not expand continually for the duration of their existence. There may have been a slight increase in population densities in some areas toward the end of the MP, but this could be explained by the influx of invading Upper Paleolithic (UP) peoples at about the same time (from northeast Africa, southwest Asia, or both).[36] Like most other animals, MP foragers generally responded to fluctuations in environmental productivity and consumer-resource imbalances through localized depopulation or moving to other areas. They did not, to the best of archaeologists' knowledge, squeeze more out of local food supplies by processing or storing food.

As for meat, Middle Paleolithic people hunted whatever animals were available, so long as they were big: deer, wild cattle, wild boar, and so on. Strangely, at least in comparison to recent hunter-gatherers and traditional farmers, they seldom made use of small animals except for those that were very easy to collect, such as tortoises and shellfish.[37] MP populations, like large carnivorous mammals, occupied the upper tiers of the terrestrial food web. They lived at very low densities over vast areas of Eurasia, and their potential for population increase was small.[38]

The pace of change in Paleolithic material culture increased rapidly after roughly 70,000 years ago in Africa and 50,000 years ago in Eurasia. Technical innovations such as durable art objects or ornaments and bone spear points first appeared in disparate "hotspots" across the three continents.[39] These precocious developments are surprisingly discontinuous in time and space, as if the innovations were fragile and easily snuffed out: they seem to represent not a few great ideas rapidly becoming established over large areas, but rather many isolated experiments. After about 50,000 years ago, however, regional variety in human material culture became the rule, based on the development of recognizable styles and stylistic turnover.

The people of the Upper Paleolithic were big-game hunters, as were those of the MP before them, but they also hunted or gathered a wider range of small animal and plant species. Although MP folk apparently recognized birds, lagomorphs, and other small animals as potential food, they only rarely pursued them, probably because hunting these quick animals requires more effort in relation to energy gained. In other words, UP diets tended to combine low-cost (slow-moving) and high-cost (quick-moving) prey. These shifts in human predatory patterns began in the eastern end of the Mediterranean basin and eventually spread northward and westward.

The broadening of the Paleolithic diet is not explained by climate oscillations that could have affected the diversity of small game animals in the region. Moreover, the technological innovations that would have mitigated the costs of capturing small, quick animals and increased hunters' efficiency (such as snares, deadfalls, and nets) generally *postdate* the diversification of diets. In addition, the observed shifts to foods with lower net yields of energy often involved foods, like rabbits, that can breed rapidly, which increased access to meat. Behaviors that reduce the variance in the costs of acquisition can lead to a more consistent supply of animal protein and fats. This can greatly improve survival rates of a population without increasing the birth rate.

The diversification of UP foraging regimens may reflect the growing use of mechanisms for managing economic risk and fluctuations in supply and demand. Here we return to the coevolutionary theme of this section, for risk pooling can be achieved through diversified socioeconomic roles, food sharing, and cooperative labor even when food is scarce. Another method of risk management and buffering among recent foragers involves the formation and maintenance of geographically extensive social alliances and networks of reciprocity. Such practices are evidenced in the UP from the circulation of designs or art objects through large areas of the Old World.[40]

A third method of risk management involves insulation mechanisms practiced at the level of the individual or the group—food storage, intensified food processing, and improving technological efficiency. Storage buffers human groups against seasonal fluctuations in resource abundance, especially in situations where residential mobility, exchange, or sharing cannot resolve this problem. More efficient methods for extracting all potential value from animal carcasses—including meat, fat, and bone grease (the fat embedded within the structure of the bone itself)—may have increased the yield of any given animal caught, although the gains in food supplies would have been offset by the greater amount of work required.

Although individuals during the MP certainly shared food and cooperated while hunting, there is little evidence of diet diversification or intensified food processing during this period. Neither were food-acquisition roles highly specialized by sex or size: the fates of MP women and children were closely allied to those of hunting males, although they almost certainly took fewer risks during hunts and did more work in carrying carcasses and processing meat and bones. Thus labor was cooperative but not especially diversified. Artifactual evidence meanwhile tells us that MP social networks were limited in comparison to those of later cultures. Because MP populations were constrained by the high day-to-day variation in the availability of meat and by frequent residential moves, they would have seldom attained large sizes and were subject to frequent local crashes.

The shift in predatory economics between the MP and UP not only increased environmental carrying capacity for UP populations but also had social ramifications. The addition of novel resources to human diets may have allowed a wider range of individuals in human groups to become productive, quasi-independent foragers. As foods came from a wider range of foraging substrates and habitats, different techniques were required to obtain them efficiently. Because no single forager could have hunted and gathered this entire range of animal and plant foods, dietary changes must have been accompanied by role diversification.

The modern pattern of cooperative labor divided by age and gender could have been a historical accident, stemming in part from the tropical and subtropical environments where *Homo sapiens* first evolved.[41] Low-latitude ecosystems offer a wider range of plant foods and therefore provide consistently rich opportunities for dietary diversification, should natural selection favor this behavior for any reason. The spread of "collaborative economies" into temperate and eventually high-latitude environments could only have been fueled by the demographic advantage they conferred. The diverse, collaborative character of these foraging systems was sustained because of the competitive advantage of greater efficiency. In higher-latitude environments, tasks such as producing clothing and shelter eventually became as important as foraging.

The demographic advantage of UP foragers over neighboring MP populations was probably quite subtle, yet enough to make a difference over a few thousand years. It was likely less a matter of reproducing faster than of being less vulnerable to oscillations in population size. Stylistic evidence and the widespread use of ornaments suggest that micropopulations of the UP were also more closely connected. UP groups often responded socially and technologically (rather than simply demographically) to the periodic scarcity of resources.

One of the great lessons of the Paleolithic story is how demographic factors affect the potential for connectedness among social entities and for human participation in environmental systems. For a long time hominins were of little significance in ecosystems in which they lived. Distinctly human impacts on community structure and prey populations first become detectable with the onset of the UP. The fact that UP humans spread so quickly across Eurasia, quietly snuffing out or absorbing populations of indigenous hominins, shows that UP groups were adept at both colonizing and holding onto any territory gained. The plasticity of UP cultural systems allowed them to reorganize frequently in the service of demographic robustness.

The MP-UP cultural transition in Eurasia raises a fascinating paradox. The adaptive systems of the MP were persistent in time and space: over their 200,000 years of existence, MP populations dealt successfully with the many challenges of Ice Age environments. Yet the populations who made MP artifacts probably were not particularly robust. In fact the rather narrow set of behavioral responses that characterized these groups would have rendered them susceptible to localized extinction. The larger social networks of UP populations may have allowed them to grow somewhat faster, or at least to experience fewer oscillations in population size. At the same time, the interconnectedness among UP social groups would have allowed ideas to spread, facilitating rapid change. In other words, the dispersal of UP groups presented MP populations, capable as they were in so many aspects of adaptation, with a new challenge that they could not quite overcome: competition from an invading cultural system with a slightly more efficient and plastic organization. This cultural flexibility and demographic persistence allowed UP groups to flourish at the expense of the Neanderthals and underpinned the extraordinary cultural developments to come. Cultural flexibility and demographic persistence mark the beginning of the explosive growth of humans' ecological footprint.

DOMESTICATION: COEVOLUTION NEAR AND DEAR

The human domestication of animals and plants is but one outcome of small-scale strategies for risk pooling and management. Other outcomes include changes in and diversification of socioeconomic roles and new patterns of food sharing and cooperative labor. By comparison to early coevolutionary relations between hominins and other large carnivores, human interactions with the organisms that became domesticated in the terminal Pleistocene and early Holocene involved cohabitation, increasingly anchored to human settlements.

As Jared Diamond remarked in 1994, the interval in which humans domesticated most of the important large animals that we continue to manage today is surprisingly short—between roughly 10,000 and 4,000 years ago. By that end point the species with the most suitable predispositions had already been drawn into the human orbit. Why domestication did not occur earlier is a separate question and requires information on the unique interactions of human ecological history and selective mechanisms. For P. J. Wilson, domestication began when people lived in houses grouped in small hamlets.[42] Others would say that it began earlier, mainly on the grounds that domestication does not necessarily require captivity to isolate a reproducing group of animals or plants. We can be sure, however, that domestication of plants and animals is the result of many isolated experiments that ultimately reordered human participation in ecosystems and the mode and scale of our energy consumption relative to that of other species.

Morphological changes brought about by domestication normally emerge rather late in the process. Fortunately, peculiar shifts in genetic diversity, geographic range, and spatial associations with humans normally precede the morphological changes, and it is these that researchers use to establish the beginnings of domestication processes. The dog is widely considered to be the first domesticate.[43] The earliest known domesticated dog skeletons come from the Near East and are associated with the Natufian culture approximately 11,000 years BP.[44] Estimates of the timing of the genetic divergence of dogs from wolves vary from 100,000–40,000 years ago to 40,000–15,000 years ago, but archaeological evidence generally argues for later dates, probably between 14,000 and 11,000 years ago.[45]

Domestication has been a mainstay of world histories that feature human beings as the tamers of nature, enabled by superior cognitive abilities to dominate lower life forms and turn them to their own purposes. Indeed, a recent issue of *Science* magazine, focusing on the latest results in sequencing the bovine genome, states as much in the caption to its cover photograph, a close-up of a heifer in a plastic halter, the glint of life in its eye replaced by a glittering helix of man-made DNA:

"Animal domestication has been key to the development of human societies."[46] Yet our growing understanding of domestication, based on skeletal, archaeological, paleoecological, genomic, retroviral, and other data, belies those common claims.[47] Domestication, like every other aspect of hominin existence, arose out of coevolutionary relations of mutual dependence, and the process continues to change both us and our partners in domestication today.

The role of human intention in domestication has long been questioned, though usually by lone voices at the margin of mainstream beliefs. Darwin developed his model of natural selection in *Origin of Species* on the basis of British farmers' and herders' practices of artificial selection.[48] Darwin recognized farmers' deliberate modifications of their animals and plants, but he pointed out that these practices created a mixture of desired and unanticipated results, only some of which proved useful to humans.[49] By contrast, he argued, natural selection was "unconscious" and not guided by a grand design. Following Darwin, more than a century later, David Rindos, a formative thinker on the subject of domestication, insisted that human breeders of animals and plants are unaware of the full range of effects of their actions.[50] In addition to providing benefits to humans, domesticated animals and plants have benefited in many ways that are potentially harmful to humans in the long run. A variety of powerful pathogens have also evolved and flourished in economies built on domesticates.

Domestication is not limited to human beings but is found among a number of other organisms. Ants protect and exploit certain aphids, and aphids thrive under this protection.[51] According to Hiroshi Sakata, female worker ants of the species *Lasius niger* make simple decisions every day to either eat or protect aphids.[52] The ant colony collectively tends and milks several aphid species for their sugary secretions (honeydew), but each worker ant tends just one kind of aphid. She also leaves unmolested any aphid that has been tended and milked by other ants in the colony. Such a relationship can alter both ant and aphid populations over many generations, leading, for example, to more productive aphids and better-nourished ant colonies.[53]

The fact that plants or animals can be domesticated in the absence of human partners demonstrates that human design is not required, even if it remains true that humans have many more domesticate partners than any other species. Dmitry K. Belyaev's forty-year fox-domestication experiment changed many minds about how domestication could come about in the absence of an overarching human plan.[54] He showed how remarkably simple selection rules can arise naturally from the practical challenges of interacting with or handling animals. Selection for less fearful behavior in caged foxes over many generations resulted in submissive, friendly foxes, and along with these behavioral changes came changes in physical features. The foxes became more doglike; some had curled tails, floppy ears, foreshortened or infantile faces, simplified dentition, and broken or spotted coats. Some of these foxes bounced before their human keepers, wagging their tails. By consuming or culling difficult-to-handle individuals for meat or fur, keepers leave gentler individuals to reproduce under human protection. In a similar manner, the dog may have been domesticated from wolves following the simple rule of raising only animals that did not bite. This approach could work in both captive and free-ranging situations, such as selection among the numerous pups that humans robbed from wild dens, or observation of less aggressive tendencies among certain wolves that hung around and scavenged near human settlements.

At the heart of nearly all of the outward changes in Belyaev's foxes were subtle shifts in the endocrine system, which helps to control the pace and extent of physical and psychological development. The outcomes of this experiment have been replicated in numerous contexts and species, resulting in a virtual sea change in our perceptions of the earliest processes of domestication. No more can we be satisfied with the view that people finally saw the light and chose to bring productive animals into their yards and homes. Domestication, instead, took place at the interface between humans and animals and was the by-product of selection processes that formed naturally in that space. Humans are evolutionary partners in domestication relationships. We must recognize that we are as deeply affected by these relationships as are the animals and plants that we manipulate. Certain metabolic changes in humans, for example, are clearly a result of domestication relationships over the long term, such as the coevolution in Neolithic Europe of milk protein genes in cattle and lactase genes in humans.[55]

One further insight, perhaps the most bruising to the human ego, is that many of the same traits that arise from domestication in mammals have also appeared in humans. Darwin and many biologists since have noted that a wide range of animal species undergo similar physiological changes in the context of domestication.[56] It is difficult to account for these commonalities in light of the great variety of roles that domesticates play in human lives, from hunting companion or guardian to walking meat larders and chattels, to load bearers and producers of eggs, milk, hair, and fertilizer. The progressive reduction and smoothing of the human face over the last 40,000 years, its retreat under the brain case, the general gracilization of the postcranial anatomy, broken pigmentation (freckling, for example), and the progressive reduction of human dentition over the last 10,000 years might also fit the model of selection for tolerance to social stress and living at close quarters with ever-larger groups of people. We can expect that there have been important alterations to human endocrine systems to alleviate the panic reaction in crowded social situations. H.M. Leach, following P.J. Wilson, argues that human beings developed their juvenile features in tandem with those common in the domestication of animals, specifically as a result of changes in diet, housing, and the increased rates of social interaction associated with sedentary living.[57]

While acknowledging that human beings are neither omniscient nor prescient about the processes of domestication, the zooarchaeologist Melinda Zeder argues that intentionality is what differentiates human forms of domestication from those of other organisms: "The uniqueness of the relationship comes from its cultural component and the dominant role humans play in consciously and deliberately perpetuating it to their own advantage."[58] Contrary to Rindos's emphasis on largely unconscious selection in domestication, Zeder and colleagues argue that humans deliberately shaped the niches of tended species to enhance their numbers and productivity.[59] It may be this element of conscious human intent—or *agency*, to use a fashionable term—that forms the interface between the overarching forces of domestication on the one hand and the highly localized ways that food production economies developed in different world areas on the other.

Today, information about animal and plant management is conserved and disseminated in many cultures through common knowledge, agricultural science, stud books, and seed banks. These institutions have developed over thousands of years of living with domesticated species, and the scale of conscious management and design has expanded so much that this knowledge has become highly specialized. The scope of intentionality inherent to modern animal and plant management is unlikely, however, to represent the initial conditions of domestication thousands of years ago. Early attempts at domestication would have been short-term in scope: feeding captive wild lambs, expanding the number of nesting spots for doves in a cliff face, removing weeds from a patch of wild barley, setting aside some of the best of wild seed to sow on fertile ground. Unintended outcomes in the early stages of domestication would have been inevitable.

The earliest attempts at domestication of animals such as sheep and goats of the Fertile Crescent may not have been intended to create a better meat animal, but rather as solutions to an impending tragedy of the commons.[60] The supplies of large wild game were already compromised in the eastern Mediterranean area by burgeoning human populations whose diets were supplemented in large part by grains and legumes (see chapter 10). As hunters encountered progressively fewer wild sheep and goats, the benefits of controlling access to the remaining harvest would have been amplified, specifically the locations and movements of the animals and their availability to competing hunters. "Ownership" of valuable prey animals might have been indefensible within small, egalitarian communities but easy to rationalize between communities.

With the coalescence of the Neolithic package of technologies and associated behavioral patterns in Eurasia, domestication became one of the main vehicles of the expansion of the human footprint.[61] Domestication relationships have opened new worlds and niches to humans and their coevolutionary partners. Our indisputable gains from domestication relationships have been matched by losses in other aspects of life. As for grand designs, we must acknowledge the wisdom of Darwin's contemporary, George Eliot, when she wrote in *Middlemarch*: "If we had a keen vision and feeling of all that is ordinary in human life, it would be like hearing the grass grow and the squirrel's heart beat, and we should die of that roar which lies on the other side of silence. As it is, the quickest of us walk about well wadded with stupidity."[62]

CONSERVATION AND EXTINCTION

The growth of the human footprint, coupled with a wadding of stupidity, has not been a good recipe for nature conservation. In recent years, a soul-wrenching debate involving social scientists, biologists, economists, and lawmakers has emerged over whether it is reasonable or useful to assume that human beings are capable of conserving natural resources, and whether they may have done so in the past. Some small communities have sustained relatively constant environmental relations over centuries. But in circumstances that push human beings beyond sustainability, efforts to conserve resources are rare, almost nonexistent, in comparison to efforts at innovation and compensation.[63] The consequences, as many have argued in the popular media, can be catastrophic.

Two related issues merit consideration in any discussion of conservation: the actual limits of conserving behaviors in humans (rather than the basic capacity to conserve) and the scale-sensitive nature of cooperative networks. Humans squirrel away all sorts of things, from food and baubles to information. Hoarding behaviors are also widespread elsewhere in the animal world (though rare in primates).[64] Fallowing of fields is arguably a measure intended to conserve and enhance soil fertility over the long term, but the delayed advantages to be gained from fallowing are generally protected by rules of land tenure that prevent another user from planting the area. Conservation or management of free-ranging or common resources is a separate matter and is conditioned to a great extent by one's faith in the stability of the resource and its vulnerability to theft. Even animals that share extensively, as humans certainly do, rarely succeed in conserving open resource pools. The capacity and inclination to conserve varies among the many levels of human sensibility, from the individual to small sharing groups to large social units. The inclination to conserve often fades as the consumer group gets larger.

Garret Hardin's essay "The Tragedy of the Commons" describes a classic dilemma in which multiple individuals acting independently and rationally in their own self-interest will ultimately destroy a shared finite resource, even with the knowledge that the exploitation is in no one's interest over the long run.[65] This tendency has been proved again and again, not because humans are inherently greedy but because they must weigh immediate consequences against future odds. This dilemma shows us that rational choice is limited by uncertainties inherent to the natural systems of which humans are a part. As Hardin observes: "The population problem has no technical solution; it requires a fundamental extension in morality. . . . [T]he commons, if justifiable at all, is justifiable only under conditions of low-population density. As the human population has increased, the commons has had to be abandoned in one aspect after another. . . . Every new enclosure of the commons involves the infringement of somebody's personal liberty."[66]

Rather than showing a flair for conservation, humans have become a powerful extinction force on every continent. Admittedly, massive human impacts on ecosystems during the Pleistocene remain in doubt. On the one hand, the latest data suggest that the extinction of the Tasmanian megafauna was caused by human activity.[67] In Australia, R.G. Roberts and B.W. Brook have argued, "human impact was likely the decisive factor" in megafaunal extinctions 50,000 years ago, through "imperceptible overkill" and "habitat disturbance, most likely by burning vegetation."[68] On the other hand, the latest research on North America, where most of the megafauna were thought to have gone suddenly extinct 15,000 to 13,000 years ago, now shows that they persisted several thousand years after the arrival of human beings.[69] An alternative explanation is that an earlier trend toward demographic collapse and "functional extinction" may have spelled the demise of American megafauna several thousand years before their final disappearance from the fossil record around 10,000 years ago.[70] If so, perhaps Paleoindians simply nudged them over the precipice.

But even if the evidence for human predation in quaternary extinctions is equivocal, it is impossible to dismiss the human element in later extinctions, such as on Pacific islands. Overhunting brought on the demise of moas not long after humans colonized New Zealand, and the introduction of mainland mammals was disastrous for Hawaiian birds.[71] Other examples come from the Metal Ages of mainland Eurasia, where mobility, technology, and a more crowded world sent humans in relentless pursuit of the great cats.[72] Originating from human competition with both wild hoofed animals and the large predators that eat them, the biggest hit to the populations of magnificent carnivores is associated with increasingly stratified societies and powerful political hierarchies that commanded huge territories. Rare, beautiful, or iconic parts of dangerous animals were and still are in high demand as displays of power and wealth.

Relations between humans and animals can be both synergistic and destructive, as is evident, for example, in hominins' long-time relations with fish, shellfish, and other marine organisms.[73] Yet archaeologists have also documented the role of humans in conserving and tending some marine ecosystems, for example through the creation of clam gardens that once ranged from the San Juan Islands, off the coast of Washington, to Alaska. Specialists argue that a long-term historical perspective is essential to fathoming anthropogenic and other effects in marine ecosystems. The effects of human exploitation, for example, may be masked for decades or centuries if trophically similar fish replace overfished species until they too are fished out.[74]

Because some human habits can transform landscapes and habitat structures on a grand scale, humans' role in extinctions has grown in tandem with human population densities. With deliberate modifications of the physical environment to enhance the productivity of preferred economic species, we diminish habitat space or area for other species. This is an effect of scale. It does not derive from our having transcended ecosystems or, even less, from our having conquered nature.

PATTERNS OF SOCIALITY
BETWEEN HUMAN AND NONHUMAN BEINGS

One outcome of domestication during the Neolithic in the Middle East and the population growth that resulted from it was the eventual transformation of egalitarian into hierarchical human societies. Subsequent historical evidence shows that humans also exerted ever-tighter controls on reproduction in domesticates. Darwin himself recognized that domestication had a long and changing history in Europe.[75] From animal breeders, veterinarians, investigative reporters, and others involved in agricultural improvement from the late 1700s to the mid-1800s, he learned that methods of breeding in confinement were historically new developments derived in part from the earlier shift to enclosures throughout the British Isles. These enclosures enabled much closer controls over animal breeding precisely because the animals could not wander.[76]

The butchering of animals and the culling of the unfit has always been a part of humans' involvement in domestication partnerships. We don't just milk, as the ant does to the aphid; we kill as well, and not always for food. However, some scholars would argue that the killing of animals in contemporary life is "without precedent . . . on such a scale that is almost beyond comprehension. It is not just the statistics that are staggering, but the fact that almost all areas of human life are at some point or other involved in or directly dependent on the killing of animals."[77] Such treatment has early correlates in the extermination (bounty hunting) of wild pests, but dogs and cats euthanized each year in the United States currently number almost 4 million (albeit less than the estimate of more than 20 million in the 1970s, before the widespread use of sterilization). Humane shelters have called for the development of new kinds of contraceptives for domestic pets, because immunocontraceptives, originally developed for human females and adapted for use on feral horses in the 1970s (which at the time were hunted for pet food) do not work on cats and dogs.[78]

Yet despite this apparent ruthlessness, humans have developed emotional and spiritual feelings about the animals with whom they live, and some of these attitudes have in turn influenced human social relations. Inspired by Darwin's *Origin of Species,* the Scottish lawyer John McLennan conjectured in 1870 that ancient and non-Western ideas about human-animal kinship, typically involving respect for nonhuman beings—what McLennan saw as "worship"—represented the earliest stage of religion in the worldwide evolution of religion into science.[79] In his *Primitive Culture,* published in London one year later, Edward

Burnett Tylor acknowledged the depth of feeling for animals in a back-handed way by coining the term *zoolatry*, or animal worship, which he distinguished from *zoology*, in his view the civilized stance toward animals. "To the modern educated world, few phenomena of the lower civilization seem more pitiable than the spectacle of a man worshipping a beast. We have learned the lessons of Natural History at last thoroughly enough to recognize our superiority to our 'younger brothers,' as the Red Indians call them, the creatures whom it is our place not to adore but to understand and use."[80]

We define humanity in relation to our concepts of other-than-human beings. Some people—for example, the Ojibwa and the people of the Kluane First Nation in western Canada—put human and other-than-human creatures in the same social field.[81] Others, like Tylor, define humans and animals oppositionally and hierarchically. The Linnaean system, for example, is categorical, and the boundaries between taxa cannot be overcome except through processes of speciation and hybridization that are not expressed in the system itself. Especially in cultures where social inequality is rife, human relations are projected onto animal relations (categories of higher, lower, and so on). These projections are then used to manipulate human relations of hierarchy and inequality through social processes that scholars have variously described as "naturalizing" (feminists took the lead on this), "brutalizing," and "animalizing."

In short, whether human beings select or reject, conserve, let die, or extinguish other biological populations, these behaviors are inextricable from the ways they evaluate and rank relations among themselves. Elinor Melville's study *A Plague of Sheep* analyzes the effects of the Spanish conquest of Mexico on the ecology of a valley north of what is now Mexico City, then occupied by Otomi irrigation farmers.[82] Inspired by Crosby's *Ecological Imperialism*, Melville argues that the Spaniards' introduction of sheep into the area, combined with lumbering and human population losses to epidemics, resulted between 1530 and 1600 in the radical transformation of the land, water, people, plants, and animals.[83] The Otomi seem to have taken up sheepherding because the land, so quickly transformed, could support no other form of subsistence.

For contemporary examples illustrating how societies are defined by the ways in which humans relate to animals, we need only look around us. A century and a half after Darwin's time, animals are not only bred in confinement but raised and killed there. Factory farms produce 75 percent of the world's poultry, more than 66 percent of all eggs, and 40 percent of all pork, and "virtually all of the growth in livestock production" occurs in industrial systems.[84] The globalization of agriculture—crops and livestock—that has come about through commercial efforts to cut costs by shifting factories to places with lower rents and labor costs has severed many of the links, both substantive and conceptual, that once existed between livestock and land. Naylor and colleagues argue that the result has been still greater ecological costs, combined with a greater ignorance of biological relations between animals and land in particular. The long-term ecosystem costs are therefore passed on to the poorest countries, and especially to the poorest women and children, thus impoverishing them further.[85] Meanwhile, the amount of food wasted per capita in the United States (a source of energy loss as well as methane and carbon dioxide emissions) increased by about 50 percent between 1974 and 2003, accounting for more than one-quarter of the nation's total freshwater consumption and "approximately 300 million barrels of oil per year."[86] Agricultural lands for crops and livestock, mainly in private hands, now cover about 40 percent of the world's land—almost as much as forests and wooded areas, about 86 percent of which are owned by national governments. The demands of food production, in short, have fostered a massive redistribution of landed resources within nation-states and internationally, benefiting corporate wealth at the expense of the common wealth.[87]

CLOSING THE TEMPORAL BREACH

We have wrestled over several centuries in the sciences and historical disciplines with two false dichotomies: man versus nature, and history versus prehistory. What has changed most in reality is the complexity of the interactions between humans and their ecosystems and the solutions required or historically predicated as new problems of adaptation have emerged. The products of these processes are cumulative, but many of the processes are essentially timeless. The collective effects of human actions—intended and unintended—cannot be avoided by human communities once they begin to unfold. Through continuous interaction, the relationships develop an impetus of their own, with humans and the environment being necessary partners in the dialogue.[88]

Evolution is a process highly sensitive to history. This is because, to quote a biology-classroom adage, natural selection and random drift operate on existing variation. As a process of change, evolution is timeless, and there is no logical distinction between the recent and the remote past. Humans interested in these processes face the challenge of lower information resolution in the deep past—hence the diplomatic distinction between prehistory and history, the lack of writing and the emergence of writing, and the Dark Ages and the dawn of reason. Any artificial compression of history denies us critical opportunities to discover how changes in human societies may come about through the spiraling interactions between ourselves and other species and between ourselves and the physical environment. If our eyes are trained only on the outcomes, we cannot detect the processes at work.

Scholars advocating the use of the term Anthropocene, referring to the era in which humans have themselves become geological agents, argue that human beings have succeeded in domesticating all of nature, and therefore we should reconceptualize ecosystems in terms of what some now call ecosystem services, a perspective emphasizing the benefits we can draw from the environment if only we learn to be appropriate stewards.[89] A significant drawback to this worldview is the reduction of all life forms, including our own, to codes that are construed as intellectual property. From a deep-time perspective, such an approach risks transforming ecosystemic relations into tradable and heritable bio-wealth—or bio-capital—a transformation not unlike the age-old processes by which land has been transformed from a matter of rights and obligations into heritable material wealth.

A deep-time perspective also shows that human involvement in ecosystems, as devastating as it has been to increasingly large numbers of human and other organisms, is still narrow, even blinkered, in its scope. Although we now realize that we inhabit the Earth with some six million other species, compared to Linnaeus's estimate of twenty thousand, our knowledge of other organisms is limited mainly to the ones we consider "free-living," by comparison to the "parasites" involved in some 75 percent of the links in the world's food chains.[90] We are just becoming acquainted with the microbiota that inhabit the exterior and interior landscapes of our bodies, outnumbering our cells by an estimated ratio of ten to one.[91] We have come to know and control some of our animal partners so intimately that we can harvest their body parts for our own use.[92] Yet we are just beginning to grasp the complexities of the webs that bind our being to those of others.[93] As Leach argues, what we may least understand about our coevolutionary relationships with other organisms is how those relationships subtly change us as they unfold.[94] What we perceive so readily as mastery is but an illusion born of dependence.

CHAPTER 5

Language

APRIL McMAHON, THOMAS R. TRAUTMANN,
AND ANDREW SHRYOCK

A NEW KEY TO THE REMOTE PAST

Well before the time revolution of the 1860s, the comparison of human languages and the discovery of their historical relations was the first effective foray into deep history. Language comparison—comparative philology, or historical linguistics—was already under way in the eighteenth century, seeking to push the frontiers of deep history beyond the limit of the written record. By the early nineteenth century, comparative philology had gained a sterling reputation as a key to the remote past.

There were several reasons for this success. Language comparison could be used to study times and places before and without writing. It constituted a new record, stored in living languages of the present, of a time before alphabets, syllabaries, and ideographs. It could even be applied to languages for which there was no writing—those of the Americas, for example. Within the confines of the short chronology made popular by biblical scholars (see chapter 1), historical linguistics promised to extend the reach of history to cover all humans, not just those who lived in the literate world. Moreover, comparative philology developed an exactness of method and a unity of conception that inspired confidence in its conclusions and put an end to the undisciplined pluralism of the amateur study of language. As to conception, it adopted the model of a family tree. As to method, it adopted the comparison of vocabulary and grammar. An early discovery clinched its reputation: namely, that divergence had a certain regularity to it that could be described by the "laws" of sound shifts. Increasing refinement of these laws increased the power and trustworthiness of the method.

Comparative philology's reputation did not, however, go unchallenged after 1859. As history deepened drastically in response to Darwinian ideas, the inability of linguists to examine and account for the whole of the newly christened territory of prehistory grew increasingly apparent. The origin point of language receded into an indeterminate past, and it began to seem that the evolution of the human species had begun long before the advent of language. Following the discoveries of 1859, historical linguistics was no longer the key that opened the door to a universal past. The methods of archaeology, Darwinian biology, and genomics eventually overshadowed it.

In this chapter we trace the early and permanent successes of language comparison. We also examine the nature and limits of the tree model and its associated methods, and the emergence of a network model to account for what the tree model leaves out. Finally, we discuss new approaches to the study of the evolution of language that work through simulations. The enduring potential of language as a framework for the study of deep history is based not only on the gains made in recent centuries of linguistic research, but also on the kinds of problems—those of exchange, connection, difference, and patterning—that language repeatedly creates and solves for humans.

LANGUAGE TREES

Working out the historical relationships among languages and arranging them in family trees was a European intellectual project that, in an age of worldwide expansion of European power, was carried around the globe. This project led to real scientific breakthroughs, and in the early nineteenth century it was the leading means and model for the exploration of the deep human past.

Three major examples of this endeavor are found in places as far apart as Russia, America, and India. Catherine the Great, empress of Russia, directed an ambitious project for the comparative study of the languages of the world through the collection of vocabularies by the officials of her expanding empire and by correspondence with statesmen and scholars around the globe. The results of this enterprise were published in two volumes, grandly titled *Linguarum Totius Orbis Vocabularia Comparativa* (1786–89), by her assistant, Stephen Pallas.

In America, Thomas Jefferson, president of the American Philosophical Society, inaugurated a similar attempt to collect vocabularies of American Indian languages and compare them against a standard list of words in English, impelled by the belief that uncovering the historical relationships among the languages would reveal the historical relationships of the tribes that spoke them. This project, first sketched in his *Notes on the State of Virginia,* launched the comparative study of American languages that continues to this day.[1]

In India, at Kolkata (Calcutta), the Indian headquarters of the British East India Company and capital of British India, Sir William Jones took up the study of Sanskrit. Recognizing its similarity to Latin, Greek, Gothic, Celtic, and Old Persian, he proposed that all these languages must be descended from an ancestor language, now perhaps lost. He made this proposition in his address to the Asiatic Society, of which he was the president and founder.[2] In doing so, Jones outlined the conception of the Indo-European language family, the study of which led to rapid advances in comparative philology.

It was no coincidence that these three projects sprang up in distant places more or less simultaneously: they were instances of the more general project of tracing the historical relationships of languages, a project whose long, complex history reaches back to the medieval period. It promoted not only the collecting of word lists but the writing of dictionaries and grammars for all the languages of the world as a basis for study. The comparative method, to give it a name, conceptualized historical relations through the model of a branching family tree. Languages grew in time from one to many, and all, in theory, were siblings or cousins to one another and codescendants of ancestral languages. The tree model was ideal for mapping relations of *divergence,* but it had no means of accommodating contact and *convergence.* The branches of the tree never grew together; they only grew further apart.

This model and method achieved spectacular results, many of which remain valid today. The tracing of the Indo-European language family is the leading example (see figure 12). No previous mapping of the world had grouped India and Persia with Europe, skipping over the Turks and Arabs who occupied the territory between the two wings of the new language family. This peculiar linguistic geography led to the hypothesis of a Central Asian homeland for the speakers of Proto-Indo-European—a name linguists invented for the ancestral language Jones had originally proposed—and the migration of different fractions of this population in different directions.

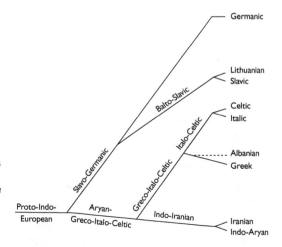

FIGURE 12. August Schleicher was one of the first philologists to portray the evolution of the Indo-European language family using tree models, which he developed in the 1850s. This famous tree appeared in his classic work *A Compendium of the Comparative Grammar of the Indo-European Languages* (1861).

The genealogy of Indo-European languages is surely one of the most important results of the European language project, but it was hardly the most surprising. That the language of the Roma, or Gypsies, of Europe was a descendant of Sanskrit was equally significant, precisely because the Roma had no tradition of a homeland in India, and their common name in English expressed a presumption that they came from Egypt. These new findings were especially impressive because they showed that language could illuminate history beyond the reach of collective memory. Even more startling was the discovery of historical relations linking languages of what we now call the Malayo-Polynesian family, stretching from Madagascar off the east coast of Africa through Malaya and Indonesia to the Maori of New Zealand and the Tahitians and Hawaiians far to the east. Here again was an unanticipated addition to deep history.[3]

In the two and a half centuries since Empress Catherine, Thomas Jefferson, and William Jones made their contributions, linguists have carried this project forward, extending its reach and enhancing the accuracy of its results. Given the revolutionary success of their efforts, the tree model and the comparative method deserve a closer look. As chapter 2 shows, the family tree as a frame for universal history has biblical roots. In Genesis, the story of humankind unfolds in a genealogy of nations starting with Adam but ramifying with Noah and his sons, the only human survivors of the Flood. By continually extending the branches of this vast genealogical tree, Jews, Christians, and Muslims created universal histories (and geographies) in which all peoples of the world could be located.

Yet in the biblical accounts, the genealogy on display is one of nations, not languages alone. What is the relation between these two trees?

William Jones and other early linguists assumed the tree of languages to be completely isomorphic with the tree of nations. For this reason, knowledge of language history was considered a way to repair the defects of, or move beyond, the historical memory of the nations that spoke the languages in question. In other words, the eighteenth-century project of comparative philology was always concerned first with the deep history of nations: language history illuminated national history. The project was not a self-contained inquiry into historical linguistics per se. Furthermore, the impulse to write grammars and dictionaries of other languages was a project inspired and made possible by a unique combination of Abrahamic cosmology and European expansion. The ancient Greeks and Romans took little interest in the languages of others, and, although all the "people of the book" (Jews, Christians, and Muslims) shared the biblical model of the tree of *nations,* the tree of *languages* developed only in Christian Europe, on the brink of the global extension of European power, which opened the entire world to the languages-and-nations project.

The European impulse to collect and compare languages first took the form of publishing polyglot Bibles or collections of paternosters, but these were not very effective instruments for discovering the historical relations among languages. The word list, on the other hand, proved a simple and effective tool for the comparative method. Indeed, the novelty and durable results of the languages-and-nations project seem out of all proportion to the simplicity of the word lists from which they came, and we need to take a close look at them.

One of the earliest word lists, devised by the German philosopher Gottfried Wilhelm Leibniz, was published in 1718. Leibniz selected words that he believed would determine the scope of German and its close relatives as well as of the Slavic and other language families of Eastern Europe and the Russian empire. His list, "expressing common things," consisted of numbers, kin terms, body parts, actions, necessities of life, and phenomena of nature.[4] Leibniz was interested in the language of common people, not of the learned; in words describing the immediate needs of life, not luxuries or complex notions of art and science; in words from the earliest times, not recent coinages; and in native words rather than words borrowed from foreign languages. These choices reflect the notion that there is an ancient, native core to a language that the vocabulary list seeks to capture.

The comparative method was applicable to grammar as well as vocabulary. Jones had discovered early on that the ancient Indo-European languages shared not only similar words but also grammatical structures and the roots of verbs. A few decades later, Franz Bopp showed that similarities among the Indo-European languages in the conjugation of the verb *to be* could be explained by a tree model. He developed this insight into a comprehensive comparative grammar of the language family.[5] Another area of research concerned the "laws" of sound shifts, again in Indo-European languages. Word lists arranged in parallel columns made visible a pattern of systematic sound shifts that occurred as the languages diverged over time. In 1819, Jacob Grimm published his massive historical grammar of German: enriched by the emerging knowledge of the Indo-European comparative context, it was among the first works to observe these regularities and bring them to bear on the analysis of a single language.[6] An example of Grimm's Law is the "f" sound in Germanic words, such as English *foot* and *father,* answering to a "p" sound in Latin (*pes, pedis,* and *pater*) and Sanskrit (*pada* and *pitr*), a pattern suggesting that the Proto-Indo-European ancestral language had a "p" sound that changed to an "f" sound in Germanic languages.

There were exceptions and problem cases that Grimm's Law could not account for, and efforts to refine the law and realize its analytical promise were a significant part of nineteenth-century comparative philology, leading to a multiplication of laws of sound shifts in Indo-European. Unlike the laws of physics, the regularities governing sound shifts in Indo-European were not universal; they were historically contingent, sequential, and specific to Indo-European languages. Nonetheless, wider application of the comparative method proved immensely fruitful, establishing beyond doubt that regular sound shifts were also a feature of other language families.

Refinements in the use of word lists continued as well. In the 1950s, Morris Swadesh developed a master vocabulary of two hundred words for the comparison of languages. His list retained elements of Leibniz's list but included many additions, including pronouns and prepositions. These words were taken to represent the basic lexicon of a language: the first words learned in childhood, the words least culturally specific and most nearly universal in meaning. We see a great change in conceptualization here; the eighteenth-century word list was designed around what was thought to be the primitive vocabulary of a language, that core of words a language possessed at the moment of its creation—perhaps at the Tower of Babel, when God confused the tongues of the nations. Now the core vocabulary was conceived as a kind of elementary standard for children, or for foreign adults trying to learn the language and communicate at a simple level. From this basic list, Swadesh developed *lexicostatistics,* a technique for determining the closeness of the relationship between pairs of languages, and *glottochronology,* which measures replacements in core vocabulary against an empirically determined rate of fourteen words per thousand years.[7]

The comparative method lies at the center of historical linguistics today; lexicostatistics is further toward the edge, and glottochronology is located at the fringe, refined by some scholars but viewed with skepticism by the majority. The Swadesh list persists but does not prevail, kept alive by the quantum of truth it contains. The strength and weakness of the comparative method is the idea that languages have a durable, inner core surrounded by newer materials that are somehow less essential to the work of comparison.[8] The not-core aspects of a natural language include borrowings and contact phenomena of all kinds, which may be extensive: they may arise through geographical contiguity, the formation of pidgins (simplified trade languages) and creoles (languages formed from the mixture of two or more languages), and many other effects unaccounted for by the comparative method or the core vocabulary of the Swadesh list.

Even if we ignore the limits imposed on the comparative method by its strict linearity, other constraints have undermined its goal of uniting all the language families in a single superfamily. Simply put, the further back in time comparisons reach, the fuzzier and more indeterminate are the facts on which they operate. Joseph Greenberg is famous for proposing the method of *mass comparison* to work around this problem, arguing for the existence of macrofamilies of languages, such as Amerind (comprising all the Native American languages other than Eskimo-Aleut), Indo-Pacific, and Eurasian, and reducing the language families of Africa to four.[9] These consolidations have met resistance from other linguists, and the issue remains unresolved. It would seem that further illumination of the deep history of human language requires either a Greenberg-like method that can be applied across large numbers of languages or some new method working along different lines altogether.

NOT SEEING THE WOOD FOR THE TREES: LIMITS TO THE COMPARATIVE METHOD

The comparative method attained its status as the gold standard in historical linguistics by way of rigorous application. It relies not on superficial similarity but on the demonstration of regular and repeated correspondences across basic vocabulary lists.[10] The method requires ample data of sufficient diachronic reach. For many languages today, because of the effects of globalization, the social pressures on speakers to opt for an "international" rather than a local language, and the continuation of many languages only in oral form, such data can be sparse, their preservation piecemeal and happenstance.[11] It is no accident that the comparative method was pioneered on Indo-European, with an unusual abundance of written historical data and a long history of study of both daughter and intermediate ancestral languages (Latin, Greek, and Sanskrit).

A second challenge to the comparative method is the cumulative effect of language change. Few changes are totally homogeneous, affecting every instance of an eligible sound in every single word. If they were, they would leave no evidence. Limited irregularity in language is the rule, and most changes affect sounds only in certain contexts. Historical linguists can see these changes and use them to reconstruct earlier forms. Sometimes the remaining evidence is from other members of a language family or other dialects of a single language—so, whereas Southern British English varieties have lost the [r] after a vowel in *star, sure, for,* Scottish and many North American varieties retain it, providing evidence that the ancestral form is r-ful. We can use the same example to show the other sort of evidence we commonly find, namely, the preservation of a sound in certain contexts. The loss of [r] after a vowel was restricted to contexts preceding a consonant or at the end of an utterance, so Southern British English still has [r] pronounced before a vowel, as in *red, very, starry, I'm sure it is,* and *for example.*

Many sound changes are conditioned in this way, allowing us to reconstruct the operation of a change, and the situation before the change, through comparison of alternative forms of the same word.[12] Such reconstructions would be easy if there were an infinite number of sounds. However, the number of sounds in any language is small.[13] The Caucasian languages can have more than eighty distinct consonants, but this number is low compared to the thousands of words in which we would expect to find those sounds. Hawaiian has only five distinct vowels and eight consonants. Because the territory in which sound changes can operate is tightly circumscribed, a sequence of changes will often affect the same historical sound in the same or overlapping sets of contexts. As long as the affected sounds or contexts are slightly different, we can still hope to reconstruct the changes involved; but over time, it is almost inevitable that later changes will obscure some earlier ones. The temporal reach of the comparative method is therefore naturally limited, no matter how carefully we apply it. The timescale over which the method can be expected to work is often stated as around 10,000 years.[14] The size of the sound inventory, the availability of comparative evidence, and the specific sound changes found in the history of the language concerned all affect the possibilities for reconstruction. The general point, however, is clear.

The most important limitation of the family tree model and the comparative method is that both are aimed at reconstructing only one aspect of history: the innovations that take place in one set of dialects of a protolanguage, distancing these from their relatives and cumulatively separating the branches of the tree. The underlying model, borrowing a term from biology, is one of isolation by linguistic distance: gradual change becomes cumulative, and over time the nodes at the ends of branches grow farther and farther apart. These splits are irreversible; they lead over time to distinct dialects and mutually incomprehensible languages. However, language histories involve not only splits and divergence, but also convergence through borrowing. Trees are easy to read, make clear predictions, and echo real-world notions of family membership and the transfer of names, resemblances, character traits (and, these days, genes) down through generations. The tree model does not exclude the effects of contact between speakers and languages, but it does require us to downplay them. This is particularly difficult to do for languages from those parts of the world, notably Australia and South America, where our oldest linguistic data come only from the oldest living speakers. In such cases, distinguishing between similarities based on common ancestry and those based on contact can be difficult; it cannot be achieved through the tree model and the comparative method alone.[15]

CONTACT VERSUS COMMON ANCESTRY: DUAL-PATHWAY APPROACHES

The comparative method encourages us to distinguish linguistic similarities that are evidence for common ancestry from those that derive from borrowing, chance, or other factors. The latter are typically regarded as marginal and beyond the reach of the most reliable methods of comparison. However, what we might call the "sociolinguistic turn" in historical linguistics has, over the past twenty years, led to attempts to reintegrate different aspects of the histories of languages into a whole picture and to shift our emphasis from the system to the speaker. As Brian Joseph and Richard Janda put it, "Our view on the identity of the parties most responsible for linguistic change is . . . : we think speakers have something to do with it."[16] Because speakers interact with other speakers, only some of whom speak the same variety of a language, the effects of contact are inevitably part of this more inclusive historical linguistics, which also includes changes within the life span, not just across generations.[17]

There are good reasons not to exclude contact-induced change. For one thing, it is difficult to be sure we have factored it out. The older view that privileging certain sorts of data (basic vocabulary, for instance) protects against contamination by borrowing is coming under attack.[18] Sarah Thomason argues that "when contact is intense enough, there appear to be no absolute linguistic barriers at all to borrowing."[19] This view is still controversial. It is certainly true that contact is more common in some regions of vocabulary and grammar than others, but propitious social circumstances do override these tendencies in some cases.

Thomason is careful to distinguish contact languages—pidgins, creoles, and bilingual mixtures—as special cases.[20] They do not fit the family-tree model, which requires one system to divide into many, rather than several to combine into one. However, even here there are difficulties of delimitation. Contact languages are outcomes of processes that affect all languages, and it is often impossible to distinguish between contact languages and cases of heavy borrowing.[21] Worse, we categorize pidgins and creoles as such because we typically know their history from other sources, or we have earwitness accounts of their formation and of the contributory languages. However, this practice implies that the formation of such contact languages is a recent reflex of globalization; if we cannot definitely identify a creole by looking at it only linguistically, it is possible that earlier examples do exist but have continued to develop and change in their postcreole phase, increasing in complexity and in their contexts of use and becoming progressively distanced from their contact-language origins. Some language family trees might already contain supposedly incompatible contact languages without our knowledge, and some apparent cases of regular correspondences on which family classifications have been built may be due in part to contact.

A response to these doubts about the tree model and its methods has been to develop "dual-pathway" approaches, which retain the divergent patterns found in trees but also factor in convergences caused by contact, borrowing, and the parallel innovations that occur often in phonology, where several languages share certain developments simply because they occur frequently. The breakthrough here is itself a result of borrowing: the more interdisciplinary environment since the late 1990s, which has seen historical linguists increasingly working with geneticists, evolutionary anthropologists, and archaeologists in the pursuit of convergent approaches to population histories (see chapter 8), has led to the adoption and adaptation of network methods from biology.

The developing field of quantitative phylogenetics is already too complex to describe fully here, but overviews and illustrations of different approaches can be found in several sources.[22] There are two main innovations in this work. First, it is based on explicit measurements of similarity, derived either from a set of predetermined features (*character-based*) or from a composite measure over a whole area, whether lexical or phonetic (*distance-based*). Second, it usually involves the application of computer programs first developed for population biology, which generate many possible trees or networks and then select those that are consistent with the most data. Rather than consider the available data and drawing the tree we think fits best, we adopt a more objective approach to tree and network selection.

The character-based alternative is best illustrated by the "perfect phylogeny" approach based on first-order branching relationships in Indo-European, where a range of features or characters is chosen to give the best possible resolution for comparisons within this family only.[23] Although the great majority of these characters are lexical, involving a basic vocabulary list similar to the Swadesh list, there are also morphological and phonological characters specifically designed to reflect changes that have taken place in some Indo-European subfamilies but not others.[24] Clearly, this approach works only *within* language families, as the characters must vary from one family to another; furthermore, initial research in this vein focused on trees, only recently extending to networks to accommodate cases of, say, suspected dialect continua. The work of Ringe, Warnow, and their colleagues adds only minimally to family-tree models; still, it does show that by generating many possible trees and selecting the best, we can identify the features and languages that are most treelike, and those (notably Germanic languages) that seem not to fit into a neat tree.

Perhaps more common now are approaches that are distance-based, often involving cognate counts across Swadesh-type vocabulary lists, which are also called meaning lists. The preexisting method in this case is lexicostatistics: we establish an agreed meaning list, count the cognates, and arrive at a final, composite measure of distance between the languages being compared. The new step is to feed these distance scores into a program like Neighbor-Net (part of the SplitsTree suite of programs).[25] This program has the great virtue of producing a result that looks treelike when the relationships between the languages concerned are straightforward and familial, but weblike in cases where several languages share affinities that are not compatible with a single tree. If we have six languages, A–F, and there are numerous links between A, B, and C on the one hand and D, E, and F on the other, we might see a basic treelike pattern with two branches; but if C and D also show affinities, they will be connected by a reticulation, or boxlike link between the branches.

In several recent studies, data have been drawn from a 200-item meaning list for Indo-European; the results have then been used for different purposes.[26] For example, Gray and Atkinson use meaning-list calculations in association with some glottochronological assumptions to date Proto-Indo-European to 7,800–9,800 BP; they conclude that this dating supports Renfrew's argument that the spread of Indo-European accompanied the spread of farming (beginning in Anatolia roughly 9,000 years ago) rather than Gimbutas's identification of the Indo-European languages with the spread of Kurgan horse cultures from the Russian steppes (beginning in the sixth millennium BP).[27]

In other studies, McMahon and McMahon consider how quantitative language data of the sort used for network analysis can be compared with data from genetics; and Wichmann considers improvements in these methods following from the development of large, shared typological databases.[28] McMahon and colleagues generate networks from different subsets of the 200-item meaning list, finding different patterns for the subset of meanings most readily borrowed and for those most resistant to borrowing.[29] For Romance and Greek language data within Indo-European, McMahon et al. find a lexical similarity of 52 percent for the most conservative items and 32 percent for the most borrowable ones; this result shows that for closely related languages, stronger similarity scores are yielded for those meanings that are less likely to be borrowed, or indeed to change at all.[30] This outcome is absolutely what we would predict if we assumed that Romance and Greek started out from a position of 100 percent similarity at the common ancestral stage, with erosion of that initial identity taking place more quickly in the more changeable, more easily borrowable part of the lexicon.

On the other hand, for the South American languages Quechua and Aymara, McMahon and colleagues find similarity scores of only 20 per-

cent for the most conservative meanings but 54 percent for the most borrowable ones, the opposite pattern from the Romance and Greek cases.[31]
Here the best hypothesis seems to be that there was no original common
ancestor for Quechua and Aymara, which have instead had a long history
of contact and borrowing; reasonably enough, this has mainly affected
the meanings most susceptible to borrowing, with a lower, though still
discernible, impact on meanings that are more resistant. These quantitative approaches, then, both confirm our existing hypotheses based on
the comparative method and extend our reach into parts of the linguistic world where the comparative method has proved inconclusive, partly
because of the lack of appropriate data.

The distance-based, networking approach to linguistic similarity also
allows us to consider similarities not just between languages but also
between dialects and even individual speakers. Such investigation is consistent with the "sociolinguistic turn" in historical work, where concerns
focus not only on distant prehistory but also on the inception and initial spread of change. Indeed, it is perhaps only by focusing on change in
progress that we can fully understand how change begins; we can then
apply that knowledge to linguistic prehistory and areas about which
we have relatively little data to see whether similar patterns emerge.
Whereas conventional family trees tend to stop at the language level,
networks can and do include much finer-grained variation; and although
such variation would be difficult to calculate using lexical data, because
the requisite levels of variation are unlikely to occur between dialects or
individual speakers, McMahon and colleagues argue that the right level
of resolution can be achieved through phonetic comparison.[32]

The Sound Comparisons project (www.soundcomparisons.com) is
based on a purpose-built computer program designed by Paul Heggarty
and a series of transcriptions for more than ninety varieties of modern
English produced, mainly on the basis of interviews with individual
native speakers, by Warren Maguire. Although the detail of this work is
beyond the scope of this chapter, the results can be illustrated by means
of a network (figure 13).

At the top right of the diagram, we see a group of Scottish and Irish
Traditional dialects; adjacent to these are the Scottish and Irish Typical
varieties, which are closer to the English English varieties in the lower
half of the network. Longer branches are typically associated with the
Traditional English Englishes, so that overall, the extreme positions are
occupied by the "broadest" British dialects. Varieties toward the top
of the network are *rhotic,* that is, pronouncing a sound for the letter *r*

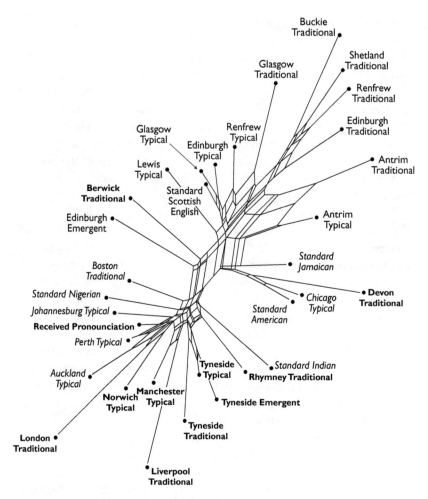

FIGURE 13. Neighbor-Net for a selection of varieties of English, based on phonetic comparison across a list of 110 Germanic cognates. This figure shows a subset of varieties, mainly from the United Kingdom but with examples from the rest of the English-speaking world. Varieties are labeled as *typical* (the normal, local pronunciation for the area); *traditional* (a "broader" set of pronunciations, characteristic of older, working-class male speakers); and *emergent* (transcribed from younger speakers between ages sixteen and twenty-five). Transcriptions of the cognates were first passed through Paul Heggarty's articulation-based phonetic comparison program, then through the Neighbor-Net software. Relative closeness between varieties in the network is established by the shortest distance between them; two varieties on opposite sides of the diagram may be closer than two immediately adjacent varieties. (www.soundcomparisons.com.)

everywhere it appears in the spelling, while those at the bottom (including Boston, for instance, among the North American varieties) are *non-rhotic,* having lost [r] after a vowel, except where a vowel also follows. In an intermediate position we find Berwick Traditional, from the border region between Scotland and England; and Edinburgh Emergent, which is unlike the other Scottish varieties in having become almost entirely non-rhotic; this result reinforces findings by Stuart-Smith, Timmins, and Tweedie for Glasgow, where younger speakers are also losing several phonetic features of historical Scottish varieties.[33]

It follows that phonetic comparison combined with network analysis can help us understand the initiation and progress of change and the relationships between present-day varieties of a language. However, although Neighbor-Net diagnoses and displays connections of all kinds, it cannot separate links that reflect common ancestry from those that arise from contact or parallel innovation; we must take further analytical steps to make these distinctions. This work requires the expertise of historical linguists who know the languages concerned, showing conclusively that quantitative phylogenetic approaches should be an *addition* to methods we already have rather than a *substitute* for them.

Further developments and applications of these phylogenetic and computational methods will strengthen the implications we can draw from them. We should aspire to work in future with both sound and word comparisons, as well as, perhaps, the internal structure of words and how they are put together to form phrases and sentences (morphosyntax). Comparisons of varieties, languages, and even language families will help us trace the weblike relations that result from interactions between speech communities, which may result in sounds, words, and elements of grammar jumping across distant branches of phylogenetic trees. We happen to know, from a rich historical record of invasion, cultural exchange, and literary development, why so many of the words in this paragraph are of Romance, not Germanic, origin. Similar histories of borrowing, contact, and parallel development are perhaps more common than phylogenetic models have allowed us to see. Research conducted rigorously using branching and network models can serve as an alternative form of historiography, especially when conventional written records of language change are absent, but also when the findings produced by computer programs cast well-established language histories into doubt. As we pursue dual-pathway research in ever-larger domains of linguistic comparison, we may find that the emergence of reticulations and network patterns challenges prevailing views on the antiquity and consequences of language contact, and even posits the existence, in deep time, of apparently modern constructs like pidgins and creoles.

ON NOT STARTING FROM THE PRESENT: EVOLUTIONARY LINGUISTICS

One intrinsic limitation to all phylogenetic methods involves the inevitable gap between the most distant common ancestor we can reasonably reconstruct in any detail and the beginnings of human linguistic communication. Greenberg and Ruhlen have claimed to be able to group all human languages into a single macrofamily and even to reconstruct aspects of the ultimate common ancestor; but the methods involved are so disputed, and the detail of what can be reconstructed so sparse, that these approaches may not be worth developing further.[34] Undoubtedly there is productive work to be done on determining the relationships between language groups that are not yet clear, through a combination of the comparative method and quantitative phylogenetics; this is especially true for the languages of South America and Australia.[35] However, the lack of data in some areas of the world, and the cumulative nature of language change, which obscures some previous developments and shortens the reach of any classificatory method, creates an unbridgeable chasm between our reconstructions, which use contemporary and recent data to model a distant past, and the findings of paleontologists, who use physical remains from the remote past to build family trees that grow forward to the present.

Attempts to bridge this gap are increasingly coming from the domain of evolutionary linguistics, using simulations to overcome the lack of empirical evidence and the limited backward reach of reconstructions. The evolution of language was a topic actually banned from its publications by the Linguistic Society of Paris in 1866 because it had spawned increasingly bizarre speculations, but matters have improved considerably since. We consider recent approaches to bridging the gap, pioneered by linguists in the Language Evolution and Cognition research unit at the University of Edinburgh (www.ling.ed.ac.uk/lec/LEC/Welcome.html).

The first generation of computational simulations tended to involve artificial agents and focused on the initial emergence of language structure. This was a particularly lively field in the first years of this century, and understandably so. Simon Kirby provides a very helpful overview of how techniques from the study of artificial life have cast light on the evolution of natural language and concludes that such approaches can help linguists solve "the methodological problem of linking theory and prediction for complex dynamical systems involving multiple interacting components."[36] Often, such work involves artificial agents that develop an ability to communicate in an increasingly structured way, in a context where the experimenter controls all the other parameters in the simulation.

Such simulations, to be sure, have their critics. Derek Bickerton, commenting on Kirby's work, might have been discussing almost any contribution to the simulation literature at the time:

> Kirby (2000) begins with an artificially limited corpus of five proper nouns (which may be "Agents" or "Objects") and five action verbs, giving rise to a hundred possible three word sentences. Simulated individuals are repeatedly asked to produce a string corresponding to one or other of these hundred possible meanings, but since they have neither words nor grammar, they say nothing. From time to time, however, they produce at random "some invented string of symbols" (Kirby, 2000: 308) which may consist of multiple units (e.g. ecdeaabdda) or single units (e.g. d). If you go on doing this for long enough, apparently, populations of simulated individuals will converge on the same string for the same meaning. But what is the likelihood that actual hominids randomly produced invented strings of symbols for indefinite periods of time? When nobody could figure out what they meant until a stable structure had developed?[37]

Of course, this is exactly how such work has to progress—researchers change one thing at a time and see how it affects the outcome. If they alter too many variables simultaneously, they cannot tell what is affecting what. On the other hand, it does make the first generation of work on simulations a relatively easy target for criticism: if the initial conditions imagined are not realistic, they reduce the value of the exercise for explaining language evolution.

This accusation has clearly had some effect on the emerging field of evolutionary simulation, and it is acknowledged by its practitioners, who have been considering ways of introducing more realistic conditions while exploring issues that really cannot be investigated in any other way. For instance, Kirby, Dowman, and Griffiths characterize language as a balance between innateness and culture. Although it has been understood for some time that human language must arise "from biological evolution, individual learning, and cultural transmission," they argue that little attention has been given to cultural transmission.[38] The main issue here is that languages are not randomly and endlessly different from one another; instead, they manifest various universals. Some of these might be derived from constraints that are not specific to language, including memory, but others seem to be structural and specific to language as such. Generative grammar—the dominant model since Noam Chomsky's early work in the 1960s—holds that these universals reflect innate constraints imposed by the biogenetic structure of our language faculty. The main explanatory factor for the development of human language, it follows, is biological evolution.

Kirby, Dowman, and Griffiths, however, propose that cultural transmission is more important than hitherto thought. A learner is exposed to linguistic input that is the output of learning by others, and the language that a learner acquires becomes data for a later generation of learners.[39] Kirby and colleagues refer to this sequence as iterated learning, a process by which one acquires a behavior by observing a similar behavior in another, who acquired it in the same way.[40] They envisage the necessary interaction as a process in which the learner's learning depends solely on the language spoken by the previous generation. Languages are seen as pairings of meanings and classes, where a class is a set of possible ways of expressing a signal (such as past tense). Learners are exposed to a random subset of these pairs, and the smallness of the subset imposes a bottleneck on cultural transmission. More regularity in the language corresponds to greater predictability between pairings. Perhaps most notably, "It is the number of training examples, the cultural bottleneck, that determines how systematic languages become."[41]

Regularity can thus be seen as an adaptation: "Regularity is adaptive for infrequently expressed meanings because it maximizes the chance of being understood by another individual with different learning experience to you. It is less relevant for frequently expressed meanings because there is a greater chance that two individuals will have previously been exposed to the same form. In fact, irregularity might be preferred for these meanings if, for example, it enables the use of a shorter and therefore more economical form."[42] So weak biases can result in strong universals, and not necessarily because of innate, biological predispositions. Thus the main issue in language evolution is not necessarily that humans have evolved to be able to learn languages, but rather that human languages evolve to be learnable. This view provides an original and fresh perspective on the earliest prehistory of language.[43]

However, as long as simulations of this kind are being conducted in silico, with artificial agents, they are subject to the same Bickertonian criticism of lack of realism: who is to say, after all, that people (or early hominins) would have reacted in just such a way to just such a set of stimuli or just such a context? The latest and very recent innovation is the development of in vivo experimentation, where investigation moves away from artificial agents to the way human subjects learn and develop "alien" languages in the laboratory. This work is in its infancy, but it is possible to give two illustrations here.

Kirby, Cornish, and Smith claim to have produced "the first experimental validation for the idea that cultural transmission can lead to the appearance of design without a designer."[44] This experiment involves a diffusion-chain study: the first participant observes the experimenter doing something and is required to replicate the task so that a second participant learns it. A third participant then observes and learns from the second, and so on. Each of these iterations is taken to replicate a single generation. The experiment, which involved ten generations, was based on learning an "alien" language, where a range of objects having distinctive color, movement, and shape were labeled with strings of written nonsense syllables; thus, a red bouncing square might be labeled *kihemiwi*. The first set of labels was generated randomly and used to train the first participant, and each subsequent generation was trained on the output of the final testing of the previous participant. However, participants were not told they were being trained on the basis of what someone else had managed to do; they simply thought they were learning the language as best they could, so that they would reproduce the language and not try to improve it in some way.[45]

The researchers hypothesized that they would see cumulative adaptation across generations, that the learnability of the language would increase, and that the predictability of the mapping between meaning and signal would improve. This is exactly what happened. For instance, from an unstructured starting point, one language had stabilized by generation 8 such that any object moving horizontally was labeled *tuge;* any spiraling object was *poi;* and bouncing objects were divided into squares (*tupim*), circles (*miniku*), and triangles (*tupin*). In a second experiment, there was an initial stage of filtering, whereby "if any strings were assigned to more than 1 meaning, all but 1 of those meanings (chosen at random) was removed from the training data."[46] This measure ensured that systematic underspecification could not be adopted as a strategy for learnability; as a result, unambiguous labeling would also be permitted to develop. This is what did happen: the output of a participant at generation 9 is shown in figure 14.

The authors conclude that "the culturally evolving language has adapted in a way that ensures its successful transmission from genera-

	Green	Blue	Red	Symbolic object
moves forward	n-ere-ki	i-ere-ki	renana	□
	n-ehe-ki	i-aho-ki	r-ene-ki	○
	n-eke-ki	i-ahke-ki	r-ahe-ki	△
bounces	n-ere-plo	i-ane-plo	r-e-plo	□
	n-eho-plo	i-aho-plo	r-eho-plo	○
	n-eki-plo	i-aki-plo	r-aho-plo	△
spirals	n-e-pilu	i-ane-pilu	r-e-pilu	□
	n-eho-pilu	i-aho-pilu	r-aho-pilu	○
	n-eki-pilu	i-aki-pilu	r-aho-pilu	△

FIGURE 14. Generation 9 of an evolved language, from the second experiment in Kirby, Cornish, and Smith. (Kirby, Cornish, and Smith 2008, 10684.)

tion to generation, despite the existence of a bottleneck on transmission imposed by the incomplete exposure of each participant to the language." Cumulatively, this evolution results in increasing learnability and increasing structure. Overall, the experiment demonstrates successfully that "just as biological evolution can deliver the appearance of design without the existence of a designer, so too can cultural evolution."[47]

Though convincing, this experiment tells only part of the story. It involves languages, or rather participants, developing similar ways of signaling that something is the same; yet speakers also diverge. Sociolinguistics and studies of change in progress show that differentiation, and the emergence of ways of speaking that are different, also form a part of historical linguistics; moreover, differences between speakers allow us to draw important social conclusions about one another. Work exploring such divergence is only now beginning; one example is provided by Roberts, this time involving a competitive team game involving another "alien" language.[48]

In Roberts's pilot experiment, players in an online game had to negotiate for resources (meat, grain, fish, water, and fruit) by using an invented language. The game consisted of several rounds of trading, and players were divided into teams. At the start of a round, each player was paired with one other, who might be either a teammate or an opponent, except during the first round, when the opposite player was identified as a teammate. In subsequent rounds, players could choose to give resources to their randomly selected trading partner, and any resource given away would have twice the value to the receiver as to the giver. At the end, the team with the most resources won: hence it was beneficial to give resources to a teammate and to receive resources from anyone else. It follows that it is a very good idea to be able to tell when you are trading with a teammate and when you have been paired with an opponent. Because players could not see one another, played the game online, and were not permitted to use English or any other natural language, the only way they could identify a teammate was through modifications to the alien language.

Roberts identified five strategies by which participants identified one another as allies: "secret handshakes," or shared greetings; mimicry; identifying salient features of another's language use; using the language themselves in a noticeably different way; or changing the language to increase expressivity.[49] The most successful team used all of these strategies, and most notably established the simple and reliable innovation of repeating the name of a resource the appropriate number of times to signal quantity. There was a great deal of innovation: in the third game, for instance, 120 unique forms were used. However, there was no evidence that players changed features of language simply for the sake of being different.[50] Any changes in meaning followed naturally from the original meaning of an item, and many of the changes in form were easily interpretable as initial errors that were copied and established. Yet these simple strategies were highly effective in differentiating and identifying groups and in allowing members of a group to identify one another.

REVERSE BABEL

The artificial languages that evolve during these in vivo simulations are ingenious inversions of the biblical story of human linguistic diversity. Comparative philology began its career in close conversation with Abrahamic scriptural tradition, and this peculiar affinity remains crucial to the way language works as a framework for deep history. In the Book of Genesis, we are told that humankind once spoke a single language, a capacity that enabled them to settle and work together. They decided to build a city, Babel, with a tower that would reach the heavens. God was disturbed by this project, so he confounded their speech. No longer able to communicate, humans abandoned their city and scattered. Today's language simulators turn this scenario upside down, creating a situation in which people who do not share a language arrive, by trial and error, at a pre-Babel state of mutual intelligibility. Despite moving in opposite directions, the authors of the Babel story and the designers of evolutionary language simulations seem to agree on fundamental points.

First, they assume that *language enables cooperation.* The participants in language experiments trade objects as members of teams, or they fit objects into categories, trying to reproduce someone else's effort accurately. The humans in the Genesis account make bricks and mortar, which they use to build a tower. Although language entails faculties of mind, and no doubt requires abstract categories, it becomes consequential when humans use it to plan, organize, and act. It is also assumed that *language involves the exchange of physical objects that are classified in meaningful ways.* Words and things combine to form a medium in which both can be given, received, and returned. When this process is disrupted or incompletely systematized, social relations that depend on durable chains of exchange and transmission are not possible. Likewise, both approaches assume that *predictability in language is essential to the creation and mastery of larger worlds.* The architects of Babel exhibit godlike powers, which originate in language: once their shared language is lost, humans can no longer stack one brick on top of another. Similarly, the participants in language simulations cannot trade, determine the value of traded objects, or distinguish friend from foe without linguistic conventions.

Finally, in both the simulation lab and the Bible, *human community depends on language, and communities and languages are interactively modified through reproduction.* Intelligibility is crucial to all social projects, which is why the builders of the tower of Babel do not simply halt production when they lose their shared language: rather they disperse, forming new language communities that develop new linguistic differences as they multiply. This process, as depicted in Genesis, is identical to genealogical reproduction. The subjects of language simulations, for their part, show a genius for reproduction and modification. They are quick to establish conventions, normalize mistakes, and invent expressions, all in order to accentuate differences that confer advantages on individuals, teams, and languages. In the real world, most of these modifications would lead to differential reproductive success, as Darwin conceived it.

The family resemblance between these very different ways of explaining language origins is not accidental. The nations-and-languages project is the child of a specific kind of literate society, working with very specific notions of how a language and a people are related in time. The eighteenth-century Europeans who undertook this project finally broke through the barrier of the written word, but their ability to speculate about the origins of languages before writing was utterly dependent on textual traditions of scholarship. Their breakthroughs began with the study of the great scriptural languages of the Semitic and Indo-European families. Their work was also part of an imperial impulse, a desire to bring diverse populations into a single, universal scheme of classification that would render them more governable. This impulse also motivated the Genesis account, which for millennia functioned as a social register of nations for "peoples of the book," ranging in size from the rather parochial kingdoms of David and Solomon to vast, transcontinental Islamic and Christian civilizations. The Babel story is itself a frank assessment of the prospects for any city-state that cannot manage its sociolinguistic diversity. As practiced today, historical linguistics is still answerable to the long-standing relationship between language as a subject of knowledge and languages as an object of rule.

None of these associations changes the fact that the comparative method is reliable and effective, but its ten-thousand-year purview limits its scope to a post-Neolithic world, what we might call the "old" deep history—a period in which urbanism, universal genealogies, and literate culture gradually generated the conditions of possibility for a study of language that focused on words and grammars. This is a rich but narrow seam of human communication. The qualities that give words and grammars their rule-like aspects are part of larger systems of predictability. Attempts to simulate the evolution of language are valuable precisely because they are a step away from a tradition that localizes language within certain ways of describing human speech and a step toward a new framework in which human language is connected to the more general problem of predictability and repeatability in social life. The simulations we describe produce data that are as much about material objects and their placement in space as they are about speech, and this outcome brings the simulators into the intellectual company of scholars interested in the materiality of culture—not to mention archaeologists, who routinely contend with material evidence that resembles the patterns of knowing arrangement that result from (successful) language simulations.

If language is inseparable from our material worlds and social relations, then some aspects of language can be studied in deep historical frames, even when speech is not available for scrutiny. The radical increase in hominin brain size over the last 2.6 million years, the increasing size of social groups in hominin lineages ancestral to modern humans, the geographic spread of networks through which materials and people are exchanged, changing engagements with plants and animals: these trends are all contexts in which human language can be historicized. The communicative tricks that emerge in experimental language simulations have very old material correlates. The use of red ocher to adorn the human body, a habit established among humans 100,000 years ago, might have functioned originally as a visual cue announcing someone's status and group membership. Mimicry, another popular tactic in language simulations, is obvious in the shape of Acheulean hand axes, which were manufactured in roughly the same way for almost a million years. The use of expressive variation to signal identity is evident in Upper Paleolithic cave paintings, figurine carvings, and toolkits. These objects were produced by humans who, most paleoanthropologists agree, were behaviorally modern. The fact that cave painters had a fully developed language capacity cannot be proved using linguistic evidence from the Upper Paleolithic: there is none, if such evidence is restricted to communication through speech. Yet the material culture of Europe thirty thousand years ago is so thoroughly saturated with representational effort, both abstract and naturalistic, and is so clearly part of a regional complex tied to ritual aspects of group identity and subsistence economy that we are eager to assume language was present.

For earlier periods, this assumption is harder to justify. And again our doubts are dependent not on linguistic evidence but on our ability to imagine language as a quality increasingly absent from the material remains we analyze. Could this biface have been produced without words? Could that horse have been hunted and butchered without elaborate verbal communication? Could those bodies have been buried without even the simplest liturgy? When our intuitive response is yes, we have carried out an informal language-simulation experiment, concluding that the materials on display were not organized by a system of communication that would produce elaborate kinship terminologies, organize long-distance trade in shell beads, or build a tower that reaches the heavens.

These conclusions might be anachronistic, mistaking what language later became for what it might have been in the distant past; but it would be wrong to dismiss them as evolutionary prejudice. They are provoked, instead, by intense moments of recognition. Unlike the early comparative philologists, who worked before Darwin, we now know that the human language faculty evolved over time. When very old hominin remains show signs of behaviors later associated with language use—cooperation, exchange, repetition, classification, and productive modification—we are confronted with the basic elements of a developmental narrative. The circumstantial nature of the data, and the great temporal and spatial gaps between bits of evidence, does not disqualify them as a historical resource. Flaked stone, cooked seeds, bodily adornments, carvings of the human form, pictures of animals, and the size and shape of hearths are data embedded in a relational matrix that turns artifacts into signs and signs into evidence. Closer in time to the world of *Homo sapiens,* these signs become more intelligible, and evidence can be interpreted with greater certainty. The factors that lead to more confident interpretations of material remains are the very factors that contribute to a successful language simulation.

Historical linguistics requires scholars to connect missing and present data—indeed, to generate one kind of data from the other—and it entered the modern era purpose-built to escape the limits of contemporary history writing. The accounts of the remote past devised by comparative philologists have been used to conjure grand stories of Aryan invasions, the spread of Bantu villagers across Africa, and the peopling of the Pacific islands, but the sorting of languages into families does not presuppose a detailed knowledge of the geographic distribution of human groups over time. It is based instead on the assumption that certain likenesses and differences among languages are genealogical and have accumulated in a particular sequence. Grimm, Jones, Schlegel, and Bopp described human languages as if they were bodies, and they believed that, like bodies, languages have anatomical features that offer proof of their shared descent. Most contemporary linguists would modify this claim, pointing out that languages are not anatomical in a metaphoric sense alone but are physically located in our bodies and distributed in our social relations. It might be more accurate to say that our bodies, like our social forms and material cultures, are deeply historical precisely because language (simulated and real) has become an essential component of their reproduction. The implications for historiography are profound, and we have only begun to explore them.

PART THREE

Shared Substance

CHAPTER 6

Food

FELIPE FERNÁNDEZ-ARMESTO WITH DANIEL LORD SMAIL

Some prejudices seem ineradicable. The contempt that formerly banned the study of nonliterate societies from history departments persists. Its target, however, has shifted from the allegedly meaningless "gyrations of barbarous tribes" to the peoples of the deep past.[1] As it happens, the "barbarous tribes," and all those whom they can be said to represent, have now been recognized as the proper subjects of colonial history. By contrast, the peoples of the deep past were never anyone's victims, and nothing makes a people historical so much as victimhood. They fall short in other ways as well—supposedly changeless, unmoving, responding only to the rhythms of their environment. Their relatively modest levels of material culture seem—to scholars and students who evince no interest in them—devoid of lessons for the modern world.

Outside the narrow world of history departments, however, the lessons are more evident. Evolutionary psychology and, even more, cognitive archaeology have helped to make our remote ancestors seem relevant. The discovery of "stone-age affluence" has cast considerable doubt on the perspicuity of all who have imagined a poor and brutish world.[2] The accumulation of ever-earlier evidence of leisure time that could be exploited for art—whether in the form of what look like deposits of body paint or forms of flutes—makes Paleolithic life seem rich and "cultured" in the most refined sense. The abundance of food—we now have evidence of feasting on the threshold of the cave of Altamira in Spain—nourished lifeways we might not hesitate to call civilized.

Perhaps the biggest and most venerable reason for the positive public reevaluation of pre-Holocene antiquity has been a new respect for the foodways of deep time. In the nineteenth century, Sylvester Graham and W.K. Kellogg, with their legions of followers, counseled the public to follow the diet of our ancestors, which they understood to be a diet low in meat and rich in cereals and fruits. The "Stone Age diet," the latest in this long-standing trend, has become fashionable, or at least faddish. The supposedly healthy lifestyles of Paleolithic peoples offer an antidote to the excesses of modernity and subvert the old master narrative of progress, in which changes in food production—from scavenging to hunting, from hunting to herding, from garnering food to growing it, and from agriculture to agroindustry, the Green Revolution, and genetic modification of crops—marked supposedly ameliorative stages. Common assumptions about food, not to mention the everyday evidence provided by bathroom scales, now amply support an alternative narrative of decline.

In this chapter, without subscribing to any judgments of value about the foods of the last two million years, we hope to show that deep time really is part of history: by tracing the history of what humans eat over the very long run, we can identify continuities with the recent past that make modern foodways more readily intelligible. We chart the emergence of a distinctively human diet, of diverse cultural ways involving food (including trade and other forms of cultural exchange), and of the ecological basis of modern diets. Because humans' relationship with the ecosystems of which we form a part is at its most intimate when we eat from them, the history of food exemplifies perfectly the question at the heart of this book: how and how far human agency combines with environmental or evolutionary influences in effecting change. Food ought to be historians' most important topic, partly because it has mattered the most to most people, and partly because, of all the elements that make human life possible—the sun, the biosphere, evolution, and the vital spark itself, wherever that comes from—it is the only one humans can influence to a point close to control. Considered out of the context of deep time, the history of food remains incoherent and imperfectly intelligible.

CARNIVORY AND ITS CONSEQUENCES

Humans are ill equipped to eat. We have only one stomach—which means that, compared with ruminants, we have access to only a limited range of plant foods. Our digestive systems have become small and rudimentary compared with those of other primates. We have modest fangs and talons and weak lips and jaws, incapable of providing our digestive systems with much help by way of crushing, shredding, and masticating food. To some extent we make up for these evolutionary deficiencies by eating a range of foods that is exceptionally wide by comparison with the diet of other creatures—and in particular with other primates.

Alone among primates, we are dedicated carnivores who eat meat from large carcasses. Even chimpanzees, who, among the surviving primate species, most resemble humans in body and behavior, consume meat relatively rarely. We do not know whether chimpanzee carnivory is a recent development—a response, perhaps, to environmental stress and the depletion of their foraging territories by human incursions—or a custom that reaches far back in time. Chimps' favorite prey is the colobus monkey. No carnivorous chimps have been known to take anything larger than a small antelope, and the contribution of meat to the chimpanzee diet, even in communities that practice hunting fairly intensively, is paltry.[3] Among human societies, by contrast, carnivory is universal in the sense of having been practiced everywhere at some time (though certain groups and generations may reject it), and in all known societies it supplies at least a third and typically more than half of people's caloric intake.

The remotest origins of prehuman carnivory presumably lie in untraceable experiments with foraging for mollusks and insects, which early eaters might have classed among "hard" plant foods; but we can properly leave these out of account, because the nutritional benefits of grubbing for such easily appropriated foods are not likely to exceed those of gathering the inert plant items they supplemented.[4] Proof in the form of butchery tools and animal bones marked with the signs of cutting and chopping date the human consumption of meat from large carcasses to about two and a half million years ago.[5] We can reasonably imagine an indeterminate period of furtive and hurried scavenging, with scraps of meat torn away by hand, before the craft of butchery developed. So although *Homo sapiens* is the only carnivorous primate to have survived, and the chimpanzee is the only other primate to exhibit what may be the beginnings of a similar trajectory, there were carnivorous primates, with the potential to become hunters, for more than two and a half million years before the appearance of our species in the fossil record.

Causes and consequences are hard to separate, but the existing literature acknowledges aspects of human behavior that are inseparable from our species' carnivorous past and antecedents.[6] Even at the scavenging stage of the hominin past, meat eating fostered the evolution of relatively large, relatively collaborative social units, organized for defense. Such groups had specialized functions, which may have introduced forms of sexual specialization as well as systems for distributing the meat and for consuming it by turns—some individuals guarding the carcass while others helped themselves. The relative complexity of human and hominin societies, compared with those of other primates, can be fully understood only in this context. Activities associated with the pursuit and defense of scavenged carcasses and, even more, with hunting for meat favored species with a marked capacity for throwing missiles and for long-distance running, cooled by perspiration. These are among the few (perhaps the only) examples of physical prowess in which humans excel other surviving primates.[7] Butchery, the making of butchers' tools, and hunting demand, in more marked degree, the same qualities as scavenging. Protein-rich diets are well suited to the shrunken digestive tracts we have inherited from a remote past: small stomachs, small colons, and small guts. They supply the surplus energy that, in human bodies, sustains brains of egregious proportions—far greater than necessary by the standards of all other animals.

Meat eating therefore probably helped to launch humans' long and distinctive trajectory as a relatively big-brained and dexterous species with convoluted guts. The concentrated energy derived from meat enhanced humans' capacity for survival. Plants indigestible by humans could be retrieved, half-digested, from the stomachs of dead animals. Energy-packed fat helped humans compensate for their relative slowness, feebleness, and lack of agility in competition with other predators.

Above all—though this is a new suggestion, unsupported by the existing literature but offered here as a subject of future research—carnivory may have made the rest of human history possible by demanding from humans, as from all scavenging and hunting species, a keen capacity for anticipation, which in turn may have led to our capacity for imagination. Humans lack many of the resources with which evolution has equipped other predators: swiftness, nimbleness, sharp and powerful claws and teeth, and an acute olfactory sense. Hunters need to anticipate—more speedily, more acutely, and more reliably than eaters of immobile foods—the behavior of prey and of rival predators, as well as the effects of relevant changes in the environment. Anticipation may be defined as the property of seeing what is not yet present to the senses. Imagination is a kindred property, or perhaps a substantial endowment or superabundance, of anticipation: it is hard to explain in evolutionary terms, except as a by-product of anticipation. If we are the most imaginative of animals, perhaps this is why. It is probably also why our societies are so much more complex than those of other primates, who resemble us so closely in almost every other respect: we hunt far more than they do. Humans' highly charged imaginations are the starting point for most of the changes we commonly designate by the term *history*. We can imagine the world differently from the way it is and then act to realize our imagined ideas: hence our mutable, volatile societies and our dangerous, unstable relationship with the rest of nature. These are features of human history unreplicated in the past of other cultural species.

COOKING WITH FIRE

Humans are adept at preparing food to make it more digestible and thereby extract more energy from it: methods include washing, rotting, fermenting, masticating, wind drying, burying, curing with acids and salts, and selecting food partly processed by natural fires or by semidigestion in the stomachs of animal prey. Most of these techniques have parallels in the behavior of nonhuman animals. The most efficient method of all, however, is unique to humans: cooking with fire. The consequences have been transmutative. "Cooked food," in Richard Wrangham's summary, "makes our food safer, creates rich and delicious tastes, and reduces spoilage . . . [and] increases the amount of energy our bodies obtain from our food." The results include "a new kind of species tied to the use of fire by our biological needs, relying on cooked food to supply adequate amounts of energy to our bodies," because "a strict raw food diet cannot guarantee an adequate energy supply."[8]

The chronology of cooking is inseparable from that of the domestication of fire. Broadly speaking, as more data accumulate, they push the scholarly consensus about the date of the earliest use of fire ever further into deep time. At a site occupied by *Homo erectus* at Gesher Benot Ya'aqov, on the River Jordan, remains of kindled fire date from about 790,000 years ago.[9] Wrangham has argued persuasively that the peculiar physical characteristics of *H. erectus,* compared with predecessor species—including relatively small teeth and guts and relatively large brains and bodies—as well as the unprecedented success of the species in populating diverse environments suggest that "cooking was responsible for the evolution of *Homo erectus.*"[10] Cooking would unquestionably favor the relevant bodily adaptations. Cooked food is easier to chew with small teeth and to digest with modest intestines; it enables favored creatures, including humans, to free up energy consumed in maintaining gut tissue and internally processing fibrous foods; and it imparts the energy boost that large brains and adventurous migrations demand. Abundant research supports these claims. Human energy expenditure on digestion is 10 percent less than that of great apes.

Cooked foods confer enormous advantages in digestibility and the release of energy. Heat gelatinizes starch, making it vulnerable to enzymes and thereby speeding digestion. It denatures proteins, making them more available to the body: cooking increases the protein value of eggs by around 40 percent. Between about 60 and 100 degrees Celsius, depending on the length of time of the exposure, it hugely increases the food value of meat, turning collagen, an otherwise indigestible form of fibrous protein, into jelly.

If cooking significantly affected human bodies and patterns of nutrition, it also transformed technologies and helped to effect the construction and use of containers that, at an uncertain date in deep time, made human tool use uniquely sophisticated.[11] A dearth of evidence compels caution in reconstructing how cooking might have stimulated the invention of technically complex containers. Of course, cooking with embers, naked flames, and heated stones, in pits or over open fires, predated specialized cookware. Presumably early cooks appropriated skins, tripes, cauls, or stomachs of animals for cooking in. The skin is of limited usefulness as a sealant in most species: it is frequently more valuable if it is stripped off the carcass before cooking and tanned for garments, pouches, and awnings. The internal organs, however, are nature's cooking vessels—impermeable and elastic enough, in most quadrupeds, to contain all the other edible parts of the animal and more. Because they can be filled with water, they can function as boilers. A small intestine packed and placed inside a large one can make a serviceable bain-marie, as long as the cook has some method of shielding it from damage by excessive direct heat. Traces of this early style of cookery survive in even the most sophisticated cuisines. The best sausages are still made with strips and tubes of innards.

Though shells may have made good stockpots in antiquity, few places in the world yield shells large enough for economical cooking. Only those of turtles and similar creatures can have preceded the manufactured pot. At an unknown date, pots hewn from wood supplemented them, along with woven fronds or grasses. These can produce watertight vessels: examples are still in use among peoples of northwest America.

The invention of earthenware pottery in remote antiquity is often surmised to have begun with wicker vessels that were smeared with clay as insulation so that they could be suspended over a fire. The alternative technique is to place hot stones inside a vessel: this method is serviceable but slow, as the stones have to be heated first.

The social effects of cooking with fire are as important as the bodily and technical effects. Cooking is one of the great revolutionary innovations of history not only because of the way it transforms food—there are plenty of other ways of doing that—but also because of the way it transformed society. Recognizably human culture, in a sense, begins when the raw is first cooked. The campfire becomes a place of communion when people eat around it. Society takes shape around communal meals and predictable mealtimes. Cooking with fire introduced new specialized functions and shared pleasures and responsibilities. It was more creative, more constructive of social ties than merely eating together—which collaborative bands of scavengers already did, as they guarded each other from rival predators around a dead carcass. Once fire became manageable, it began to bind communities—literally providing a focus, because tending flame demands a division of labor and shared effort. Fire was socially significant for all the reasons that people gather round it still: for light and warmth, and for protection from pests and predators. Cooking intensified fire's social magnetism by making eating an activity practiced in a fixed place at a fixed time.

Cooking can even replace eating together as a ritual of social adhesion. When Bronislaw Malinowski, the pioneer of Pacific island anthropology, was at work in the Trobriand Islands, one of the ceremonies that most impressed him was the annual yam-harvest festival in Kiriwina, where most ceremonies took the form of food distribution. To the accompaniment of drums and dancing, prepared food was arranged in heaps and then carried off to the various households to be eaten in private. The climax of what most cultures think of as a feast—the actual eating—"is never reached communally. . . . But the festive element lies in the preparations."[12] In any case, by providing a locus for cooking and eating, the use of fire helped to divide the spaces humans inhabit into areas devoted to specific activities.

Cooking stimulates salivation and appetite, enhancing humans' relationships with other species and enriching the metaphors with which we express our relationships with each other. In some cultures cooking itself becomes a metaphor for the transformations of life: California tribes, for instance, used to perform a ritual in which women who had just given birth and pubescent girls were put into ovens dug in the ground and covered with mats and hot stones.[13] In other cultures food dressing becomes a sacred ritual that not only shapes society but also nourishes the heavens with sacrificial emissions of smoke and steam. According to Claude Lévi-Strauss, Amazonian peoples who see "culinary operations as mediatory activities between heaven and earth, life and death, nature and society" generalize a notion that most societies apply to at least some acts of cooking.[14]

EATING FOR MORE THAN NUTRITION

One particular form of eating—cannibalism—is a distinctive, even a defining, feature of humanity. No other mammal routinely practices cannibalism. Cases have been observed among chimpanzees, but the practice seems to be regarded by most chimps as what we might call a psychopathic aberration, or to represent the culmination of strategic acts of infanticide, which—though their purposes remain unclear—seem to be purposeful.[15] Small mammals may indulge when in extremis or, as among hamsters, may cannibalize their young to control scant resources—behaviors that have parallels among humans in times of famine, siege, or other dire emergency. According to the "custom of the sea" in most Western law codes until the late nineteenth century, for example, cannibalism was sanctioned as a survival strategy among shipwreck victims.[16]

Among humans, however, cannibalism is not always an aberration but sometimes part of the moral order. As far as we can tell, every known society of *Homo sapiens* has practiced it at some time: under the stones of every civilization lie the bones of cannibal feasts. Though the literature on the subject encompasses every imaginable opinion—from characterizing cannibalism as a colonial myth to ascribing its prevalence to a strategy of protein substitution—a scholarly consensus has emerged to explain its origins and nature. Though experts have bickered over the significance of evidence gathered from *Homo erectus* sites, discoveries reported at Atapuerca, Spain, in July 2006 leave no doubt that the hominins who occupied the site 800,000 years ago (generally regarded as ancestral to *Homo sapiens*) regularly butchered children over a period of hundreds of years. Moreover, as in most recorded cases of human cannibalism, the cannibals ate individuals of their own species, as one of the excavators reportedly said, not for "gastronomic, but cultural reasons."[17] Cannibalism can be dangerous: the eating of human brains promotes a brain disease called kuru. Genetic evidence, which dovetails with the archaeological evidence, has suggested that a mutation in the prion protein gene conferring some resistance to kuru evolved more than 500,000 years ago.[18]

Cannibalism is practiced for its symbolic or magical power: human flesh is consumed with as much moral self-consciousness as vegans bring to eating beans. "Famine cannibalism" was until recently a regular feature of life in the islands of the Massim near New Guinea and of some other societies of Southeast Asia and the Pacific.[19] But most peoples who tell ethnographic enquirers that they eat their enemies "for food" seem to have concealed the symbolic and ritual logic underlying the act.[20] For the Orokaiva people of Papua New Guinea, cannibalism is a means of "capturing spirits" in compensation for lost warriors. The same country's Hua eat their own dead to conserve supposedly irreplaceable vital fluids.[21] Until the 1960s the Gimi women of the Papuan highlands used to eat their dead menfolk. The practice is still enacted in mime with dummy corpses. "We would not have left a man to rot," protest the women. "We took pity on him!"[22] Their explanation recalls the sages who told Alexander the Great that they ate their honored dead out of respect and could not bear to burn or bury them.

Though cannibals may and sometimes do eat people for simple bodily nourishment, that is not why cannibal practices have become enshrined in some cultures. Most cases concern other aims: self-transformation, the appropriation of power, the ritualization of the eater's relationship with the eaten. Some cannibals eat their honored dead to save them from desecration by vermin or destruction by fire. Others eat admired enemies to absorb their virtues, or reviled enemies to maximize revenge. For others again, the ingestion of a body, or parts of it, is symbolic or mimetic of sex or impregnation. For almost all cannibals, the practice enhances life in ways that transcend bodily nourishment. This puts human flesh on the same level as many other foods that we eat not because we need them to stay alive but because we want them to change us for the better: we want them to give us a share of their virtue. In particular, it aligns the cannibals with their real modern counterparts: those who follow particular diets in pursuit of self-improvement, worldly success, moral superiority, enhanced beauty, or personal purity.[23]

Cannibalism typically occurs in the context of war. Fighting is not like hunting for food: it is a clash of rival predators. Cannibalism is not usually lightly undertaken even by its most enthusiastic practitioners, and the parts of the victims consumed at cannibal meals are often highly restricted. The most frequently consumed part is the heart. The whole business tends to be highly ritualized. Among the Aztecs, ingesting the flesh of a captive was a way of acquiring his prowess: in a complementary gesture, the captor also donned his victim's flayed skin, with the hands flapping at his wrists like trinkets. Even in Fiji before the coming of Christianity, when cannibalism was practiced on a scale which suggests that some people—the chiefly and warrior elites—were getting a useful dietary supplement from human flesh, the surviving bones are always marked by signs of torture and sacrifice: these marks distinguish them from the remains of other animal foods, killed cleanly for speed and efficiency. A visitor in 1847 was told that Chief Ratu Udre Udre of the Rakiraki district recorded each body he ate with a stone: his tally was nine hundred stones.[24] But the fact that cannibal meals were worthy of such special commemoration distinguishes them from ordinary eating. Human meat was the gods' food and cannibalism a form of divine communion. Cannibalism makes sense as part of a pattern of what Peggy Sanday refers to as "metaphors symbolizing dominance."[25] Alternatively, as in Marshall Sahlins's view, it is part of a "mythical charter of society" sustained, again in Fiji, by "an elaborate cycle of exchange of raw women for cooked men."[26]

Cannibals and their critics have always agreed about one thing. Cannibalism is not neutral: it affects the eater. Critics claim the effect is depraving, as in the story of Sinbad the sailor: his companions began "to act like gluttonous maniacs" as soon as they tasted human flesh and "after a few hours of guzzling" became "little better than savages."[27] Cannibals, on the other hand, see the practice as a means of self-improvement. Cannibalism is a conspicuous instance of a food reinterpreted as more than bodily sustenance: the practice of eating not for physical nutrition but to gain symbolic power. It embodies the discovery that food has meaning. No people, however hungry, has escaped its influence, for there is now no society in which people normally eat merely to live.

If food can change bodies, inspire minds, transform relationships, and provide a focus for rites, it becomes a source of magic—useful for rationally inexplicable self-transformations, including the sacramental, the symbolic, and the curative. Everywhere, eating is a culturally and sometimes a magically transforming act. It has its own alchemy. It transmutes individuals into a society and sickness into health. It changes personalities. It can sacralize apparently secular acts. It functions like ritual; it becomes ritual. It can make food divine or diabolical. It can release power. It can create bonds. It can signify revenge or love. It can proclaim identity. A change as revolutionary as any in the history of our species happened when eating stopped being merely practical and became ritual. From cannibals to vegans, from practitioners of Galenic or Ayurvedic medicine to homeopaths and health-food enthusiasts, from Pythagoreans to followers of modern dieticians and nutritionists, eaters select foods that they think will burnish their characters, extend their powers, and prolong their lives.

The extent to which food-related behavior is cultural among humans raises the question of whether other cultural species have food practices that transcend instinct or "mere" ethology. The current state of the evidence suggests that they do. Japanese primatologists, for example, observed macaque monkeys transmitting across generations the technique of washing sweet potatoes.[28] The way chimpanzees distribute food, especially meat in hunting communities, seems to be related to other ways in which their societies are organized. So to understand fully our cultural relationship with food—indeed, to understand fully the history of culture in any respect—we shall probably have to go deeper into deep time than the origins of *Homo sapiens* or even of the genus *Homo*.

RITUALIZED EATING

To the extent that food prescriptions and prohibitions mark and communicate social relationships, they act as carriers of what Émile Durkheim called social kinship (see chapter 7). Food taboos are as universal and at least as various as incest controls. Rational or scientific explanations have always been sought as to why certain foods are proscribed. Cicero was first in a long line of theorists who have explained prohibitions as economically motivated: bovines, for instance, are too valuable to eat, and the societies that sacralize them are practicing a conservation measure.[29] Yet beef is eaten in many places where bovines are vital for plowing, transport, and dairying; and in communities where they are sacralized, as among Hindus, their practical value is much diminished in consequence. Prohibitions on eating some creatures are explained on grounds of their intimacy with humans, yet dogs and cats are treated as food animals in some societies.

Hygiene is often invoked as the basis of some taboos, especially in connection with the puzzlingly selective prohibitions enjoined on the Jews in Leviticus. "I maintain that the food which is forbidden by the Law is unwholesome," wrote Maimonides. "Pork contains more moisture than necessary and too much superfluous matter. . . . [The swine's] habits and its food are very dirty and loathsome."[30] This is well-intentioned nonsense—on a par with Maimonides' contention that women had two wombs, corresponding to the number of breasts—because there is little or no difference in cleanliness to distinguish the meats forbidden in the book of Leviticus from those allowed. The most convincing explanation is the view of the anthropologist Mary Douglas, who argued that the prohibited creatures are anomalous in some way: integrity, necessary for holiness, is violated by terrestrial creatures that wriggle, like snakes, or airborne ones with four feet (Leviticus 11:20 mentions insects), or those that are cloven-hoofed but nonruminant, like the pig and camel.[31]

If taboos served some rational end, such as hygiene, purity, consistency, integrity, or economy, they would be widely imitated and would not differentiate their practitioners from everyone else. To function as identifiers, they have to be capricious. It is pointless to seek rational and material explanations for dietary restrictions, because they are essentially suprarational and metaphysical. Meanings ascribed to foods are, like all meanings, agreed conventions about usage: ultimately, they are arbitrary. Nevertheless, food taboos are socially functional because all of them are totemic: they bind those who respect them and brand those who do not. Permitted foods enhance identity; excluded foods help to define it. Food taboos are usually related to, and supportive of, the collective beliefs that help a society keep going. Dietary restrictions often forbid foods that are thought to impede access to the sacred world by conveying "impurities." There are even devil's foods, like the apple of Eden, which are seemingly wholesome but which degrade men or alienate deities, and dishes which can be polluted by association, or which can be either good to eat or fatal, depending on the circumstances.

The most spectacular example, perhaps, occurs among the Batlokwa of Botswana, who prescribe and proscribe different foods for every stage and rank of life. Pubescent boys may not have honey. Teenage girls are not allowed eggs or fish. New mothers may not eat with their hands. The people justify these rules on specious grounds of health, but their obvious function is to mark individuals' places and roles.[32]

In Hindu society, as C. E. McDonaugh has argued, "the rules concerning food are extremely important for marking and maintaining social boundaries and distinctions. Castes rank themselves in terms of purity, and this is reflected in the kinds of food which may or may not be shared with other castes. . . . Raw food can be transferred between all castes, whereas cooked foods cannot, since they may affect the purity status of the castes concerned." Cooked foods are further subdivided. Those cooked in water are distinguished from those fried in clarified butter:

the latter can be exchanged between a wider range of groups than can the former. Moreover, eating habits and dietary prescriptions are specific to groups of certain status. Vegetarianism, for instance, is proper to the highest and "purest" castes, "while meat-eating and alcohol consumption are associated with less pure status. Certain untouchable castes are marked most obviously by the eating of beef."[33] The Tharu, the third rank in Dang, Nepal, will not exchange food with lower castes or feed them in their houses but will eat pork and rats. The complexity of Fijian taboos has made them popular with anthropologists as objects of study. In Fiji, when particular groups eat together, the members of each group are confined to the foods appropriate to them. In the presence of warriors, chiefs eat the captured pigs, but not fish or coconuts, which are reserved for the warriors.[34]

In some modern societies, food taboos have become virtually indistinguishable from vague cultural preferences. This diminution is a process proper to but neglected by historical inquiry. Hospitality, on the other hand, is an enduring context for the ritualization of food habits in almost every known human society. Historians notice it quite as much as anthropologists and archaeologists, because it shapes power relations. Although feasting has many functions—it formalizes relationships and helps groups manage waste—its history seems inseparable from that of power.[35]

Its beginnings surely predate agriculture. Records and direct observations document the joy and sharing that accompanies a kill among hunting peoples, as does the archaeological evidence of large-scale repasts at Paleolithic sites. Hambledon hilltop in Dorset is a transitional site, showing how feasting was compatible with both food gathering and food producing. Here, early in the third millennium BCE, in a complex of ceremonial enclosures and defensive earthworks, hundreds, perhaps thousands, of people gathered for purposes we can no longer identify. One thing, however, is obvious from the archaeological record: they ate and drank. They brought a variety of foods with them. Some, like venison, were obtained by hunting. Other items, such as the large quantity of hazelnuts, were gathered. But these people also ate foods produced by herding and tillage: enormous livestock animals and large amounts of wheat and barley.

These eaters were engaged in a huge, centuries-long transformation of their way of life—from foraging for food to growing and breeding it.[36] That transition is now characteristic of most of the Earth's inhabitants. Where food is scarce, individual entitlement is commonly contested. In abundance, the right to distribute the food and the responsibility of warehousing and guarding it become foci of political ambition. In all circumstances, feasting confers or confirms leadership: it has to be organized. The organizer gains power over the eaters and, by way of reciprocation, asserts claims on their loyalty and services.

Early agrarian sites show unmistakable signs that feasting had a political function. The redistributive palace-storehouses operated by elites are conspicuous: the labyrinth of Knossos contained no minotaurs, but it was filled with oil jars and bins of grain. In Egypt the pharaonic economy was dedicated to a cult of abundance: not individual, everyday abundance, for most people lived on bread and beer in amounts only modestly above subsistence level, but a surplus garnered and guarded against hard times, at the disposal of the state and the priests.[37] In an environment of scorching aridity periodically doused by promiscuous floods, triumph over nature meant not only refashioning the landscape and punching pyramids into the sky but also stockpiling against disaster, to make humankind indestructible even by the invisible forces that controlled the floods. The temple built to house the body of Rameses II had storehouses big enough to feed twenty thousand people for a year. The taxation yields painted proudly on the walls of a vizier's tomb are an illustrated menu for an empire: sacks of barley, piles of cakes and nuts, hundreds of head of livestock. The state stockpiled food, it seems, not for regular distribution—the market took care of that—but for famine relief. When "the starvation-year" was over, according to a text of about the late second century BCE, people "borrowing from their granaries will have departed."[38]

The royal banquets of Mesopotamia originally functioned as means of distributing food according to a hierarchy of privilege determined by the kings. Like everything else in the Assyrian world, these feasts grew to gigantic proportions when an imperial system replaced the city-states. When Ashurnasirpal (883–59 BCE) completed the palace of Kalhu, he had 69,574 guests at a banquet that lasted ten days. It included 1,000 fat oxen, 14,000 sheep, 1,000 lambs, hundreds of deer, 20,000 pigeons, 10,000 fish, 10,000 desert rats, and 10,000 eggs.[39]

In the Old Norse *Prose Edda*, the heroes Loki and Logi engaged in an eating contest that the latter won by eating "all the meat and bones and the platter itself."[40] This triumph of heroic eating was not considered selfish. In a more equivocal instance, Nero's banquets, according to his enemies, lasted from noon until midnight. Rules composed two thousand years ago in India specified rice, pulses, salt, butter, and ghee for everyone; but a menial should receive only one-sixth of a gentleman's allowance of rice and only half his measure of ghee. Some differentiation on grounds of quality was also made: laborers, who needed plenty of nutrition, got the rice husks and slaves the broken bits.[41] Although the excluded may evince resentment, rulers' feasts bind political alliances and create affinities, retinues, patronage networks, and household aristocracies.

The banqueting halls of the medieval West were designed for meals of allegiance, at which food was cooked and served in stunning quantities to demonstrate largesse. Meals exhibited lords to their followers and bound the followers to the lords. They were often occasions of oath taking, most famously exemplified by the occasion when diners at the court of Philip of Burgundy took the Vow of the Pheasant to go on crusade, rather as modern fundraisers extort pledges at charity dinners. Philip's hospitality was as extravagant as the oath. According to a participant, "There was even a chapel on the table, with a choir in it, a pasty full of flute-players, and a turret from which came the sound of an organ and other music." The duke was served by a pantomime horse and elephant, ridden by trumpeters. "Next came a white stag ridden by a young boy who sang marvellously, while the stag accompanied him with the tenor part. Next came an elephant . . . carrying a castle in which sat Holy Church, who made piteous complaint on behalf of the Christians persecuted by the Turks."[42]

The tradition of banqueting as showmanship and of conspicuous consumption as a means of power continued through the banquets of Renaissance Rome, when gold plate was cast into the Tiber—carefully, so as to be caught in thoughtfully disposed nets below the surface of the water—to the era of extravaganzas in the Jay Gatsby style.[43] The financier James Buchanan Brady, the "Diamond Jim" famous for his ability to consume four dozen oysters as a first course at dinner, was a guest at the legendary Horseback Dinner hosted at Louis Sherry's New York restaurant in 1903 by Cornelius Kingsley Billings, who made his fortune generating light from coal gas in Chicago. On floors overlaid with real sod and turf, the guests ate pheasant and drank champagne astride horses that were lifted to the third-floor ballroom via the elevators. Thus the history of the power lunch, the state banquet, and the "princess parties" that waste the wealth of so many wealthy Americans today encompasses elements of a vast story traceable back to deep time.

FOOD PRODUCTION

Although ours is not the only species to manage food, or even to produce it, humans have a unique propensity for these activities. Food management predates agriculture. Hunters improve species by culling weak or old animals, set fires to control grazing (and perhaps in some cases to encourage the growth of particular plants), and drive herds down lanes or into corrals for slaughter. Yet the switch from managing food sources to controlling them—from procuring food to producing it—is one of the great revolutions of the human past. It enabled populations to explode and concentrate, states and cities to rise and grow, economic specialization to develop at unprecedented rates and scales, and all the consequent history of sedentary and pastoral societies—which have increasingly dominated the history of the last ten thousand years or so until they have almost entirely replaced hunter-gatherers—to happen.

When the last ice age ended, a productive zone between forest and grassland stretched across the eastern shore of the Mediterranean and the region that is now Iran, eastern Turkey, and Iraq. Food was so plentiful that foragers did not have to move around much. By about 14,000 to 15,000 years ago, permanent settlements arose throughout the region.

Similar evidence of preagricultural settlements exists in central Honshu in Japan, where the Jomon culture occupied permanent villages about 13,000 years ago, feeding themselves by fishing and gathering seeds and nuts.[44] In the Egyptian Sahara, at Nabta Playa, about forty plant species, including sorghum, grew alongside hearths and pit ovens from about 10,000 years ago. At Göbekli Tepe, in southeast Turkey, gatherers of wild wheat built on a monumental scale, hewing seven-ton pillars from limestone.[45]

Although foraging produced abundance and security in deep time, early attempts at farming, surprisingly, seem to have had disastrous consequences almost everywhere.[46] Reliance on a few cultivated staples exposed societies to increased risk of famine; the yield of energy per unit of effort fell; nutrition declined; domesticated animals became reservoirs of disease. The need to organize labor and to police warehoused food favored authoritarian or despotic political systems.[47] Yet not only has almost the entire human world adopted agriculture, but many peoples have come to it independently, in a range of regions and a variety of environments. In environments that produce little plant food digestible by humans, such as tundra, taiga, and grassland, people adopted herding as a way of life. Tilling appeared independently in swamplands, upland valleys, and forest clearings as well as in alluvial plains.

Nineteenth-century scholarship explained the origins of agriculture as an accident. A primitive forager might have observed how dropped seeds germinated in fertilized soil. More recent theories have emphasized stresses—especially population pressure, climatic lurches, and diminished availability of wild foods—that might have driven people to experiment with food production, or, conversely, abundance that might have provided experimenters with leisure to develop new techniques. Some theorists have emphasized political or religious circumstances: chiefs might have needed to supply feasts and bind followers by increasing food supplies, and sacred foods would naturally have required tending and replanting in special enclosures. Any explanation must take account of two inescapable contexts.

The first is the global warming that—with some fluctuations—dominated the early millennia of the Holocene era. Warming can drive humans and other creatures into closer relationships by increasing their dependence on shared sources of water. It can also threaten stands of vegetation on which foragers rely and force them to take greater care of them, tending and weeding them, improving strains by selection, and perhaps transplanting them to more favorable locations. In these circumstances, farming was not necessarily a revolutionary innovation but a conservative response to environmental change.

Foraging and farming are similar activities that shade into one another. Plant gatherers often replant the seeds or roots of the species they gather and may shift them to more favorable plots or encourage them to grow in easily managed stands. Some gatherer peoples reserve seed crops to plant when emergencies or opportunities arise. Hunting communities often corral their prey and use fire to manage the species' grazing. If they are wise, they will also encourage the species to breed fatter, meatier varieties by sparing the best specimens. Hunters who used dogs were familiar with the principles of breeding for thousands of years before agriculture began, using them to improve the obedience and specialized talents of their hounds. These techniques can gradually mutate into farming without any intervention from ecological crisis or cultural interchange. Humans and the species they eat are locked in a relationship that some specialists call coevolution. Gradually, as the relationship becomes closer, humans lose their ability to survive without particular sources of food, and the species that provide those foods become so dependent on cultivation by humans that they would cease to exist without it (see chapter 4).

Gathering, hunting, herding, and tillage, which conventional chronologies usually place in sequence, were and are complementary techniques of obtaining food. They developed together over thousands of years. The warming, drying effects of the post–Ice Age world multiplied the opportunities and incentives for people to experiment with food strategies. David Rindos describes early farming as a case of human-plant symbiosis, in which species developed together in mutual dependence.[48] Eventually, foodstuffs developed that needed human involvement to survive and reproduce. For instance, emerging kinds of edible grasses would not survive independently of human intervention because their seeds would not fall to the ground unless someone removed the husks.

The continuities between the worlds of food procurers and food producers are in many ways more impressive than the differences. The settled way of life, the art, the religious cults, and even the kinds of foods (though obtained by different means) are commonly of the same order. The similarities suggest a new way to look at the transition to agriculture: as an attempt to stabilize a world convulsed by climatic instability. Both those who switched to herding and tilling and those who stuck to hunting and gathering wanted to keep what they had. Instead of seeing the coming of agriculture as a revolution, we might call it a long period of climacteric, poised between different outcomes.

Revolutions—enduring, fundamental, human-induced changes—in the availability, procurement, and preparation of food started in deep time. "If there was a neolithic revolution," said Fernand Braudel, "it is still going on."[49] The changes introduced at the dawn of farming—specialization, domestication, selective breeding, and the multiplication of cultigens—have continued to our own day. The great revolutions, as they are commonly characterized, of the nineteenth and twentieth centuries—in industrialization, energy production and distribution, agriculture, and the genetic modification of food sources—were in a sense extensions or further stages of the process launched at the beginnings of farming, by which humans became producers of their own food: a sort of "unnatural selection," which replaced the impersonal role of evolution in changing and launching species with the power of the human hand.

Whereas farming began in a symbiotic relationship or coevolution between humans and other life forms, industrialization and its successor revolutions were innovations exclusively attributable to human agency. By the nineteenth century, the nature of the food market was changing globally: a vast increase in volume was combined with new patterns of concentration that defied existing structures of production and supply. The population of the world, especially the developing world, was in the early stages of an unprecedented and sustained expansion, demanding equally unprecedented levels of production. In the early nineteenth century, the population of the world probably reached a billion. Over the course of the century it rose to 1.6 billion. The birth of the world's six-billionth baby was announced in the year 2000. The growth of huge, industrialized, and industrializing cities has had to be fed by new methods.

Early in the period, from the time of the introduction of the *levée en masse* in the French revolutionary wars, armed forces, on a scale never experienced in the recent history of Europe, had anticipated the trend. Like cities, these armies were immense concentrations of people, often located far from the sources of food. Wartime logistics provided the models and sometimes the forges of innovation for the people who devised new ways of producing and supplying food in nineteenth-century Europe. Food factories, for instance, were inspired by the huge production lines first employed in state bakeries producing hardtack for navies. The need for campaign provision stimulated the development of canning. Demand for grease for the maintenance of firearms added to the pressure to develop new sources of fat. Margarine was first devised for the use of the French navy.

From 1815 to 1914, city growth replaced army growth as the motor of change in Europe. By 1900 nine European cities had populations of more than a million people. The land, where food was produced, lost labor to the towns, where food was eaten. Most of the population of Britain, by the end of the nineteenth century, had forsaken agriculture for industry and rural for urban life. In the rest of industrializing Europe, the same trend was evident. In 1900, two-thirds of the inhabitants of St. Petersburg were classified as former peasants. Today, country by country, 2 to 4 percent of people in the "developed" parts of the world remain engaged in agriculture; 20 percent at most live in areas that, for statistical purposes, count as rural.

Towns cannot feed themselves. The result of urban growth was a potential food gap that only industrialization could bridge. With the enlargement and concentration of markets, food itself became industrialized. Food production became ever more intensive. Processing conformed increasingly to the patterns set by industries producing consumer durables. Supply became mechanized. Distribution was reorganized. Mealtimes shifted with the changing patterns of the working day. Over the past half-century or so, we can even speak of a trend toward the "industrialization" of eating, as food has become "faster" and households have come to rely more heavily on dishes prepared outside the home to uniform standards.

Increasingly, in the late nineteenth and twentieth centuries, the capital investment necessary for higher agricultural output came from huge industrial companies that made fertilizers and animal feed. The first chemical fertilizer was invented by John Lawes when he dissolved phosphate-rich ore in sulfuric acid in 1842. The process was not much used until the last few years of the nineteenth century, when phosphate mines were discovered and developed on a large scale. Meanwhile, mountains of guano and potash nourished the world's fields. The real chemical revolution in fertilizer technology came in 1909, when Fritz Haber found a way of extracting nitrogen, the basis of nitrate fertilizers, from the atmosphere. His admirers said he had plucked "bread from the air."[50]

Ultimately, farms became stages in a sort of conveyor belt: chemical fertilizers and industrially processed feed went in at one end, and edible—though sometimes barely so—manufactured products came out at the other. The trend approached culmination in 1945, when the "Chicken of Tomorrow" contest was announced in America. Three years later it produced the battery hen.[51] In combination with "growth vitamins" marketed from 1949, and feed laced with antibiotics employed from 1950, this innovation led rapidly to chicken houses containing 40,000 birds. By 1954, there were 5 to 6 million chicken-breeding businesses in the United States. Some farmers had ten million chicks.[52] Betty MacDonald, a chicken-rancher's wife in Washington State, looked back unsentimentally on the old-style "chicken house knee-deep in weasels and blood" where "stupid" chicks would devote themselves to contriving self-immolation in their drinking fountains or under their brooders or "pick each other's eyes out or peck each other's feet until they are bloody stumps."[53] The advocates of the new methods disingenuously claimed that the chicken came to "cover the globe" because of its unique merits: an undiscerning appetite and its own "refrigeration and heating," supplied by its feather coat.[54] A ruthless new mode of production made chicken the cheap treat of the modern world. In the factory farms that now supply most of the meat, eggs, and dairy products of industrial society, animals are treated like machines: anonymous units of production confined in ergonomically minimal spaces to yield the maximum output per unit of cost.

In the late nineteenth century, the railroads linked up with steam-powered sea routes. Land transport could now take bulk cargoes across continents as easily as across seas. The great food-producing and consuming belt of the Northern Hemisphere, from Vancouver to Vladivostok, was linked by steam transport. As Charles Wilson observes, "The flow of trade was no longer governed by Nature."[55] The results included a new form of worldwide specialization, as food no longer had to be produced near the point of consumption. In industrializing areas, agriculture declined. British agriculture virtually collapsed in the last generation of the nineteenth century. All over Western Europe, wheat production was abandoned in favor of cheap imported grain. The rock-ribbed farmland of New England began its long, slow reversion to forest as food production shifted west.

Distribution, however, still needed to be local. In the urban environments, new ways of shopping evolved. Markets built under new municipal dispensation became, in their very structures, monuments to the wonder of industrial technology: palaces of abundance set under elegant glass and cast-iron arcades. Together with railway stations, winter gardens, and shopping arcades, these were industrializing Europe's equivalents of the aqueducts and agoras of antiquity. Food manufacture imitated other industries: it powered production with steam in the nineteenth century and with electricity in the twentieth, using mechanized assembly lines and producing a standard product.

THE EXCHANGE OF FOODS AND FOODWAYS

If the modern history of food production becomes more readily intelligible in the context of deep time, so, more surprisingly, do the economic and cultural history of food exchange—with respect to both trade across distances and influence across barriers of class and culture.

Food became a social differentiator—a signifier of class, a measure of rank—at an undocumented moment when some individuals began to command more food resources than others. There was never a golden age of equality in the history of humankind. Whenever hominin remains provide sufficient data for comparison, differences in nutrition levels appear. Many Paleolithic burials show correlations between levels of nutrition and signs of status. In early agrarian societies, elites literally commanded abundance, because the warehousing, guardianship, and distribution of stored food were their responsibility.

In some societies, the amount consumed remains the measure of rank. Jack Goody documents that in West Africa, his friend Chief Gandaa of Biriku "lived just like everyone else, but with more of everything."[56] Yet even there, chiefs' tables attracted peculiar rituals and special comestibles: chiefs commonly eat in secret. Yoruba chiefs consumed their predecessors' hearts. In societies blessed with abundance, frugality can become an elite characteristic: a qualification for buddhahood, sanctity, or secular leadership.

So even if social differentiation in matters of food initially focused on quantity, it almost always acquired other characteristics: elite foods tend to be different, differently prepared, and eaten in different ways. The earliest surviving courtly recipes, from Mesopotamia, emphasize painstaking preparation. They advise browning meat or birds before boiling in water thickened with blood and adding flavorings of garlic, onion, leek, and turnip and dressings of cheese or butter; braising in fat and water is also recommended.[57] From ancient Egypt no direct evidence survives, but medical treatises sometimes refer to courtly recipes, such as the dish of minced pigeon cooked with liver, fennel, chicory, and iris recommended by a physician from Krokodilopolis on the grounds that the broth was thought to be good for stomachache.[58] Dishes to celebrate the completion of the harvest and tempt the souls of the dead back to Earth were listed with obvious yearning by a Chinese poet of the second or third century BCE: "The cunning cook slices pigeon and yellow heron and black crane with peppered herbs into millet pies. He concocts badger stew, fresh turtle, sweet chicken cooked in cheese, pickled suckling pigs and the flesh of newborn puppies floating in liver sauce, with radish salad and Indian spices, roast daw, steamed widgeon, grilled quail, boiled perch and sparrow broth—in each preserved the separate flavor that is most its own."[59] Apparently elaborate preparation did not compromise the ritually necessary purity of the ingredients.

Around the turn of the second and third centuries CE, Athenaeus of Naucratis combined all the elements of the emerging haute cuisine into his sketch of the most luxurious meal he could imagine: copious amounts, distinctive dishes, exquisite service, impressive variety, and inventive cookery. In the banqueting room he envisaged, on well-polished tables, under hanging lamps which "shone on festive crowns," "well stuffed conger" would be served in a glistening dish "to delight a god," along with snowy-topped loaves.[60]

The emergence of elite cuisines led to the rise of a culinary profession of high status, a litany of techniques, and a code of kitchen practice. Livy dated the decline of Rome from the moment when banquets became elaborate, because it marked the point when "the cook, who formerly had the status of the lowest kind of slave, first acquired prestige."[61]

The impossibility of preserving hieratic or esoteric foodways may help explain the importance of etiquette. Even the most elaborate secret recipes are usually divulged eventually, so that ethereal sauces trickle down from kingly tables to become bourgeois treats. Like other forms of technology, cuisine is easily imitated and transferred. Courtly cuisine spread through society, becoming first a standard of aspiration and then—surprisingly quickly—the norm for a bourgeois family. Louis XIV's kitchen kept no secrets: they were diffused by cookbooks, beginning with *Le cuisinier françois* by François Pierre la Varenne, cook to a noble household, in 1651. By 1691, when François Massialot published a work whose title summed up the process of social diffusion—*Cuisinier royal et bourgeois*—one hundred thousand copies of such works were in print.[62]

Courtly eating styles in the West have always been borrowed from other cultures. In classical antiquity, upper-class foodways were denounced by Horace as "Persian" and by a Greek proverb as "Sicilian." Medieval Western courts looked to Islam for culinary inspiration. For most of history, long-range trade in food was limited to luxury items. Trade hovers and shimmers like a waiter at the table of world food, carrying surprising dishes to unsuspecting diners, or shuffling seating for unexpected guests. Global circulation of ingredients by way of trade is assisted by the "stranger effect"—the tendency to revere the exotic.[63] Ingredients brought from afar at trouble and cost, or exchanged as gifts with alien plenipotentiaries, derive prestige from their journey out of all proportion to their intrinsic value or their practical merits. They are received as flavors of the divine horizon, treasured as mirabilia, or prized, at least initially, for their exclusivity. This effect is similar to the added interest that travelers acquire according to how far they journey: pilgrims gain sanctity, leaders charisma, warriors fearsomeness, and ambassadors attention. Unfamiliarity forestalls contempt. Sometimes the stranger effect is strong enough to overcome the ingrained hostility that most cultures have for foreign food.

Every society grows its own staples, unless and until they can be imported cheaply. A common motive for the expansion of empires is the diversification of diet by imposing ecological collaboration on regions specializing in different foodstuffs. Andean imperialism, from the age of Tiahuanaco to that of the Incas and Spaniards, was based on enforced exchanges of food and, when necessary, of labor between producers at different altitudes or among the different microclimates that are characteristic of mountainous terrain. For much of Chinese history, northern and southern China have been linked by the supply of southern rice for northern consumption. In the Roman world, provinces specialized in the supply of basic products to the rest: Egypt, Sicily, and the North African littoral were the granaries of the empire, Betica its olive grove. In the Aztec empire, shifts of tribute between ecologically specialized zones supported the hegemony of a few communities in and around Lake Texcoco (the site of present-day Mexico City). At more than seven thousand feet above sea level, where local agriculture was confined to garden mounds dredged and piled from the lake bottom, the environment was incapable of feeding the huge population—probably at least eighty thousand people—concentrated in the capital at Tenochtitlán. The city's tribute rolls show 240,000 bushels a year of maize, beans, and amaranth levied from subject communities. The cacao needed for the elite drink consumed at every ceremonial occasion would not grow in the region at all and had to be brought in vast quantities by bearers from the "hot lands" of the far south.

ECOLOGICAL EXCHANGE

Although just about every historical topic benefits from consideration in the context of the very long run, not everything began in deep time. The biggest rupture between modernity and deep time in the history of food occurred in a context only partly shaped by human agency. From the time of continental drift, perhaps about 200 million years ago, until the sixteenth century, evolution generally followed a broadly divergent course. The biota of each land mass grew ever more distinctive. When European voyagers traversed the world and linked formerly isolated regions by sea routes, the process went into reverse: biota began to shift around the globe in a convergent pattern. The relatively sudden severance of a 200-million-year trend deserves to be called a revolution.

Now, for instance, the descendants of Merino sheep from Spain graze the Southern Hemisphere. There are wallabies in English parkland. The American prairie, which never saw a grain of wheat until the sixteenth century, has become the wheat bin of the world. Coffee, which originated in Ethiopia, is sought from Java, Jamaica, and Brazil. Texas and California produce one of the world's most popular kinds of rice, which was once an exclusively Old World crop. Chocolate and peanuts, both formerly peculiar to the New World, are among the most important products of West Africa. The potato, staple of the Incas, sustains Ireland and typifies the cuisine of Bengal. Ingredients indigenous to the Americas are now strongly associated with other regions: tomatoes with Italy, chocolate with Switzerland and Belgium, peanuts with Southeast Asia, and chiles with Thailand and Szechwan.

Foodstuff migrations have occurred throughout history. The diffusion of the great, gramineous staples of early farming presupposes ecological as well as cultural transmission. The plant most prized for flavor in ancient Rome was silphium, a weed never successfully domesticated. It was exported from Cyrene after introduction from its homeland in nearby Libya, presumably by self-seeding. The natives, and the Greek gourmets for whom they harvested the plant, only nibbled the extremities, but Romans ate the whole stem and root, sliced and preserved in vinegar.[64] Grapes advanced with the Roman colonizers as far as the local climates would allow. Alexander's balm, balsam, coriander, dill, fennel, garden leek, garlic, hyssop, marjoram, mint, mustard, onion, opium poppy, parsley, rosemary, rue, sage, savory, and thyme were all probably introduced to Britain by the Romans.[65] None of these, however, nor any subsequent transmissions within the Old World or the New, can compare in importance with the exchanges that began with— or about the time of—the voyages of Columbus.

In part, this is because more recent ecological exchanges have occurred over unprecedented distances on an unprecedented scale. In part, too, it is because of the role of human agency in facilitating and promoting such exchanges. Although there is room to debate the exact chronology and means of transmission of many of the plants in question—the sweet potato, for instance, may have crossed the Pacific on driftwood without human involvement—the great ocean-borne exchange of biota of the last five hundred years constituted the biggest human intervention in environmental history since the beginnings of species domestication.

Ecological exchange on this scale could never have happened without human vectors. The stars of the story, however, are surely the plants and animals themselves, who survived long and stressful journeys and achieved leaps of acclimatization. Sometimes seeds traveled without intentional human help, in the folds of the clothing of unwitting carriers, or in the weft of bales and sacking.

The effects of the exchange were most dramatic in the field of human nutrition. The sudden increase in the species available for exploitation in different parts of the world meant that the total nutritional value of the world's food production could expand enormously. The transport of crops and livestock opened up vast tracts of previously unexploited or underexploited lands for farming or ranching. Farming could climb up mountainsides and colonize deserts. Varied diets became accessible to populations previously reliant on particular staples. Wherever the effects of the ecological exchange were felt, more people could be fed. This is not to say that the exchange of biota "caused" population to increase; but it facilitated the expansion. There were countercurrents: among the exchanged biota were not only foodstuffs but also people, who tend to be destructive; disease-causing microbes, which inflicted terrible losses on populations unused to them; and species, introduced deliberately or accidentally, which can become invasive. Nevertheless, in most places, to begin with—and, eventually, just about everywhere—the multiplication of foods fed the great demographic expansion of modern history.

There were also obvious political consequences. The people who controlled the routes of transmission could, to some extent, manipulate the consequences, shifting food production and concentrations of labor to the places that suited them. The maritime enterprises of modern times began as desperate efforts at self-elevation by poor, marginal communities on Eurasia's Atlantic rim; but the perspectives opened up by their privileged access to the benefits of long-range ecological exchange helped the Spaniards, Portuguese, English, and Dutch to become imperialists, shifting sugar production to their American colonies or creating new spiceries under their own control. The power of garnering plants and creatures from a dazzling variety of environments was a boost to Europe's incipient scientific revolution. Every courtly *Wunderkammer* became a repository of specimens for scrutiny and experiment. Nothing like this global range of knowledge had ever been available before. As Richard Grove puts it, privileged acquaintance with "plant and faunal occurrence and distribution constituted a first step towards an ability to determine the influence of man on the environment."[66] Worldwide ecological exchange made a major contribution to the long-term shift in the balance of knowledge and power, tilting it increasingly toward the West.

The transformation of North American grasslands stands out as the most conspicuous arena of ecological exchange and the most striking modification of a biome ever effected by human intervention. For most of the short human past, on the Great Plains of North America three conditions inhibited the introduction of tillage. There was ample game— giant quadrupeds in Paleolithic times, which were succeeded by great herds of bison. The soil, unaffected by the last ice age, was tough and invulnerable to preindustrial tools and did not support an abundance of any plant edible by humans. Even as late as 1827, when James Fenimore Cooper wrote *The Prairie,* it seemed a place without a future, "a vast country, incapable of sustaining a dense population."[67] The habitat lacked the ecological diversity that encouraged civilization in the Sahel. It could and did serve, like the Eurasian steppe, as a highway between the civilizations that flanked it: but even at the height of their wealth and grandeur a thousand years ago, the cities of the North American Southwest, between the Rio Grande and the Colorado, and those of the mound builders of the Mississippi bottom to the east, were relatively small-scale ventures that never generated the copious and productive exchanges of culture and technology that rattled back and forth between Old World cultures and made the steppe a vital link.

At the very moment when Cooper described it, the prairie was beginning to experience a slow invasion of white usurpers, which would eventually contribute to a new look for the plains as a land of rich farms and cities. Today the Great Plains are dubbed the "breadbasket of the world," with some of the most productive farming ever devised in the entire history of humankind. The relatively new practice of ranching is still prodigiously successful on the high plains in the west and south of the region. It may seem incredible that a land now so thoroughly adapted to human needs should for so long have been the domain of nature, where farming was confined to a few poor and tiny patches and where sparse populations trailed the great American bison. A similar revolution has overtaken the South American grasslands known as the pampa, which were even more wretchedly endowed by nature than the prairie: instead of big, meaty bison, their native grazer was the small, skinny guanaco, a kind of wild llama, which the natives encouraged and in some respects managed but never domesticated. Now the region supports the world's most productive beef industry.

Only invaders from the Old World—ecologically intrusive species, human and nonhuman—could have effected this transformation. The first stage was colonization by European weeds and grasses, which enabled the pampa and prairie to support sheep, cattle, and horses. Purslane and Englishman's foot created what A. W. Crosby calls "the empire of the dandelion."[68] Weeds made the revolution work, healing "the raw wounds that the invaders tore in the earth": they bound soil together, saved it from desiccation, refilled vacated eco-niches, and fed imported livestock.[69] The conscious transpositions followed. Horses and cattle came first—domesticable quadrupeds of a kind unknown in the New World since the Pleistocene. Then came people and wheat: after Juan Garrido's efforts, the lower levels of the central valleys of Mexico proved highly suitable for wheat, and although most of the population continued to rely on maize, wheat bread became a badge of urban sophistication. Within a few years of the Spanish conquest, the city council of Mexico demanded a supply of "white, clean, well cooked and seasoned bread."[70] The valleys supplied wheat to Spanish garrisons all over Central America and the Caribbean.

Not all efforts to introduce wheat in other parts of the Americas were successful, at least initially. The Spanish colonists of Florida in 1565 brought wheat seed, together with vine cuttings, 200 calves, 400 pigs, 400 sheep, and unspecified numbers of goats and chickens; in 1573, however, "herbs, fish and other scum and vermin" sustained them when rations were short. Cornbread and fish, foodstuffs copied from the indigenous diet, were their mainstays.[71] Similarly, the first English colonists in Virginia were unable to grow food for themselves and relied on precarious handouts from the natives to see them through their "starving time." Investors and imperialists back home blamed colonists' moral deficiencies for these failures; but the problems of the mutual adaptation of Old World agronomy and New World environments were formidable, especially for settlers of exposed seaboards in an era of imperial competition. Colonies sited for defense, behind marshes or swamps, in enervating climates, needed generations of investment before they became agriculturally productive; the remarkable thing is not the high rate of failure but the perseverance that led to ultimate success.

The Mexican model—exploitation of wheat lands for export and for feeding a few urban centers, with transitional or marginal ranching perpetuated on unfarmed land—was transferred to the North American plains as soon as the requisite technology became available: powerful steel plows to turn the sod and strains of wheat bred to flourish in a capricious climate and unglaciated soil. The enterprise had to be underpinned by an industrial infrastructure. Railways were needed for the economical long-distance transport of grain. Lightweight balloon frames for houses, made from precision-milled sticks and cheap nails, housed settlers and spread cities in a region bereft of most construction materials.[72]

FOOD HISTORY AND DEEP TIME

For historians whose watchword is *nihil humanum alienum,* the history of food can hardly be understood as exclusively a story of *Homo sapiens;* the food practices of hominin predecessors and other cultural species are inescapable parts of the context. Other species are part of the story because we eat them; human lives must be considered in the ecosystems in which they are enmeshed. The history of food evidently needs a generous time frame if we are to understand it fully. Most of its stories started in deep time. Awareness that human food production is part of a process of coevolution with other species makes it untenable to treat the inception of farming as a "Neolithic revolution" characterized by an abrupt rupture with the food-getting strategies that preceded it. Something similar can be said of the great ecological exchange of the sixteenth century and after: although it was a genuinely new phenomenon—a break with the past, with only shadowy precedents in deep time—and, for the most part, a result of human agency, some of the most influential biota involved, including weeds, vermin, and microbes, took part in it in indifference to or despite humankind. Even if one were to reject coevolutionary models, the striking continuities and overlaps between garnering food and producing it invalidate the notion that the story starts at a discernible moment or in a discrete period. The survival of hunting and gathering throughout the periods historians commonly traverse is an invitation to consider all hunters and gatherers as part of historians' subject matter. Even today, the most highly industrialized societies hunt for wild food when their trawlers gather fish—though to a diminishing extent, as aquaculture adds another chapter to the story of food production.

Like food production, almost everything else that historians generally admit as a proper topic of enquiry in connection with food turns out to have begun much earlier than traditionally supposed. Cooking with fire should probably be reckoned as a story unfolding over many hundreds of thousands—perhaps millions—of years. If we accept that carnivory is historically important, our study of human eating must grapple with millions of years. The history of food as a cultural device—as magic, as rite, as a locus for behavior that is not just instinctual—must take hominin cannibalism into account. For the history of food, as for all the other themes of this volume, historians' traditional prejudices against encompassing deep time look increasingly like self-denying ordinances—arbitrary in nature, irrational in origin—that can only narrow our vision and impair our understanding.

CHAPTER 7

Deep Kinship

THOMAS R. TRAUTMANN, GILLIAN FEELEY-HARNIK,
AND JOHN C. MITANI

Kinship suffuses human sociality; it is the central story in the deep history of humankind, but so far we do not have a well-settled history of kinship. There are many obstacles to constructing such a history, and most of them center on what the terms *history* and *kinship* actually mean. How can kinship be a part of history? What conception of kinship is needed for kinship to have a history?

In the 1830s the philosopher Georg Friedrich Hegel situated history and nature on opposite sides of a great divide.[1] Nature he considered a realm of necessity whose only mode of change is cyclical; it reproduces itself without change. Nature encompasses ceaseless movement without forward motion, change without alteration. History, by contrast, is a realm in which creative human agents, conscious of their innovation, make progressive change. At the heart of such originary making is the state; and politics, in this view, is the site of true history. Hegel explicitly ruled out the family, and by implication kinship, for family life is an attribute of nature. Species reproduce without net change, he thought; so when humans reproduce, they are merely behaving in a way natural to all species. Hegel could envision no deep history of kinship exactly because history breaks out of the necessity of nature: developmental, directional progress is the defining property of history. The nature-versus-history distinction runs right through humans, who are products of both nature and history.

Hegel's conceptualization of history was powerfully influential. It was taken up and further propagated by Karl Marx, so that all across the political spectrum, history became the story of human progress and emancipation from nature. This imagery would inspire political action for the next two centuries.

The paradox of this formulation is that it circled the wagons of history into a small, defensive perimeter at the very moment when historical consciousness was expanding into the territory of what became the social and natural sciences. Hegel was highly successful in articulating the political philosophy of modernism, delineating the borders of what became the discipline of history, but he was not a good theorist of the new historical sensibilities that were growing up outside the discipline. Shortly after Hegel's intervention, L.H. Morgan, in a massive worldwide survey of kinship systems, showed that the family is not an institution that simply reproduces itself in biological fashion but instead has a history that is varied and deep.[2] And Charles Darwin, working at roughly the same time, showed how spectacularly wrong Hegel had been to think that species merely reproduce themselves exactly.

In the late nineteenth century, anthropology crystallized as a new discipline centered on the study of kinship, and biology experienced a huge paradigm shift that refashioned it on the basis of the theory of evolutionary change through natural selection. Even cosmology was taking on a developmental dimension. Nature, it seemed, had a history after all: it showed a pattern of developmental change, a history without agents. As historical thinking came to permeate the natural sciences and social sciences, however, the discipline of history stayed within a narrow, Hegelian frame. Only recently has it ventured widely beyond topics of state and statecraft, which still dominate the field, and almost all contemporary historiography is conducted within the limits of biblical chronology, whose origin no longer has any bearing on method but whose constraints on temporal coverage seem, for today's historians, almost sacred. The department of history, for these reasons, is not the place to find a deep history of kinship.

To construct a deep history, we must turn to anthropology and biology. Paleoanthropology, the study of the human fossil record, supplies invaluable clues and benchmarks. But kinship is a pattern of ideas and behavior: its traces cannot be captured and read from fossil remains alone. Our most telling evidence comes from primatology, the study of living primate populations—especially our nearest cousins, the chimpanzees, bonobos, and gorillas—and from the anthropological study of human kinship systems. Exploring the deep history of human kinship requires coordination between these two disciplines. This hybrid approach presents problems of chronology and of the conceptualization of kinship itself.

THE PROBLEM OF CHRONOLOGY

Throughout this book we face the challenge of writing history across the chronological gap separating the natural and social sciences. Humans and their nearest primate relatives branched off from one another 5 to 8 million years ago; consequently, the time depth of the primatological evidence bearing on human kinship is extensive indeed. The comparative study of human kinship systems implies a time depth that, although much greater than history based on written records, is relatively shallow. Insofar as human kinship systems involve the teaching and learning of concepts that were eventually articulated in words, the study of human kinship can take us back perhaps hundreds of thousands of years to the origins of language. How can we coordinate findings on these two very different temporal scales?

THE PROBLEM OF CONCEPTUALIZING KINSHIP

With the challenge of chronology comes the equally vexed problem of the relationship between biological and social kinship, which has dogged the study of kinship virtually from the beginning. The difference between kinship as a social fact and as a biological process requires us to write across the Hegelian gap separating nature from history. In the study and everyday experience of kinship, there is a sense in which every living being has relations of shared substance with others and is the product of those relations, which can be described in biological terms or with reference to shared blood, bone, or flesh. But human kinship is also something learned and lodged in consciousness, a set of rules that can be applied, through marriage or adoption, to people who are not biological kin. These rules vary widely among humans, such that close kin in one society are not considered relatives at all in another.

Kinship studies have been greatly shaped by the work of the American anthropologist L.H. Morgan (1818–81). The discovery that kinship is not simply a measure of biological relatedness involved the recognition of patterns in Iroquois kinship that seemed, to Morgan, nonnatural and contrived, even a stupendous act of invention. The leading example of this is the merger of kinship categories Morgan considered distinct: "The father and his brothers [are] equally fathers" and the mother's sister is equally a mother, as he put it.[3] Morgan puzzled over the fact that, among the Iroquois, some kinds of uncles and aunts are called father and mother, some cousins are called brother and sister, and some nephews and nieces are called son and daughter. To explain the difference between

Iroquois and Euro-American kinship, Morgan undertook a global survey of kinship systems, eventually devising a series of hypothetical evolutionary steps from an original state of primitive promiscuity to the most advanced stage, monogamy. His unpublished manuscripts, however, show that he first conceived the English and the Iroquois kinship terminologies as *natural* and *artificial,* respectively.[4] He regarded the Iroquois merger of father and father's brother as an imaginative invention, not a spontaneous effect of human biology.

The French sociologist Émile Durkheim criticized Morgan's published evolutionary theory for having too biological a conception of kinship: kinship "is social, or it is nothing," he said.[5] This distinguishes the kinship we have by virtue of inhabiting reproductive bodies from the kinship we consciously know and practice. Durkheim left the first to biologists and psychologists and identified the second as the proper object of the new discipline of sociology. In the twentieth century, cultural anthropology was strongly oriented toward the study of social kinship, but on the relationship between social and biological kinship there were divergent views. Some scholars sought to connect the two; some treated the variability of social kinship as evidence for human freedom from the constraints of nature. The emergence of sociobiology in the 1970s occasioned a strong clash within anthropology over the exact relation of biological and social kinship.[6]

The tension between advocates of kinship as culture and kinship as biology has only recently begun to fade. It now seems possible to entertain simultaneously two views, both of which are essential for the analysis of kinship, neither of which is true in isolation from the other, and each of which becomes self-contradictory when taken to the extreme: first, that social kinship is the social construction and elaboration of biological relations, that is, biological precedes social kinship; and second, that biological kinship is a form of social kinship developed in the idiom of modern science, that is, kinship is social all the way to the bottom. Given the explanatory potential of these approaches, how can we coordinate the results of human kinship studies, which focus on distinct classes of relatives articulated in speech by way of logically integrated categories, with the results of primatology, which addresses the patterned behavior of biological kin whose conscious recognition of their relationship, to the degree that it exists at all, is formed without benefit of language? Any answer to this question that takes deep time into account must also incorporate the findings made possible by new technologies for tracking genetic relatedness through DNA. Genomic research has revolutionized the study of the evolution of all living species. A rigorous, singular, and universal conception of biological kinship is needed as the basis of such studies.

The appearance of two recent books that attempt to speak across these gaps of chronology and conception is a hopeful sign. Both draw upon the structuralist theory of Claude Lévi-Strauss, which posits a radical discontinuity between human and prehuman kinship by a kind of invention that amounts to a leap from nature into culture.[7] Nicholas J. Allen and colleagues offer an interdisciplinary mix of perspectives on the development of early human kinship without an overall synthesis.[8] Its starting point is the "tetradic theory" of Allen, a social anthropologist, which posits the simplest possible system of kinship categories as one that has only four kinship terms—roughly, "my group/other group" and "my generation/other generation"—and which in the course of development opens out through the breakdown and multiplication of terms to produce the diverse kinship systems found among humans today.[9] This formulation, too, represents something of a leap into culture, a moment of discontinuity from biology, though Allen does not treat culture as a negation of nature, as Lévi-Strauss does.

Bernard Chapais, by contrast, gives a synthetic account of "primeval kinship" from the perspective of an accomplished primatologist with a good grasp of the anthropological kinship literature.[10] He combines the conspicuously social, nonbiological, nonevolutionary theory of Lévi-Strauss with the necessarily biological kinship of primatology. In doing so, Chapais contends that nonhuman primates are capable of "kinship recognition," incest avoidance, pair bonding, and other behavioral patterns that can be seen as precursors of the institutions of human kinship. In other words, he tries to show a gradual, continuous transition from prehuman to human kinship, making use of Lévi-Straussian ideas of exogamy and marital exchange between groups. Analysis of this sort requires a close look at how other primate societies are shaped by kinship and the extent to which human kinship is intelligible as a graded variant of, or a radical departure from, these primate trends.

PRIMATE KINSHIP

Human kinship extends well beyond genetic relationships. The existence of culturally constructed kinship categories, the development of novel reproductive technologies, and changes in gender relations and marriage patterns mean that human relatives may not always share genes. Because these issues do not apply to nonhuman primates, most primatologists have defined kinship exclusively in terms of genetic relatedness: kin are individuals who share genes inherited from a recent common ancestor.

Although seemingly straightforward, kinship defined in this manner is not easy to determine. Pedigrees derived from observations of individual animals furnish a means to establish who is related to whom. The long life spans and slow reproduction of primates, however, make collecting this information extremely time-consuming. Even in rare cases where pedigrees exist, they can be used to ascertain kinship only through the mother. In many primate species, single females mate multiple males, making it impossible to employ behavioral observations alone to determine paternity. Recent advances in genetic technology allow us to genotype primates in the wild.[11] In principle, these data can be used to estimate the relatedness of individuals, but in practice, a prohibitive amount of genetic information is required to refine estimates with any degree of precision.[12] In general, the best way to determine kinship in primates is to combine pedigree data based on long-term behavioral observations with genetic information.

Two factors, dispersal and mating behavior, influence kinship patterns. Most primates live in groups. These groups are not closed but open because of a process of dispersal. On reaching sexual maturity, members of one or both sexes typically leave their natal group. In some species, where individuals of one sex stay and the other leaves, the individuals remaining in the group are usually more closely related to each other than are those who leave.[13] Mating behaviors also have strong effects on the genetic relationships of individuals living in primate groups. If, for example, one male sires a large number of infants, his progeny will form age cohorts consisting of paternal siblings.[14] By contrast, mating between animals who live in different groups, which occurs in some primate species, reduces the degree to which individuals living together are related.[15]

KIN RECOGNITION

Humans do not find it particularly difficult to distinguish kin from nonkin. Family ties validated and reinforced through language usually make clear who is related to whom. But do primates recognize their kin? If so, what mechanisms do they employ to discriminate kin from nonkin? What, if anything, do primates know about the kin relations of others? Experiments with captive monkeys show that they are unable to discriminate unfamiliar kin from unfamiliar non-kin.[16] Surprisingly, females appear to be incapable of recognizing their own offspring: they readily serve as foster mothers to unfamiliar infants, of the same and different species.[17] Yet primates discriminate relatives from nonrelatives during their normal, day-to-day affairs, providing prima facie evidence for kin recognition. For example, female monkeys can discern the calls of their own infants from those produced by unrelated individuals.[18] In many species, individuals associate with and maintain proximity to kin more frequently than to non-kin.[19] Relatives groom each other more than do unrelated individuals. Kin selectively share food and aid each other in fights.

Such recognition occurs largely through the maternal line. Female primates form enduring relationships with their offspring, making maternal relationships easy to determine for the animals themselves as well as for human observers. In contrast, mating associations between male and female primates are typically ephemeral, with females frequently mating multiple males. As a consequence, it is unclear whether primates can distinguish their paternal relatives. Recent studies nevertheless suggest that paternal kin relationships affect the behavior of primates in some unanticipated ways. Male baboons and capuchin monkeys avoid mating their paternal half sisters and daughters, respectively.[20] Female macaques and baboons affiliate preferentially with their paternal half sisters, and male baboons selectively aid their own infants when they are threatened by others.[21]

These findings remain controversial, as the mechanisms primates employ to identify their paternal kin are unclear.[22] Other studies indicate that individuals in other primate species fail to recognize their paternal kin. For example, female pig-tailed macaques and female baboons do not recognize their paternal half sisters.[23] Male chimpanzees and female capuchin monkeys affiliate with their paternal half siblings and unrelated individuals equally often.[24] Taken together, these conflicting results indicate that, in the absence of a convincing mechanism of identifying kin, questions about paternal kin recognition by primates will remain open.

In contrast, a relatively simple mechanism exists to explain how primates recognize their maternal kin. Here it is generally assumed that primates learn to recognize their maternal relatives through association and experience obtained during development.[25] In primates, prolonged periods of infant development, extended periods of maternal care, and long life spans create social groups whose members consist of overlapping generations of related individuals. Kin thus have ample oppor-

FIGURE 15. The mothers, sisters, and daughters in this wild gelada group in Ethiopia have formed a "grooming train." Geladas live in matrilineal societies in which female kin form the core of each group. (Photo by Jacinta Beehner.)

tunity to become intimately familiar with each other as they interact daily and repeatedly over long periods (figure 15).

Primates not only recognize their relatives but also possess knowledge about the kin relations of others. Tape-recorded screams of juvenile vervet monkeys played back to females cause them to look toward the juveniles' mothers, suggesting that females recognize the bonds between mothers and their offspring.[26] Similarly, female long-tailed macaques distinguish pictures of mothers with their infants from those of unrelated individuals.[27] On hearing calls mimicking a fight between two individuals, female baboons gaze at the contestants' relatives.[28] In disputes involving female pig-tailed macaques, participants may redirect aggression toward the kin of opponents.[29]

EFFECTS OF KINSHIP ON BEHAVIOR

Some of the first systematic studies of primates revealed the powerful effects of kinship on behavior. Pioneering research by Japanese primatologists more than fifty years ago showed that social groups of Japanese macaques were organized around subsets of genetically related females.[30] In this species, males leave their natal groups at maturity, whereas females stay. Females who remain are closely related to each other through the maternal line and form strong friendly ties, displayed in association and grooming behavior.

Subsequent research has shown that matrilineal social networks are characteristic of additional Old World monkeys, such as baboons, vervet monkeys, and other macaques.[31] Social bonds between maternally related female baboons are extremely robust, in some cases enduring as long as seven years.[32] Maternal kin frequently support each other in coalitions, groups of two or more individuals that direct aggression toward third parties.[33] Female monkeys intervene in disputes between their relatives and unrelated animals, typically favoring kin and occasionally taking considerable risks by supporting them against opponents who are much higher-ranking than themselves.

Nepotistic support plays a critical role in the acquisition and maintenance of female dominance rank. In several species of Old World monkeys, status is inherited through the maternal line, with youngest daughters acquiring ranks immediately below their mothers.[34] Young females ascend the dominance hierarchy because their older kin protect them and furnish aid in conflicts with others. As these processes operate over time and across families, females of one matriline come to occupy adjacent ranks, with members of the same matriline dominating individuals of other matrilines. The resulting dominance structure influences the reproduction of females in important ways, as high-ranking individuals mature faster, give birth to healthier infants, and experience shorter interbirth intervals than do low-ranking animals.[35]

Old World monkey females provide some of the best examples of nepotism in primates. Kin biases in behavior are also displayed in solitary species and other primates whose females disperse from their natal groups. In grey mouse lemurs, females forage alone at night but sleep with others during the day. Sleeping groups are relatively stable, and nestmates are maternal relatives who raise their infants cooperatively.[36] Females groom and communally nurse related infants and adopt them if their mothers die. Additional research has shown that female gorillas, who typically disperse from their natal groups, occasionally move to adjacent areas that contain relatives.[37] Studies of red howler monkeys in South America furnish a particularly compelling case of female nepotism.[38] In this species, most females disperse at a young age. Dispersing individuals compete vigorously with females already living in social

FIGURE 16. Among chimpanzees, maternal brothers, such as the pair depicted here, are long-term allies. Females leave their natal group at adolescence, but males stay. As a result, enduring bonds between adult brothers and sisters (common among humans) are exceedingly rare among chimps, our nearest primate relatives. (Photo by John Mitani.)

groups and gain entry into a group only by forming one themselves. Related individuals are selectively recruited into new groups, with the result that established groups consist primarily of close kin. Female kin who live together over long periods reproduce more than individuals who associate with non-kin.

Although the effects of kinship on the behavior of female primates are well documented, scant data exist on nepotism in male primates. The paucity of data may reflect the fact that males derive few benefits by acting nepotistically because they compete for fertile females, a resource not easily shared. Empirically, the inability to recognize paternal kin might place further limits on nepotistic behavior. Long-term studies of wild chimpanzees provide a good illustration of male nepotism (figure 16). Male chimpanzees typically live with close relatives because females in this species are the dispersing sex. Like female Old World monkeys, male chimpanzees form coalitions, but they also engage in other forms of cooperation, including food sharing and group territorial behavior.[39] Maternal half siblings cooperate in all of these contexts more often than do unrelated individuals.[40] As with female baboons, kinship affects the development and maintenance of social bonds between male chimpanzees; strong bonds form selectively between maternal brothers, with some persisting for seven years.[41]

Kin biases in male behavior have been documented in other primate species characterized by male dispersal. Male Hanuman langurs in India and squirrel monkeys in South America form "migration alliances" by dispersing together, and allied males are assumed to be paternal brothers.[42] Studies using genetic data suggest that closely related male gorillas disperse to adjacent areas. Perhaps as a consequence, relatively peaceful interactions occur during subsequent intergroup encounters involving these males.[43] Finally, male red howler monkeys cooperate with kin to defend groups of females.[44] Related males form alliances that last longer than those between non-kin, dominance-rank relationships are relatively stable between kin, and dominant males sire most, if not all, of the infants. These observations suggest that subordinate males cooperate to help related dominants, who reap most of the benefits of group life.

KIN SELECTION AND ITS LIMITS

Around the time that Japanese primatologists were making their seminal observations on macaques, a British biologist, W. D. Hamilton, was developing a simple, elegant, and compelling evolutionary theory to explain why animals typically exhibit kin bias. Hamilton reasoned that although individuals are the units on which the process of natural selection operates, they are not the units of inheritance.[45] Instead, the entities passed from generation to generation are genes, and genes are shared differentially with others: relatives share more genes with each other than do non-kin. From this reasoning, Hamilton concluded that natural selection would lead to the evolution of traits that increase the survival and reproduction of kin. This process, dubbed "kin selection," predicts that beneficial acts will occur primarily between close genetic relatives. This prediction has been empirically validated not only in primates but also in insects, birds, and additional mammals.[46]

Although empirical observations generally conform to predictions derived from kin-selection theory, several factors other than kinship exert a strong influence on the behavior of primates. Recent studies of wild chimpanzees show that male chimpanzees, which are known to bias their behavior toward their maternal brothers, fail to affiliate and cooperate preferentially with their paternal brothers because they appear unable to recognize their paternal kin. Thus the impact of kinship on behavior is limited to only half the population. Demographic factors place additional constraints on the opportunities for maternal kin to interact. There is a 50:50 sex ratio at birth among chimps, with females producing infants only once every five to six years.[47] Coupled with high rates of infant mortality, these statistics make it likely that adult males will not possess maternal siblings. Lacking close relatives, some male chimpanzees cooperate frequently with non-kin.[48] Similarly, strong social bonds do not exist exclusively between close kin but occur among related and unrelated individuals alike.[49] Long-lasting bonds develop between unrelated males who maintain equitable social relationships, as evidenced by balanced grooming interactions.

Additional research indicates that female chimpanzees may also form strong social bonds in the absence of kinship.[50] Females are the dispersing sex in this species, and recent genetic analyses indicate that females seldom move into communities with their relatives.[51] As a result, long-lasting relationships develop primarily between unrelated individuals, although, like male chimpanzees, females maintain strong bonds with their kin.[52]

Long-term social relationships are a prominent feature of primate behavior, and factors other than kinship affect their formation and maintenance. Primates cultivate relationships with non-kin to obtain adaptive benefits.[53] For example, unrelated individuals reciprocate grooming and exchange it for coalitionary support, tolerance at feeding sites, and access to newborn infants.[54] Female baboons gain protection against infanticide and aggression by establishing long-term bonds with unrelated males.[55] Unrelated male chimpanzees trade meat, a scarce resource, for help in fights.[56] In baboons, females who form strong social bonds with others produce more offspring than other females.[57]

Social relationships between unrelated primates may also have significant emotional and psychological effects. Female baboons who groom with a small number of predictable partners have lower levels of stress hormones than do animals with more diverse grooming networks, and females display high levels of these hormones after the death of preferred grooming partners.[58] These results suggest that, as is the case in humans, social bonds may play an important role in mitigating stress.[59]

This review suggests that primate life is embedded in networks of social relationships in which kin are distinguished from non-kin. Kinship affects the development and maintenance of these relationships. Despite its deep roots in our primate past, however, kinship is only one of several factors that influence the behavior of our closest living relatives. These observations lay the groundwork for understanding the role of kinship in human societies.

THE EVIDENCE OF KINSHIP CATEGORIES

Mapping the social traits of primates, Rodseth and colleagues find that the majority (thirty-six out of forty-eight species) live in communities practicing male dispersal, in which female kin form the core of society.[60] Facts of this order have led some authors, including Chris Knight, to propose that early human kinship was matrilineal.[61] Yet our closest relatives, chimpanzees, have female dispersal and enduring male relationships. Neither scenario can be entirely ruled out for the starting point of the evolutionary story of human kinship, though the second seems more likely. Inevitably, an element of uncertainty dogs our attempts to trace the deep history of kinship through primatology.

We have already mentioned the imaginative attempt by Chapais to combine primatology and social anthropology to reconstruct the evolution of modern human kinship. The "leap" into kinship that we find in the theory of Lévi-Strauss assumes that human kinship is without precedent among other animals, posing reciprocal exogamy as a complex, integral package of traits best treated as a stupendous human invention. Chapais's principal move is to turn the leap into a gradual evolution by decomposing the uniquely human configuration of reciprocal exogamy into twelve elementary building blocks, which he arranges as an ordinal set. By way of this twelve-step program, a human-chimp ancestor is turned into a reciprocal-exogamic modern human being with a kinship terminology. The twelve steps, from earliest to latest, include:

multimale-multifemale group composition

kin-group outbreeding

uterine kinship

incest avoidance

stable breeding bonds

agnatic (patrilineal) kinship

bilateral affinity

the tribe

postmarital residence patterns

the brother-sister complex

descent

matrimonial exchange

Chapais gives extensive evidence and causal argumentation for these steps in his book. He argues for a tendency toward agnatic kinship in our primate ancestors, not the matrilineal tendency that is more widespread among primates. We also observe that Chapais finds in the "brother-sister complex" a prelinguistic tendency toward exchange and incest avoidance, consistent with Lévi-Strauss's view of early kinship. The argument has the appeal of continuity, in that it shows how a momentous transformation could have emerged from a series of simple changes. However, these changes are numerous in the aggregate, and each moving part would have to work for the whole machinery to have functioned as proposed.

Taking the primatological evidence as a rough guide to the state of kinship among our earliest human ancestors, we may assume at the bare minimum both the recognition of kinship relations between a given individual and some close kin, and recognition by a given individual of some close kinship relations among others. Moving to the more recent past, the advent of language had the potential to greatly expand the reach and multiply the categories of kinship over time, enabling an almost unlimited attribution of kinship to other humans and other-than-human entities, including gods, animals, and plants.

The study of language is central to the scientific study of human kinship, and it was a deep-history project from the outset. Seeking the earliest forms of human kinship relations, Morgan modeled his project on comparative philology, which constructed family trees of languages around the world.[62] As chapter 5 shows, a simple early device for comparing languages to determine their historical relationships was the word list, a vocabulary of words thought most likely to be primitive and conservative: words for numbers, parts of the body, and the like. Among these words were kinship terms, such as *father, mother, sister, brother, son,* and *daughter.* Although cognates of such terms are often obscured by sound shifts or borrowing of new words, it is striking that, for example, the equivalents of these in Sanskrit, in use three thousand years ago, are still recognizable as cognates of modern English: *pitr, matr, svasa, bhratr, sunu, duhitr.* Such resemblances were the basis for the claim that English and Sanskrit, in spite of the time and space separating them, belong to the same family of historically related languages, called Indo-European.

Realizing the power of this simple analytical tool, Morgan applied it in a new way. He took the kinship terms of the word list and conceived them as a set. For example, the kinship terms above can be arrayed in a matrix:

father	mother
brother	sister
son	daughter

The terms in each row are distinguished by gender, and those in columns are distinguished by *generation*. Gender has two values, male and female; and generation has three values, parents' generation, my generation, and children's generation. The six terms form a set. People I call *father* and *mother* call me *son* or *daughter;* the terms form a reciprocal set, and the terms *brother* and *sister* form another. Taken together, the terms constitute a map of social location. Morgan had discovered that kinship terms form a set, or system, and he put this knowledge to use in a worldwide comparison of kinship terminologies, or, as he called them, "systems of consanguinity and affinity of the human family," a phrase that provided the title for his great book.[63]

The set can be expanded by adding another dimension, which doubles the number of items:

father	mother	uncle	aunt
brother	sister	cousin (male)	cousin (female)
son	daughter	nephew	niece

What is the new dimension? We could call it *lineality* and say that the first two columns are relatives in the same line, or *lineals,* and the other two are *collaterals.* The category *cousin* is unmarked for gender in English. The collateral categories contain people related in different ways; for example, an uncle can be a father's brother or a mother's brother, or even the genetically unrelated spouse of a father's sister or a mother's sister. My lineal kin are few—one father and one mother, a few siblings and children—but my relations with them are intense, whereas my collateral kin may be more numerous, but my relations with them are less intense.

These relationships are all familiar to English speakers. What Morgan found surprising about the Iroquois was that the father's brother was called *father* and the mother's sister was called *mother;* an individual could thus have multiple fathers and mothers and correspondingly fewer uncles and aunts. Indeed, insofar as these kinship categories were applied to all persons of the older generation, one might even have fathers and

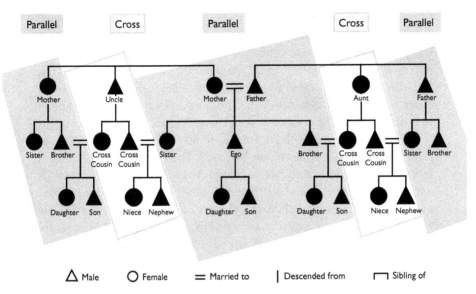

FIGURE 17. Genealogical chart showing cross and parallel kin.

mothers one had not met in another village. The children of all these fathers and mothers were, logically, one's brothers and sisters, as opposed to a roughly equal number of cousins. Thus the English-language dimension of *lineal* and *collateral* is here replaced by a different dimension, which we call *crossness* (see chapter 2). The lineal categories have been redefined and enlarged; they comprise *parallel* kin, whereas the redefined and reduced collateral kin have been turned into *cross* kin.

The principle involved in crossness was named "same-sex sibling merging" by Floyd Lounsbury.[64] The father's brother, a same-sex sibling of the father, is merged with father; the same goes for the mother's sister. As for my sibling's children, if I am female, by the same principle my sister's children are called *son* and *daughter,* and I call my brother's children *nephew* and *niece.* If I am male, my brother's children are son and daughter, and my sister's children are nephew and niece. The whole three-generation set is divided into cross and parallel kin. This distinction is extended to the most distant relatives in these generations, so that the social map is divided like a checkerboard into squares of cross and parallel relations (figure 17).

Crossness comes in several varieties, the differences among them having to do with the logic by which crossness is extended to distant relatives. Viveiros de Castro recognizes eight different patterns of crossness, all of them having real-life examples, and Tjon Sie Fat finds sixteen logical possibilities.[65] All are similar in dividing the most distant relatives into two social categories. In all, parallel kin are forbidden to marry, and marriage is permitted only with cross kin or strangers. The main difference concerns systems of the Iroquois or Dravidian types, linked to a difference in the treatment of relatives by marriage—affines or in-laws. Where the Iroquois have a separate set of terms for in-laws, as in English (father-in-law, mother-in-law, etc.), Dravidian systems of South India and others like them have a rule of cross-cousin marriage, according to which a brother and sister, and all other kin described as parallel, may not marry, but their children, who are cross kin, *should* marry. The rule of marriage is reflected in the kinship terminology: all in-laws are merged with blood relatives, and there are no separate terms for in-laws.

N. J. Allen's tetradic theory proposes a deep history of human kinship that carries this compression of categories to the extreme. Allen posits as a starting point the most highly compressed system of categories possible, an ideal type having only four categories, which he calls the tetradic system. He achieves this compression by merging in-laws and blood relatives (as in the Dravidian system) and reducing the generations from three or more to only two, my generation and the other generation; that is, he posits a scheme of alternating generations by which I, my grandparents, and my grandchildren belong to one generation, and my parents and children belong to the other (there are real-world examples of this scheme). He proposes that the history of human kinship begins with a tetradic system and proceeds by the opening out and multiplication of categories. Thus two alternating generations give way to a lineal series of generations, and in-laws are decoupled from blood relatives. Previously, to facilitate understanding, we analytically transformed English to Iroquois to Dravidian, but Allen's theory holds that the deep history of kinship goes in the other direction, from tetradic to Dravidian to Iroquois, and through further steps to English.

Lévi-Strauss's alliance theory operates on rules of marriage rather than categories of kinship, but the two theories offer a similar trajectory for the deep history of kinship, moving from something like Dravidian to something like English, deemed "elementary" and "complex" respectively by Lévi-Strauss. Both are theories of discontinuity, in which kinship comes into existence by a leap. Lévi-Strauss treats the causes of the leap as a mystery; Allen imagines the leap as being performed in space, by the moving bodies of dancing relatives arranged in pairs. The cross-cutting dimensions of kinship were spontaneously performed by opposing sets of dancers long before the system was articulated as categories of thought, rather like Diaghilev's primitive dancers performing *The Rite of Spring* or, more to the point, the seasonal gatherings of foragers in the Kalahari Desert or in Australia, during which collective effervescence took the form of dancing. Neither of these theories speaks across the divide separating the natural from the social sciences, but we have already seen how Bernard Chapais does so, turning the alliance theory of Lévi-Strauss into a theory of continuity through a series of small steps.

Lévi-Strauss, Allen, and Chapais agree on the overall direction of the deep history of kinship. For Lévi-Strauss the progression is from elementary, direct forms of marriage exchange to complex, indirect forms; for Allen it is from simple terminologies having few categories to complex ones having many. But we are a long way from being able to ground these shifts in evidence drawn from deep history. Until such evidence is found, we need to consider alternatives. To be sure, crossness is widespread in the world. But it is a curious fact that the lineal pattern, considered complex by Lévi-Strauss, is shared by speakers of English, the Khoisan hunter-gatherers of southern Africa, and numerous Arctic hunter-gatherer societies; indeed, anthropologists call kinship terminologies of this type *Eskimo*. This fact alone shows that there is no simple connection between kinship terminology and subsistence economy and, conversely, that kinship terminologies are platforms on which the most diverse kinds of economy, in very different climates, can be built.

To complete the picture, we should mention two other kinship systems that are familiar to ethnographers. In moving from lineality to crossness, from English to Iroquois, lineal categories are enlarged at the expense of collateral ones. Suppose the lineal categories were enlarged without limit until they absorbed all collateral kin, and all my kin became fathers, mothers, sisters, brothers, sons and daughters. That would be the type of kinship that anthropologists call *generational,* or *Hawaiian.* Or suppose, in contrast, that the collateral kin were subdivided by finer discriminations, so that cousins on my father's side and mother's side were designated by different terms, and so forth. That would be of the type of kinship anthropologists call *bifurcate collateral,* or *Sudanese.* These systems, as their names indicate, have real-world examples.

How do we trace the overall arc of kinship history among these types? How do we identify the starting point and rule out other possibilities? Alan Barnard, for one, argues for the precedence of Hawaiian, Eskimo, and Sudanese types over those with crossness.[66] There is no simple way to decide between these possibilities without comparison, careful mapping of the distribution of kinship terminologies in time and space, and related methods for determining the character of kinship relations at great temporal distances. To date, even the boldest analyses, based on the emerging synthesis of genomic, archaeological, and linguistic data, can take us back only about fifteen thousand years; and even at this early date, all the kinship systems discussed here, from the lineal Eskimo to the crisscrossing Iroquois, already existed on the continent of Africa, the point of origin for the global expansion of modern *Homo sapiens,* sixty thousand years ago.[67]

WHOLE-BODY KINSHIP

Most anthropologists would probably agree that Darwin's "hidden bond of descent" uniting Morgan's "Human Family" is but a subset of the "infinitude of connecting links, between the living and extinct inhabitants of the world" proposed by Darwin.[68] Social anthropologists since Morgan have also argued that the bonds uniting the human family are socially constructed. Anthropologists differ over whether kinship involves the social recognition of biological ties or is largely independent of biological relations and processes.[69] The latter view originated with a contemporary of Darwin and Morgan, Sir Henry Maine (1822–88). Maine's *Ancient Society* (1861) is a study of kinship among the ancient Romans as expressed in their legal codes, which he took to be the historical source of kinship in Europe.

Out of all possible ways of conceptualizing family ties, the ancient Romans combined agnation, or patrilineal descent, with adoption, whence their "memorable legal maxim, 'mulier est finis familiae'—a woman is the terminus of the family. A female name closes the branch or twig of the genealogy in which it occurs." Maine then posed a question that has preoccupied students of kinship ever since: "What then is the reason of this arbitrary inclusion and exclusion? Why should a conception of Kinship, so elastic as to include strangers brought into the family by adoption, be nevertheless so narrow as to shut out the descendants of a female member?"[70] Maine's answer was that Roman kinship was based not on biology but on power: what the ancients called *patria potestas,* or "power of the father." Feminist anthropologists reanalyzing Nuer society as described by Evans-Pritchard—a paradigmatic case of agnation in anthropology—came to the same conclusion and went further.[71] Descent through males, they argued, is the dominant ideology of kinship among the Nuer. However, it coexists with other ways of reckoning kinship, for example, through women, residence, surrogate forms of procreation, and multiple forms of marriage.[72] As it happens, the Nuer term for an agnatic lineage (*thok dwiel* or *thok mac*) also means the doorway to a house or its hearth; kinship among agnates (*buth*) is called "sharing" and is conceptually linked to diverse forms of support and mutual caring.[73] We may call the tendency of these developments "whole-body kinship" for its way of viewing categories, practices, and bodies together. Taking a whole-body perspective, how might we understand the workings of plural systems of kinship in deep time?

Maine conceived deep time as the Before and After. Before, humans followed the law of the wild, like animals. After, they developed codes of behavior and became "stationary" like the Romans. They were on their way to becoming "progressive" by shifting from kinship to contract through the use of "legal fictions."[74] For Maine, adoption was "fictive" kinship because it did not conform to reality as defined in law and supported by the *potestas* of some over others. Based on the research that Maine's work inspired, we can see that official forms of kinship never embrace the entirety of a society's kinshipping practices, and thus systems are always plural.

Like the Roman laws separating Maine's Before and After, dominant forms of kinship are apt to be hedged round with words—legal codes, genealogies, histories, and the like—more than their alternatives, whether the alternatives are deemed illegal, unreal, tabooed from speech, or simply less spoken and more enacted, as are behaviors like sheltering, feeding, and grooming. We have been speaking for at least 200,000 years, so none of our more recent ways of kinshipping can be called pre- or nonlinguistic.[75] Yet recognizing the extent to which we relate through our whole bodies may provide clues to our deeper history, of some 2 million years, and perhaps bring our speaking years into sharper relief. Because human kinship involves the exercise of power in which some thrive while others dwindle, a whole-body approach may help us understand "fitness" in terms of both political and biological factors.

KINSHIPPING IN SPACE-TIME: HOUSES AND HOUSE LIFE

People everywhere praise speech as the epitome of humanness, however diverse our conceptions of humanity might be. Yet recent research shows that the development of speaking in children is associated with pointing, and thus language is not limited to vocal and auditory behavior but includes gestures and other bodily movements.[76] Speech is inherently spatial; and so kinship, as developed in speech, is developed in space as well. Morgan's wonder at the matrilineal kinship of the Iroquois, for instance, extended to their housing and hospitality. They laid out their longhouses with apartments for members of a matrilineal clan segment on one side and hearths on the other, with two families to a hearth. The Iroquois imagined clusters of longhouses as a body extending the length of their home country, from its feet at the Hudson River to its head at Niagara Falls. As for their hospitality: "Perhaps no people ever carried this principle to the same degree of universality, as did the Iroquois," who made their houses open day and night to kin and strangers alike.[77] After running out of room in *Systems of Consanguinity and Affinity* (1871), Morgan published a deep history of *Houses and House-Life of the American Aborigines* (1881), which was based on archaeological as well as ethnographic data. He felt that the "law of hospitality" indicated "a plan of life" that was the foundation of kinship.[78]

For Morgan, "houses and house-life" existed alongside descent and marriage. For Lévi-Strauss, whose comparative analysis of "house societies" (*sociétés à maison*) was inspired by the great named houses of the Kwakiutl (*Kwagu'ł*) people of the Pacific Northwest coast (now part of the Kwakwaka'wakw First Nations), houses in their social and historical materiality stand as alternatives to structures of descent and alliance, containing if not resolving their contradictions.[79] For Morgan, hospitality is the heart of the house; for Lévi-Strauss, houses shelter wealth, their growth and inheritance enduring beyond the lives and deaths of their inhabitants.

In Florence in the fourteenth and fifteenth centuries, houses were made by men and *were* men. The *casa* comprised the building, the domestic group, and the entire agnatic kin group—"all ancestors and living members of a lineage, all those in whose veins the same blood ran, who bore the same name, and who claimed a common ancestor"—and their collective wealth.[80] Women were noted by their "entrances" and "exits" (*entrate* and *uscite*) into and out of the houses of their families of origin or alliance.[81] Val Daniel's study of Tamil speakers in a Hindu village in southern India shows beautifully how a Tamil house acquires the attributes of a living, breathing person whose "horoscope, *kunam* [qualities, dispositions], and even 'feelings' (houses can have evil eye, feel lonely, and so on)" are intimately related to the health and well-being of its residents in ways that they try to control, without always succeeding.[82]

Houses too have their systems. Their kinshipping logic is multiscalar, extending from familial dwellings to communitywide structures articulating relations among people deemed kin or strangers, grand or small, living, dead, or ancestral, in shallow time or deep. Archaeologists now believe that the great Bronze Age monuments of the British Isles, like Stonehenge (built around 4,500 years ago) and Avebury (built 4,400 to 4,000 years ago), were oriented toward the dark moon as a source of ritual power while incorporating new solar cosmologies associated with cattle herding. Based on archaeo-astronomical and other data, Sims argues that Silsbury Hill, a cropped chalk cone in the Avebury complex, aligned with the dark moon on the longest night of the year and located along a downward slope to a river, enabled pilgrims from all over southern Britain to enter the "underworld" of their forebears and then return to the world of the living.[83]

Such landmarks show how houses become worlds and worlds become houses, a transformation that is not confined to modern human societies. The ranging patterns of chimpanzees in Gombe National Park, Tanzania, are shaped largely by the need to find food. Murray and colleagues found that male chimpanzees typically forage widely across the entire territory of their community.[84] During periods of food shortage, however, they restrict their movements to smaller parts of the territory, especially areas where they followed their mothers when young and dependent. The pattern of returning "home" during food-poor times occurs even when mothers have died, suggesting the importance of social memory in retaining parental teaching across generations. If we consider nonhuman primates' territories as "houses," or more generally as "containers," in Gamble's sense, we might be able to integrate the analysis of settlement and ranging patterns across hominin and other primate groups in deep time.[85]

Evidence of "locales" in the form of scatters—for example, the cluster of wood and flint chips, seeds, and nuts at Gesher Benot Ya'aqov in what is now Israel—dates back to some 780,000 years ago; evidence of multiple hearths to 400,000 ya; burials in caves to 350,000 ya; hearths in caves to 160,000 ya; and cooking hearths to 80,000 ya.[86] Recently archaeologists at Gesher Benot Ya'aqov have argued that the scatters in layers dating to about 790,000 to 690,000 years ago represent separate food-preparation and hearth work areas.[87] Yet the patterns of materials associated with hearths during and after that period elsewhere, perhaps for lack of evidence, still seem so idiosyncratic and unfamiliar that they are rarely identifiable either as apes' nests or as shelters. Kolen describes them as "centrifugal living structures" that accumulated as hominins dropped and tossed things about them in their living and dying.[88] Even the so-called housepits at the open-air locale of Kostenki (in modern Ukraine) of some 28,000 ya, which contain exotic shells and amber as well as broken bits of figurines, seem to be the outcome of accumulating rather than building.[89] Expanding our understanding of dwelling in terms of what Ingold calls "way-finding" (perhaps comparable to range finding among other primates or the social carnivores with whom hominins were closely involved) may help to explain how these paths and places of accumulation developed into the shelterlike containers that began to appear some 20,000 ya. Structures that we would recognize as houses began to appear only in the last 11,000 years, in agricultural settlements associated with the intensification of containments and accumulations of all kinds.[90]

KINSHIP, SEXUALITY, AND SOCIAL REPRODUCTION THROUGH FOOD

Are you still one house? In Madagascar this is a blunt way of asking if you are still married. Linguistic systems of kinship, gender, and sexuality—like terminologies, genealogies, and naming systems—must also be understood in terms of what happens in and about the house: eating, feeding others, and often, but not always, sex. In Zhizao in southwest China (where adolescents move to the barn), it is embarrassing and potentially dangerous even for the married couple of the household to sleep on the man's bed at the higher, upstream end of the house, overlooked by paternal ancestors and guardian spirits. "To have sex there would be as offensive as to give birth or menstruate there."[91] Housing articulates these relations as powerfully as the speech in which they are expressed or tabooed from expression.

Studies of kinshipping through housing show that oral and aural modes of articulating kinship through kin terms are associated with other forms of orality, like eating, which are far older than speaking or housing. "Milk kinship"—the bond between a woman and her nursling—is one of the most widespread forms of kinship established through food. In Islamic law, relations of closeness (*qarābah*) are distinguished according to whether they are through descent (*nasab*), through alliances like marriage (*musāharah*), or through breastfeeding (*ridā*). Marriage is forbidden between nurse and nursling and between nurslings who have suckled at the same breasts, even when the nurse is not the birth mother of the infants who shared her milk.[92] Milk kinship, along with other forms of fosterage, was basic to forming tributary political alliances throughout Eurasia, Africa, and Oceania over the past 2,000 years.[93] Although milk kinship is no longer the basis of far-flung alliances, it retains its legal significance in many Muslim settings. In Lebanon, for example, milk kinship is crucial in resolving ethical issues involved in new reproductive technologies like in vitro fertilization and surrogacy.[94]

The association between food and sexuality may be universal in humans. The commonest way of articulating restrictions on sexuality and marriage is through food taboos. These have commonly been interpreted as metaphorical, in contrast to the biology of sexuality. Yet cross-cultural research shows that notions of food and sex cannot always be easily distinguished in this way. In the Trobriand Islands, for example, sexual intercourse between a woman and a man is crucial to creating children because it is believed to be a nourishing act; the man's semen feeds the maternal ancestral spirit that the woman is growing in her womb.

Intercourse is one among many exchanges of food through which the couple and their kin are linked. Intimate, if not sexual, relations between a sister and her brothers in the matrilineage are essential to a proper death, because only by returning the equivalent of the gifts from the father and his kin (mainly in the form of foods and banana-fiber cloths, which Trobrianders see as related to the substances of human bodies) can the spirit of the dead person be returned to its matrilineal kin to rejoin its ancestors.[95] Throughout Southeast Asia, couples use brother-sister terms as endearments, suggesting the value of taking a broader view of social reproduction in which pair bonds between spouses or mates may be structurally and historically related to pair bonds between siblings.

The earliest hominins found so far in Eurasia provide a striking example of caring through feeding. The cluster of five small-brained, short-armed, long-legged, and highly sexually dimorphic fossils found near Dmanisi (in present-day Georgia) in the foothills of the Caucasus Mountains, and dated to 1.77 million years ago, are thought to be a very early form of *Homo erectus*. The remains include a rare example of an adult incapable of chewing. All but one of its teeth are missing, and bone had actually reformed around the holes in the jaw, suggesting that the teeth were lost long before the individual died. The altitude of the site, associated animal bones, and stone artifacts show that these hominins were hunters. Lordkipanidze and colleagues believe their carnivorous diet must have required mutual care, especially the care of indi-

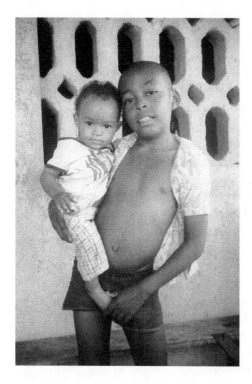

FIGURE 18. Brother and baby sister, northwest Madagascar, 1989. Humans are the only living primate species in which close brother-sister bonds are sustained throughout life. They are also the only primates among whom juveniles know and regularly interact with their mothers' male kin. (Photo by Gillian Feeley-Harnik.)

viduals who could eat only soft foods (like brains, bone marrow, and plants).[96] If kinshipping is caring in some ontologically basic way, perhaps derived ultimately from mother-child relations, then we might see pair-bonding siblings and spouses as divergent elaborations of intimacy expressed in new patterns of caring, which eventually became the multiple systems of kinship and affinity we know now (figure 18).[97]

BINDING TIES: KINSHIP AND MEMORY

Relations of caring and affection are held together by powerful combinations of containers and instruments, to use Gamble's terminology.[98] In Renaissance Florence, necklaces, diadems, belts, and especially rings—as many as twenty or thirty made of precious metals and stones—were the most important gifts from the groom and his family to the bride on the day she moved from her father's house into her husband's. Their circular form, encircling the body of the bride, bound her to her husband, his father, and their family—including the women who married into the house before her. These women gave her the rings they received at their own *nozze,* thus renewing the many alliances through which the agnatic house endured and grew over time.[99] Traditions of this sort can be followed deep into the human past, as can the objects central to them. Steven Kuhn and Mary Stiner interpret the beads of shell, horn, bone, and stone that begin to appear in exchange networks in Africa and Eurasia around 90,000 to 100,000 years ago, and in Europe by 40,000 years ago, as "information technology," varying in their "durability," "standardization," "quantity," "expression of investment differential," "transferability," "cost," and, we should add, extent of wear and repair.[100] How do we understand the mnemonic properties of artifacts deliberately intended to bind relations over time and space?

Their spatiality seems to be one key factor. The centuries-old "method of loci" or the "memory palace" known to the Greeks and Romans and revived in Renaissance Europe is a memory-enhancing technique based on visualizing items to be remembered in a sequence of places, like tokens (or instruments) in containers, then recalling the items by mentally revisiting the places and removing them in the same order.[101] The places visualized may be real or imaginary. The predilection for using houses or even imaginary palaces as settings for this exercise is a striking comment on how we have grown accustomed to ordering the world as a series of nested containers. Putting containers within containers seems to have increased the number and complexity of items we can remember.

An outstanding ethnographic example of the method of loci in practice can be found in Joëlle Bahloul's *The Architecture of Memory,* a study of an extended family of Jews who moved to France from Algeria in 1962.[102] These immigrants and their children remember their common origin in *Dar-Refayil,* "the house of Raphael," a multifamily building in Sétif, where their maternal grandfather's family lived with other Jewish and Muslim families. Now settled in Nice, Lyons, Marseille, and Paris, "the children of Dar-Refayil" (who follow the old country custom of identifying themselves by house rather than surname) remember their origins in the men's house as if it were a womb. The tokens from the house include old photographs, clothes, pots, and other mementos, the most inclusive of which are foods. The children of Dar-Refayil are reborn through the regular consumption of *t'fina,* a lamb stew cooked on Thursday and Friday and served on the Sabbath, as well as on other ritual occasions. The sensory experiences of tasting, touching, smelling, seeing, hearing, and speaking are associated with pots, rooms, and houses. They bring individuals living in far-flung cities into one cosmic place.

Ecologists would describe the *t'fina* and other ritual foods as "sensory traps," as "signal mimics that elicit out-of-context behaviors by exploiting the adaptive, neural responses of signal receivers."[103] In this case, the "signal mimics" of current houses and foods facilitate the memories associated with sensory patterns laid down in actual childhood. Ecologists have long studied how animals attract mates and prey using sensory traps. David Edwards and Douglas Yu argue for the importance of sensory traps in the development and maintenance of mutualism among animals and plants.[104] Sarah Blaffer Hrdy argues that babies are sensory traps that facilitated cooperative behavior in our early human ancestors about 2 million years ago.[105]

Perhaps kinship terminologies evolved to articulate the power of sensory traps like babies, mothers, meals, hearths, pits, and houses. Given the increasing significance of language in hominin relations over the past 200,000 years, basic systems of kin terms might have developed as memory traps, counters to the massive migrations that saw our forebears disperse over 75 percent of the globe in 1 percent of the time elapsed since their divergence from other primates.[106] Kinship has certainly done heavy memory work in more recent times. For the past several thousand years, genealogies have been important mnemonic forms, closely associated with the exercise of religious and political power in all historically documented societies. Among the first forms of knowledge to be committed to writing, genealogies now flourish on the Internet. Genetic pedigrees, widely believed to root people deeply in time, are major expressions of a very old human commitment to remembering our ancestors.[107] These genomic data are housed within our own bodies, but they are also kept in powerful institutions, from public hospitals to private businesses with rival claims to define our humanity (as illustrated in the debates raging among bioethicists over the merits and abuses of genetic testing).[108] The steady fading away and rejuvenation of human memory, an existential problem to which kinshipping was perhaps our earliest and most durable solution, is evident in the very question that prompts this book: who are we?

WAYS FORWARD

Let us now gather up the threads of discussion and look for a way forward to a deep history of human kinship. The results of comparative primatology suggest that at the point where chimps and humans branched off from one another, 5 to 8 million years ago, there already existed a limited recognition of kin, and, more important, a higher-order recognition of the kinship relations of others. In addition, there must have been many affiliative relations with individuals who were not close genetic kin. One way of expressing the primatological data would be to say that chimpanzees have affiliative relations with some (genetic) kin and some (genetic) non-kin, but a better way would be to say that chimps have a sense of *social* kinship that they share with humans.[109] Social kinship is decidedly oral, involving vocalizing, nursing, and grooming, even when it lacks spoken language. We might say that primate dispersal patterns create metaphoric houses and house life for members of one sex or the other, resulting in different patterns of affiliation. When males leave and females stay, females are generally more sociable than males. Communal nursing occurs in a few primates and other animals, leading to social bonds among females and youngsters formed directly through food. Primates occasionally form groups consisting of individuals of entirely different species. There are many ways in which primate comparisons can be seen as tracking the expansive kinship of humans, though in more limited ways.

However, we should probably avoid making too much of similarities between humans and other primates. The differences, which are many, can be summarized as the limited extent and effects of social kinship among primates other than humans. With respect to extent, kinship is often manifest only in the mother-child relation, even within chimp social groups based on male solidarity; with respect to effects, kinship sometimes seems to make a difference in behavior, other times not. Human kinship is vastly more extensive. It creates relations on the maternal and paternal sides and frequently extends far back in time, through descent, or laterally, through crossness. Language and the ability to use symbols generally allow humans to develop the more extensive and pervasive effects of kinship, both social and biological. Less clear is the matter of chronology. It is inherently difficult to date the emergence of language, and it may be pointless to try, as our linguistic abilities have been evolving in tandem with our brains, our diets, and our modes of social interaction for hundreds of thousands of years.

One way forward may be to try to understand the deep history of human kinship by a gradual thickening of social kinship, a concept that has clearly played a fundamental role in our biological evolution. Widening the framework of human kinship to include relations among species and the environments they share would create a more expansive ecology of kinship, one that necessarily includes closer attention to the materiality of caring over time. Kinship, in this view, could be reconceptualized as the outcome of coevolution between human beings, the object worlds they have made through interaction, and the plants and animals they gathered, hunted, and eventually domesticated. For this approach to work, the old Hegelian divide will have to be demolished and new relationships between nature and history will have to be worked out in a language that human kinship has already equipped us to devise.

PART FOUR

Human Expansion

CHAPTER 8

Migration

TIMOTHY EARLE AND CLIVE GAMBLE
WITH HENDRIK POINAR

Darwin's bulldog, Thomas Huxley, knew something of world travel and exploration, but he was scathing when it came to speculative theories about human migrations in the past. In *Man's Place in Nature,* with his guns trained on the ethnologists (those trying to make sense of the miscellany of newly "discovered" world societies) and particularly their views on cradles of the human race, Huxley growled, "It is one thing to allow that a given migration is possible and another to admit there is good reason to believe it has really taken place."[1] At a time of few fossil skulls and no science-based dating for the emerging discipline of archaeology, he demanded evidence, not opinions. Yet his experiences while sailing on *HMS Rattlesnake* in 1846 had introduced him, as they had Darwin in the 1830s, to the bald fact that humans were found nearly everywhere. Humans had come from some place, and Huxley assumed that their global journeys had begun in remote antiquity, when people were not "impelled to wander by any desire nobler or stronger than hunger."[2] He vehemently opposed attempts to explain ancient migrations based on superficial biological observations and spurious histories of the deep human past. He railed against the "intellectual hocus-pocus" that surrounded ethnology, a field beset by its fascination for (perfectly Caucasian) Georgian skulls, the Asiatic origins of humanity, and the notion that shared languages, skin colors, or toolkits were compelling evidence of shared biological descent. From an evolutionary perspective, Huxley realized that human migration provided opportunities for natural selection to produce the physical variation visible among contemporary human populations. Yet once the prejudices of popular ethnological frameworks were effectively exposed, he lost interest in migration.

Over the past century, as scientific methods have improved, our ability to collect reliable information on the movement of peoples in the deep past has attained a rigor Huxley could not have foreseen, and migration has once again assumed a central place in our understanding of human evolution.[3] We now realize that migration across great distances is one of the fundamental processes of human history. By a thousand years ago, people had journeyed to the uttermost ends of the Earth. From their African homeland, humans have colonized all continents and inhabitable islands, from seashores to alpine mountains, from high-latitude arctic tundra to tropical deserts and forests. They have done this remarkably quickly. In only 1 percent of the time since we split from the great apes, humans have covered the Earth. Starting some 60,000 years ago, entire hemispheres, continents, and oceans were traversed for the first time, often by people using only hunting and gathering technologies. The descendants of these early travelers were waiting on the shore to be "discovered" by James Cook, Darwin, Huxley, and all the other European explorers, scientists, missionaries, and imperial adventurers who, like London buses, took a long time to arrive but then came all at once.

The history of human migration is dauntingly complex. Even with the first settlement of regions, new migrations continued often at even greater rates, displacing earlier settlers, forcing removals and relocations, creating regional movements of marriage partners and workers, funneling vast populations through colonial and postcolonial global economies, and creating diverse, intermingled diasporas. In recent historical periods, rich documentary evidence allows us to reconstruct the details of human migration, including the numbers of people involved, prevailing social and economic conditions, and the most compelling reasons for movement. For earlier periods, for which written sources are fragmentary or absent and biological and archaeological remains are the only data available, understanding patterns of migration presents formidable challenges. Using new molecular, linguistic, and archaeological evidence, we can broaden our understanding of the role of migration in deep history. To this end, we propose an approach that emphasizes how migration has been affected by changes in human densities, scales, and institutions over time. We link these changes to three key transitions: the development of technology and symbolic communication among early *Homo sapiens;* population increase and the growth of settled communities among early farmers; and the emergence of political economy in complex societies. These are only signposts along a network of trails that winds through human history, but they can help us understand processes that have dominated our recent and remote past, casting us in the roles of settlers, occupiers, conquerors, slaves, laborers, and entrepreneurs.

METHODOLOGICAL ADVANCES IN THE STUDY OF MIGRATION

The challenge for migration studies is to bridge the gap between shallow and deep histories based respectively on documentary and material evidence. This was Huxley's dilemma as well: he knew that human migrations had occurred, but he rejected the just so stories that, when concocted without solid evidence, led inevitably to conclusions that justified the present. In keeping with the precedent set by Huxley, British social anthropology rejected the study of early human migration. A.R. Radcliffe-Brown famously argued that an ahistorical, structural-functional approach was necessary because nonliterate peoples had not produced historical records, by which he obviously meant textual evidence and written accounts.[4] Since World War II, however, radical changes in the tempo and direction of scientific inquiry have opened up new possibilities for deep-time studies of migration, and these openings are based on research techniques that no longer privilege the distinction between literate and nonliterate peoples.

First, archaeological research has expanded dramatically over the past sixty years. Support from private and public funding has grown as archaeology has become an indispensable asset to nation builders, tourism boards, and the managers of heritage politics worldwide. Comprehensive fieldwork is now being done throughout Europe, North America, Australia, the Middle East, Asia, Africa, and the Pacific. The blank spaces on the map of world history are being filled in at a rapid pace. With this research has come a proliferation of new science-based dating methods.[5] Since the 1950s, archaeologists have used radiocarbon dating to determine the age of organic materials ranging from charcoal from prehistoric fires to preserved seeds, wood, and bone. By now the procedure is well known. The radioactive (unstable) isotope of carbon (C^{14}) decays at a regular rate; once the ratio of C^{14} to C^{12} in past atmospheres has been established, the date of organic material can be determined by measuring the extent of C^{14} decay. New techniques have lowered costs, improved accuracy, and broadened the range of time and of datable materials for radiocarbon determinations. Other methods of absolute dating now include dendrochronology (tree rings), obsidian hydration, thermoluminescence (TL), optically stimulated luminescence (OSL), and potassium-argon.[6] The result has been an ability to order archaeological sites and assemblages according to a much firmer chronology.

Other technical advances have been similarly impressive. Ancient ice-core sampling, paleo-pollen work, and glacial geography allow us to reconstruct macro- and microclimatic patterns.[7] Stable-isotope research has enabled the analysis of prehistoric diets among humans and other animals. The logic here is that we are what we eat. Because there are particular trophic pathways for stable isotopes, especially of carbon and nitrogen, it is possible to reconstruct the character of a human diet by the stable-isotope ratios found in human bone. By combining climatic and dietary data, archaeologists can reconstruct the foodways and thus the nature of the overall adaptation of any prehistoric population. For example, direct measurement of the isotopic composition of human bone reveals the changing balance of plant food and animal protein in early hominin diets as populations dispersed and displaced existing groups.[8]

Still other techniques can pinpoint the origin of archaeological materials using trace-element analysis.[9] Elemental analyses allow us to match stone, metal, and ceramics to particular sources. Instrumental neutron activation analysis (INAA), for example, identifies a wide range of elements in obsidian that can then be used to trace the material to a specific geographical location, suggesting patterns of movement or exchange. Likewise, elemental analysis of human tooth enamel (which is stable in form after adolescence) can actually identify where people grew up, and this information allows us to gauge how far individuals moved in their lifetime.

With improvements in our ability to determine the age and geographic origin of material remains have come radical increases in the amounts and kinds of physical evidence archaeologists can now study. Huxley could not have imagined the complex assemblage of hominin bones stored away in labs and museums around the world, a grand ossuary whose relics date back some 5 million years and include samples from at least three genera and more than a dozen species (figure 19). Although fossilized bones are essential to paleoanthropological models of human evolution, it is now possible to reconstruct the hominin past using evidence drawn from genetic material present in living humans (as

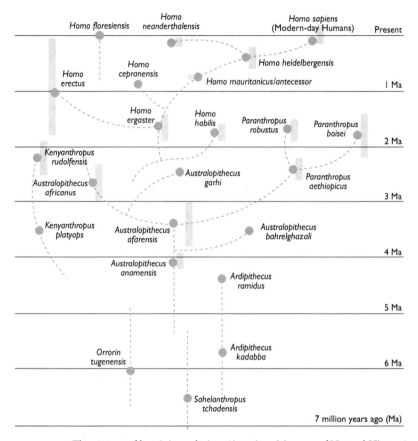

FIGURE 19. The pattern of hominin evolution. (American Museum of Natural History.)

well as ancient genetic material found in bones). By comparing small changes that occur within the mitochondrial genome, which is inherited along the female line, and by studying changes in sections of the Y chromosome, which is present only in males, geneticists can piece together detailed human lineages, tracing the nearest common ancestor of modern humans to Africa between 120,000 and 200,000 years ago.[10] By charting the types and numbers of these genetic changes within human populations around the world, one can essentially track human movements across the planet. Because these mutations occur at rates whose tempo can be estimated from familial genealogies, we can estimate when populations diverged in the deep past (coalescence), in what directions they traveled, and even how large they might have been, a figure called effective population size.[11]

Genetic research is similar to the comparative method devised by philologists in the eighteenth century to map the historical relations between human languages (see chapter 5). Changes in a sequence of DNA, like variations in a Swadesh word list, can determine distance from a common point of origin. Genomes and languages are reproduced by radically different means, but the geographical distribution of both begins to overlap in measurable ways about 10,000 to 15,000 years ago, after which the global flow of genes, languages, and cultural forms can be correlated with increasing precision. The articulation of deep and shallow histories is currently based on explanatory models that, as previous chapters show, are genealogical in design, as were older biblical accounts of human variability over time. Theories of ancient migrations first developed by linguists—stories of Indo-European homelands, Aryan invasions, Bantu expansions, and waves of Amerindian settlement—are still prominent in genetic research on population movements and the reconstruction of paleogeographies.[12]

A DEEP HISTORY CHRONOLOGY
OF HOMININ MIGRATIONS

The conceptions of geography and movement needed to understand human migration in the deep past are somewhat different from those familiar to scholars who work in shallow time. A few definitions suggest the nature of our argument. Under the cover term *migration,* we discuss three modes of human expansion across the globe: dispersal, displacement, and diaspora. These processes are sequential, but they are not mutually exclusive. Dispersal is always operating, but it results in displacement and diaspora under specific economic and institutional conditions. Dispersal is the expansion of populations into unoccupied areas, requiring access to these areas and triggering biological and cultural adaptations. The prehistoric movement of humans into North and South America, where they encountered new climates, new animals to hunt, and new plants to gather, is an example of dispersal, as were the movement of people back into Northern Europe after the retreat of the ice sheets sixteen thousand years ago and the voyages into remote Polynesia that began some three thousand years ago.

Displacement is the dispersal of a population into areas that are already occupied, entailing the competitive replacement of existing hominin populations. When members of *Homo sapiens* first entered the Middle East and Europe, for instance, they encountered Neanderthals, whom they eventually replaced. Evolving cognitive abilities and technocultural innovations, such as agriculture, have allowed human populations to exclude others with less effective adaptations. People who live in the political systems we now call *states,* for instance, have been displacing and incorporating the world's tribal and foraging populations for thousands of years.

Finally, diaspora involves rapid movements of people through political economies of trade, colonization, and slavery. New institutional settings create spaces and uses for these people in motion, who retain their cultural distinctiveness but often interbreed with coexisting populations. The last five hundred years of European expansion, for instance, have witnessed the creation of trading and production colonies, often as the extension of homeland states. Slaves were sold broadly in these colonies, and immigrants were brought in or kept out to meet the demands of global labor markets. These three processes of migration must be understood as a package that represents both substantial continuity and selective change over time.

We consider patterns of human migration against the backdrop of three landmasses, Terra 1, Terra 2, and Terra 3, each of which is more expansive, ecologically and culturally, than the last (see figure 20).[13] These configurations allow us to create geographies that are not dependent on modern political divisions or climate zones. They should be thought of, instead, as the paleo-continents of hominin evolution or the successive stages of an expanding frontier. We have pieced them together much as geologists have reconstructed the supercontinent of Pangaea, which existed 250 million years ago, before the continental plates started drifting apart. Unlike Pangaea, however, the archaeological landmasses we explore have no hard and fast boundaries. Hominins are highly mobile, and it is the pattern of their global journeys that has created these three great landmasses. We are especially interested to know what environmental factors—such as the presence of food, carnivores, water, glaciers, and other hominin competitors—for so long ensured that hominins would remain an Old World species, and largely a southern one at that. We also want to consider the biological and social adaptations—large brains, tools, kinship, language—that enabled hominins to overcome these geographical restrictions.

Terra 1 encompasses sub-Saharan Africa, the Arabian Peninsula, the northern extension of the Rift Valley, and the Plio-Pleistocene lakes of the Sahara. From 6 to 2.5 million years ago, this was the likely region for speciation of *Pan* (the genus that includes modern chimpanzees) and

Chronological movements	Hominin worlds	Continents inhabited	Technologies	Indicative species
6–2.5 Ma	Terra 1	Africa	Primate technologies (probes, hammer stones)	Early australopiths; preaustralopiths (e.g., *Ardipithecus ramidus*)
2.5–0.05 Ma	Terra 2	Africa; Asia 1; Europe	Instrument technologies (stone and wooden tools)	Large-brained hominins; later australopiths; early *Homo*
50 ka–present	Terra 3	Africa; Asia 2; Europe; Australia; Americas; Pacific; continental islands	Domestication and container technologies (fibers, textiles, skin, clay)	*Homo sapiens*; extinction of regional small- and large-brained hominins

FIGURE 20. The three worlds of hominin migration. Asia 1 recognizes the limit to northern occupation and includes western Asia (Near East). Asia 2 includes northern and eastern Siberia. Exposed continental shelves are also considered. The continental islands are Madagascar and Greenland.

the australopiths, whose shadowy forebears, now illuminated by the 4.5-million-year-old ancestor from Ethiopia, *Ardipithecus ramidus,* produced several hominin species, including the lineage that was ancestral to our genus, *Homo.*[14]

Terra 2 encompasses Terra 1 and adds the temperate grasslands of the Old World and the tropical regions of India and Southeast Asia. From 2.5 million until 50,000 years ago, this was the region of speciation, dispersal, and extinction for several varieties of the genus *Homo,* including *H. erectus, H. ergaster, H. antecessor, H. heidelbergensis, H. neanderthalensis,* and *H. sapiens.*

Terra 3 is the world of modern humans: it encompasses all the globe's land surfaces except Antarctica and the Arctic ice cap. From 50,000 years ago to the present, this was the stage for *H. sapiens'* dispersal and technological development, allowing for an extraordinary range of effective adaptations. Although no hominin speciation has taken place during this period, a closely related species, *H. neanderthalensis,* and perhaps others, went extinct.

Terra 1 (6–2.5 Ma)

Based on current evidence, hominins originated in Terra 1. It is humanity's Eden, both the place of origin and the place of creative evolutionary trajectories. At about 7–8 Ma in Terra 1, according to genetic evidence, the hominin line diverged from its great-ape relatives. Some of the major features distinguishing this new line included increasing cognitive abilities and tool use, a changed diet, and considerable migration. Humans are an unusually mobile species. Beginning nearly 2 million years ago with the initial dispersal out of Africa by genus *Homo,* humans have continued to wander wide and far. Our taste for mobility stands in sharp contrast to the sedentary ways of many other animals. For example, our closest living relatives—the chimps, bonobos, and gorillas—generally occupy relatively small, circumscribed home ranges or territories. They traverse these areas day in and day out and remain in or near them throughout their lives. To be sure, in all primate species some individuals, typically members of only one sex, disperse from their natal homes on reaching sexual maturity, but often they do so by moving only to an adjacent range. Most primates, apart from macaques, have not ranged into the wide variety of habitats and environments that humans have known throughout our history.

Australopiths evolved in and dispersed throughout savannalike environments of sub-Saharan Africa, extending northward into Chad during wetter periods, when large lakes formed there. Living in patchy, rapidly changing environments, australopiths utilized a fairly wide range of food resources based on evolving cultural and cognitive capabilities. Terra 1 was apparently the location for the evolution of the genus *Homo* and the origin for its dispersal into Terra 2.[15] The appearance of larger-brained hominins required changes in diet, because big brains need more and higher-quality energy. The result was a shift from plant to animal foods, the evidence for which is being teased out of the skeletons by stable-isotope work. This transition was also accompanied by stone tools, the earliest of which were flakes and pebble tools used to sever and pound animal and plant tissue. The oldest of these stone tools, which date to 2.6 Ma, have been found in Ethiopia.[16]

Even with such simple technologies, hominins could become brazen in their competitive dealings with other large carnivores. Stone tools helped them reduce the dangerous time spent parceling kills and moving them to safer feeding locales, and they might also have been used to fashion wooden spears or clubs, although such tools have not been found. Conditioning these developments was a global trend toward colder and drier climates; major habitat changes within Terra 1 resulted in a latitudinal shuffling of populations that no doubt increased the chances for speciation through geographical isolation (allopatry).[17] Although Africa currently holds all the early hominin evidence, the movement of large mammals between the African and Asian parts of Terra 1 is well documented, showing that dispersal was normal within this paleo-continent. Hominins could very well have been part of this pattern. Populations such as *Homo* explored the boundaries of their geographical worlds under selective pressures to disperse.

Terra 2 (2.5–0.05 Ma)

With the evolution of the genus *Homo,* populations spread out of Africa repeatedly to inhabit the paleo-continent of Terra 2, which became the expanded hominin world of speciation, dispersal, and population replacement. The first to leave Africa was the complex of species known as *H. erectus,* which spread through the temperate grasslands and certain tropical environments of Asia and Europe before 2.0 Ma.[18] Regional evolution occurred, resulting, for example, in the distinctive Eurasian hominins known as Neanderthals. First results from the Neanderthal genome project point to a last common ancestor with humans some 300–500 ka, and fossil ancestors of these socially skillful people, dating to at least 400 ka, have been found at locales such as Swanscombe, in an ancient terrace of the Thames River east of London.[19] Most classic Neanderthal remains, however, date to less than 200 ka, when the number of samples preserved increased dramatically because of their habit of burying bodies in protective caves. It comes as no surprise that these big-brained, robustly built, cold-climate specialists, who wielded stone-tipped projectiles with immense physical power, were dedicated meat eaters; isotope studies reveal that they were at the top of the food chain. However, the distances over which Neanderthals obtained the stone points for their lethal spears indicate a local focus; materials obtained from more than 100 km away are rare, and most stone sources were within 20 km, or a day's walk from where tools were found.[20]

While Neanderthals were regularly feasting on bison, horse, reindeer, and even mammoth, our direct ancestors were emerging in Africa. These so-called modern humans (*H. sapiens*) were late developers in the dispersal stakes. Excavations at Blombos Cave on the coast of South Africa have produced a wealth of novel cultural materials dating to 80 ka, including bone awls, well-fashioned ("Still Bay") stone projectile points, and, most significant, pierced shells for necklaces and many pieces of engraved ocher. The Blombos collection, matched piecemeal elsewhere in Africa, suggests a population engaged in the material representation of symbolic codes. For other Terra 2 populations, such as the Neanderthals, the search for symbolic material culture of this kind has so far produced little evidence.

Despite signs of a complex cultural package for modern humans at around 80,000 years ago, it was not until some 50 ka that *H. sapiens* began to disperse steadily across Terra 2, displacing existing populations of *H. neanderthalensis* and contributing to their extinction by 25 ka.[21] As they moved, modern humans developed new cultural patterns of technology, social organization, and meaning systems that allowed for rapid adaptations to climate and environment. In particular, the distances over which material goods traveled now radically exceeded the limits set in earlier times. Shells picked up on the beaches of the Mediterranean, for instance, have been found 1,000 km to the north at sites associated with modern humans, pointing to extensive networks of movement and exchange.

Throughout Terra 2, patterns of dispersal and displacement must have been extraordinarily complex, and they are difficult to imagine with the present fragmentary evidence. They were certainly repeated many times, creating a landscape of multiple hominin dispersals.[22] A marker of evolutionary success, dispersal can but does not always result in speciation. It can also be traced archaeologically, whereas speciation cannot. A well-worked example of patterned dispersal is provided by research in Britain covering the period after 800 ka. At Pakefield, on the eastern coast of Britain, dated to 750 ka, flake tools were excavated from sediments indicative of Mediterranean rather than temperate conditions, suggesting that this early dispersal northward may have followed an ecological shift during a warming trend.[23] These finds contrast with those from the later occupation at Boxgrove, on the southern coast. Boxgrove is dated to 500 ka, a period of warm, interglacial conditions but without the Mediterranean component. Archaeologists excavated a collection of symmetrically fashioned stone hand axes associated with the hunting of large mammals, including rhino. Fossil evidence is sparse, but these locales were visited by *H. heidelbergensis,* ancestor to later Neanderthals.[24] The dispersal events represented at Pakefield and Boxgrove were achieved by large-brained hominins who relied on stone tools, but the latter shifted to hunting in order to occupy an environmental zone more extreme to the African-origin animal.

How can we make sense of such outcomes? Perhaps we can modify our narrative to incorporate changing cognition.[25] Between the periods of settlement of Pakefield and Boxgrove, brain size significantly increased, and the ability of local groups to integrate into larger hominin communities improved.[26] It is tempting to conclude that changes in social cognition coevolved through the selective pressures of dispersal to form new adaptations in diet and technology. For example, fire is more frequently found at the locales of these large-brained hominins after 500 ka. Not only would it provide warmth in northern latitudes and defense against large predators, but it also had biological and social ramifications. Cooking meat in a fire is a form of external preliminary digestion.[27] Such assistance is important for an expanding, energy-hungry brain, which can grow only at the expense of other organs. Fire was a cultural extension for the gut, which shrank in size as brains grew larger, overcoming a key biological constraint to increased energy intake.

Furthermore, dispersal into northern latitudes would have meant a shorter day length for several months of the year. Hominins who had evolved in the tropics were faced with new problems of budgeting time. They had to find, prepare, and consume food during a shorter period of daylight, all the while pursuing the important business of interacting with other members of the group to create and sustain social bonds. Fire provided a way of adapting to these time constraints by lengthening the hours available for visual contact and by creating a highly charged, affective place in which it could occur.

These early moves northward, whether at Pakefield, Boxgrove, or among later Neanderthals, pale in comparison to the global dispersal and displacement wrought by modern humans. Why did modern humans take so long to expand out of Africa? How much social and cultural gestation was needed before humans like ourselves, who first appeared some 200,000 years ago, could become a global species, replacing all other hominins? Explanations for our sudden geographic expansion range from neural mutations for a language gene to the creation of population bottlenecks after the eruption of the Toba supervolcano 73,000 years ago and to the development of new technologies that allowed us to procure highly productive aquatic and small-bodied food resources, broadening the human diet and sustaining larger populations.[28]

Hunting smaller prey such as fish, tortoises, and rabbits and then moving even further down the food chain to shellfish, grasses, roots, and tubers created an ecological bonanza. This diet was more abundant. It could feed more people and allowed more food to be stored against shortages. The accumulation of stored foods, in turn, encouraged people to concentrate around them in settlements. Such abundance from diversification and intensification, however, was hard-won. Workloads increased, especially for women responsible for collecting and laboriously processing these new foods. Archaeological evidence points to work-related traumas in the bones of people who adopted a broader diet, and evidence from cemeteries along the Nile and the Murray River in Australia point to violent deaths from fighting. The human ability to experiment with diet and intensify food production long predates the appearance of agriculture. It goes hand in hand with our displacement and dispersal, and it distinguishes the modern human migration out of Africa from earlier hominin dispersals, which were conservative and gradual by comparison.

The ability to crank up the business of getting food does not in itself explain why the Grand Tour of *H. sapiens,* beginning rather late in our evolution, at 50 ka, has such a special place in the history of hominin migrations. Cognitive changes were essential to the development of social relationships that could function locally and on a larger regional scale. These long-distance social forms were essential to the global distribution of modern humans. Rapid fission and fusion of camp groups was necessary to cross vast expanses of unpopulated ice, grasslands, and forests, and these spatial dispersals may have required the ability to retain fairly stable relations over prolonged spatial and temporal separations.

Terra 3 (50 ka–present)

The geographical gains of modern humans over the past 50,000 years are impressive (see figure 21). For the first time the harsh environments of central and eastern Siberia were populated, an accomplishment that opened up several possible routes into the Americas. A well-used hominin dispersal route along the coast of Arabia through India and down to Southeast Asia was traveled again. This time, however, the dispersing population did not stay on the beach at Phuket. They crossed 80 to 100 km of open water and made landfall in northern Australia, then in part of the great, low-lying continent of Sahul (encompassing New Guinea, Australia, and Tasmania). They continued to the islands of Melanesia, reaching New Ireland more than 30,000 years ago, and then to the more distant Solomon archipelago. These dispersals into virgin territories depended on social relationships and in particular on the development of kinship systems.[29] To break out of the bounds of Terra 2, humans needed to replace and elongate their social networks, a process that would enable them to transport more of their cultural repertoire and to overcome the constraints of separation on the conduct of social life.

Genetic evidence allows us to set the human occupation of Terra 3 in deep historical perspective. The level of detail now possible is shown in figure 21, which charts the spread of modern humans out of Africa, and figure 22, which juxtaposes the estimated ages and geographical locations of divergences in mitochondrial DNA. The expansion starts with the mitochondrial Eve, humanity's most recent common female ancestor, who lived in Africa almost 200,000 years ago. The movement out of Africa can then be traced by the new genetic lineages that resulted as populations budded off, were separated over time, and reconverged. These lineages appear as groups or bundles of genetic changes (known as haplogroups), represented in figure 22 by the letters that mark the major groups. For example, the L3 group coalesced in Africa about 65,000 years ago and in turn gave rise to the major mitochondrial DNA haplogroups outside Africa (M and N) between 40,000 and 50,000 years ago.

These haplogroups reveal the direction of the initial movement out of Africa, through the Near East and into South and East Asia. Indeed, the evidence suggests a rapid coastal settlement of Asia (the data indicate an annual dispersal rate of about 4 km a year) with later migration into the interior of the continent.[30] A few thousand years after leaving Africa, modern humans had made a 12,000 km journey into Terra 3, fueled by rich coastal and marine foods, that ended with the crossing over open water to Australia.

The movement west was slower. Without the riches of the marine environment, and with the presence of well-adapted indigenous populations of Neanderthals, the dispersal into Europe and the continental landmass of Asia, particularly Siberia, took place later. The genetic evidence for human dispersals into Europe hinges on haplogroup U, which points to arrival of modern humans between 55 and 30 ka. The archaeological evidence shows a major change in technology and lifestyle, referred to as the Upper Paleolithic revolution, after 40 ka.[31] The subsequent history of Europe is complex, as traced through haplogroup H, which records the ebb and flow of populations before, during, and after the maximum extent of the ice sheets some 19 to 25 ka.

The third great arc of movement led humans to the Americas through the harsh continental environments of Siberia, which they had settled by 30 ka. From there they headed into the Americas, traveling along the western coastline and migrating through gaps in the Cordilleran ice sheet. The age of the first peopling of North America is hotly debated, but there is good archaeological evidence that humans had progressed

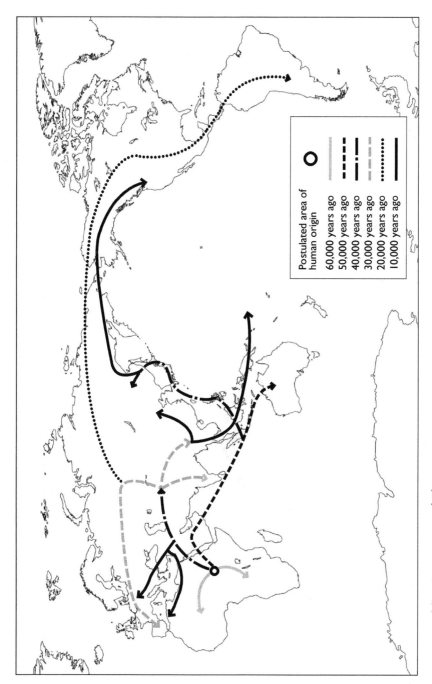

FIGURE 21. Migration routes out of Africa.

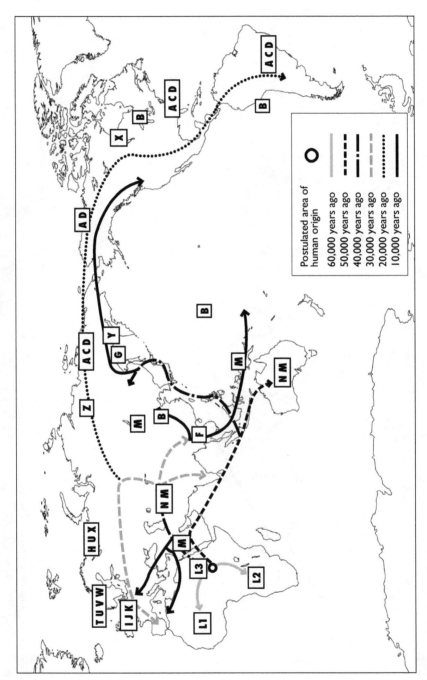

FIGURE 22. Human haplogroups.

south of the Cordilleran ice sheet between 16 and 19 ka. The genetic data show a major expansion at 14 ka and an impressively rapid rate of advance through both continents, perhaps spurred on yet again by an abundance of coastal resources.[32]

Dispersal: Human Populating of the Old and New Worlds

Dispersal into Terra 3 was achieved as part of a coevolutionary process. Changes in social cognition interacted with core hominin abilities to create and reproduce material culture, a process that fed back into social organization and long-range planning. Each new environmental zone and its associated animal and plant species required deliberate innovation. Snowy wastelands and expansive bodies of water called for novel means of transport as well as alterations in clothing and tools. New animal species—the formidable plains bison, the coastal sea lion, the fast jackrabbit or salmon—required specific technologies for capture, processing, storage, and preparation as food. These adaptations would not have been possible without steady cognitive and cultural change. In particular, the pattern of group fission and fusion necessary to cross oceans and adapt to low-resource environments at the heart of continental landmasses would have created problems of separation and reacquaintance. The frameworks of social life could no longer be negotiated in face-to-face communities, where daily interaction reduced the cognitive demands of remembering and acting out social relationships. Human society now had to be imagined and enacted in absentia.

The centrality of an expanded social imagination to the success of human dispersal can be seen in a comparison of *Homo sapiens* to the Neanderthals they encountered in Europe and Western Asia. The differences were marked, less in brain size and technological skill than in the scale of social life and the devices used to support it. Neanderthals were well suited to local conditions. A Neanderthal tooth at Lakonis Cave in Greece yields strontium isotope evidence that this individual died no more than 20 km from its birthplace.[33] The raw materials Neanderthals used to manufacture stone tools come predominantly from local geological sources (within 100 km).[34] Transfers of material over longer distances are known, but nothing we know of Neanderthal travel suggests that it came close to the hundreds of kilometers over which *H. sapiens* obtained shell and amber to make into ornaments for display or the even greater distances over which stones were transferred for tools. The evidence points to a geographically constrained existence for Neanderthals and limits to their imaginary universes. These restrictions did not apply to the well-traveled *H. sapiens,* whose global dispersal brought a whole new meaning to the idea of "keeping in touch": contact was maintained not only through frequent, face-to-face interaction but also by extendable webs of relationship based on the transregional exchange of goods and ideas.

This expansion of the social universe was accomplished by amplifying the emotional and material basis of human relationships. To make separation both possible and desirable, it was critical to develop "containers" of diverse sorts, ranging from the physical to the metaphorical.[35] Some containers sped human migration in ways that were eminently practical. Boats carried humans to Australia and other islands. Shelters protected people from cold, rain, ice, and snow in harsh environments. Skins, baskets, and, later, ceramic pots held food for cooking and stored it away for use in lean times. But containers could also have psychological and social functions. A set of beads stores the memories of ancestors, friends, and family members. Other containers produce music that helps to bind communities together. Still other containers, serving as totemic devices, work to keep individuals or communities apart. All of these trends point to hominins who were not only speaking language but also exploring its metaphorical and symbolic potential for shaping worlds. In short, the proliferation of containers marked a significant development in social cognition. Ideas of containment could now be applied to novel categories such as kinship, laying the groundwork for rule-based marriage systems and the constant exchanges of gifts and people that accompany these systems.[36] Ties of kinship pulled humans steadily across Terra 3, ensuring the simultaneous flow of people, their goods, and the networks of shared experience that kept them all in motion.

Displacement: The Spread of Agriculturalists

The story of migration through Terra 3 was, for more than 40,000 years, dominated by hunting and gathering populations. Between 10,000 and 5,000 years ago, however, the Neolithic revolution brought about the dramatic displacement or incorporation of foragers by farming societies. The domestication of plants and animals allowed for the emergence of more densely settled and centrally organized populations. Villagers could use their superior numbers to seize and develop the lands once used by foragers, steadily pushing the former occupants into lands less suited to agriculture, or incorporating them as specialized hunters and fishers within a more complex economy. Foragers also interacted with farmers as a source of mates and extra labor.

Throughout Terra 3, adaptive radiations, multiple dispersals, and a growing pattern of displacement culminated in the prehistoric movements of what appear to be cultures and, moving into shallow time, the historical migrations of named peoples. Such cultural shifts and inferred migrations in the Old World were studied closely by the archaeologist V. Gordon Childe, who made explicit the assumption that some of the evidence archaeologists were digging up showed different peoples, or cultures, moving and replacing each other. "We find certain types of remains—pots, implements, ornaments, burial rites and house forms—constantly recurring together. Such a complex of associated traits we shall term a 'cultural group' or just a 'culture.' We assume that such a complex is the material expression of what today would be called a 'people.'"[37] The entire social system, the culture complex, became a container for ideas and relationships that were essential for local adaptation and enabled one group to replace or incorporate another.

Moving cultures (migrating peoples) have been represented in two models. Using the Fisher-Skellam wave-of-advance model, Albert J. Ammerman and Luigi Cavalli-Sforza produced an account of the spread of agriculture from the Near East into Europe beginning about 8,000 years ago.[38] They used the relatively new radiocarbon evidence from the Neolithic to estimate rates of advance of about 1 km per year and combined this with molecular and genetic evidence that indicates the direction of movement from southeast to northwest Europe. Inexorably, like a slow tsunami, the population wave covered all of Europe from Greece to Scandinavia, filling all environments and leaving almost no trace of previous hunting and gathering economies.

The second model, which is based on saltation (or leapfrogging), recognizes that the earliest forms of agriculture took advantage of selected places on the landscape.[39] Low-intensity food production was particularly dependent on fertile soils in small alluvial basins. These conditions are not continuous, especially in southeast Europe. As a result, the earliest farmers in the region jumped from one productive agricultural area to another, leaving the spaces in between to foragers.

The complex processes of assimilation and acceptance between populations of farmers and foragers have been investigated archaeologically in northern Europe.[40] Forager resistance and accommodation are built into the model of expansion to produce, over several thousand years, a varied Neolithic world in which the overall pattern was a cultural mosaic.[41] Northern hunter-fishers lived off a rich seafood diet of oysters, eels, and herring, leaving southerners to toil in their fields cut from the forests and live on a cuisine dominated by tasteless millet gruel. As multiple dispersals of farmers and herders took place across most of Europe, Asia, and the Americas, foragers were incorporated as specialists and interbred with the newcomers. Only in Australia, in substantial parts of America—such as the west coast, from California to Alaska—in the deserts and tropical forests of the Old World, and in the high latitudes did foragers retain their nonagricultural economy and the freedoms (and risks) of such a life.[42] These agricultural expansions, whether they entailed the movement of people or the diffusion of subsistence technologies and domesticated animals and plants, resulted in a broadly dispersed social order of local groups engaged in farming and pastoralism.[43]

In Peter Bellwood's early farming dispersal hypothesis, the spread of early farming lifestyles is documented by combining data from archaeology, historical linguistics, and genetics.[44] Following the wave-of-advance model, Bellwood argues that agriculture spread by means of demographic replacement, as farming populations moved ever outward, overwhelming foragers (their languages, genes, and cultures) in all directions. Yet the model pays little attention to human distributions before the evolution of farming. Rather, the interdisciplinary mix is used to sustain a master narrative of prehistory that equates the origin of our (modern) world with the origin of farming.[45] "The overall shape of the past," Bellwood writes, was "one of dispersal-based pulsation at intervals, with reticulation in the periods (often extremely long periods) between. We cannot expect that the results of all past dispersals will be unambiguously obvious in present-day linguistic and biological patterns. But the major ones should be."[46]

Bellwood's model identifies agricultural homelands, the points of origin for domesticates like wheat and barley in the Middle East and taro in Melanesia. Once dispersal was under way, the expansion of farming populations had a starburst quality, which Bellwood describes as spread zones at "full-steam ahead." The Neolithic revolution is, according to this framework, a process that triggered dramatic migrations, which in turn brought the benefits of agriculture to the world at large. It brings to mind an old set of ideas about imperial expansion, informed by the values of the so-called civilizing process, by which the benefits of a civilization are bestowed on a subjugated and increasingly dependent hinterland. The lure of this familiar imagery is seductive. The potential for anachronism, however, is great.

Key features of the early farming dispersal hypothesis are problematic. For example, a study using a similar interdisciplinary methodology confirms the fact of a dispersal but suggests that it took place much earlier, during the European Late Glacial period.[47] This correspondence was determined using radiocarbon dates to fix the time and direction of population movement after 16,000 years ago and mitochondrial DNA to reconstruct a contemporaneous phylogeographic pattern. Contra Bellwood's "full-steam ahead" model, molecular evidence shows that up to 75 percent of the genetic history of Europe dates to the population expansion that occurred 16,000 years ago, when hunter-gatherers dispersed north from a southern glacial refugium thousands of years before sedentary agriculture came into the region.

This conclusion does not downplay the importance of agriculture from the Near East when it finally did arrive in Europe, an idea central to Bellwood's hypothesis. It simply highlights the possibility that the movement of agriculture into Europe did not require a massive importation of people and genes from elsewhere. It might have been accomplished without radical displacements of local foragers, who could have adjusted steadily to the arrival of farming communities and technologies as populations increased in both Europe and the Near East. This situation is better interpreted, from the vantage of deep history, as the latest element in a long series of population diasporas, in which settled and mobile populations were mixing and remixing for a wide range of social and political reasons.

A review of the genetic evidence for early animal and plant domestication points strongly to variable geographical and temporal patterns.[48] Domestication of animals such as pigs, for example, occurred independently in multiple locales. Across a huge "wild" range of the pig genus *Sus,* domestication occurred independently at least six times based on genetic evidence, or four times according to archaeological evidence. Most striking is the genetic evidence for much earlier dispersals of domestic plants than had been anticipated from the archaeological evidence.[49] It was thought that the African bottle-necked gourd, for example, reached the Americas as flotsam, but genomic analysis suggests that, along with the dog, it may have come overland in the Late Pleistocene from Asia.

The genetic evidence for domestic animals shows a palimpsest of dispersal tracks that follow the ebb and flow of economies and peoples. Each species belonged to a network of relationships and resources; each had a distinctive biography. Animals moved with people, were given as gifts to build alliances, and were stolen by competing groups.

M.A. Zeder reviews genetic and archaeological evidence for the "first global economy" that linked Eastern Africa to India.[50] The genetic evidence indicates that Zebu cattle, bananas, yams, and taro were all introduced into Africa; sorghum, millet, and donkeys went the other way. According to archaeological evidence, the Indian Ocean track involved not only transport by many small ships but also overland movement, which overlaid a much older track—the southern coastal route—that acted as an ecological conduit for many species, including hominins and modern humans, to disperse out of Africa and probably move back again.[51] It was also a foundation for the integrated trading networks that emerged with the development of more complex societies.

Diaspora: Human Migrations with the Emergence of Political Economies

In complex societies, which are often called chiefdoms and states, leaders used political economies to employ staples and wealth to finance emergent institutional systems of rule (see chapter 10). As a result of these economic restructurings, human migration patterns became increasingly complicated and intertwined with the political process. Starting at least 6,000 years ago, leaders of complex societies attempted to control bottlenecks in the economy so as to take advantage of a surplus that could support new methods of governance.[52] Increasingly, political leaders targeted populations and regions for migration, turning mobility into a tool for generating revenue and solidifying social control. The new political economies were typically based on surplus agricultural staples, which were often produced on newly acquired lands that required displaced populations to farm them. Variants of this system, which appeared in such diverse areas as the high Andes, Mesopotamia, and the Pacific Ocean, developed independently and by imitation wherever complex, surplus-based polities had spread. Human diasporas arose from colonization, population displacements, trade in slaves, and labor migration. Below are some examples of these diasporas linked to early archaic states under differing forms of political economies.

Early chiefdoms, city-states, and some empires were heavily based on staple finance. In simplest terms, elites in chiefdoms and archaic states, like the Hawaiian paramount chiefs encountered by Captain Cook, developed intensive agriculture, often irrigated, and claimed ownership over those highly productive resources. Populations were then moved onto these engineered landscapes, often from some distance. Farmers gave elites a percentage of their produce or labor as a rent in return for access to land. Generally, such political systems have expanded, displacing or subsuming simpler agricultural and herding societies.

Fredrik Barth describes the ethnic and ecological mosaic of populations in the now-famous Swat Valley in Pakistan.[53] Presumably the result of dispersals and displacements, three ethnic populations lived in close proximity to each other, based on their distinctive subsistence economies (irrigation farming, dry hill farming, and pastoralism). The densest and most highly organized group, based on irrigation farming, had competitively excluded simpler farmers and pastoralists from the valley bottom, where surplus from the irrigation systems supported local landlords. Each group identified, across broad regions, with pockets of similarly organized populations, with whom it shared cultural beliefs, economic adaptations, and tribal affiliations. The configuration is thousands of years old.

In ancient Mesopotamia, early city-states were based on irrigation; as they expanded, their rulers built new irrigation systems, moving populations out from the core, bringing marginal dry-farming and pastoral communities into the system, and rapidly expanding their staple finance base.[54] A warrior elite, supported by the revenues of the staple finance system, engaged in the conquest and expansion of political systems, which often involved population replacements.

Subsequent states and empires, which were based on staple finance, often reshuffled populations to increase surplus production and to tighten control. Inca imperial policy and its military moved populations around the empire, creating a mosaic of diasporas.[55] The *mitmaqkuna* were the mobile class of specialists and administrators who performed specific military and economic functions for the state. As foreigners to the regions in which they lived, these internal migrants had no rights to land or means of support except those provided by the state. Groups were moved to pacify populations, to provide specialists in certain crafts (potters or metallurgists), to support newly engineered agricultural developments, and for military support. In the valley of Cochabamba, in present-day Bolivia, the Inca state forcefully removed an indigenous low-density population, constructed a massive new agricultural landscape, and then placed a new farming population on the land. Empires often encouraged internal migration in pursuit of specific imperial objectives and to create populations committed to the state superstructure.

In these complex societies, stratification provoked intense internal competition for power. Elites often fought among themselves for control of a chiefdom or state.[56] An option for aspiring leaders, especially those defeated in battles of succession, was to lead expeditions of exploration and conquest to obtain new lands in which to establish a new political society. This was the probable motivation for the very rapid colonization of the deep Pacific by Polynesian chiefs.[57] In less than two thousand years, Polynesian explorers located and occupied all habitable islands, from Fiji to Easter Island, from the Hawaiian Islands to New Zealand. This is one of history's great examples of systematic, comprehensive colonization. We can imagine fairly small-scale chiefdoms involved in both internal and interpolity competition for power on each Pacific island. An aspiring leader always had the option, based on the historical example of other chiefs, of setting forth to find a new island over the horizon, where he could establish his own polity. As a result, a single cultural group established new homelands across the open Pacific, often heading into the unknown across expanses of water more than 500 km wide.

Similar processes have unfolded across the inner reaches of the Eurasian land mass, where pastoral chiefdoms engaged for centuries in another kind of island hopping, moving from open steppes to the shores of the great urban civilizations to overrun, dominate, and eventually blend with Roman, Chinese, Abbasid, Byzantine, and Persian societies. During the turbulent demise of the Western Roman Empire, for instance, such rapid migration occurred throughout Europe. Entrepreneurial chieftains led small-scale warrior groups that plundered unprotected lands, seized local territory, and established new polities. Chieftains wanted to establish new networks of power, and their followers saw the opportunity to obtain unprotected wealth and rich farmlands. Somewhat later, Viking chieftains explored and colonized the sub-Arctic fringe of the Atlantic, including the Faroe Islands, Iceland, Greenland, and Newfoundland. Throughout Europe, their raiding ships were feared, and their chieftains conquered sections of Ireland, England, and France.

Other major conquests included the historic movements of the Magyars, Mongols, Arabs, and Berbers, all of which triggered population displacements, diasporas, and mixtures. The outcome of these conquests during the Middle Ages was a rapid reshuffling of populations across Europe, Asia, and Africa and eventually into the New World. Typically, these conquests involved the raiding of unprotected (or poorly defended) wealth and the establishment of staple-based local polities weakly tied to broader political alliances and relationships.

For complex societies, an alternative strategy to control over staple production was wealth finance, involving control over systems of trade, especially the traffic in luxury goods. With the establishment of staple-based political economies in the Middle East about 7,000 years ago, demand increased for luxury goods made with special materials of semi-precious stones, ivory, metals, and textiles. The demand for luxury goods created new systems of specialization and trade dedicated to providing these goods, and with these trade networks came new bottlenecks in the flow of wealth that elites might control. As watercraft moved luxury goods along rivers and coastlines, and camel caravans hauled them from oasis to oasis, flows gradually concentrated in a few profitable routes, where bandits and other skimmers of wealth could settle down to expropriate some of the goods. In the Middle East, demand for a wide range of foreign goods eventually established trading networks from China and India to Europe and Africa. Early on, trading colonies were established in hinterland regions, well away from direct state presence but nearer to the sources of scarce metals and precious stones.

"Trade-diasporas arise," Gil Stein tells us, "in situations where culturally distinct groups are engaged in exchange under conditions where communication and transportation are difficult, and where centralized state institutions are not effective in providing either physical or economic security to participants in long-distance exchanges."[58] In the fourth millennium BCE, the Uruk trading colony of Hacinebi consisted of a small population living in southern Turkey, well removed from their homeland in the irrigated zones of Mesopotamia. The later expansion of the Egyptian empire placed a string of trading colonies along the eastern Mediterranean to supply the pharaonic elite with specialty goods, including the famed cedars of Lebanon. Similar trading colonies characterized the Assyrian Empire. These colonies were protected by warriors, but they appear to have included a broad mix of people from different areas, each involved in specialized activities ranging from metalwork, pottery, and glass making to boat maintenance and handling to the mass processing of commodities like metal and wood.

As the agrarian states of Mesopotamia established broad networks of trade in luxury products, secondary chiefdoms and states grew up, each controlling smaller routes of trade in animal products, metals, salt, and slaves. A series of chiefdoms expanded along the caravan routes to the east. City-states dependent on water-based trade emerged around the Mediterranean. Sequentially, Minoan, Mycenaean, Phoenician, and Greek trading states forged chains of new colonies to organize commerce and guarantee the safe shipment of luxury goods. Starting in the ninth century BCE, for example, Greek city-states established coastal colonies around the Black Sea and into the eastern Mediterranean on the coasts of Sicily, Italy, and France.[59]

Strategies of establishing trade-based political economies caused substantial movements of people in three distinct contexts. First, they moved colonizing populations of Greeks, Phoenicians, and others to designated enclaves; second, they created new opportunities for production and trade with local populations that created extensive population dislocations; and third, they created markets for slaves, which coercively removed substantial populations from Europe, the Caucasus, and Africa.

Although slavery was already common in complex human societies, the creation of trade states fundamentally changed the nature of the practice. To produce specialty products, like olive oil and wine, for an export market, slaves were obtained by the Greek, Roman, and eventually Ottoman empires through conquest (as prisoners of war) and purchase (as new chattel commodities). Slaves filled the ranks of low-skilled agricultural workers, artisans, household servants, and the military. Slavery was the preindustrial means to attain and defend an economy of scale in the export production of agrarian and craft goods. In the age of European empires, captive labor was deployed with a similar goal in mind: to produce highly valued commodities, including sugar, cotton, and tobacco, on a global, industrial scale.[60] Over the past 4,000 years, large-scale slavery has created massive Eurasian and African diasporas.

With the development of political economies, migration has become both a means and an unintended consequence of such governmental strategies as colonization, slavery, trade in elite goods, warfare, and the dislocation of weaker populations. These processes have deep histories, and our understanding of migration in the modern era can be greatly enriched by a consideration of how and why people have moved in the past. Dispersal has always been influenced by family decisions (and kinship systems may, in fact, have evolved as dispersal and displacement strategies). Specific group identities facilitate and prevent human migration today as in the distant past, when tribal agriculturalists displaced and absorbed foraging populations; and political factors promoting migration that have been heightened by industrialization and the large-scale flow of commodities in capitalism can be traced back to the expansionist logic of early complex societies.

Labor migrations, for instance, have shaped the culturally diverse populations that flourish today in North American and European nation-states, but such large-scale migrations are not new to human history. They have parallels in early episodes of colonization, the spread of agrarian populations, and the political movements of archaic chiefdoms and states. People of the past weighed similar options and faced similar constraints when deciding to migrate. If modern populations are distinctive, their distinctiveness perhaps lies in the fact that they are generally less adventurous in their movements, traveling to well-known destinations by well-traveled routes and maintaining close ties to their homelands via telephone, e-mail, transnational media, and frequent return visits. Recent claims about the novelty, transformative power, and unprecedented nature of human mobility in the age of globalization sound a bit strange given the more or less relentless movement of humans whenever opportunities for subsistence, political advantage, and the accumulation of wealth appear to have existed. We seem to be made for travel; we evolved in transit. Migration has shaped and continues to shape the deep and shallow histories of humanity.

CONCLUSIONS

One of twentieth-century archaeology's great achievements was to dispel the notion that prehistoric humans populated the world in entirely natural ways. New evidence has shown that peoples were not blown to the ends of the Earth by the winds, by hunger, by population explosions, or, as Darwin once believed, by floating on vegetation mats from one continent to another. We now see a different, more intentional character in even the earliest dispersals. Evolutionary success went to those hominins whose abilities to disperse and displace earlier populations were enhanced by selective pressures. New social technologies that operated across time and space, such as kinship and the conventional exchange of people and goods, supported the ability of human groups to travel across vast expanses and difficult terrain.

Human displacements and diasporas over the past 8,000 years can be tracked linguistically, genetically, and archaeologically. The populations involved are larger, the webs of exchange more complex, the advantages to be gained from trade and political effort more immense. The world is now dominated by populations who have perfected the arts of displacement. Nowhere are these encounters more striking than in those that have taken place since 1492, when Western explorers led an expansionist wave of conquerors, missionaries, traders, and settlers into a world of indigenous populations. In many cases, the indigenes had reached their homelands as a result of long-term selective pressures, with advantages of dispersal: they were strangers to the methods of expansion and dispossession Europeans had developed in their historically recent career as colonial powers.

It is this conjunction of long-separate worlds that should inform our new sense of history. During the modern era, the global intersection of colonizing and colonized populations, each shaped by different historical and evolutionary pressures, has repeatedly led scholars to claim (or emphatically deny) that one party was more primitive than the other. Such assertions are themselves shaped by an imperial politics of displacement and difference. More fundamental questions are possible. Like two continental plates slipping past each other, the perspectives of deep and shallow history promise to generate friction, but they will also create new intellectual landscapes and new temporal frames in which to contemplate the dynamics of human migration.

CHAPTER 9

Goods

DANIEL LORD SMAIL, MARY C. STINER,
AND TIMOTHY EARLE

The shells of mollusks, like teeth, can have fascinating life histories. Although formed by organisms, they have a hardness approaching that of ceramics and of gemstones like lapis lazuli and turquoise. To the mollusks who make them, shells serve many purposes, including armor, camouflage, and warning. But once the shells are picked up by beachcombers, they embark upon a new life as beautiful and valued objects. They are fun to gather and useful for purposes of ornamentation. If they are rare or taken far from their point of origin, they also serve as the carriers of costly signals in a semiotic system as old as culture itself. As early as 70,000 to 90,000 years ago, shells were drilled and strung together as beads, no doubt traded or exchanged as gifts. They were then lost or discarded, only to be found again, collected, and stored as precious objects in museum drawers thousands of miles from home. The dramatic *Spondylus* (or thorny oyster) was independently adopted for human use in North and South America, Europe, and the Pacific. For example, the shells were harvested off the coast of Ecuador 3,000 years ago and then cut, shaped, polished, fashioned into jewelry, and widely exchanged in the Andes. *Spondylus* was used broadly in the Early Horizon (900 BCE–200 CE) to mark elite status, and it was a key religious symbol in a complex iconography that linked up local chiefdoms and legitimized their political order.[1] Cowrie shells can be found today in countless millions in parts of West Africa, thousands of miles from their place of origin in the Indian Ocean, thanks to the role they played as commodity money in the early modern slave trade.[2] The history of shells, as these fragments suggest, is a history that connects humanity across the globe and across time.

This chapter is not about shells. It is about the category to which shells belong, namely the goods that circulate in human societies. The shells of mollusks, the teeth of elephants and walruses, the threads that encase the larvae of certain caterpillars, the fibers of many plants, the feathers of birds, and inorganic materials such as metals, stone, and clay take form as tools, clothes, ornaments, books, and weapons. Living things, too, can also be goods: cattle and pigs, pets, slaves, even wives and retinues. They can all be displayed, hidden away, exchanged, sold, given as gifts, stolen, pawned, admired, destroyed, or recycled. Such processes have much occupied the anthropological literature.[3] Closely linked to language and the creative genres of social communication, the objects of material culture became containers for meanings that express social relations across both time and space. The evolution of human social institutions, from intimate, small-scale family groups to complex global systems, has been materialized, in the fullest possible sense, through the creation of new cultural forms that carry meaning and relationships into new and expanding social and political arenas.[4]

Goods are woven into the deep history of humanity. Their own history is an incremental and additive one. It begins with a trickle of decorative items, like shells, paintings in ocher, and other signs of personal display, and symbolic objects, like ritual spears and axes. The trickle of goods became streams, expanding to include amber carvings and mammoth tusk beads and, later, hair ornaments, figurines, textiles, and ceramics. The streams turned into the rivers of stuff that mark Neolithic, Bronze Age, and Iron Age societies—some of it displayed on bodies, some of it packed into the households and other architectural forms whose history parallels that of goods. The rivers debouched into the oceans of goods and trash in which we have wallowed ever since those who made the Industrial Revolution found clever ways to transform coal, oil, uranium, wind, and water into commodities shipped across land and sea to consumers who were then taught, and ceaselessly reminded, to desire them.

The history of goods cannot help being a history of more and more stuff. Archaeological horizons vividly illustrate scalar leaps in the quantity of goods in historically unrelated areas around the globe. As goods have multiplied, so have the varieties of goods, like organisms that migrate, speciate, and gradually fill every available niche of an abundant ecosystem. The world's buttons and fasteners, at one time, were nothing more than pins fashioned of bone and probably wood. The pins, in time, gave rise to clasps and buttons, and the buttons diversified to include toggles and other closures and eventually an array of objects made of wood, silver, tin, ivory, shells, pearl, and mother-of-pearl. This is to say nothing of the zippers, elastics, plastics, Velcros, and other fastening devices of the present day. It is a rich phylogeny indeed.

But if the history of goods is necessarily a history of more, it is also a history of the enduring semiotic system in which goods have always been entangled. This is a system for communicating information about status and prestige as well as identity and belonging. An act of semiotic gymnastics often allows the same thing to convey both messages at once. It is tempting to speak of a great transformation whereby the logic of belonging gave way to the logic of prestige. In the hierarchical societies that have emerged in the past few thousand years, prestige goods have become especially visible, and for that reason ever more subject to political controls on their distribution. But this is a temptation we should resist. The logic of belonging that characterizes the ornaments of the Upper Paleolithic has continued to suffuse the mass production and consumption of identical objects in complex societies. The use of the lustrous red-deer canines known as pearl teeth, collected and strung together in a necklace that was exactly like every other pearl-tooth necklace, is echoed today in coins, newspapers, soup cans and grocery carts, and rows of desks in a classroom, all exactly alike. The history of goods may be a history on the move, but it is also a history that explores startlingly familiar patterns operating at different scales, a history that stretches over vast reaches of human time.

COMPETITIVE PRESTIGE

When James Cook first arrived in the Hawaiian Islands, he needed no translator to understand that the paramount chiefs' feather mantles and helmets marked a social elite, although he probably would not have grasped that the mantles were the clothing of gods on earth. People in all human societies are accustomed to the idea that status and prestige can be displayed by means of material objects. So are some animals. Male bower birds display fitness by collecting objects and mounting them in their display arenas. Chimpanzees impress their subordinates by dragging branches about. When people use goods for display, the objects become extensions of the human body (see chapter 3): the feathers harvested from the bird of paradise play much the same role for humans as for their original makers. Goods allow everyone, from the cabaret dancers of the Moulin Rouge with their feathered headdresses to Hawaiian high chiefs with feather mantles, to stretch the edges of the human phenotype. In this role, goods join with postures, facial expressions, and vocal tonalities in composing the symphony of social signals that fly about in the space between individuals.

More than a century ago, Thorstein Veblen, writing partly with tongue in cheek, built a framework in which the central "forward" impetus for human history was generated not by some ceaseless Hegelian synthesis between two opposing forces but instead by the individual's ceaseless urge to outspend others competing for status.[5] Veblen was interested in any pattern of use or consumption that was conspicuous. His rather mischievous goal was to suggest that historical change was generated not by noble sentiments but rather by sheer envy. Or perhaps, as Fernand Braudel conceived it, modernity itself is the product of the inflationary spiral that is generated by the slavish pursuit of fashion. "Is fashion in fact such a trifling thing?" Braudel once asked. He responded in the affirmative, but for him, the future belonged to the trifling societies. To explain this disturbing realization, he offered a mechanism similar to Veblen's inflationary spiral of competitive consumption.[6]

The model of competitive prestige developed by Veblen and Braudel, in which change is driven by fashion, is a captivating one. It maps well onto trends and processes documented in societies all over the world. Consider, for example, the emergence of chiefdoms and early states several thousand years ago. In a sign of the growing prominence of prestige goods, the objects with distinctive decorative content found in Bronze Age societies—including metal serving vessels, mirrors, earrings, bracelets, weapons, and precious body parts of rare animals—became more common and more richly elaborated. The political institutions that emerged in this period, that expanded from small family groups to embrace thousands and eventually hundreds of thousands and more, required radically new structures that could embed independent village communities into regional polities, creating centralized political decision-making hierarchies and facilitating a form of social stratification based on wealth accumulation.

This process of institution building relied on material culture in familiar ways, but with important new twists.[7] The emergence of hierarchies of power within the new regional polities was enabled by the manufacture and control of high-end objects denoting status and distinction. Early in the process, "aggrandizers" competed for leadership

concept

status by channeling the flow of primitive valuables.[8] The emergence of fully fledged chiefdoms, in turn, was associated with the ability to control the flows of valuables across entire regions.[9] Also important was a would-be leader's control over productive land, which became materialized in an elaborate built environment. Local ritual sites continued to be marked with rock art and communities with village walls, houses, plazas, and cemeteries. But new monumental constructions were built as arenas for polity-wide ceremonies of legitimatization and for houses and burials of high-ranking political personages. The political and social order of the polities was visible to all, a permanent presence inscribed on public activities and the landscapes of power. The role of both objects and the built environment in the construction of regional polities is well illustrated by the archaeological record in Europe.[10]

In this kind of environment, as Veblen perceived from his armchair more than a century ago, goods speciated rapidly and intensively, necessarily becoming more numerous, more conspicuous, more refined and tasteful, larger, and more delicate. Much the same kind of selection pressures, operating in different realms, were responsible for increasing the tail of the peacock and the girth of the sea lion. Competitive consumption fashions an escalating spiral that mimics that found in coevolutionary processes (see chapter 4). In *Brave New World*, Aldous Huxley grimly predicted that the spiraling competition could not sustain itself. It would end, he suggested, with a biologically ordained caste system, with each tier defined by specific patterns of consumption that its members were programmed to enjoy.[11]

MEMBERSHIP GOODS

Totalizing narratives are never wholly successful. As Mary Douglas and Baron Isherwood perceived, the ramifying world of goods of the past few thousand years has been generated as much by the demands imposed by groups on their members as by patterns of competitive consumption.[12] Goods communicate belonging. In the form of gifts, dowries, and legacies, goods define and reify kinship. They pass from parents to children, distinguishing the legitimate descendants from the illegitimate. They move from generation to generation, as part of individual or group heritage. They accompany or cross with brides—and if they don't, the woman in question is a concubine rather than a bride, and therefore someone who does not create kinship.

In the Upper Paleolithic, gifts of special objects like decorative shells

def link w/ kinship

and small carved objects helped fashion broad social networks of a sort we never find among other great apes (see chapter 8). Beads and beaded objects could be transferred with ease from one individual to the next and from one individual to many others at once, a trend that persists in contemporary ethnography and more recent archaeological data. The *kula* valuables exchanged by Trobriand Islanders, for instance, carry specific biographies of manufacture, use, and possession that establish the political reputations of influential men and their followers. As red shell necklaces are traded clockwise through the islands for white shell armbands that move counterclockwise, they form "*kula* rings," grand circuits of exchange that knit dyadic relationships into transregional social networks that define local groups.[13] With the formation of village life in Europe (between 9,000 and 4,500 years ago), people increasingly used objects and the built environment to materialize affiliations linking individuals to small corporate groups centered on the family. Material culture, in this context, both integrated the group and excluded others from it. Group membership in early European villages became essential to individuals and their families as they sought access to farmland and hunting areas. The integrating function of goods became part of all group occasions, from everyday activities to calendric ceremonies.

In Neolithic Hungary, regional cultural groupings became identified by distinctive and elaborate styles of ceramic vessels, stone tools, dress, and houses. Everyday life, such as the preparation and eating of food, involved elaborate vessels, utensils, and other devices for reinforcing a family's local identification. Spaces could be used in much the same way. The villages in the Hungarian plain formed tell settlements, artificial hills built up by many generations. These tells stood distinctively above a seasonally inundated plain: in small clusters of houses (consisting of perhaps a few hundred inhabitants each), people lived packed together, looking down on their rich agricultural and grazing lands. The houses, built of wattle and daub, lasted for perhaps a generation. When a new house was needed, it was simply built on top of its predecessor. At each village site, which was often occupied for hundreds of years, an elaborate structure of families developed. The village was structured defensively, and its group was closely associated with the place. Land was held corporately and defended cooperatively. A proliferation of distinctive figurines and other ritual objects and the emergence of village cemeteries demonstrate regular rituals conducted by households according to local ceremonial practices.

Families and groups in all societies, not just in Neolithic Hungary, are

role of goods: create community / class

defined by patterns of sameness: the sameness of goods, the continuity of spaces, and the persistence of similar memories and customs. Douglas and Isherwood explain how goods, in particular, provide marking services when they are shared across a group. Members of the British working class buy inexpensive ceramics made in exactly the same style as those of their neighbors, because, pace Veblen, they do not want to emulate the aristocracy: they want to emulate each other. To serve an integrative role, goods must have similar characteristics. A few hints of individuality may be allowed, but with too much variation or embellishment the object in question ceases to mark membership and instead connotes prestige.

The uniformity essential for membership, importantly, can be generated by premodern industries; it is not a quality limited to highly mechanized industrial production. The famous African red-slip pottery of Mediterranean antiquity, like all mass-produced ceramics, was remarkably uniform, and the fact that it can be found across an enormous geographical range is a sign of how Rome itself was bound together as an imagined community. We can detect a similar urge for uniformity from the outset of the Upper Paleolithic and the later part of the Middle Stone Age, though the dynamics of production and distribution were very different.

2 types

Both prestige goods and membership goods convey signals, but the signals point in different directions. Membership goods unite, triggering emotions like affection, trust, and possibilities for marriage or cooperation. Prestige goods, by contrast, pull apart and trigger emotions like envy, fear, and tension. Goods were readily swept up into the age-old semiotics of division and union and are readily transferred across generations. It comes as no surprise, therefore, that chiefdoms and states, hierarchical societies that rely on an ethic of membership, are keenly interested in producing, using, and controlling goods. So too are egalitarian hunter-gatherer societies, although to a much lesser degree. In fact, practically everyone is interested in regulating everyone else's goods, if only because my prestige, or our collective need, requires that you knuckle down and behave as a consenting member of the group. Because of the extensive social implications of goods, all human societies hedge them about with a vast array of rules and controls, customs and laws.

Although the logic that drives the consumption of membership goods is different from the logic of competitive consumption, both contribute equally to the growing presence of goods in human societies. As large-scale political societies emerged after the Upper Paleolithic, they did not dissolve the smaller-scale entities characteristic of earlier societies (see chapter 10). Modern citizens can and do identify with the imagined community of the nation, but they also identify with smaller and psychologically more manageable units. Indeed, the number of small units of membership has probably multiplied in the past few hundred years. Symbols of membership, often carried by goods (though not always), play a huge role in determining the boundaries of groups. The multiplication of these groups has been a powerful force for accelerating consumption patterns in modern demographic conditions.

MATERIAL SUBSTRATES

Goods constitute signals by virtue of the materials they are made of, particularly if those materials are rare. Rare goods whose substrate has no apparent use value, like cowrie shells, can readily acquire value, and goods that do have use value, such as textiles, acquire added prestige value that can eventually swamp the use value. In the Upper Paleolithic, the work of collecting shells to make necklaces and clothing added value to the shells. Collectors in search of uniformity often selected comparatively rare shell types of similar size. They drilled the shells to make beads and then traded them in areas where they were naturally rare. In the chiefly societies of the Danish Bronze Age, metal could be obtained only by long-distance trade. The metal imported into Denmark was manufactured into fine swords and daggers, fasteners and belts, arm and neck rings, and other impressive objects. These objects signaled wealth. Gifted craftsmen fashioned them for the chiefs to whom they were apparently attached, and the chiefs displayed them publicly and distributed them to supporters and allies as a way to establish and represent regional political networks. Weapons were also used in war and raiding to reinforce power relationships.

Earlier, during the Neolithic, weapons and decorative items were certainly important. We find beautifully knapped flint daggers, often of considerable size; elaborately flaked arrow points; and ground stone battle-axes. Bodily decorations included amber collected from beaches and crafted into beads. But because the weapons and bodily adornments of Neolithic people were manufactured locally from local materials, it was impossible for a would-be aggrandizer to control their production and distribution.[14] With the shift to bronze, bottlenecks in the circulation of metal allowed chieftains to control the distribution and hence the meaning of metal goods.

Because the substrate is not essential to value, almost everything, including foreskins (that of Jesus, at least in legend) and feces (Hitler's), can be turned into an object to be traded or treasured. The identity of the thing is changed in the process. When it starts being a unit of currency, a cowrie becomes something more, or less, than a shell. This change is most evident where humans themselves become commodities. The commodity nature of some goods is conferred when the goods are exchanged between traders or sold at markets. For slaves the process can be complicated, as something that we might call personhood, or autonomy, has to be taken away from the material substrate—the body—to make it a slave. Thus, in fifteenth-century Valencia, a Christian could not simply seize *mudejars* (Iberian Muslims) and put them up for sale.[15] Something had to happen first. The circumstances that could transform *mudejars* or Berbers into slaves, including seizure during a just war, felony, and insolvency, were regulated by law. Slaves, moreover, have at least a nominal ability to cease being goods. Enslaved *mudejar* women often tried to get impregnated by their masters, because, by local statute, bearing a master's child automatically conferred liberty. In other respects, slaves make excellent goods, or so humans have thought for a long time. Slaves were a key commodity in the early medieval European economy.[16] In the antebellum South, owning a slave was a sign of prestige.[17] Moreover, slaves have a special kind of economic value, because they can be harnessed to the task of producing more goods—not only in the fields of cane and cotton but also in the sweatshops, mines, and brick factories that produce many of the goods we consume today. Slaves can also be made to breed more slaves and thus supply new goods for the market.

The nature of the material substrate matters to the history of goods in one very important way, because materials have different longevities. A visit to any museum containing Etruscan goods from the Iron Age suggests a society utterly obsessed with pottery and carved rock, and to a lesser extent with bronze, and it is difficult to remind oneself to put the surviving materials in conversation with those that did not survive. Similarly, the physical remains from later medieval Europe suggest a society captivated by ceramics, ecclesiastical ornaments, and book treasures, like the glorious books of hours from the fourteenth and fifteenth centuries.[18] The odd rusty spearhead, belt buckle, or dagger hilt indicates how greatly iron weapons were treasured as well. Here, though, the written evidence tells an entirely different story. If this world was obsessed by anything it was clothing, especially fancy outerwear. Clothing dominates the intimate records of households and acts of debt

FIGURE 23. Chopines were the platform shoes of medieval and Renaissance Europe. Status was not conveyed solely by the height of the chopines; costume historians have theorized that the elevation also allowed the wearer to display more costly, elaborate fabric trains. (Image copyright © 2010 Bata Shoe Museum, Toronto.)

recovery, acts in which ceramics and pottery were almost totally insignificant. Beds and bed accoutrements—cushions, mattresses, blankets, sheets—run a close second.

Material substrates matter in another way, too, because they help determine how well an object performs its intended function.[19] We have touched on two related characteristics already: durability and transferability. A third is standardization or formal redundancy, a prerequisite for information-carrying units of many types. Without some redundant patterns, goods can have no consistent symbolic content or shared sense of meaning. Collectors of natural forms for use as ornaments during the Paleolithic appear to have had distinct preferences in size, form, and color.[20]

A final salient characteristic of materials and objects is their ability to express amplitude, as this affects how forcefully the messages can be broadcast by the medium. The use of three hundred red-deer pearl teeth to make a necklace inevitably evoked thoughts of the 150 male deer that had to be killed or scavenged to provide them. The chopines or platform shoes that emerged in fifteenth-century Europe, some of them more than 50 centimeters tall, allowed wearers to display that much more fabric in the train of their skirts (figure 23). Quantity affords considerable opportunity for the expression of investment differentials; so does cost. Where Upper Paleolithic ornaments are concerned, we cannot speak of commodities or currency, but we can talk about the cost of searching for raw materials and the time and expertise required in their manufacture. Cost may be expressed by the selection of rare types of shells (such as colorful carnivorous species) and rare minerals, or the time-consuming manufacture of artificial forms.[21] In the European interior, people carved hundreds of ornaments of very similar form and size from mammoth ivory, and spent countless hours doing so.[22] These costs were as legible to the peoples of the Upper Paleolithic as were the costs of the luxurious woolens worn by the women who tottered about on chopines, and observers would have noted the costs with the same interest that Italians, today, note the value of your shoes and your watch.

SEX AND GENDER

Goods can be set to work in the semiotics of sex and gender. Clothes, in particular, have been infused with expectations about gender for a very long time. Joan of Arc got in a great deal of trouble because she shamed the English, but the proceedings of her trial show that the clerics who nominally ran the inquest were also indignant about her spectacular violation of sumptuary norms through wearing men's clothing. Inventories from Mediterranean cities and towns in the later Middle Ages routinely distinguish between male and female clothes, and in Lucca they did not stop there: even beds, blankets, and mattresses were gendered. The distinctions of male and female are highly variable by social and political rank, and they originate deep in human history, as evidenced by the extreme patterns of body fat and dress of the Venus figurines of Upper Paleolithic Eurasia.[23]

In Bronze Age Europe, the dress and equipment of male warriors and elite women were highly distinctive. A warrior was buried with his sword, sword belt, special clothing, and personal grooming equipment, including razors and tweezers. Because gendered clothing is meant to distinguish the sexes, in the same way that white gloves signal membership in an elite caste, it has aspects of uniformity, as evidenced in the sameness of men's ties today and women's wimples in past centuries. But in these later societies, clothing also marks social status. Female bodies have long served as sites for the materialization of prestige, not only in women's roles as wives and concubines but also as household slaves and domestics—and as art objects. The emergence of mass consumption in the twentieth century, notably the rise of department stores, targeted women's bodies more than men's. This trend was a vast change from earlier centuries, when men's bodies were the sites of the most conspicuous forms of sartorial consumption.

THE DEEP HISTORY OF ORNAMENTS

In contemplating the deep history of goods, it is difficult to know how far back to go. The example of bower birds suggests that material ostentation did not begin with humans: ecological circumstances have long induced a few species, perhaps those with the necessary cognitive and morphological traits, to integrate goods into their systems of communication. The archaeological record of humanity reveals stone tools from at least 2.6 million years ago. Whatever their functional characteristics, tools also have discernible forms that themselves constitute signs. To focus on the archive of ornamentation, then, is a somewhat arbitrary choice. Yet ornaments are one of the earliest and most widespread forms of a special kind of good, a good that has the qualities of an art form.

Beads or objects of similar artistry and form date back 70,000 years or more in Africa and southwestern Asia.[24] With the exception of the cave paintings in southwestern Europe, in fact, most Upper Paleolithic art took the form of small and portable beads whose formal properties were imposed repeatedly through human manufacture.[25] Beads were made from a range of raw materials, such as shell, soft stone, mammal teeth, bone, amber, and ostrich eggshell. Many were taken directly from nature, such as red-deer pearl teeth and small shells. Other beads were carefully made to *resemble* something taken from nature, such as the objects laboriously carved from mammoth ivory or soft stone to look like red-deer pearl teeth or sea shells.[26] Some of these beads were assembled in very artistic ways, judging from rare examples of preserved necklaces and belts or aprons. These include the spectacular double burial at Sungir in Russia, in which a boy and a girl were buried with grave goods that included more than nine thousand mammoth-ivory beads sewn to their funerary vestments. Each bead probably took an hour to carve. Beads were the most basic units of ornamentation (see figure 24). Archaeologists normally find them as isolated objects in the camp litter, where they are found whole, burned, or broken; they are rarely found in graves. These objects are abundant in some Upper Paleolithic sites but strangely absent from others of the same period and region.[27]

Beads, like other forms of Paleolithic art (such as cave paintings and small figurines), were objects for communication. In the modern ethnographic record, ornaments and certain everyday tools similar to those we find in the Paleolithic frequently serve as media in token exchanges, meant to formalize expectations of delayed reciprocity between trade partners.[28] The intended audiences for and information conveyed by Paleolithic goods are a matter of speculation, though the objects often have fairly explicit forms or evocative colors. The messages themselves are clear enough. A pair of pearl teeth was surely meant to gesture to the large buck that was killed to obtain them; the claw of an eagle hints

FIGURE 24. Shell beads from the early Upper Paleolithic (Aurignacian) layers of Klissoura Cave 1 in southern Greece, dated by radiocarbon technique to between 33,000 and 35,000 years ago. The holes in the shells were made by humans, using a punch technique. The beads were then strung on a cord; some of the holes show signs of wear. (Photo © M. C. Stiner.)

at the precision of a powerful hunter. We find objects that have a breast-like form and mollusk shells selected for a particular blood-red color.

The use of these noneconomic objects as communication media during the Late Pleistocene raises a number of fascinating questions about the early development of a technology for visual communication as well as the contexts in which such practices first emerged. To begin with, careful analysis of substances and isotopes has allowed us to track the movements of goods and materials, although it remains difficult to distinguish materials that moved with migrating peoples from those exchanged between distant parties. Some information on intergroup contact nonetheless is suggested by the movement of distinctive types of tool stone (e.g., flint, chert, and basalt), amber, and mollusk shells that originated from discrete and distant sources.[29] The quantities of these materials moved from one location to another were small.[30] Even so, the *geographic* extent of exchange or transport of ornaments during the Upper Paleolithic was considerable, perhaps exceeding that of high-quality tool stone.[31] The maximum distances over which stone raw materials were moved indicate that Middle and Upper Paleolithic groups had fairly similar territory sizes. However, the pattern from the Middle Paleolithic (ca. 300,000 to 30,000 years ago) suggests that the raw material was progressively consumed as it was carried farther and farther from the source.[32]

The objects that moved in the Middle Paleolithic were strictly economic items whose utility could be exhausted through use. In the Upper Paleolithic, the transported goods included beads. Ornamental objects like beads are distinctive in that they generally were not subject to physical exhaustion as they were carried or traded away from a raw-material source. They cost little, if anything, to move on account of their small sizes and quantities, and they tended to be visually arresting. Many archaeologists have marveled at the blossoming of artistic traditions in the early Upper Paleolithic—in beads, pendants, bone pins, small sculptures, and wall paintings—and the lack of durable art objects in the Middle Paleolithic before it.[33]

Some archaeologists have argued that the similarities in ornament raw material, shape, and size in northern and southern Eurasia reflect a common ethnic and linguistic heritage, deriving from early Upper Paleolithic populations that branched out from an unknown center of origin.[34] An alternative explanation is that these similarities were maintained inadvertently as part of loose, long-distance networks that people used to manage risk through alliances and marriage ties. The raw materials used for ornament making exert a strong local signal, whereas the resemblances in form and size reflect human links between distant areas.[35] The uniformity of shapes and sizes of Paleolithic beads stems in part from the use of a few highly favored natural forms, but it extends well beyond these prototypes because of the artificial replication of these shapes in other materials. In this sense, the beads may even suggest the existence of a lingua franca of sorts, though it is not clear how such uniformity was maintained across disparate groups.

The emergence of Paleolithic art represents a profound evolution in the nature of social messages that could be conveyed. Red ocher and other mineral pigments occur in earlier sites dating to the Middle Paleolithic and early Middle Stone Age, and pigment-based ornamentation on the skin may have been practiced.[36] If so, the extent of these practices would have been mostly limited to face-to-face interactions. Kuhn and Stiner suggest that pigment-only decorative systems would have been oriented largely toward increasing an individual's visual impact.[37] Fugitive media were not well suited for conveying standardized social messages.

By contrast, the widespread appearance of Paleolithic beads, in particular, implies that different kinds of information were being conveyed through body ornamentation, and probably to a larger and different audience. Body ornaments are most important for communicating to people "in the middle distance" socially: individuals who are close enough to the wearer to understand the meaning of the ornaments but who do not know her or him personally.[38] The durable and transferable nature of beads and beaded objects frees communication from dependence on direct interaction with other people. The circulation of ornaments allows information to be transferred and expressed over larger spatial and temporal domains. The messages encoded in body ornaments and decorated objects can be expressed even when the individuals involved are absent or dead. This characteristic is vital to the use of communication technology for establishing and maintaining relationships over large areas of space or over a human life span.

The fact that these early technologies for visual communication were amplifiable implies cultural notions of value.[39] At the very least, the appearance of this new medium of ornamentation implies that there was an advantage to expressing certain kinds of information in semipermanent media and thus suggests that such information might itself have been longer-lasting and more structured. The sudden appearance of transferable, durable objects therefore seems to imply an expanded scale of social interaction in the late Middle Stone Age of Africa and the early Upper Paleolithic of Eurasia, with messages or iconic objects exchanged over larger areas and among a wider variety of people.

Ethnographic studies assure us that ornaments can be put to double uses, as both individual and group expressions of style.[40] Although these uses are not easy to distinguish archaeologically, the contexts of ornament use and larger patterns of uniformity tell us something about the dynamics of within-group and intergroup communication. Because ornaments can efficiently convey information about quantity or cost, they are also useful in the forms of social competition described by Veblen, including "costly advertising" or conspicuous displays that imply something about an individual's fitness.[41] Because Paleolithic ornaments are unevenly distributed in the Old World, it is also possible that early beads mark heightened levels of within-group competition played out in the social and symbolic rather than purely physical arena.

This analysis of changing technologies for body ornamentation in the Paleolithic raises the question of why the scale and complexity of social interactions might have increased during the Upper Paleolithic and late

Middle Stone Age and expanded further in later periods. Here we run up against one of the basic challenges of paleoanthropology, that of distinguishing the consequences of evolutionary changes in fundamental human capacities from the effects of changes in the external conditions of life. The observed developments in technologies for social communication and inferred changes in the nature of social interaction could reflect a heightened need to communicate with ever-growing numbers of people, strangers and friends alike, and to exert greater control over the outcomes of those interactions.[42]

These exigencies in turn may have been responses to increasing population sizes and other causes of resource decline and shrinking territories.[43] Some researchers have cogently argued that the technological shifts indicate a fundamental change in hominins' abilities to conceptualize and execute social action. For example, the use of long-lasting, exchangeable objects to communicate across large areas or across generations may require higher-order executive functions than do direct face-to-face communications.[44] This debate will see no immediate resolution, but we can examine the probable relation between the pace of culture change and demographic increase (see chapter 10). Should the data coverage ever be sufficient, we may find a good correspondence between areas most heavily populated by Paleolithic foragers and the rate of bead production and use. Changes in the pace of life and its consequences were as important to quantum culture change in the remote past as they have been in the recent past. This phenomenon is at least partly independent of human neurological structures and cognitive capacities.

SAMENESS AND REPEATABILITY

In 1845, John Franklin set sail from England on a mission to discover the Northwest Passage. The expedition's two ships carried a sampling of the products of what has been called, not without reason, the "consumer revolution" of the eighteenth century.[45] These goods included a large selection of the new canned foods that would provide much of the sustenance for the 129 members of the crew. The first year of the expedition was uneventful, if unspeakably cold. During the second and third years, however, contrary winds kept the expedition icebound and immobile in the high Arctic, and by April 1848, twenty-four men had died, including Franklin. The survivors decided to abandon ship for the mainland. They came ashore on King William Island, scarcely halfway through the tangle of islands that make up the high Arctic, and a few, despairing of their prospects for rescue, broke from the main group and headed south. They took lifeboats and fashioned them into sledges with leather harnesses, to be drawn by the only beasts of burden available: the men themselves. Into the sledges they piled things they might need, including cans of food, canteens, a sextant,[7] chronometers, shotguns and pellets, and a medicine chest. They also took thousands of personal items, including Franklin's gold watch, eating utensils emblazoned with the family crests of the officers who used them, a family Bible, prayer books, Oliver Goldsmith's novel *The Vicar of Wakefield,* a hairbrush, carpet slippers, a tea canister, and decorative stars that adorned the hats of the Royal Marines.

Days or weeks later, as their appalling situation became apparent, the men gradually began to discard the things they had brought with them. The medicine chest was one of the first things to go, along with the sextant and unopened tins of food. The discarded goods formed a trail across a hundred miles of ice and snow. Many were picked up by members of the local Inuit population as curiosities. Enough of this jetsam remained, however, to allow a rescue expedition to follow the last steps of the doomed expedition. At the end of the trail, in 1853, the rescuers came across one of the lifeboat sledges, and inside they found, to their horror, the bones of the last survivors scattered among the few goods that had survived the journey, among them *The Vicar of Wakefield.*

The book's journey across the snowy Arctic is a reminder of how goods, like parasites, have embedded themselves in human culture. Before 1845, few books were taken on journeys: they were too valuable. This book's initial voyage out of England in 1845, therefore, is an indicator of the emergence of books and reading materials as a different kind of consumable, a trend that had begun earlier in Europe and Ming China.[46] The shift from rag stock to wood-pulp paper helped make this shift possible. But why should it have occurred to anyone threatened by frostbite and hunger to carry a book across the icy wastelands of the north?

The Vicar of Wakefield, first published in 1766, quickly became one of the most popular novels in Britain. By 1845, it had gone through more than one hundred new editions or printings. It even makes a cameo appearance in the library of a farmer in Jane Austen's *Emma.* To this extent, the book itself was an emblem of Englishness, an object that, by virtue of its enormous distribution, connected its author to household libraries across Britain. This connection to home, presumably, is part of the reason why *The Vicar of Wakefield* lasted longer in the sledge than the sextant.

According to Benedict Anderson, the ability of industrial manufacturing to replicate identical objects is crucial to the formation of the imagined communities of the modern world.[47] The capacity to imagine oneself as part of a vast community is bolstered by the knowledge that everyone is sharing, looking at, yearning for, or learning from exactly the same object. As we have seen, though, the quality of repeatability has been found from the beginning of the Upper Paleolithic. It was an important feature of the ceramics, temple forms, and other objects manufactured during the Bronze and Iron Ages. To this extent, the mass production and circulation of repeatable objects is something that can emerge in any political ecology where there has been a release from proximity, where individuals have developed far-flung connections and networks defined by goods and kinship. The repeated object itself is a crucial feature of this release, as it can travel across considerable distances, carrying with it threads of connection by virtue of its sameness.

The deep history of repeatability offers us the kind of stable context that is necessary for the writing of any history. This is true even though we are dealing with a process or a behavior rather than one of the backdrops more usual to the writing of history, such as a geographical entity (e.g., the history of Britain), an institution (e.g., the history of banking, slavery, or warfare), or a social category (e.g., the history of women or the working class). Knowing the deep history of repeatability allows us to explore the process at work in particular situations and use the distinctive features we find at the heart of our histories.

In this vein, consider the history and anthropology of the object of religious veneration in the Christian West, from the fall of Rome to the fifteenth century. In the wake of the collapse of the western Roman Empire, the nature of the holy underwent a profound transformation: it came to center on the relics of the very special dead.[48] These could consist of either body parts (typically bones) of saints and other holy persons or objects they had touched (contact relics). Because Jesus and Mary were assumed bodily into heaven, they left behind only contact relics, such as the True Cross, bits of cloth blotted with Mary's breast milk, and the like.

Relics are a special kind of good. Their substrate generally has no intrinsic value, and the objects themselves are indistinguishable from one another. As a result, a huge emphasis was placed on authentication. The emerging cult of relics, which dominated the religious scene in Europe for half a millennium, centered on the veneration of a massive number of sacred objects, each believed to have different properties. Veneration, in turn, generated tremendous mobility. Pilgrims criss-crossed Europe.[49] The relics themselves, echoing a pattern of ossuary mobility from earlier ages, were sometimes highly mobile, being sold, traded, given as gifts, and, often enough, stolen.[50]

By the thirteenth century, this culture of veneration had undergone a transformation. The relics were still there, but a new object, the eucha-rist, was crowding them out as the central objects of veneration.[51] The eucharist, a small, flat wafer deemed to be Christ's body, is an extraor-dinarily dull object of an appalling sameness—and this, of course, is exactly why it was and is meaningful. The eucharist had always been important to Christianity, but over the course of the twelfth century an occasional partaking turned into the regular communion rite that most present-day Christians are familiar with.

The population of Europe in 1300 was in the range of 73 million, of whom the vast majority were Christian. Even leaving aside the children not yet old enough to receive communion, the heretics, the excommuni-cants, and of course the Jews and Muslims, the ecclesiastical bakeries of Europe were probably churning out tens of millions of wafers for each of the three major feasts when Communion was normally taken by the laity. In addition, wafers were displayed and consumed by the clergy at mass every day. It is hard to calculate the total number of wafers required annually: 100 million? 200 million? Whatever the sum, the scale of production dwarfs that of the next most commonly replicated object in 1300, namely the coins issued by kingdoms and cities.

Coins, in striking contrast to commodity money like cowries, do symbolic work by virtue of carrying the stamped symbols of sovereignty to the edges of a realm and beyond. The eucharist does symbolic work even though it is not stamped like a coin: the symbolic importance is provided by the ceremony of the mass, which does not simply invest the eucharist with the image of Christ's head but transforms it into his body. It does symbolic work not because it is durable and lasting but for exactly the opposite reason. The act of consumption continuously gen-erated the need for more.

The imagined community of Latin Christendom, indeed the very con-cept of Europe itself, emerged in tandem with the rise of eucharistic devotion in the twelfth century. Papal monarchy was eclipsing the epis-copal regionalism that had hinged on local control of unique local rel-ics. This transformation should be considered from the perspective of the deep history of uniqueness and repeatability. In a general sense, it can be seen as simply one instance in an age-old oscillation between the unique and the repeated, an oscillation generated by the long-standing tension between membership goods and prestige goods. The sameness of the eucharist, in this view, laid the basis for the patterns of consumption and waste that are distinctive features of the fourteenth century and beyond.

EMULATION AND CONSUMPTION

From the twelfth century onward, a tide of sumptuary legislation rose, not ebbing until the seventeenth and eighteenth centuries, as eucharistic devotion, along with church attendance, began to fall.[52] By the later Middle Ages, the sort of status emulation that Veblen had predicted took shape in the form of a wider distribution of luxury goods across different social strata and especially an emerging industry devoted to luxury knock-offs. Archaeologists studying deposits from later medieval London, for example, have discovered a growing array of fasteners and fittings made from tin and base alloys that mimic the silver accessories found on the hot new fashions among the elite: namely, the tight-fitting, body-hugging sewn clothes that replaced the draped garments of the thirteenth century.[53] The fashion for heraldry and lineage spilled over into the households of the only moderately well-to-do. Inventories reveal that the dining halls of artisans and tradesmen in Mediterranean Europe were adorned with *pavices,* the decorative shields bearing a family's seal or coat of arms. According to Alan Hunt, legislation against this sort of imitation reached its peak in the fourteenth and fifteenth centuries, as legislators sought to restrain *sumptus,* excess in all its forms, including forms of consumption that mimicked or mocked aristocratic or clerical monopolies.[54]

Sumptuary law lingers on in the form of school dress codes, customs governing business attire, and "sin" taxes on luxury goods. But the formal disappearance of sumptuary law and the consequent unfettering of the market look very much like a bourgeois victory over the aristocracy. The pattern neatly fits a model of history writing that demands a progressive movement from something to something else. This model, however, loses shape when framed in deep time. Rather than the J curve of modernity (see chapter 10), such trends describe a bell curve, in which state or social regulations governing the production and circulation of repeated objects and prestige objects emerge, become dominant, and then decline, or more accurately take different forms. In early modern Europe, printing as well as the printlike qualities of mass-produced ceramics, such as Delft ware and Wedgwood, took up the task of supplying the membership goods. Membership goods, in this sense, were being supplied by individual producers rather than state-level agents interested in monopolizing the production and circulation of both prestige goods and membership goods. In a political sense, the shedding of market controls saw a return to the conditions of production and consumption of the Upper Paleolithic.

Competitive consumption and, especially, luxury knock-offs signal a different use for goods, a world of taste and fashion in which the consumption of goods begins to matter more than the goods themselves. It produces trash.[55] Archaeology, like history, used to ignore or even discard the junk, but as the theory and method of excavation have changed in recent decades, archaeology has become the science of the discarded object. Broken ceramics, enough to constitute small mountains, were definitely thrown away by their owners. Other items may have been lost or discarded by accident. Medieval coins recovered from the fields of England presumably fell out of the pockets of peasants.[56] Some of the best finds in early American archaeology consist of objects that fell into privies and latrines and were not retrieved by their squeamish owners.[57]

Before the modern era, recycling was the norm. Household inventories from later medieval Mediterranean Europe—few of which survive, probably no more than a few tens of thousands—reveal households bulging with clothing, linens, curtains, beds, mattresses, cushions, utensils, fine storage chests, belts, and so on; but along with all the linens and fineware are listed a considerable number of items described as broken, torn, worn, old, and, most evocatively, "sad." A vast system existed for recycling all this material, ranging from rag pickers to smiths who reworked metals. The households found in certain favored modern economies contain a lot of stuff, but no more than the households of any reasonably well-to-do house in late medieval Mediterranean Europe. The velocity of circulation, of course, is much faster today. Now that we realize that we must recycle to avoid drowning in trash, we are becoming medieval again.

GOODS AS PARASITES

If goods are like people—if goods are imbricated in the relationships of family and kinship and, along with pets, can be treated as members of the family—then disposable goods are not unlike slaves who have been denied personhood. If the affirmation of social hierarchies requires the

hm

trashing of some beings, if freedom can only be celebrated when some people are systematically deprived of it, then the history of trash takes up where emancipation leaves off. The very perception of freedom is the freedom to be able to consume and discard. Perhaps the most poignant observation here is that goods are now more firmly entangled in slavery than ever before, because much of the slavery (or semislavery) in the modern world is practiced in the factories and mines that generate consumer goods.

The copy of *The Vicar of Wakefield* that accompanied the rump of the Franklin expedition somehow avoided being turned into trash. The explanation for this apparent anomaly, or at least part of the explanation, lies in our coming to terms with the depth of the human dependence on goods. We have already seen how the freedom to consume goods is entangled with the freedom to consume slaves. Goods are addictive. The anticipation of shopping and the use of electronic devices is known to lead to high levels of dopamine in some people. This is clearly a learned behavior that emerges when the desire to use goods and read goods interacts with changes in the distribution of them. Goods, in this sense, are not all that distinct from viruses or prions: strings or bundles of molecules, lacking DNA, that nonetheless have a talent for co-opting the metabolic energy of other organisms and using that energy to reproduce themselves. The infection, to continue with this playful metaphor, is very old, perhaps 2.6 million years or older. It has intensified in leaps and stages across human history: in the upper Paleolithic; in conjunction with the rise of early chiefdoms; at points in time scattered across the face of a young global history; and in the past few hundred years.

Goods and humans, in this vision, have been dancing a coevolutionary dance for a long, long time. Other pairs engage in the same dance: towering trees and strangler figs, ruminants and gut fauna, ant colonies and aphids. We can leave aside here the question of whether the spiraling process involving humans and goods is symbiotic or parasitic (and in the latter case, the delicate question of which is the parasite and which the host). But whatever the results of that inquiry, we can see how the deep history of goods invites us to contemplate a world that erases firm distinctions between animate and inanimate material. At the core, after all, we are all just strings of molecules. We readily acknowledge our kinship with chimpanzees, fruit flies, and even bananas. The inexorable logic of comparison suggests that it is self-centered to make the possession of DNA the measure of worth.

The object of this exercise is not so much to deny us our free will, agency, or soul, or any other quality of autonomy, but rather to grant agency to the other things around us. The agency does not lie in a thing per se. It is instead an illusion that we perceive when we contemplate the phylogeny of goods in its full majesty: for goods adapt, evolve, and speciate in a way that closely resembles the phylogeny of a DNA entity. In the same way that we have to accept that there is no sharp line that marks the break between biology and culture, between nonhistory and history, so too there is no clear rupture between what is animate and what is inanimate, between humans and their goods, or between goods and their humans.

CHAPTER 10

Scale

MARY C. STINER, TIMOTHY EARLE, DANIEL LORD SMAIL,
AND ANDREW SHRYOCK

Scholars of the modern era, like policy makers, are fascinated by the notion of take-off. The idea is a simple one. At some point in the past two centuries, humanity burst through a ceiling and embarked on a novel path toward an exhilarating, uncertain future. This metaphor has been applied to numerous research topics, including energy consumption, global temperature, species extinction rates, income level, land clearance, and dietary protein. The data generated in these fields lend themselves to graphs that illustrate scalar leaps, sharply angled moments of take-off that produce the distinctive J curve of modernity. The exact date of the take-off varies, but the time axis of the graph usually emphasizes the past two hundred years.

Consider the widely cited graph generated by the economist Gregory Clark to depict trends in per capita income over the past three thousand years (figure 25). It is striking on two accounts. First, it vividly illustrates Clark's point that the Industrial Revolution inaugurated a spectacular ascent in per capita income. Second, it provides visual support for Clark's key assertion that the existence of a Malthusian cap blocked all previous income gains. The left tail of the graph, reaching back to 1000 BCE, shows the history of these disappointing setbacks; if the data were available, the left tail, with its minuscule oscillations, would extend indefinitely back in time. Other graphs, such as those charting energy consumption (see figure 26), also suggest an infinitely long, and inexplicably flat, left tail.

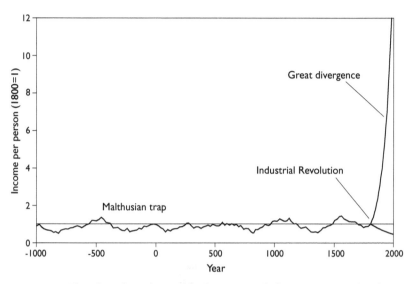

FIGURE 25. The release from the "Malthusian trap," with the year 1800 as a baseline for income levels. (Clark 2007, 2; used by permission of Princeton University Press.)

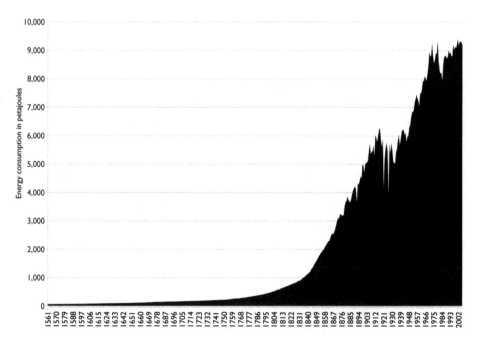

FIGURE 26. The rising curve of energy use. (Adapted from Warde 2007, 72, incorporating new data.)

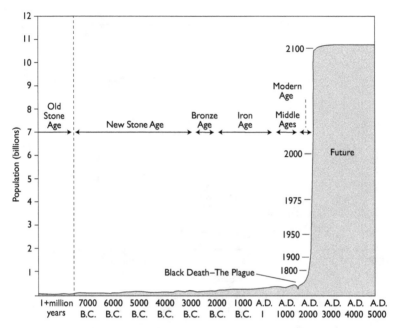

FIGURE 27. The J curve of world population growth. (Population Reference Bureau, www.prb.org, accessed 6 October 2009.)

Some of the most arresting graphs are those illustrating the rapid increase of human populations. A sigmoidal graph of population growth widely used on Internet sites (figure 27) characterizes the genre. The left tail extends back more than 1 million years into the Old Stone Age, although the scale fails to represent the immensity of this time period. To give the plotline verisimilitude, the illustrator adds rises and dips that have no statistical or chronological meaning. According to the graph, human populations rise slowly and uncertainly until 1750 or thereabouts, following which comes the vertiginous ascent. The bumps then disappear from the plotline. The new smoothness, here and in Clark's graph, represents the moment at which humans escape from natural forces.

Viewed in their totality—and there are thousands of examples available in print and electronic forms—these J curve graphs yield a compelling picture of modernity on the move. They point to something vast and new happening simultaneously all over the globe, something of critical importance. When the actions of multitudinous humans directly or indirectly change levels of atmospheric carbon dioxide, melt glaciers, and cause the rise of seas; when they denude landscapes, dry up aquifers,

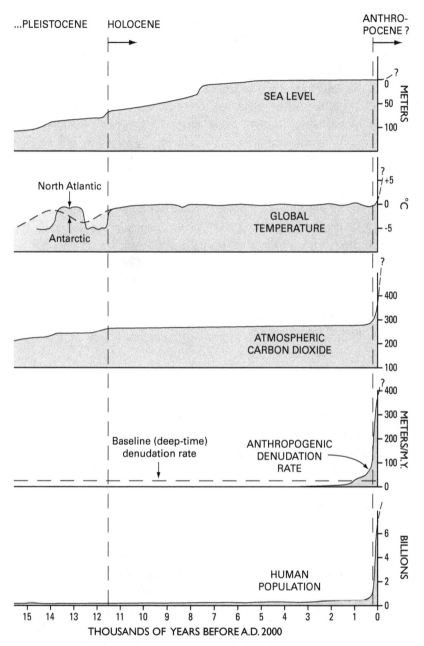

FIGURE 28. The J curves of the Anthropocene. (Zalasiewicz et al. 2008; used by permission of *GSA Today*.)

trigger extinctions, and meddle with rates of mortality and natality, then humanity itself appears as more than a biological entity. Leaving behind the rhythms of the natural world, we have become a geological agent in our own right, responsible for ushering in a new age: what some scholars call the Anthropocene (see figure 28).

The idea of the Anthropocene is a powerful tool. It lends gravitas to policy discussions concerning global climate change and sustainability. Yet the narrative arc suggested by the J curve of modernity, with its sudden, sharp and usually upward trend, is problematic for the framing of a deep history. Attempts to model this dramatic take-off posit a sudden, artificial shift in the timeline of the human endeavor, a monstrous leap in the scale at which things happen. In this worldview, humans have created a remarkable set of new conditions and then adapted to them using cultural mechanisms, somehow leaving behind—in fact becoming masters or destroyers of—the nature that for so long held humankind in its grip. Everything before this point of transition is visually flattened out into a prehistory of little interest. At the moment of take-off, new forces come together to create the modern world, whose rich, eventful history merits more of our attention.

DEEP HISTORY, UNFLATTENED

This chapter is about the unexamined left tail in the graph of human history. Contrary to the impression created by the iconic graphs of modernity, the left tail is not flat at all: it only appears so at the scale on which the graphs are drawn. Both the drawings and the scale bespeak a singular preoccupation with the place of modern humans in the world. We moderns are intensely tribal. We identify with our own kind, and we are fascinated by the historical processes that set us apart from others— from people who lived in the past, or live today on the margins of the global system—whose relationship to nature, and to their own societies, seems less disruptive and less susceptible to the ills and advances of "civilization," "progress," and other, world-altering forms of "agency." This worldview is meaningful to us because scalar increases are built into its key terms, which liken modernity to maturation and development. But scale can be a deceptive thing. The seemingly radical transitions that created the modern world emerged out of nested hierarchies of pattern and form; they were additive as well as transformative. We now know that systems with emergent properties can generate nonlinear trends at any scale of analysis. In other words, we must look at what was happening prior to the radical inflection that defines the J curve of social or economic change. Little is learned by using the transition to modernity to render earlier periods flat, unknowable, and historically insignificant.

The goal of this chapter is to show that deep human history, too, is punctuated by momentous leaps in population, energy flow, efficiency, levels of political organization, and degrees of connectivity. Our relationship to the ecosystems we and our ancestors have inhabited is marked by scalar leaps in extractive capacity: the harnessing of fire, for example, enabled early humans to extract significantly more calories from foods. Seen through the optic of deep history, what matter are the processes that produce the leaps and change the state of existence. The size of a leap relative to later events is unimportant. A leap from human communities numbering in the tens of people to those numbering in the thousands may be just as momentous for social relations as the leap from millions to hundreds of millions; indeed, the smaller shift probably required more complicated and durable alterations in human interactive styles. Likewise, a jump from 0.1 percent to 1 percent in the amount of biomass humans extract from an acre of land can have effects no less revolutionary in natural systems than a jump from 10 percent to the more than 90 percent that agricultural systems manage today.

Viewed in sequence, scalar leaps suggest a metaphor for human history that follows the pattern of a fractal, in which the same pattern is repeated at every level of magnification. Smaller scales do not simply vanish as larger ones emerge. Historians have long been fascinated by the idea that human history is the story of how small family groups turned into nations: they imagine that identities were transformed, made, or remade in the process. But we have never stopped living in groups reminiscent of the families, clans, and tribes described by political anthropologists. As scales of political organization increase, we add new levels of behavior; in the process, we invent new social actors and larger, more inclusive contexts in which they can act. Sociopolitical life, in this view, has been multiscalar since at least the Upper Paleolithic. Historically, each new level of social integration is shaped by the dynamics of the social forms that predate it and may still, in diverse ways, be embedded within it.

To make additional sense of these ideas, we need to explore cases in which scalar increases are demonstrably real but their causes and effects are likely to be misdiagnosed. These misinterpretations occur because the processes that triggered the increases in scale unfolded in a historical time frame that is much deeper, and often less dramatic, than the cumulative moments in which "revolutions" and "great transitions" can finally be perceived and narrated as historical events. We begin with population growth, a domain of obvious relevance whose data lend themselves to graphs illustrating scalar leaps.

POPULATION AND THE ENERGY BASE

Human populations across the Pleistocene were never stable; they responded to imperceptible shifts in climate as well as catastrophic events, such as the explosion of Mount Toba about 73,000 years ago and the sudden, brief return to cold, dry conditions in the Younger Dryas about 11,000 years ago.[1] Genetic data indicate several demographic bottlenecks in the human past, some of which were dangerously narrow. With dispersal out of Africa (see chapter 8), humans experienced the sort of population bounce that often follows an escape from old pathogens and predators and contact with new, untapped food resources. In Eurasia, additional pulses in population growth have been detected between 50 and 40 ka and again in the latter half of the Upper Paleolithic, roughly 25 to 22 ka; and a very large burst occurred in the millennia after the Last Glacial Maximum (after approximately 18 ka).[2] Yet another episode of population growth took place about 13 to 10 ka in many parts of Eurasia. The story of the human population in Africa is less well known, but Nile Valley and South African populations underwent a series of early pulses as well.[3] The number of humans worldwide increased by several orders of magnitude, but never to the extent we are familiar with today.

With each population increase, wherever it occurred, more individuals required resources from the environment. Yet resources are finite. Only changes in the ways that humans extract energy from the natural world could account for unprecedented bursts in human population growth. The Green Revolution of the 1960s and 1970s, for example, raised the carrying capacity of farmland by the use of pesticides and fertilizers and by improvements in domestic stock. A major challenge for archaeologists has been to understand how, in the Pleistocene, *before* the domestication of plants and animals, environmental carrying capacity was also raised, stage by stage. The full picture of these successive transformations is not yet clear. One thing is certain, however: the lifting of the ceiling was, at least in part, the product of human creativity.

Let us begin with what, for want of better terminology, we call the social dimensions of this emerging history. More than a century of ethnographic research among hunter-gatherers has shown how they insulate themselves from adversity and risk through exchange and reciprocity and through the maintenance of interactive networks that span great distances, producing both social and genetic relatedness.[4] Connections are maintained through gift giving, sharing, marriage, hospitality, and all the other modes of "kinshipping" that humans have created during their evolution as a species (see chapter 2). Because these social practices do not always leave obvious archaeological signatures, it is difficult to understand how they might have operated in Paleolithic societies. Even so, we can tease out evidence for the degree of social connectedness in the Upper Paleolithic from the presence and quantity of decorative and iconic objects in different areas (see chapter 9). New forms of decoration appeared, radiated, and were abandoned at an accelerating pace during the Upper Paleolithic, a pattern that hints at the dramatic changes afoot.[5]

Economic factors alone cannot explain the existence of decorative items, and archaeologists now lean toward the conclusion that they served as key elements in a technology of social communication.[6] The novel importance of beads and baubles perhaps reflected a heightened need to communicate with an ever-growing number of people, strangers and friends alike, and to exert greater control over the outcome of those interactions. In Eurasia, the impact of the Upper Paleolithic social transformation on population was twofold. First, increasing levels of connectedness provided a buffer against periods of hardship, thereby reducing mortality rates. Second, and perhaps more important, new habits of connectedness, together with the technologies for making those connections tangible, provided social infrastructure that would accommodate local resource stresses, future migrations, and population surges. In short, human populations emerged from the Pleistocene socially adapted for transformations to come.

The people involved in the "decorative revolution" were not entirely at the mercy of their environment. Like the British working class during the early decades of industrialization, Upper Paleolithic foragers had a hand in their own making.[7] The social worlds they created did not flow automatically from earlier cognitive, demographic, or social revolutions. They emerged instead as the innovative reworking of contexts and materials and the unleashing of latent abilities. The human brain, for example, may have been adapted for social connectedness and symbolic display, but this adaptation was meaningless without the historically contingent transformation that brought it to life. After all, the brain was also adapted for playing chess and contemplating nuclear physics, but neither was on the horizon in the Upper Paleolithic, nor was there anything inevitable about their eventual invention several tens of thousands of years later. The task of explanation is not satisfied merely by pointing to the existence of a set of adaptations. The explanation lies, instead, in the history.

THE FALL OF TEMPERATE-ZONE HUNTER-GATHERERS

What, then, of the invention of agriculture, the great transition celebrated by V. Gordon Childe and the generations of Western Civilization instructors who followed him? Toward the end of the Pleistocene, the foraging systems that characterized the subsistence economies of the eastern Mediterranean basin began to collapse, and out of the wreckage emerged the Neolithic revolution, which then spread like wildfire through Europe, western Asia, and parts of Africa. In the same way that the Anthropocene can be defined by J curves, so too can the rapid emergence of the Neolithic. Consider, for example, an upside-down J curve: such a graph illustrates the decline in the availability of wild hoofed animals, including deer, aurochs, and the ancestors of pigs, goats, and horses, in the Mediterranean world toward the end of the Pleistocene (figure 29). These data come from studies that measure the percentage of bones and teeth from large hoofed mammals relative to small animal remains found at hunter-gatherer sites. The biggest drop in large hoofed mammal remains occurred around 10,000 years ago.[8] Widespread and catastrophic, it punctuates a long trend toward broadening diets and led in to the emergence of farming in the Fertile Crescent. It also coincides with the beginning of the Holocene epoch, when global temperatures approached those of modern times.

Which of these factors, the warming climate or the shift to agriculture, was responsible for the collapse of big-game populations? The answer is neither. Changing climate conditions during the Pleistocene can be measured against similar studies of prey biomass over the same period. As it turns out, no clear relationship exists between global climate change, as represented by multiple marine oxygen-isotope cycles, and the percentage of large hoofed mammals in Paleolithic human diets.[9] For the last 350,000 years of the Pleistocene, ungulates always constituted 95 percent or more of the prey biomass eaten by humans, regardless of warming or cooling trends. Signs of change begin to creep in around 35,000 years ago; by 15,000 years ago, the decline was marked. From this point forward, the biomass of large hoofed mammals dropped steadily at most Mediterranean sites, and humans increasingly hunted rabbits,

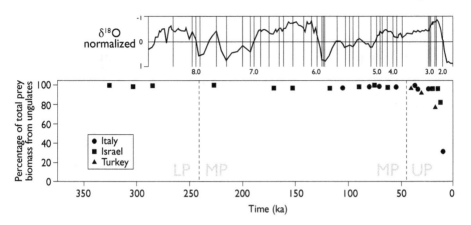

FIGURE 29. Percentage of prey biomass obtained by Paleolithic hunters from large hoofed mammals (ungulates) versus small animals over the past 350,000 years in several Mediterranean regions, relative to broad climate oscillations based on global marine oxygen-isotope (MIS) chronologies. The figure illustrates that hunters' preference for large hoofed mammals was unaffected by fluctuations in climate between 350 ka and 30 ka. After 30 ka, however, the percentage of large hoofed mammals in the diet decreased dramatically. Given previous trends, it is unlikely that climate change was the principal factor behind the shift in hunting patterns. LP: Lower Paleolithic, MP: Middle Paleolithic, UP: Upper Paleolithic. (MIS data from Martinson et al. 1987.)

turtles, fish, and other small animals. The rather sudden emergence and spread of farming seems not to have been a factor in the declining role of large game in the human diet at all.

Thus, we turn to a third hypothesis: humans, as hunters, are the likely culprit for the declining population of large hoofed mammals. After roughly 14,000 years ago (during the Epipaleolithic), human population densities in the region were rising quickly, and the preferred prey (which large hoofed mammals certainly were to Pleistocene hunter-gatherers) were being overhunted. The decline in large game populations—first the largest species and then medium-sized species—took place in several regions, including peninsular Italy, southern Greece and Portugal, Levantine Turkey, and Israel. The prey animals did not go extinct, but their distributions were severely thinned, making human reliance on them less and less sustainable.

Oddly, some human populations did not shrink in response to the decline in large game, despite its high value in human diets. Studies of modern hunter-gatherers have shown that they buffer themselves from adversity not only through careful management of social connections but also through physical solutions that include food storage, intensive food rendering, and broadening of diet. These habits and technologies, too, appear to have coalesced during the Upper Paleolithic, filling in the food gaps and limiting mortality in relation to birth rates. The process began with a simple but profound reorganization of human labor around 45,000 years ago, probably during the Middle to Upper Paleolithic cultural transition, specifically in how (and with how much versatility) people supplemented large game in their diet with alternative foods—mainly small animals but eventually also plant seeds and nuts.[10] They pooled both labor and risk. Innovations spread quickly: tools used for specialized tasks were frequently abandoned in favor of newer designs, and the implements used for getting food and preparing it proliferated.[11] Methods for storing food and extracting more calories from each food item helped free humans from strictly time-based constraints on foraging, a path of change made necessary by shrinking territories in a world now thicker with people. The emerging practices raised the environmental carrying capacity in stages throughout the remainder of the Paleolithic. The catastrophic drop in the large game available to Mediterranean hunter-gatherers at the end of the Pleistocene was a long-term outgrowth of small, iterative innovations in the ways small social groups procured, processed, and preserved their food in unpredictable environments.

In recent years, some archaeologists have argued that the decline of large game was a necessary precondition for the shift to agriculture and herding. By contrast, Childe described the shift to agriculture as nothing less than the idea-driven revolution that created humankind. The authors of history textbooks echoed this sentiment in the decades that followed the publication of Childe's *Man Makes Himself*.[12] The story of an abrupt Neolithic revolution was attractive to historians. It privileged a heroic model of invention, one that modern people, makers of scientific and industrial revolutions, would eventually perfect.[13] Moreover, the imagery of revolution, with its connotations of suddenness and a decisive break with the past, absolved scholars of the responsibility to write deep histories.

The scenario that emerges from recent archaeological findings, therefore, is remarkable for two reasons. First, the factors that led humans into agriculture were, for the most part, ecological. They arose from the ever-changing relationship between humans and their environment—in this case, between humans and the animals and plants that constituted their diet. To rebut Childe's idea of a revolution driven primarily by the invention of agriculture, this shift in the relationship between humans and their environments has been called the broad-spectrum revolution.[14] Second, the processes that gave rise to this monumental change were very long in the making. The groundwork for the agricultural transition was laid more than 30,000 years earlier, in cultural shifts associated with the Middle-Upper Paleolithic transition. Scalar leaps can have very long lead-ins.

SCALE AND INFORMATION NETWORKS

The data associated with the origins of agriculture—increases in population density, environmental carrying capacity, and the amount of goods circulating in human societies—suggest a take-off rivaling the modern transition. But in this case, the J curves generated by the data were built on previous J curves, such as the sharply descending curve of big-game availability and the steep increases in the spectrum of available tools and storage times for preserved foods. One J curve stands on the metaphorical shoulders of the preceding one: it is J curves all the way to the bottom. From the Upper Paleolithic forward, leaps in population play a significant role in the narrative of human history. The populations involved were minuscule by today's standards, but, again, the scale at which these transitions took place is irrelevant. It is the *leap* that matters for succeeding generations, because it increases local population densities with unanticipated consequences.

Consider the effects of population density on information flow. Archaeological and ethnographic data show that increases in the size and density of human social groups can affect innovation rates and information networks—regardless of the type or "stage" of the society. In their study of the dynamics of modern cities, for example, Luis Bettencourt and colleagues identify startling quantitative regularities in the process of urbanization.[15] Increased concentrations of people in cities create novel challenges to which humans must adapt, and rising population density makes possible new economies of scale (new levels of efficiency). Everywhere in the contemporary world, cities are associated with wealth and knowledge production, with a faster pace of life, with innovation, and with higher levels of energy consumption and environmental degradation. Close living also comes with a price: higher infection rates, more crime, new constraints on personal freedom, and increased rates of conflict. The advantages come from increasing the intensity of social interaction across a wide spectrum of human activities, which causes innovation rates to increase in response to continuous growth. Complex problems can be solved faster, and the costs of production drop as a result of design transfer; knowledge is stolen and shared; experimentation is encouraged. Cycles of innovation become shorter than individual life spans as populations (and local density) increase; information flows faster across larger populations. It is in this regard that, in today's cities, "human social dynamics transcend biology and redefine metaphors of social 'metabolism' under conditions of population concentration."[16]

These regularities in the process of urbanization exist despite marked differences in geography, culture, and local histories. Their universality is not, however, a product of hard-wired human nature. Instead, it is a property of the social systems that cities produce and in which they are embedded. Bettencourt and colleagues develop their arguments in relation to urbanism, but their findings have much wider applicability. The costs and benefits of city life can be seen, on a different scale, in the seasonal gatherings of foragers, villagers, and herding peoples, during which social life is intensified in nearly every way. With communal dancing, healing ceremonies, gift exchanges, and the arrangement of marriages come communicable diseases, intensified gossip, sexual infidelities, physical violence, and even murder. The possibilities are tantalizing, and humans have never been reluctant to explore them. Our strong desire to cluster is evident in the ritual cycles and seasonal observances that proliferate in all human societies, channeling social energies into redistributive feasting, mortuary rites, harvest celebrations, market days, and the religious and political holidays that fill the modern calendar. The moment of gathering creates an affective shift in awareness; it heightens our sense of connection across space and time, a sensibility that encourages mutual protection and risk taking, innovation and reenactment.

The transition to urbanism—a way of life now common to more than half of the world's population—is but a massive, and historically recent, pooling of the costs and benefits of scaling up. A survey of the last 50,000 years (of which only about the last 5,000 are associated with urban civilization of any sort) shows that transitions involving population density and scale have been significant and ongoing, each preparing the ground for the next. The dramatic scale transitions of the past two centuries are real. The processes they have generated—global warming, population explosions, the Green Revolution—have emergent qualities, and they will also have unpredictable consequences. But just as the agricultural transition had a long lead-in, so do the leaps associated with the highly urbanized cultures of the contemporary world. To understand them, we need to pay close attention to structural continuities of the simplest and the most complex kinds. Humans, as Aristotle assured us, are political animals, and some of deep history's most interesting lead-ins are located in our attempts to solve enduring problems of inequality in social life. The political transformations we explore next are, in crucial respects, preconditions for the population shifts that have culminated in the Anthropocene.

SCALE AND THE RISE OF INEQUALITY

To understand the roots of political hierarchy in humans, we must travel deep in time and across species boundaries. Small-scale hierarchies of males and females characterize social groups among the great apes, our closest living primate relatives, and among ground-dwelling monkeys. These hierarchies matter: reproductive success depends, in large part, on one's position in the hierarchy. Primatologists have assumed that early hominins also competed within their groups for social position and mates. This claim has fossil evidence to support it: australopith and other early hominin males were substantially larger than females, a pattern characteristic of polygynous mating systems.[17]

By contrast, the remarkable feature of small groups of human foragers and simple horticulturalists is their persistent egalitarianism, at least within the sexes. Among !Kung foragers living in the Kalahari Desert, stories are told of a camp's men joining forces to kill an aggressive member of the group, a person whose actions were very disagreeable.[18] The comparative ethnography of small-scale societies suggests that this method of social control is not uncommon. Chris Boehm describes a long interlude, lasting for much of the Plio-Pleistocene, during which human societies were characterized by "reverse dominance" hierarchies; that is, patterns of behavior that systematically prevented overreaching individuals from achieving dominance.[19] Some anthropologists have argued that the availability of lethal weapons, especially those that allow killing at a distance, may have leveled the playing field.[20]

Hunter-gatherers can be rich and not so equal in terms of individual health, reproductive success, and social connections.[21] Most of these societies do not, however, engage in large transfers of material wealth among peers or across generations. Thus "property" is not a particularly useful concept for understanding foraging societies. The same is true for more sedentary folk who engage in the small-scale cultivation of wild plants and a few domesticated ones. Horticulturalists can be as egalitarian as any hunter-gatherer group.[22] As Lawrence Keeley has shown in his careful survey of early ethnographic literature, burgeoning economic complexity and plant cultivation do not in themselves produce inequality and hierarchy.[23] This insight has been confirmed by new studies suggesting that land ownership based on low-intensity cultivation and repeated harvesting of wild tree groves and concentrated hunting and fishing grounds does not disrupt egalitarian relations. Even the presence of domesticated animals and plants does not in itself foster social inequality.[24] Rather, it is the growing presence of scarce, defensible resources that sets the forces of inequality in motion.

With these patterns in mind, let us return to the clever hunters and cultivators of the terminal Pleistocene. The cultures of the Epipaleolithic and Mesolithic periods, which developed on the heels of global warming (after 18,000 years ago), were quite complex, at least economically.[25] The Natufians, in particular, who flourished 13,000 to 10,000 years ago in the Near East, formed large communities and cemeteries in the Mediterranean hills.[26] The Natufians, more than any other group, are credited with the domestication of wheat and barley. Goats were domesticated in the Zagros arm of the Fertile Crescent, and sheep, chickpeas, and lentils almost certainly in the Taurus foothills.[27] These localized experiments in economic intensification often were accompanied by more sedentary lifestyles but not by social inequality, judging from the redundant patterns of residential architecture and grave contents.[28] Hierarchy came later, with demographic increase and the growing scarcity of agricultural lands. Some of the big Mesolithic communities on the North Atlantic coast of Europe were surprisingly sedentary as well, with huge cemeteries that clearly suggest trans-generational rights to rich fishing grounds.

These situations bear an interesting resemblance to the complex, semi-sedentary fishing cultures of the Pacific Northwest coast and Florida.[29] Uniquely positioned to harvest great streams of migratory and local aquatic animals, their food supply was rich enough to sustain communities numbering hundreds of individuals over many months or even year-round, yet elaborate social hierarchies generally did not develop among these Mesolithic communities.

Archaeologists have struggled to explain the shift from human societies that rely on broad-based foraging and simple agriculture to societies that pursue highly specialized economies, a transition that entails a parallel shift from economies that privilege common goods to those that stress ownership of scarce resources.[30] We know that plant cultivation and economic complexity go hand in hand among recent hunter-gatherers.[31] Intensive use and defense of the same patch of land from year to year might easily have evolved into ownership in sedentary populations. Meat and cropland were clearly of great value in early village communities. Given the precipitous drop in large-game availability at the Pleistocene-Holocene boundary, the social valuation of meat, and the social pressure to share and control it, likely became acute.

An egalitarian sensibility governs the consumption of large animals in recent hunter-gatherer societies.[32] J. Clutton-Brock maintains that ownership was a key feature of animal domestication in particular: rightful access to individual animals in some instances replaced the right to exploit a territory in which animal herds could be hunted.[33] It stands to reason that as human population densities increased and the distribution of animals was thinned by heavy hunting, the advantages of owning and constraining small numbers of animals increased. The largest of these animals, such as wild cattle, were the most likely to be consumed publicly and their remains to land in open trash areas. It is possible that some wild animals were captured while young and raised in pens in anticipation of major community social events or rituals. Feeding these animals, and the increasingly sedentary human populations that kept them, would have activated a feedback cycle whose by-product was perhaps the key ingredient of social inequality: "differential success in the accumulation of scarce and predictable productive resources—capital, in other words—through inheritance."[34]

SCALE AND THE EMERGENCE OF POLITICAL HIERARCHIES

Hierarchies budded and expanded dramatically from the late Neolithic onward. Agriculture increased the amount of edible biomass per acre of land, rendering control of land essential to survival. As competition for productive resources grew, so did intergroup warfare among horticultural groups.[35] Aggressive fighters became essential to a group's ability to defend and assert itself. Accompanying this shift, prestige items and patterns of ornamentation, including body paint, dress, and other devices used to signal an individual's reputation, attractiveness, and strength, begin to appear more densely in the archaeological record. By 6,000 years ago (4000 BCE), evidence of social hierarchy can be seen around the world. In coastal Peru, people planned and built impressive monumental temples.[36] In the lower Mississippi Valley, complicated earthworks were constructed.[37] In Neolithic Europe, monumental land-scapes of megalithic stones and earth were erected, and a special class of individuals were buried, with all their finery, under distinctive earthen mounds.[38] Societies of this kind are remarkably diverse, but archaeologists see telling uniformities among them and often refer to them as "chiefdoms."

Chiefdoms are political entities that organize populations in the thousands through personalized, hierarchical networks that create and distribute power. The chiefdom relies on vertical reciprocity, often called redistribution, in which a leader and his family collect goods and services from their supporters, then return a substantial portion, usually in ritualized settings that confer legitimacy and prestige to those who give, and subordination and membership on those who receive. These exchanges resemble the giving and receiving of gifts. In the literature produced contemporaneously with the rise of medieval European chieftaincies, for example, they are in fact described as gifts to God, gifts made from love, or gifts rooted in a sense of duty or honor. No doubt that is how they felt to the people involved. But the systemic effect of these exchanges, whether or not it was acknowledged by the givers of gifts and services, was to prop up institutions of power.[39] As such, they were a key component of the flow of resources within lordships and chiefdoms.

The political economy of chiefdoms, in expanded form, created the basis for later states. Chiefdoms are in fact little more than would-be states, and the "failed states" of the modern era break up into constituent segments that operate much as prehistoric chiefdoms did. Understanding the origins and political dynamics of states requires us to reengage with the world of chiefdoms.[40] Archaeologically, this world is signaled by monumental construction and elite burials with special objects of wealth, which in turn are associated with regional political organization and hierarchical social structures. Chiefs and their followers built the Easter Island statues, Stonehenge, and the towering earthen mound complex of Cahokia in the American heartland. Wherever we find them, chiefdoms have recognizable leaders who live in special residences, preside over central places for polity-wide ceremonies, and maintain specialized warriors who protect them and, as needed, discipline or kill unruly subordinates.

The Polynesian chiefdoms provide some of the most vivid examples.[41] Captain Cook, himself a specialized warrior from a class-stratified society, was greatly impressed by the chiefs he met as he traveled among the island groups; these men and their followers would eventually kill him on a Hawaiian beach. Elsewhere, European explorers, missionaries, and merchants described chiefdoms of varying types and sizes along the coasts of North America, throughout the Caribbean, in Africa, and across Central Asia from Afghanistan to Mongolia. Over the past five centuries, most of the world's chiefdoms have been conquered by or strategically contained within colonial and postcolonial state formations. In the nineteenth century, popular historical narratives came to explain how Western peoples, presumed to be racially superior, expanded with respect to primitive peoples, an idea that was translated in the twentieth century out of the idiom of racial superiority into a language of political development and modernization.[42] A shift in scale is routinely equated with progress, and this ideological commitment can obscure important commonalities between chiefdoms and the imperial dynasties and territorial nation-states that eventually came to dominate world politics.

SCALAR JUMPS IN POWER

Chiefdoms and states are fundamentally about power. This lesson is vividly taught in Machiavelli's *The Prince,* a primer that could be read with interest by a Bedouin paramount sheikh or a British prime minister but one that would certainly disturb members of small-scale, horticultural and foraging societies, who find inequality offensive and generally try to bring down men who harbor princely aspirations. To create regional political hierarchies, and to make them attractive to commoners, chiefs must strategically intertwine and institutionalize three sources of power: the economy, military forces, and ideology.[43] The development of chiefdoms requires control over some mix of these sources of power, and theoretically the initial basis of power could lie in any of them. Because economy is based on material production and flows, chiefs can, in certain circumstances, control surplus production, and effective control of this resource is the bedrock on which most complex societies are built. Chiefdoms rely on political economy to produce and direct resource flows; by manipulating political economy, chiefs can expand their spheres of influence.

To understand the emergence of chiefdoms is to understand the invention of political economy: that is, the mobilization and central channeling of resources to develop sources of power. Essential to the creation of the political economy are bottlenecks, points of control in the production and flow of valuable things. Richard Adams argues that complex, hierarchical societies depend on productive resources and the ability to organize surplus energy flows.[44] A highly productive base is necessary but not sufficient, as humans, given the choice, prefer to produce less and to enjoy their leisure, as foraging societies still demonstrate.[45] For this reason, surplus production must be encouraged—coerced, in fact— through control over economic bottlenecks.

Such bottlenecks are not universal in human economies. They require certain underlying economic conditions, but these can be built up strategically to increase revenue flows. Historically, they were of two major types. The first involved control over landed property, especially irrigation systems. The intensification of agriculture through irrigation tended to focus production on a narrow range of fertile lands that could be easily controlled by force. Richard Blanton and colleagues call this system a "corporate strategy."[46] The second strategy was based on control over trade; ownership of locally productive resources like pasturelands, water resources, or metal mines; control over movement along high-volume trade routes; or ownership of trading ships and other valuable means of transport. The development of large-volume trade allowed chiefs to extract a surplus in return for safe movement. Blanton and colleagues call this variant a "networked strategy."

Corporate and network strategies were contrasting routes to complexity. The corporate strategy was based on dense local relationships and exerted control over the flow of surplus *within* a territory. The network strategy, by contrast, focused on longer-range political and trade relationships and exerted control on the wealth that flowed *across* territories. In either case, the surplus created, either through rent or through extortion, could be invested in developing the economy in a highly selective way (building irrigation systems, harbors, mills, and the like), training and equipping a warrior elite, and supporting religious specialists who naturalized and sanctified inequalities that would violate common morality in simpler societies. Because the revenues are typically plowed back into the apparatus of power, political economies are growth oriented. If a barrier to growth is encountered, the keepers of the hierarchy, whose special status and position depend on expansion, typically work hard and creatively to overcome the blockade. Because political economies are inherently dynamic and entrepreneurial, the present world system can be seen as the continual working out of a deep history of expanding political economies. The lead-in is long, and the structural continuities are many.

PATHWAYS TO POWER

The Hawaiian chiefdoms encountered by Captain Cook and the Bronze Age chiefdoms out of which Greek civilization arose offer two compelling examples of how the exploitation of economic bottlenecks facilitated the development of political hierarchies.[47] Polynesian explorers found and settled the Hawaiian Islands about 600 CE, as part of one of the last great human dispersals to unoccupied lands (see chapter 8). Polynesian societies were organized as kin-based hierarchies and supported by a political economy that often included irrigation agriculture. To the Hawaiian Islands the colonizers brought a "transported landscape" of useful plants and animals that they cultivated and allowed to grow wild in the mountain forests.[48] Fishing was important at first but was progressively replaced by reliance on farming (especially taro and sweet potato) and domesticated animals (especially pigs). Colonists settled initially on the coasts and then, to support a growing population, expanded inland, clearing the forests for dry-land and small-scale irrigation farming. This process led to massive deforestation, extinction of endemic birds, and erosion, which filled the valley floors with silt. This new, unintended expansion of alluvial soils was the fertile medium in which farmers and chiefs constructed irrigation systems.[49] By asserting ownership over valley lands and irrigation systems, Hawaiian chiefs were able to mobilize surplus food production to support the construction of new agricultural areas and fishponds.

The surplus also supported specialized warriors and craftsmen who made weapons (large double canoes, spears and clubs, and protective cloaks). Surplus was used to support the construction of *heiau,* religious platforms of stone with frame buildings and towers. These ritual centers served as stage sets for elaborate annual ceremonies sponsored by chiefs. The high chiefs were presented as earthly gods, responsible for the productivity of the soil and for warfare against the unjust. Prior to European contact, several chiefdoms had expanded to the limits of their major islands, such as Hawaii and Oahu, then conquered smaller, neighboring islands. Each chiefdom could maintain its independence, however, because of the inability of competitors to conquer a major island across a protecting water gap. But with the arrival of Europeans, the high chiefs quickly realized that a new technology of war (including large sailing boats, guns, and swords) made further conquests possible. Boats were obtained from the Europeans, along with sailmakers and gunners, who were encouraged to jump ship by prospects of an earthly paradise complete with Polynesian maidens. Within a generation, Kamehameha, the high chief of Hawaii, had formed the new Hawaiian state by interisland conquest.

In Bronze Age Europe, state emergence followed a different but parallel trajectory. Small-scale chiefdoms had developed locally in the later Neolithic: they were based on the assertion of land ownership, marked architecturally by megalithic burial chambers and earth-bank and standing-stone enclosures, of which Stonehenge is the most famous example. Control over pasturage was probably critical here, and trade in secondary animal products (hides, cheese, and wool) and plow animals provided the basis for a regional economy.[50] Such trade would have required many routes to move goods over land, and points of control would have been difficult to maintain, resulting in a patchwork of many small-scale ranked polities.

Things changed dramatically in the Bronze Age. In the agrarian states of the Middle East (which, like the Hawaiian chiefdoms, were based on irrigation), demand for wealth objects and weaponry expanded (see chapter 9). Trade in these objects, especially new metal goods in bronze, gold, and silver, spread across Asia and into Europe.[51] As trade intensified in these formerly marginal areas, the flow of goods shifted toward more efficient water and caravan routes. Some of the long-distance trade was destined for Middle Eastern city-states, but much of it circulated among the chiefdoms of Europe. The heavier volume of trade also encouraged the use of boats along the rivers that flowed through Europe to the Mediterranean and Black seas. Water-borne transport created a more restricted and easily controlled system of trade. Chiefdoms sprang up along rivers and on islands and coasts. Along the Danube, for example, a chain of fortified central places overlooked the river, whose steady flow of wealth they both added to and siphoned off. By the Late Bronze Age, trade through the Mediterranean to Egypt and the Middle Eastern states created opportunities for secondary state formation. The Golden Age of the Minoan, Mycenaean, and related city-states was fueled by this trade. As documented archaeologically, these societies were based on traffic in specialty products, including wine and olive oil, and on the support of warriors armed with bronze weapons. The subsequent development of Greek and Phoenician colonies followed a similar pattern.

To recontextualize the rise of the West, situating it in this deeper, more pervasive set of trends, it helps to consider Europe's background as an assortment of small-scale, chiefly polities, each ruthlessly motivated by its own interests. This world is now dimly remembered as the domain of Celtic and Germanic chiefdoms. Conquered by Rome, the

Celtic chiefdoms disappeared as political entities, though aspects of their economic structure persisted in the latifundia, the great Western Roman estates. The Germanic peoples beyond the Roman *limes* were never conquered per se, though they were brought into the Roman economic sphere. The Rhine served, for several centuries, as a densely populated zone of commercial interchange. After the Western Roman Empire itself collapsed in the fifth century CE, the chiefly domains resurfaced and persisted until at least 1200, though medieval European historians, using a different nomenclature, call them lordships, castellanies, and bishoprics. Many of these polities preserved the approximate boundaries of the old Roman latifundia.

By the standards of what Karl Marx and other nineteenth-century economic theorists called the "Asiatic mode of production," in which autocratic control over highly productive irrigation systems was central to political life, the chiefdoms of Europe were utter barbarians. The states that began to consolidate after 1200 CE were unimpressive compared to those of the Middle and Far East. The development of European territorial states required that the myth of their antiquity and wholeness be asserted as public ideology, but until recent centuries, they operated as unstable confederacies of chiefly powers. The European chiefs were a motley assortment of nobles, warriors, bishops, traders, and capitalists. Their zones of influence were largely independent, their overlaps tactical and incomplete. The state, itself more an aspiration than an institutional reality, made specific demands of the chiefs—of tribute, loyalty, or temporary alliance—but, compared to today's governments, it largely left substate actors alone. This chaotic political system was extraordinarily adaptive; as centers of power failed, new actors could explore unexpected opportunities. The state, meanwhile, had only to maintain a certain (low) level of law, order, peace, and imperial expansion in order to amass and dole out the benefits needed to tame the chiefs. Not until the late eighteenth century did the unanticipated convergence of capitalism and steam power make it possible to contain Europe's multiform chiefdoms within a still highly unstable political superstructure called the nation-state. A new global political economy, visible in the transregional organization of large populations and their productive potential, grew out of the merger of large-scale industrial manufacture, steam-powered distribution by train and boat, and expansionist imperialism.

Although the lead-in to this transition was very long, the historiography of the contemporary world system tends to focus on institutions and storylines that coalesced only in the past two hundred years, the exact period in which nation-states have become a global norm. If the explanation for "the rise of the West"—a framework that is already parochial—is sought further back in time, the point of origin is typically no earlier than the European colonization of the New World. An analysis that looks even further back, emphasizing distinctions between "corporate" and "network" variants of chiefly political economies, would strike many scholars as reductionist or oversimplified. This reaction is based on persistent misapprehensions about what scalar shifts signify, the kinds of data they create, and how we can justify the insights generated by work done across scales. Again, there is a strong reluctance to engage with the flat left tail of the J curve, especially when the steep right end is defined as exceptional. This reluctance, more than any empirical aspect of method or conceptual element of theory, is an obstacle to deep historical analysis. In the concluding sections of this essay, we argue that scalar shifts can be understood as real-world processes that build over time, but they can also be conceptualized as fractal media of analysis that can be used to travel through time.

SCALING THE SOCIAL BRAIN

If there is a master J curve generating all the others, it is the upward ascent of hominin intelligence, which is typically imagined both as an increase in brain size and as the increasing complexity of social forms over time. The conceptual link between these two paths of increase and those associated with the famous J curves of the last two centuries is neatly proved in the tendency to use the term *modern* when describing the arrival, in the Upper Paleolithic, of people whose archaeological traces suggest a cultural existence very similar to our own. It is the moment in hominin evolution when the pronoun *we* can be used without reservation. Those ancestors whose bodily remains look like ours, but whose behaviors seem a bit too simple, are called "anatomically modern humans," implying that in some more essential way, they are not yet modern, not yet us. Such usages show that the term *modernity* is a fractal pattern made visible by scalar play. It can be used to describe the people of Europe 28,000 years ago, the Neolithic Revolution, the Industrial Revolution, the rise of the nation-state, or the objects on display in the Museum of Modern Art (where in fact avant-garde paintings modeled on Paleolithic cave art are given pride of place).

What is the human quality discernible in these radical shifts in context and scale? Perhaps we could describe it as activity that is highly intentional, or seems to be, because it requires social coordination, planning, prediction, and modeling. A handful of ancient shells with holes carved in them may represent symbolic intent: we can imagine that, like contemporary jewelry, they were meant to convey some kind of distinction. But thousands of ancient shells of exactly the same type, with holes carved in them, found many hundreds of miles from the sea, in dozens of contemporaneous archaeological sites, in what appear to be graves— well, *that* is culturally modern. It suggests durable exchange networks, shared ideas, and ways of seeing the world that can be expressed, with consistent behavioral outcomes, across space and time. Most significant, it suggests the development of a uniquely social intelligence rooted in a long series of changes in the shape and size of our brains. Transformations in hominin mental processes over the last several million years are clearly based on the interaction of brain expansion controlled by genes and cultural systems that promote knowledge building. Thinking of this interaction as deeply historical entails seeing it as a process in which intentionality played a necessary part. But how do we conceptualize this interaction? On what scales should it be analyzed?

Many scholars of evolution believe that sudden jumps in the complexity of human cognition, such as enhanced abilities for planning and prediction, account for the success of behaviorally modern (Upper Paleolithic) humans over the Neanderthals. Some attribute the cognitive changes to critical differences in neurological wiring or the organic bases of brain performance, a stance congruent with what Daniel Dennett has called John Locke's "mind-first model" of human history.[52] The main problem with this view is that most of the brain's hardware developed early in human evolution, whereas most mind-first models of human cultural development focus on the Late Pleistocene and later. The size of the human brain, and hence its metabolic costs, reached a plateau long before the spectacular radiations in Paleolithic material cultures, not to mention the rise of villages and cities.[53]

Subtle and important changes in brain function might have occurred later in the Pleistocene, but there is no clear behavioral division in material culture between Neanderthals and the earliest anatomically modern humans. The cases of Skhūl and Qafzeh in the southern Levant have forced us to decouple hominin types and technologies, as anatomically modern human skeletons were deposited alongside Middle Paleolithic tools 80,000–100,000 years ago, the same array of stone tools made by Neanderthals of the region several millennia later.[54] In this case, two hominin species distinguished by different skeletal morphologies relied on essentially the same technological system. Upper Paleolithic cultures, defined by the emergence of artistic traditions and other new technologies, do not appear in the region for another 30,000 years.

A strictly organic model of cognitive change leaves little room for the influence of culture, for decisions taken and plans made with the benefit of enduring knowledge. Yet a heavily cultural model encourages us to ignore the biogenetic preadaptations that make later cultural innovations possible. As a medium of intentionality, cultural transmission is shaped by the biogenetic constitution of the brain. This is highly inertial compared to the social life of intelligence, which is flexible, even frenetic. Selection for bigger brains has received more attention in discussions of human cognitive evolution, but the accelerated pace of human cultural change during the last 50,000 years cannot be explained without taking into account patterns of sociability, learning, and the effective sizes of human populations. Movement across scales of analysis can help us navigate this complex terrain of human adaptation: specifically, it can help us redraw the lines between natural and cultural change that so effectively thwart deep historical analysis.

Consider, yet again, the puzzle of expanding group size among humans. In groundbreaking research that spans a decade, Robin Dunbar has shown that the relationship between group size and the size of the brain's neocortex is constant in nonhuman primates.[55] As the neocortex (the brain area associated with consciousness and memory) grows larger, so does group size. Using observed rates of increase in brain size relative to group size, Dunbar concluded that the ideal human group size—defined as the largest group in which members could maintain steady, face-to-face interactions—is about 150, a figure we would have reached over 100,000 years ago. For Neanderthals, the number is 120; for *Homo erectus*, it is 110; for australopiths, about 65; and so on backward along the hominin line.

Because this figure of 150 (now known as "the Dunbar number") was originally determined using equations, Dunbar next went looking for empirical evidence: human groups of this size occurring "in nature" or, to put it more precisely, "in culture." Here the story becomes more interesting. Clearly, humans live in groups much larger than 150, and many of our most important communities (our immediate families, our circle of best friends, and even our academic departments) are smaller. On the reasonable assumption that the first human societies to hit 150 were simple, foraging societies, Dunbar focused his search on contemporary societies of this sort. He found what he was looking for: coresident groups of about 150 individuals are quite common among hunters and gatherers and simple agriculturalists. The number also shows up, apparently, in military organization, where 150 is a common company size. Business gurus have since adopted the Dunbar number, advising their clients to create work groups of 150 members.

The appeal of Dunbar's findings is based on their scientific rigor (his argument is very elegantly constructed) and on our age-old attraction to magic numbers. When considering the long sweep of human history, however, one is immediately struck by the aspect of Dunbar's story that receives far less attention than it should. We have been living in groups larger than 150 for at least 12,000 years, and on numerous occasions in the remote past (during rainy seasons, or salmon runs, after big kills of big game, or at ceremonial gatherings), group sizes exceeded 150 for days on end, or for predictable times each year. In other words, whatever advantages came with a highly encephalized brain that allows us to interact regularly with as many as 150 people, these advantages have long since been multiplied—and might eventually be undermined—by cognitive and behavioral innovations that allow us to live in groups numbering in the hundreds of millions. The trick lies in our ability to redefine "fellow humans" and "groups" as uniform types—stereotypes, in effect—and to alter the choreography of our daily interactions accordingly. If the human neocortex were as large as it would have to be to sustain an ideal group size of, say, 100,000 people, our skulls could not possibly accommodate it. We have solved this problem by tampering with scale, and by creating formats and subroutines that can hold us, and the worlds we create, in social containers that expand and contract many times faster than our cranial capacity can evolve.

The results of this scalar play have surfaced repeatedly throughout this book. Perhaps the earliest innovations came with the development of language and kinship, habits of mind and body that, among humans, are closely linked. By describing certain people as types of kin, and by distinguishing between kin terms (which are generalized categories) and the individuals who are called by those terms (who might be numerous in any particular category and who can belong to multiple categories at once), human groups can be conceived as larger or smaller. A forager among the !Kung, Dunbar's classic example of group sizes of 150, is able to turn nearly any other !Kung person she meets into a relative; indeed, people who share her name, or the names of her kin, become kin themselves.

Humans have also devised non-kin categories that are even more inclusive: enemy, friend, stranger, and guest. These ways of classifying others have proved so useful that we can find no living human society that operates without them. Kinship systems are routinely portrayed as the most basic (or "primitive") forms of social organization, yet it is impossible to discuss nation-state formations, economics, genetic research, dynastic rule, or the tenets of the "world religions" without constant resort to ideas of kinship. We have scaled this conceptual domain up with minimal difficulty (to constitute, in fact, the "human family"). Just as kinship served our ancestors well as they moved across the Earth's surface, it remains essential to any rigorous attempt to move analytically through time. It is not mere coincidence that contemporary historians of discourse are likely to describe their methodology as "genealogical."

The same tendency toward metaphoric extension and fractal expansion is visible in the way humans use the metaphor of the body—its strengths and weakness, its constituent parts, and its developmental cycles—to organize social processes that are physically external to the body. Not only does the invention of bodily likenesses unify sociopolitical fields that contain millions of social actors, it also brings larger social fields to bear on the individual body. To Christians, the Church is the body of Christ, and this knowledge helps them shape and control their own physical bodies, to mortify and cleanse them, and to bring them into morally appropriate relations with others. For humans, a physical body is also a social body, and the integrity of the body as both an object and a subject of social effort can help us understand why the body remains essential to the logic of even the most complex political formations. Contemporary statecraft is unimaginable without the concept of the citizen, who is always configured as a real body endowed with rights, but also as a legal abstraction, a formal stand-in for real people. The citizen is always one, always generic, and in this form can be managed (that is, brought to life, fed, educated, taxed, counted, employed, medicated, incarcerated, and put to death) within a body politic that is also constituted by a diverse, recalcitrant array of individuals and social types whose citizenship is contested, or irrelevant.

The political and economic bottlenecks that first allowed humans to explore social hierarchy, and to live in denser populations, are of recent origin. To control these bottlenecks, early practitioners of inequality (the big men, chiefs, and aspiring lords) again put scalar toolkits to use, building new ideas of rank and status into older models of kinship, gift exchange, and the body. The resulting structures were oddly conservative; with every increase in scale, streamlining reductions and simplified formats emerged at the heart of social complexity. The principalities of feudal Europe, like the kingdoms of medieval India, were quite large compared to the tribally organized herding and village populations that lived in the marginal zones of the Old World; nonetheless, they were governed as assemblages of a small number of social types, conceptualized and legally delimited as estates, castes, and orders. The terms *noble* and *priest* resemble the terms *aunt* and *cousin* insofar as they limit possibilities while allowing the number of people who fill the role to vary. Hawaiian chiefs, like the chiefly mound builders of Cahokia, ruled over thousands of people, but they did so by channeling political resources through a limited number of subordinates, who were often related to them by kinship and marriage. The ability to scale up and down, making big units out of small ones, and reducing large numbers of people to a small number of types, is essential to life beyond the "ideal" group size of 150. As human societies have grown dramatically larger over the past two centuries, we have been reluctant to jettison effective scaling techniques. They tend to live on, fractally expanded and structurally minimized, within ever-larger social configurations.

CONCLUSION

The goal of this chapter, and indeed of the book as a whole, has been to offer new frameworks for the telling of history, frames that escape the telescoping metaphors of ontogeny, genesis, and the Fall. Because they privilege the idea of birth, the point of origin, and the enduring essence, these motifs have a way of stopping history in its tracks. Each, in its way, privileges the moment of beginning, not the process of becoming that precedes it and unfolds within it. The frames we have evoked in this chapter, by contrast, suggest the pattern of the fractal, or nested scalar leaps, or expanding and contracting scales. These are base metaphors that insistently shift our attention to the flattened left tail of the J curve, a tail that turns out not to be so flat after all. Like kinshipping, genealogy, and spiraling, all of which create links between the present and the absent, our base metaphors suggest ways of writing history that move continuously between the present and a deeper, more formative past, thereby transcending the insidious tendency of nineteenth- and twentieth-century historiography to divide the past into a historical age and an age without history.

Oddly enough, the *premodern* historical tradition was far more comfortable with notions of continuity and connectedness, because Judeo-

Christian history was nothing if not an exercise in kinshipping and genealogy. Once we realize that the book of Genesis itself was innocent of the dates retroactively written onto it, we can better appreciate how early modes of history writing, including the prophetic mode, might be put to new uses. Such histories can be used not simply as evidence for the history and archaeology of the ancient peoples who wrote them but also as tools for engaging in collaborative history writing across time. The idea that human societies vary in scale, for instance, is very old, as are attempts to model the differences between "complex" societies and "simple" ones. From the Greek city-states to the Ottoman Empire, the shape of the human social order was reasonably well understood. It had even been reduced, for the benefit of sovereign and subject alike, to a simple formula. Variously known as the "Circle of Justice," or the "Eight Sentences," this ancient instruction to young rulers was traced, in legend, to the following words, spoken by Aristotle to Alexander the Great: "The world is a garden, the fence of which is the dynasty. The dynasty is an authority through which life is given to proper behavior. Proper behavior is a policy directed by the ruler. The ruler is an institution supported by the soldiers. The soldiers are helpers who are maintained by money. Money is sustenance brought together by the subjects. The subjects are servants who are protected by justice. Justice is something familiar/harmonious, and through it the world persists. The world is a garden."[56] By the time the formula reached the Arab historian Ibn Qutayba, in the ninth century CE, it was much simpler: "There can be no royal authority without men, no men without money, no money without prosperity, and no prosperity without justice and good administration."[57]

Ibn Khaldun, writing five centuries later, drew on Persian sources as well as Greek and Arabic ones. The Sasanian political philosophers, in his view, defined the Circle of Justice most precisely: "Royal authority exists through the army, the army through money, money through taxes, taxes through cultivation, cultivation through justice, justice through the improvement of officials, the improvement of officials through the forthrightness of viziers, and the whole thing in the first place through the ruler's personal supervision of his subjects' condition and his ability to educate them, so that he may rule them, and not they him."[58]

Modern readers are often surprised to discover that Ibn Khaldun, in crafting his universal history of humankind, which he deemed innovative and unparalleled, ultimately concluded that his best theories were simply "an exhaustive, very clear, fully substantiated interpretation and detailed exposition" of the Circle of Justice.[59] It is also striking to see, embedded in the Circle of Justice, the same bottlenecks that, according to contemporary archaeological theorists, produced both networked and corporate modes of early chiefdoms. The Persians, whose version of the circle emphasizes cultivation, represent the corporate model. The Greeks, whose version emphasizes money and subjects but says nothing at all of agriculture (except to insist that the world is a garden), are clearly the networkers. Both models dictate the terms of population growth, political expansion, and system collapse.

The political thinkers of the premodern, Eurasian world dealt with history on a far grander scale than do most political historians and political scientists today. They took for granted that civilization, which they associated with urban life, was nearly as old as creation. Cain, the son of Adam and Eve, built a city; and Paradise itself, in the Abrahamic traditions, is a celestial city. What we now call the "short chronology"— the calendrical residue of the Darwinian time revolution—still holds within it all the societies that endorsed the Circle of Justice, the earliest of which arose in the Middle East about 6,000 years ago. This particular location of the circle in time is opportune, as it allows us to use it as a kinshipping device, a connecting tool that enables conceptual travel through time, using existing links to generate relationships to persons and places now absent. The political world portrayed in the circle is familiar to self-consciously modern people, who, despite two centuries of ascent along multiple J curves, still have armies and rulers, agriculture and taxation, good government and bad. We even know how contemporary state formations differ from those of the circle: subjects have become citizens, dynasts have largely disappeared, and a new creature, the profit-oriented "firm," also known as the corporation, now shapes how the circle spins. The world outside the circle, likewise, was well known to Persians, Greeks, and Arabs. It was a tribal world, filled with Goths, Bedouins, Mongols, Vikings, Huns, Scythians, and other "barbarians." Writers like Tacitus and Ibn Khaldun described these societies in vivid accounts that are still widely read today, and their vexed assessment of the morality of German and Bedouin tribes—generous, brave, and virtuous as well as fractious, violent, and backward—can still be detected in contemporary accounts of peoples and places that are not fully under state control.

We are not suggesting that deep history should be written based on the Circle of Justice, an ideological tool that distorts as well as captures important aspects of statecraft. Rather, our point is that deep historical accounts are made possible by durable configurations, like the circle—and the city, the bottleneck, kinship, the body, migration, domestication, the exchange of goods, and the sharing of food—that possess long-term structural consistencies against which change can be perceived, modeled, and narrated. Unfolding on multiple spatial and temporal scales, these structures permeate the short chronology of the last 6,000 years, and the evidence we need to chart their historical development can easily be traced back to the Neolithic transition. At this point new kin-shipping devices must be found that will connect us to even more distant periods. In many cases, such devices are already present, in earlier adaptations and the long lead-ins that extend from the Paleolithic to the Industrial Revolution. As we have shown, the data, method, and theory needed to gain access to temporally distant periods already exist in abundance. What is required is a new kind of historical imagination, one that will carry us into areas of our own past that seem extremely remote but to which we are already intimately connected. Our passage through deep time is visible in the structure of our minds and bodies, and in the material and social worlds we have made. Deep history is the architecture of the present. It is the storehouse of the human experience, richly filled, constantly replenished, a resource to carry with us into the future.

Notes

1. INTRODUCTION

1. Coffman 1926, 8.
2. Albritton 1980; Rossi 1984; Gould 1987; Trautmann 1992.
3. See, for example, Cantù 1884; Ranke 1885. See also Smail 2008.
4. On strange new terrain, see, for example, Duruy 1873, Fisher 1885; on England, Goldstein 2004; on visionaries, Robinson 1912.
5. Langlois and Seignobos 1898, 17.
6. Wolf 1982.
7. Ibid., 19.
8. Michelet 1834, 9.
9. Williams 1912, 6.
10. Novick 1988.
11. Trouillot 1991.
12. See Smail et al. 2011.
13. Christian 2004; Spier 2010.
14. See, for example, Schubert 1989; a journal published since 1991 called *Journal of Evolutionary Economics;* Gruter and Bohannan 1983.
15. Spiegel 1990.
16. Dawkins and Krebs 1979, 491.
17. See, respectively, Bayly 2004; McNeill 2000; Pinker 1997.

2. IMAGINING THE HUMAN IN DEEP TIME

1. Anderson 1991, 204.
2. White 1981.
3. Anderson 1991, 36.
4. Gamble and Kruszinski 2009.

5. de Bussac 1999.
6. Livingstone 2008.
7. Frere 1800, 204–5.
8. Prestwich 1860, 309.
9. Lyell 1860, 95.
10. Lubbock 1865.
11. Glennie and Thrift 2005.
12. Rudwick 2005, 276.
13. Ibid., 349.
14. Gamble 1993.
15. Moore 1969, 63.
16. Trautmann 2006.
17. Darwin 1871, 404.
18. Wolf 1982.
19. Owen 2008; Darwin 1887, 3: 15–16.
20. Darwin 1871, 183–84.
21. Worsaae 1849, 149–50.
22. Lubbock 1865, 2.
23. Wilson 1862.
24. Lubbock 1865, 1.
25. Gamble and Gittins 2004.
26. Proctor 2003.
27. Gell 1998.
28. Gamble and Kruszinski 2009.
29. Hutchins 1995; Rowlands 2003.
30. Coward and Gamble 2008; Knappett 2005.
31. Jones 2007, 56.
32. Romm 1992.
33. Darwin 1964.
34. Darwin 1964, 422–23; see also Trautmann 1987, 215.
35. Schedel 1966.
36. Lévi-Strauss 1969.
37. Lévi-Strauss 1963, 46.
38. Chapais 2008, 259.
39. Hallowell 1991, 54–55.
40. Burling 1963; Sangma 1979.
41. Aram Yengoyan, personal communication, 2008.
42. Allen 2008; Barnard 2008.
43. Collingwood 1956, 9.
44. Rodseth et al. 1991; Gamble 2008, 32.
45. Gamble 2007.
46. Davis et al. 2007.
47. Wolf 1982.
48. Dunbar 2003.
49. Barnard 2008.
50. Mithen 2003.
51. Gamble 2007.

52. Pitt-Rivers 1977, 116.
53. Ibid., 117.
54. Jones 2007.
55. Pitt-Rivers 1977, 117.

3. BODY

1. Pfeiffer 1982.
2. Kselman 1983.
3. Keith 1931.
4. Van Loon 1921.
5. Ibid., 8–9.
6. Gerasimov 1971, xvii.
7. Kantorowicz 1957.
8. Moseley 2005.
9. On the Yanomami, see Lizot 1991; on Parsis, Luhrman 1996; on Madagascar, Larsen 2001.
10. Hodder 1990, 248; Bradley 1998, 27.
11. Chapman and Gaydarska 2007.
12. Spufford 1988; Grierson 1991.
13. Ramachandran and Blakeslee 1998.
14. Blakeslee and Blakeslee 2007.
15. Di Pellegrino et al. 1992.
16. Ramachandran 2006; see also Stamenov and Gallese 2002.
17. Arbib 2006.
18. Dunbar 1996.
19. La Boétie 1971.
20. Marx 1970, 131; Gramsci 1992; Huxley 2004; Postman 1985.
21. de Waal 2007.
22. Sapolsky 2004.
23. Courtwright 2001.
24. LeDoux 1996.
25. Anderson 1991.
26. Foucault 1977; Scarry 1985.
27. Stanley 1998.
28. Klein 1999, 364.
29. Morris 1967.
30. Wheeler 1991.
31. Aiello and Wheeler 1995.
32. Wrangham 2009.
33. Ingram et al. 2009.
34. On fibers, see Kvavadze et al. 2009; on the clothing louse, Kittler, Kayser, and Stoneking 2003.
35. Cordain 1999.
36. Lieberman 2011.
37. See, for example, Diamond 1987.
38. Ingold 2004.

39. Cordain et al. 2002.
40. Foucault 1977, 153.
41. Foucault 1978, 142–43.
42. Ibn Khaldun 1967, 136.

4. ENERGY AND ECOSYSTEMS

1. Guo et al. 2009.
2. Wrangham 2009.
3. Blondel and Aronson 1999; Redman 1999.
4. Crützen and Stoermer 2000.
5. See, for example, Blackbourn 2006.
6. Halsey 2005; Pyne et al. 1996.
7. Brown and Heske 1990.
8. Melville 1994.
9. Gould 1982, 83–84.
10. Turney et al. 2008.
11. Cf. Grayson and Meltzer 2003; Martin 1984.
12. Hallam 1979.
13. Stiner et al. 2000.
14. Broughton 1997.
15. Pianka 1988.
16. Stiner 2002.
17. Binford 2001; Kelly 1995; Hamilton et al. 2007.
18. Harpending and Bertram 1975; Winterhalder and Goland 1993. On other animals, see McNab 1994.
19. Kelly 1995.
20. McNeill 2000.
21. Foley 1984.
22. Van Valen 1973.
23. Johnston and Janiga 1995.
24. Potts and Shipman 1981.
25. Van Valkenburgh 2001.
26. Bunn 1981.
27. Stiner 1994.
28. Vander Wall 1990, 225–36.
29. Müller 1878.
30. Groves 1991; Blondel and Aronson 1999.
31. Diamond 1994; Price 1984.
32. See contributions in Hovers and Kuhn 2006.
33. See, for example, Akazawa and Muhesen 2002.
34. Speth 2006.
35. Kuhn and Stiner 1998.
36. On population density, see Lahr and Foley 2003; on invading UP peoples, Cox et al. 2009.
37. Stiner, Munro, and Surovell 2000.
38. Pennington 2001.

39. Kuhn et al. 2001; McBrearty and Brooks 2000.

40. On risk management, see Winterhalder 1998; on geographic circulation, Gamble 1986b.

41. Kuhn and Stiner 2006.

42. P. Wilson 1988.

43. Clutton-Brock 1999.

44. Tchernov and Valla 1997.

45. On genetic divergence, see Shipman 2009, 286; Wayne, Leonard, and Vilà 2006, 290.

46. See the cover of *Science* 324, no. 5926 (April 24, 2009).

47. Dobney and Larson 2006; Zeder et al. 2006.

48. Darwin 1964.

49. Ibid., 34–35.

50. Rindos 1984.

51. Janzen 1966.

52. Sakata 1994.

53. Flatt and Weisser 2000.

54. Trut 1999.

55. Beja-Pereira et al. 2003.

56. Darwin 1868.

57. Leach 2003; P. Wilson 1988.

58. Zeder 2006, 107.

59. Zeder et al. 2006.

60. Horwitz 1999; Buitenhuis 1997; Zeder and Hesse 2000.

61. Ammerman and Cavalli-Sforza 1984; Diamond 2002.

62. Eliot 1871, 1: 351.

63. Hames 2007; Tainter 2000.

64. Vander Wall 1990.

65. Hardin 1968.

66. Ibid., 1243–48.

67. Turney et al. 2008, 12150.

68. Roberts and Brook 2010, 421.

69. Haile et al. 2009.

70. Gill et al. 2009.

71. Anderson 1989; Holdaway and Jacomb 2000; Steadman 1989.

72. Diamond 1989.

73. Rick and Erlandson 2009.

74. Jackson et al. 2001.

75. Darwin 1964.

76. Feeley-Harnik 2004, 2007.

77. Animal Studies Group 2006, 2–3.

78. Grimm 2009, 1490.

79. McLennan 1869–70.

80. Tylor 1871, 2: 207–8.

81. Hallowell 1960; Nadasdy 2007.

82. Melville 1994.

83. Crosby 2004.

84. Naylor et al. 2005, 1621.
85. Naylor et al. 2005.
86. Hall et al. 2009.
87. Foley et al. 2005, 570; Agrawal, Ashwini, and Hardin 2008, 1460.
88. Odling-Smee, Laland, and Feldman 2003; White 1995.
89. Kareiva et al. 2007, 1869; see also Millennium Ecosystem Assessment 2005.
90. Dobson et al. 2008, 11482.
91. Pennisi 2008, 1001.
92. Holden 2009.
93. Lloyd-Smith et al. 2009.
94. Leach 2007.

5. LANGUAGE

1. Jefferson 1995.
2. Jones 1788.
3. Marsden 1782, 1785; Trautmann 2006.
4. Leibniz 1989, 228.
5. Bopp 1816, 1833.
6. Grimm 1819.
7. Swadesh 1952, 1972.
8. Harrison 2003; McMahon and McMahon 2005.
9. Greenberg 1955, 1987, 2000.
10. See Campbell 2000; Millar 2007.
11. Nettle and Romaine 2000.
12. Fox 1995.
13. Ladefoged and Maddieson 1996.
14. Renfrew, McMahon, and Trask 2000; Forster and Renfrew 2006.
15. Aikhenvald and Dixon 2001; McMahon 2010; Thomason 2003.
16. Joseph and Janda 2003, 10.
17. Sankoff and Blondeau 2008.
18. See Thomason 2001; Hickey 2010; Matras and Bakker, forthcoming.
19. Thomason 2003, 694.
20. Thomason 2001, 2003.
21. Thomason 2003, 706–7.
22. McMahon 2005; McMahon and McMahon 2005; Forster and Renfrew 2006; McMahon and McMahon 2008; Wichmann 2008.
23. Nakhleh, Ringe, and Warnow 2005.
24. See McMahon and McMahon 2005.
25. Bryant and Moulton 2004.
26. Dyen, Kruskal, and Black 1992.
27. Gray and Atkinson 2003.
28. McMahon and McMahon 2008; Wichmann 2008.
29. McMahon et al. 2005.
30. Ibid., 166–7.
31. Ibid.

32. McMahon et al. 2007.
33. Stuart-Smith, Timmins, and Tweedie 2007.
34. Greenberg 2005; Ruhlen 1987.
35. Bowern and Koch 2004.
36. Kirby 2002, 186.
37. Bickerton 2007, 522.
38. Kirby, Dowman, and Griffiths 2007, 5241.
39. Ibid.
40. Kirby, Cornish, and Smith 2008, 10681.
41. Kirby, Dowman, and Griffiths 2007, 5243.
42. Ibid.
43. Brighton, Kirby, and Smith 2005.
44. Kirby, Cornish, and Smith 2008, 10681.
45. Ibid., 10682.
46. Ibid., 10684.
47. Ibid., 10685.
48. Roberts 2008.
49. Ibid., 180.
50. Ibid., 182.

6. FOOD

1. Trevor-Roper 1965.
2. Sahlins 1972; see also Binford 1968.
3. Goodall 1986; Watts and Mitani 2002.
4. Hardy 2010.
5. Toth and Schick 2006.
6. Cartmill 1993; Kaplan et al. 2000; Stanford and Bunn 2001.
7. Crosby 2002; Bramble and Lieberman 2004.
8. Wrangham 2009, 13–14.
9. Goren-Inbar et al. 2004.
10. Wrangham 2009, 13.
11. Gamble 2007.
12. Malinowski 1974, 175.
13. Lévi-Strauss 1970, 336.
14. Ibid., 65.
15. Goodall 1977, 1979; Nishida and Kawanaka 1985; Watts and Mitani 2000.
16. Simpson 1984.
17. Cernuda 2006; Pancorbo 2008, 47.
18. Mead et al. 2003.
19. Sanday 1986.
20. Ibid., 6.
21. Ibid., 69; Meigs 1988.
22. Sanday 1986, 72–82.
23. Gardner 1999; Ernst 1999.
24. Derrick 1957, 22.

25. Sanday 1986, 21.
26. Sahlins, quoted in Sanday 1986, 22; see Brown and Tuzin 1983.
27. Dawood 1973, 137.
28. de Waal 2001.
29. Harris 1985, 55–66.
30. Quoted in Douglas 1984, 31.
31. Ibid., 55.
32. Kiple and Ornelas 2000, 2: 1505–7.
33. McDonaugh 1990, 46.
34. Parkinson et al. 1990, 632–34.
35. Dietler and Hayden 2001.
36. Jones 2007, 153–76.
37. Kemp 1989, 120–28.
38. Fernández-Armesto 2001, 192–200.
39. Flandrin and Montanari 1996, 55.
40. Ibid., 22.
41. Om Prakash 1961, 100.
42. Vaughan 2002, 144–45; see also Fernández-Armesto 1996, 96.
43. Partner 1976.
44. Habu 2004.
45. Schmidt 2000, 45–54.
46. Eaton and Konner 1985; Binford 1968; Sahlins 1968, 1972.
47. Scott 2009.
48. Rindos 1984.
49. Braudel 1961.
50. McNeill 2000, 24.
51. Levenstein 1988, 109.
52. Wilson and Burks 1955, 10.
53. MacDonald 1946, 65, 115.
54. Wilson and Burks 1955, 38.
55. C. Wilson 1976, 55.
56. Goody 1982, 40–78.
57. Bober 1999, 72–3.
58. Flandrin and Montanari 1996, 72.
59. Waley 1919, 13–14, quoted in Goody 1982, 112; translation modified.
60. Athenaeus of Naucratis 1928, 171–75.
61. Gowers 1993, 51.
62. Pitte 1991, 129.
63. Fernández-Armesto 2000.
64. Dalby 1996, 87, 140.
65. Déry 1997, 91.
66. Grove 1996, 93.
67. Cooper 1827, 6.
68. Crosby 2004, 7.
69. See ibid., 145–70 (quote at 170); Crosby 2003, 73–74.
70. Kiple and Ornelas 2000, 2: 1250.
71. Scarry and Reitz 1990, 351.
72. Cronon 1991.

7. DEEP KINSHIP

1. Hegel 1970, 1975.
2. Morgan 1851, 1871.
3. Morgan 1851, 81.
4. Morgan 1871.
5. Durkheim 1897.
6. E. O. Wilson 1975; Sahlins 1976.
7. Lévi-Strauss 1969.
8. Allen 2008.
9. Allen 1982, 1986, 1989, 1998, 2008.
10. Chapais 2008.
11. Morin and Goldberg 2004.
12. Csillery et al. 2006; Van Horn, Altmann, and Alberts 2008.
13. DiFiore 2003.
14. Altmann 1979.
15. Clutton-Brock and Isvaran 2006.
16. Fredrickson and Sackett 1984.
17. Bernstein 1991; Owren et al. 1993.
18. Cheney and Seyfarth 1980.
19. Silk 2001.
20. Alberts 1999; Muniz et al. 2006.
21. On female macaques and baboons, see Widdig et al. 2001; Smith, Alberts, and Altmann 2003. On male baboons, see Buchan et al. 2003.
22. Widdig 2007.
23. Fredrickson and Sackett 1984; Erhart, Coelho, and Bramblett 1997.
24. Langergraber, Mitani, and Vigilant 2007; Perry et al. 2008.
25. Rendall 2004.
26. Cheney and Seyfarth 1980.
27. Dasser 1988.
28. Cheney and Seyfarth 1999.
29. Aureli et al. 1992.
30. Kawai 1958; Kawamura 1958.
31. Kapsalis 2004.
32. Silk, Alberts, and Altmann 2006.
33. Silk 2001.
34. Chapais 1992.
35. Harcourt 1987.
36. Eberle and Kappeler 2007.
37. Bradley, Doran-Sheehy, and Vigilant 2007.
38. Pope 2000.
39. Muller and Mitani 2005.
40. Langergraber, Mitani, and Vigilant 2007.
41. Mitani 2009.
42. Rajpurohit and Sommer 1993; Mitchell 1994.
43. Bradley et al. 2004.
44. Pope 1990.
45. Hamilton 1963.

46. Griffin and West 2003; Foster, Wenseleers, and Ratnieks 2006.
47. Nishida et al. 2003.
48. Langergraber, Mitani, and Vigilant 2007.
49. Mitani 2009.
50. Lehmann and Boesch 2009.
51. Langergraber, Mitani, and Vigilant 2009.
52. Lehmann and Boesch 2009; Langergraber, Mitani, and Vigilant 2009.
53. Kummer 1978.
54. Silk 2002.
55. Smuts 1985; Palombit, Seyfarth, and Cheney 1997.
56. Mitani and Watts 2001.
57. Silk, Alberts, and Altmann 2003.
58. Cheney and Seyfarth 2009.
59. Taylor et al. 2000.
60. Rodseth et al. 1991, 229.
61. Knight 2008.
62. Morgan 1871.
63. Ibid.
64. Lounsbury 1964a,b.
65. Viveiros de Castro 1998; Tjon Sie Fat 1998.
66. Barnard 2008.
67. Jones 2003; Ehret 2008.
68. Morgan 1871; Darwin 1964, 463.
69. See Schneider 1984 for the argument that such claims are ethnocentric.
70. Maine 1963, 143.
71. Evans-Pritchard 1940.
72. Richards 1941; Gough 1971; Hutchinson 1996; McKinnon 1999.
73. Evans-Pritchard 1950, 364–65.
74. Maine 1963, 20–21.
75. Mithen 2006, S55.
76. Tomasello, Carpenter, and Liszkowski 2007; Gómez 2007; Hurford 2007.
77. Morgan 1851, 327.
78. Morgan 1881, 61.
79. Lévi-Strauss 1982, 1987.
80. Klapisch-Zuber 1987, 117.
81. Ibid., 118, 119 n. 3.
82. Daniel 1984, 115; see also 105–62.
83. Sims 2009, 405.
84. Murray et al. 2008.
85. Gamble 2007, 104–9.
86. Gamble 2007, 195, 234; see table 7.4.
87. Alperson-Afil et al. 2009.
88. Kolen 1999, 153–55.
89. Gamble 2007, 244–45.
90. Ingold 2000, 219–42.
91. Mueggler 2001, 80.
92. Clarke 2009, 40.

93. Parkes 2003, 2004.
94. Clarke 2007.
95. Weiner 1978, 1987.
96. Lordkipanidze et al. 2005, 718; Lordkipanidze et al. 2006; Rightmire, Van Arsdale, and Lordkipanidze 2008.
97. Hrdy 2009.
98. Gamble 2007, 193.
99. Klapisch-Zuber 1987, 233–40.
100. Kuhn and Stiner 2007, 48–50; Choyke 2006.
101. Yates 1966.
102. Bahloul 1996.
103. Edwards and Yu 2007, 1321.
104. Edwards and Yu 2007.
105. Hrdy 2009.
106. Gamble 2007, 211–12.
107. Pálsson 2002; Simpson 2000.
108. Lee et al. 2009.
109. James 2008.

8. MIGRATION

1. T. Huxley 1895, 245.
2. Ibid., 251.
3. Gamble 1993.
4. Radcliffe-Brown 1952.
5. Balter 2006; Brothwell and Pollard 2005.
6. Aitken 1990; Brothwell and Pollard 2005.
7. Elias 2007; Lowe et al. 2008.
8. Lee-Thorp and Sponheimer 2006.
9. Harbottle 1982.
10. Cann, Stoneking, and Wilson 1987.
11. Soares et al. 2009.
12. Cavalli-Sforza 1991; Cavalli-Sforza, Menozzi, and Piazza 1994; Renfrew 2000; Searls 2003; Jones 2003; Oppenheimer 2006.
13. Gamble 2001.
14. Gibbons 2009.
15. The earliest *Homo* specimens are represented by well-dated fossils in Africa, but evidence for early tools from Pakistan and China may call into question the Out of Africa model and open instead the possibility that *Homo* evolved in Asia and returned to Africa, perhaps with a stone technology. The African emphasis may be an outcome of disproportionate research effort; future work in Asia might challenge African hegemony (see Dennell 2009).
16. Semaw et al. 1997.
17. de Menocal 2003.
18. Dennell 2009.
19. Noonan et al. 2006; Briggs et al. 2009.
20. Gamble 1999.

21. Noonan et al. 2006.

22. Lahr and Foley 1994.

23. Parfitt et al. 2005.

24. Stringer 2006.

25. Smail 2008.

26. Ruff, Trinkaus, and Holliday 1997.

27. Wrangham 2009.

28. On neural mutations, see Klein 2000; on the Toba supervolcano, Ambrose 1998; on the broadening of the human diet, Stiner, Munro, and Surovell 2000.

29. Gamble 2008.

30. Macaulay et al. 2005.

31. Adler and Jöris 2009.

32. Soares et al. 2009.

33. Richards et al. 2008.

34. Gamble 1999.

35. Gamble 2007.

36. Gamble 2008.

37. Childe 1929, v–vi.

38. Ammerman and Cavalli-Sforza 1979.

39. Van Andel and Runnels 1995.

40. Zvelebil 1986.

41. Scarre 2005; Whittle 1996, 2003.

42. Lourandos 1997.

43. Johnson and Earle 2000.

44. Bellwood 2005.

45. Renfrew 2007.

46. Bellwood 2005, 278.

47. Gamble et al. 2005.

48. Zeder et al. 2006.

49. Ibid., 139.

50. Zeder 2006.

51. Kingdon 1993; Lahr and Foley 1994; Macaulay et al. 2005; Dennell 2009.

52. Earle 1997.

53. Barth 1965.

54. Redman 1978.

55. D'Altroy 2001, 2005.

56. Earle 1997.

57. Kirch 2000.

58. Stein 1999, 47.

59. Tsetskhladze 2006.

60. Mintz 1985.

9. GOODS

1. Paulsen 1974.

2. Hogendorn and Johnson 1986.

3. Mauss 1990; Appadurai 1986; Weiner 1992.
4. DeMarrais, Castillo, and Earle 1996.
5. Veblen 2007.
6. Braudel 1973, 235–36.
7. Earle 2002, 2004.
8. Hayden 1995.
9. Earle 1997.
10. Earle 2004.
11. Huxley 2004.
12. Douglas and Isherwood 1996.
13. Weiner 1976.
14. Earle 2004.
15. Blumenthal 2009.
16. McCormick 2001.
17. W. Johnson 1999.
18. Duffy 2006.
19. Kuhn and Stiner 2007.
20. Stiner 2003; White 1993.
21. On shells, see Stiner 1999; on rare minerals, Soffer 1985.
22. White 1989.
23. Soffer et al. 2000; White 2006.
24. Bouzouggar et al. 2007; Henshilwood et al. 2004.; Bar-Yosef et al. 2009.
25. White 2003.
26. White 1989.
27. Kuhn et al. 2001.
28. Burch 2005; Wiessner 1982.
29. See, for example, Féblot-Augustins 1993; Anikovich et al. 2007.
30. Stiner 1999; Taborin 1993.
31. Gamble 1986b.
32. Kuhn 1995.
33. Mellars 1989; White 1982.
34. Vanhaeren and d'Errico 2006.
35. Stiner 2003.
36. Barham 1998; Henshilwood et al. 2009.
37. Kuhn and Stiner 2007.
38. Kuhn et al. 2001.
39. Graebner 1996.
40. Wiessner 1989.
41. See, for example, Grafen 1990; Neiman 1997.
42. See Gamble 1999, 414–16.
43. Kuhn et al. 2001.
44. Coolidge and Wynn 2001.
45. McKendrick, Brewer, and Plumb 1982.
46. Lyons 2010; Clunas 2007.
47. Anderson 1991.
48. P. Brown 1981.
49. Sumption 1975.

50. Geary 1990.
51. Rubin 1991.
52. Hunt 1996.
53. Egan and Pritchard 2002.
54. Hunt 1996.
55. Strasser 1999.
56. Dyer 1998.
57. Deetz 1996.

10. SCALE

1. Stanley 1998; Moore and Hillman 1992.
2. On significant pulses, see Stiner et al. 1999; Cox et al. 2009. On the period after 18,000 years ago, see Gamble 1986b; Stiner, Munro, and Surovell 2000.
3. Klein 1999.
4. On exchange and reciprocity, see Kelly 1995; on social and genetic relatedness, Wobst 1977.
5. Kuhn and Stiner 2006.
6. Kuhn and Stiner 2007.
7. Thompson 1963.
8. Stiner and Kuhn 2006.
9. Martinson et al. 1987. The marine oxygen-isotope record is based on the ratio of oxygen-16 (O^{16}) and oxygen-18 (O^{18}) in the calcium carbonate shells of microfossils that accumulate annually on the seafloor. The ratio varies with subtle changes in the temperature and isotopic composition of the seawater in which the organism formed its shell. Colder water results in a richer ratio of O^{18} to O^{16}. Cyclical variation in ocean temperatures, which is linked to changes in global climate, can be inferred from the analysis of finely stratified sediment cores taken from the sea bottom.
10. On small animals, see Stiner 2001. On seeds and nuts, see, for example, Hansen 1991; Savard, Nesbitt, and Jones 2006; Wright 1994; Zohary 1996.
11. Kuhn and Stiner 2001.
12. Childe 1936.
13. See Gamble 2007.
14. Binford 1968; Flannery 1969.
15. Bettencourt et al. 2007.
16. Ibid., 7306.
17. Chapais 2008.
18. Lee 1984.
19. Boehm 1993.
20. Kelly 1995.
21. Smith et al. 2010.
22. Gurven et al. 2010.
23. Keeley 1988, 1995.
24. Gurven et al. 2010.
25. Byrd 1994; Cohen 1985; Gamble 1986a; T. Price 1991.
26. Belfer-Cohen and Bar-Yosef 2000; Henry 1985; Munro 2004.

27. On goats, see Zeder and Hesse 2000; on sheep, chickpeas, and lentils, see Buitenhaus 1997.

28. On residential architecture, see Özdoğan 1997; on grave contents, Belfer-Cohen 1995.

29. On Pacific Northwest, see Arnold 1996; Hayden 1995; on Florida, Marquardt 1988.

30. Redding 1988; Horwitz 1996.

31. Keeley 1988.

32. Binford 2001; Gurven 2004; Kelly 1995.

33. J. Clutton-Brock 1999.

34. Shennan 2010, 115–16.

35. Johnson and Earle 2000; Keeley 1996.

36. Shady, Haas, and Creamer 2001.

37. Gibson and Carr 2004.

38. Earle 2002.

39. Earle 1997, 2002.

40. Earle 1987.

41. Sahlins 1958; Kirch 2000.

42. Spencer 1967.

43. Earle 1997.

44. Adams 1978.

45. Sahlins 1972.

46. Blanton et al. 1996.

47. Earle 1997; Kirch 1985.

48. Kirch 2000.

49. Spriggs 1991.

50. Sherratt 1981.

51. Kristiansen 1998; Earle and Kristiansen 2010.

52. Dennett 1995, 26–28. See also Coolidge and Wynn 2001; Klein and Edgar 2002.

53. Klein 1999.

54. Bar-Yosef 1996.

55. Dunbar 1992, 1993, 1996, 1998, 2003.

56. Quoted in Darling 2007.

57. Ibn Qutayba 1925–30, 1: 9.

58. Ibn Khaldun 1958, 81–82.

59. Ibid., 78–79.

Bibliography

Adams, Richard. 1978. "Man, Energy, and Anthropology." *American Anthropologist* 80: 297–309.

Adler, D.S., and O. Jöris. 2009. "Dating the Middle to Upper Palaeolithic Boundary across Eurasia." *Eurasian Prehistory* 5: 5–18.

Agrawal, A., C. Ashwini, and R. Hardin. 2008. "Changing Governance of the World's Forests." *Science* 320, no. 5882: 1460–62.

Aiello, L.C., and P. Wheeler. 1995. "The Expensive-Tissue Hypothesis: The Brain and the Digestive System in Human and Primate Evolution." *Current Anthropology* 36(2): 199–221.

Aikhenvald, Alexandra Y., and R.M.W. Dixon. 2001. *Areal Diffusion and Genetic Inheritance: Problems in Comparative Linguistics.* Oxford: Oxford University Press.

Aitken, M. 1990. *Science-based Dating in Archaeology.* London: Longman.

Akazawa, Takeru, and Sultan Muhesen. 2002. *Neanderthal Burials: Excavations of the Dederiyeh Cave, Afrin, Syria.* Kyoto: KW Publications.

Alberts, S. 1999. "Paternal Kin Discrimination in Wild Baboons." *Proceedings of the Royal Society of London, Series B, Biological Sciences* 266: 1501–6.

Albritton, Claude. 1980. *The Abyss of Time: Changing Conceptions of the Earth's Antiquity after the Sixteenth Century.* San Francisco: Freeman, Cooper.

Allen, Nicholas J. 1982. "A Dance of Relatives." *Journal of the Anthropological Society of Oxford* 13: 139–46.

———. 1986. "Tetradic Theory: An Approach to Kinship." *Journal of the Anthropological Society of Oxford* 17: 87–109.

———. 1989. "The Evolution of Kinship Terminologies." *Lingua* 77: 173–85.

———. 1998. "The Prehistory of Dravidian-type Terminologies." In *Transformation of Kinship,* ed. M. Godelier, T.R. Trautmann, and F.E. Tjon Sie Fat, 314–31. Washington, DC: Smithsonian Institution.

————. 2008. "Tetradic Theory and the Origin of Human Kinship Systems." In *Early Human Kinship: From Sex to Social Reproduction,* ed. Nicholas J. Allen, Hilary Callan, Robin Dunbar, and Wendy James, 96–113. Oxford: Blackwell.

Allen, Nicholas J., Hilary Callan, Robin Dunbar, and Wendy James, eds. 2008. *Early Human Kinship: From Sex to Social Reproduction.* Malden, MA: Blackwell.

Alperson-Afil, Nira, Gonen Sharon, Mordechai Kislev, Yoel Melamed, Irit Zohar, Shosh Ashkenazi, Rivka Rabinovich, et al. 2009. "Spatial Organization of Hominin Activities at Gesher Benot Ya'aqov, Israel." *Science* 326, no. 5960: 1677–80.

Altmann, J. 1979. "Age Cohorts as Paternal Sibships." *Behavioral Ecology and Sociobiology* 6: 161–64.

Ambrose, Stanley H. 1998. "Late Pleistocene Human Population Bottlenecks, Volcanic Winter, and Differentiation of Modern Humans." *Journal of Human Evolution* 34: 623–51.

Ammerman, A., and L.L. Cavalli-Sforza. 1979. "The Wave of Advance Model for the Spread of Agriculture in Europe." In *Transformations: Mathematical Approaches to Culture Change,* ed. C. Renfrew and K.L. Cooke, 275–94. London: Academic Press.

————. 1984. *The Neolithic Transition and the Genetics of Populations in Europe.* Princeton, NJ: Princeton University Press.

Anderson, A. 1989. "Mechanics of Overkill in the Extinction of New Zealand Moas." *Journal of Archaeological Science* 16: 137–51.

Anderson, Benedict. 1991. *Imagined Communities: Reflections on the Origin and Spread of Nationalism.* London: Verso.

Anikovich, M.V., A.A. Sinitsyn, J.F. Hoffecker, V.T. Holliday, V.V. Popov, S.N. Lisitsyn, S.L. Forman, et al. 2007. "Early Upper Paleolithic in Eastern Europe and Implications for the Dispersal of Modern Humans." *Science* 315, no. 5809: 223–26.

Animal Studies Group. 2006. *Killing Animals.* Urbana-Champaign: University of Illinois Press.

Appadurai, Arjun, ed. 1986. *The Social Life of Things: Commodities in Cultural Perspective.* Cambridge: Cambridge University Press.

Arbib, Michael, ed. 2006. *Action to Language Via the Mirror Neuron System.* Cambridge: Cambridge University Press.

Arnold, Jeanne. 1996. "The Archaeology of Complex Hunter-gatherers." *Journal of Archaeological Method and Theory* 3: 77–126.

Athenaeus of Naucratis. 1928. *The Deipnosophists.* 7 vols. Ed. and trans. Charles Burton Gulick. London: W. Heinemann.

Aureli, F., R. Cozzolino, C. Cordischi, and S. Scucchi. 1992. "Kin-Oriented Redirection among Japanese Macaques: An Expression of a Revenge System?" *Animal Behaviour* 44: 283–91.

Bahloul, Joëlle. 1996. *The Architecture of Memory: A Jewish Muslim Household in Colonial Algeria, 1937–1962.* Translated by Catherine du Peloux Ménagé. Cambridge: Cambridge University Press.

Balter, M. 2006. "Radiocarbon Dating's Final Frontier." *Science* 313, no. 5793: 1560–63.

Barham, L.S. 1998. "Possible Early Pigment Use in South-Central Africa." *Current Anthropology* 39: 703–10.

Barnard, Alan. 2008. "The Co-evolution of Language and Kinship." In *Early Human Kinship: From Sex to Social Reproduction,* ed. Nicholas J. Allen, Hilary Callan, Robin Dunbar, and Wendy James, 232–44. Oxford: Blackwell.

Barth, Fredrik. 1965. *Political Leadership among Swat Pathans.* London: Athlone Press.

Bar-Yosef, Ofer. 1996. "Modern Humans, Neanderthals and the Middle/Upper Paleolithic Transition in Western Asia." In *The Lower and Middle Paleolithic: Colloquium X; The Origin of Modern Man,* ed. Ofer Bar-Yosef, Luigi Luca Cavalli-Sforza, and M. Piperno, 175–90. Forli, Italy: A.B.A.C.O. Edizioni.

———. 1998. "The Natufian Culture in the Levant, Threshold to the Origins of Agriculture." *Evolutionary Anthropology* 5: 159–77.

Bar-Yosef, O., and A. Gopher, eds. 1991. *The Natufian Culture in the Levant.* Ann Arbor, MI: International Monographs in Prehistory.

Bar-Yosef Mayer, D.E., B. Vandermeersch, and O. Bar-Yosef. 2009. "Shells and Ochre in Middle Paleolithic Qafzeh Cave, Israel: Indications for Modern Behavior." *Journal of Human Evolution* 56: 307–14.

Bayly, Christopher A. 2004. *The Birth of the Modern World, 1780–1914: Global Connections and Comparisons.* Malden, MA: Blackwell.

Beja-Pereira, A., G. Luikart, P.R. England, D.G. Bradley, O.C. Jann, G. Bertorelle, A.T. Chamberlain, et al. 2003. "Gene-Culture Coevolution between Cattle Milk Protein and Human Lactase Genes." *Nature Genetics* 35: 311–13.

Belfer-Cohen, A. 1995. "Rethinking Social Stratification in the Natufian Culture: The Evidence from the Burials." In *The Archaeology of Death in the Ancient Near East,* ed. Stuart Campbell and Anthony Green, 9–16. Oxford: Oxbow Books.

Belfer-Cohen, A., and O. Bar-Yosef. 2000. "Early Sedentism in the Near East." In *Life in Neolithic Farming Communities: Social Organization, Identity, and Differentiation,* ed. I. Kuijt, 19–37. New York: Kluwer Academic/Plenum Publishers.

Bellwood, P. 2005. *First Farmers: The Origins of Agricultural Societies.* Oxford: Blackwell.

Bernays, Edward. 2005 [1928]. *Propaganda.* Brooklyn, NY: Ig Publishing.

Bernstein, I. 1991. "The Correlation Between Kinship and Behavior in Nonhuman Primates." In *Kin Recognition in Animals,* ed. P. Hepper, 6–29. Cambridge: Cambridge University Press.

Bettencourt, L.M.A., J. Lobo, D. Helbing, C. Kühnert, and G.B. West. 2007. "Growth, Innovation, Scaling, and the Pace of Life in Cities." *Proceedings of the National Academy of Sciences of the United States* 104, no. 17: 7301–6.

Bickerton, Derek. 2007. "Language Evolution: A Brief Guide for Linguists." *Lingua* 117: 510–26.

Binford, Lewis R. 1968. "Post-Pleistocene Adaptations." In *New Perspectives in Archaeology,* ed. S.R. Binford and L.R. Binford, 313–41. Chicago: Aldine.

———. 2001. *Constructing Frames of Reference: An Analytical Method for Archaeological Theory Building Using Ethnographic and Environmental Data Sets.* Berkeley: University of California Press.

Blackbourn, David. 2006. *The Conquest of Nature: Water, Landscape and the Making of Modern Germany*. London: Jonathan Cape.

Blakeslee, Sandra, and Matthew Blakeslee. 2007. *The Body Has a Mind of Its Own*. New York: Random House.

Blanton, Richard, G. Feinman, S. Kowalewski, and P. Peregrine. 1996. "A Dual-Processual Theory for the Evolution of Mesoamerican Civilization." *Current Anthropology* 37: 1–14.

Blondel, J., and J. Aronson. 1999. *Biology and Wildlife of the Mediterranean Region*. Oxford: Oxford University Press.

Blumenschine, Robert J. 1986. *Early Hominid Scavenging Opportunities: Implications of Carcass Availability in the Serengeti and Ngorongoro Ecosystems*. Oxford: B.A.R. International Series.

Blumenthal, Debra. 2009. *Enemies and Familiars: Slavery and Mastery in Fifteenth-Century Valencia*. Ithaca, NY: Cornell University Press.

Bober, P.P. 1999. *Art, Culture and Cuisine: Ancient and Medieval Gastronomy*. Chicago: University of Chicago Press.

Boehm, Christopher. 1993. "Egalitarian Behavior and Reverse Dominance Hierarchy." *Current Anthropology* 34: 227–54.

Bopp, Franz. 1816. *Über das Konjugationssystem der Sanskritsprache in Vergleichung mit jenem der griechischen, lateinischen, persischen und germanischen Sprache*. Frankurt: Andraeischen Buchhandlung.

———. 1833. *Vergleichende Grammatik des Sanskrit, Zend, Griechischen, Lateinischen, Litthauischen, Altslawischen, Gotischen und Deutschen*. Berlin: F. Dümmler.

Bouzouggar, A., R.N.E. Barton, M. Vanhaeren, F. d'Errico, S. Collcutt, T. Higham, E. Hodge, et al. 2007. "82,000-Year-Old Shell Beads from North Africa and Implications for the Origins of Modern Human Behavior." *Proceedings of the National Academy of Sciences of the United States* 104, no. 24: 9964–69.

Bowern, Claire, and Harold Koch, eds. 2004. *Australian Languages: Classification and the Comparative Method*. Amsterdam: John Benjamins.

Bradley, B., D. Doran-Sheehy, and L. Vigilant. 2007. "Potential for Female Kin Associations in Wild Western Gorillas Despite Female Dispersal." *Proceedings of the Royal Society of London, Series B, Biological Sciences* 274: 2179–85.

Bradley, B., D. Doran-Sheehy, D. Lukas, C. Boesch, and L. Vigilant. 2004. "Dispersed Male Networks in Western Gorillas." *Current Biology* 14: 510–13.

Bradley, Richard. 1998. *The Significance of Monuments: On the Shaping of Human Experience in Neolithic and Bronze Age Europe*. London: Routledge.

Bramble, D.M., and D.E. Lieberman 2004. "Endurance Running and the Evolution of *Homo*." *Nature* 432: 345–52.

Braudel, Fernand. 1961. "Alimentation et categories de l'histoire." *Annales* 16: 723–28.

———. 1973. *Capitalism and Material Life, 1400–1800*. Translated by Miriam Kochan. New York: Harper and Row.

Briggs, Adrian W., Jeffrey M. Good, Richard E. Green, Johannes Krause, Tomislav Maricic, Udo Stenzel, Carles Lalueza-Fox, et al. 2009. "Targeted Retrieval and Analysis of Five mtDNA Neandertal Genomes." *Science* 325, no. 5938: 318–21.

Brighton, Henry, Simon Kirby, and Kenny Smith. 2005. "Cultural Selection for Learnability: Three Principles Underlying the View That Language Adapts to Be Learnable." In *Language Origins: Perspectives on Evolution,* ed. Maggie Tallerman, 291–309. Oxford: Oxford University Press.

Brothwell, D.R., and A.M. Pollard. 2005. *Handbook of Archaeological Sciences.* New York: Wiley.

Broughton, J.M. 1997. "Widening Diet Breadth, Declining Foraging Efficiency, and Prehistoric Harvest Pressure: Ichthyofaunal Evidence from the Emeryville Shellmound, California." *Antiquity* 71: 845–62.

Brown, Gordon. 2004. "The Golden Thread That Runs through Our History." *Guardian,* July 8. www.guardian.co.uk/politics/2004/jul/08/britishidentity.economy, accessed January 10, 2011.

Brown, J.H., and E.J. Heske. 1990. "Control of a Desert-Grassland Transition by a Keystone Rodent Guild." *Science* 250, no. 4988: 1705–7.

Brown, Paula, and Donald Tuzin, eds. 1983. *The Ethnography of Cannibalism.* Washington, DC: Society for Psychological Anthropology.

Brown, Peter Robert Lamont. 1981. *The Cult of the Saints: Its Rise and Function in Latin Christianity.* Chicago: University of Chicago Press.

Bryant, D., and V. Moulton. 2004. "Neighbor-Net: An Agglomerative Algorithm for the Construction of Planar Phylogenetic Networks." *Molecular Biology and Evolution* 21: 255–65.

Buchan, J., S. Alberts, J. Silk, and J. Altmann 2003. "True Paternal Care in a Multi-male Primate Society." *Nature* 425: 179–81.

Buitenhuis, H. 1997. "Aşıklı Höyük: A Protodomestication Site." *Anthropozoologica* 25–26: 655–62.

Bunn, H.T. 1981. "Archaeological Evidence for Meat-Eating by Plio-Pleistocene Hominids from Koobi Fora and Olduvai Gorge." *Nature* 291: 574–77.

Burch, E.A. 2005. *Alliance and Conflict: The World System of the Iñupiaq Eskimos.* Lincoln: University of Nebraska Press.

Burling, Robbins. 1963. *Rengsanggri: Family and Kinship in a Garo Village.* Philadelphia: University of Pennsylvania Press.

Byrd, B.F. 1994. "Later Quaternary Hunter-Gatherer Complexes in the Levant between 20,000 and 10,000 BP." In *Late Quaternary Chronology and Paleoclimates of the Eastern Mediterranean,* ed. O. Bar-Yosef and R.S. Kra, 205–26. Tucson, AZ: Radiocarbon.

Campbell, Lyle. 2000. *Historical Linguistics: An Introduction.* Edinburgh: Edinburgh University Press.

Cann, R., M. Stoneking, and A. Wilson. 1987. "Mitochondrial DNA and Human Evolution." *Nature* 325: 31–6.

Cantù, Cesare. 1884. *Storia Universale.* 10th ed. Turin: Unione Tipografico-Editrice.

Cartmill, Matt. 1993. *A View to a Death in the Morning: Hunting and Nature through History.* Cambridge, MA: Harvard University Press.

Cavalli-Sforza, Luigi. 1991. "Genes, Peoples and Languages." *Scientific American* 265: 104–10.

Cavalli-Sforza, Luigi, and Francesco Cavalli-Sforza. 1995. *The Great Human Diasporas: The History of Diversity and Evolution.* Reading, MA: Addison-Wesley.

Cavalli-Sforza, Luigi, Paolo Menozzi, and Alberto Piazza. 1994. *The History and Geography of Human Genes*. Princeton, NJ: Princeton University Press.

Cernuda, Ollala. 2006. "Canibalismo infantil en Atapuerca." *El Mundo*, 25 July. www.elmundo.es/elmundo/2006/07/21/ciencia/1153500417.html, accessed 15 December 2010.

Chakrabarty, Dipesh. 2009. "The Climate of History: Four Theses." *Critical Inquiry* 35: 197–222.

Chapais, Bernard. 1992. "The Role of Alliances in Social Inheritance of Rank among Female Primates." In *Coalitions and Alliances in Humans and Other Animals*, ed. A. Harcourt and Frans B.M. de Waal, 29–59. Oxford: Oxford University Press.

———. 2008. *Primeval Kinship: How Pair-Bonding Gave Birth to Human Society*. Cambridge, MA: Harvard University Press.

Chapman, John, and Bisserka Gaydarska. 2007. *Parts and Wholes: Fragmentation in Prehistoric Context*. Oxford: Oxbow Books.

Cheney, D., and R. Seyfarth, 1980. "Vocal Recognition in Free-Ranging Vervet Monkeys." *Animal Behaviour* 28: 362–67.

———. 1999. "Recognition of Other Individuals' Social Relationships by Female Baboons." *Animal Behaviour* 58: 67–75.

———. 2009. "Stress and Coping Mechanisms in Female Primates." *Advances in the Study of Behavior* 39: 1–34.

Childe, V. Gordon. 1929. *The Danube in Prehistory*. Oxford: Oxford University Press.

———. 1936. *Man Makes Himself*. London: Watts.

Choyke, Alice M. 2006. "Bone Tools for a Lifetime: Experience and Belonging." In *Normes techniques et pratiques sociales: de la simplicité des outillages pré- et protohistoriques*, Actes des XXVIe Rencontres internationales d'archéologie et d'histoire d'Antibes, ed. Laurence Astruc et al., 49–60. Antibes: Éditions APDCA.

Christian, David. 2004. *Maps of Time: An Introduction to Big History*. Berkeley: University of California Press.

Clark, Gregory. 2007. *A Farewell to Alms: A Brief Economic History of the World*. Princeton, NJ: Princeton University Press.

Clarke, Morgan. 2007. "The Modernity of Milk Kinship." *Social Anthropology/Anthropologie Sociale* 15: 287–304.

———. 2009. *Islam and New Kinship: Reproductive Technology and the Shariah in Lebanon*. Oxford: Berghahn.

Clunas, Craig. 2007. *Empire of Great Brightness: Visual and Material Cultures of Ming China, 1368–1644*. Honolulu: University of Hawaii Press.

Clutton-Brock, J. 1999. *A Natural History of Domesticated Mammals*. 2nd ed. Cambridge: Cambridge University Press.

Clutton-Brock, T., and Isvaran, K. 2006. "Paternity Loss in Contrasting Mammalian Societies." *Biology Letters* 2: 513–16.

Coffman, George R. 1926. "The Medieval Academy of America: Historical Background and Prospect." *Speculum* 1: 5–18.

Cohen, M.N. 1985. "Prehistoric Hunter-Gatherers: The Meaning of Social Complexity." In *Prehistoric Hunter-Gatherers: The Emergence of Cultural Complexity*, ed. T.D. Price and J.A. Brown, 99–119. San Diego: Academic Press.

Collingwood, R.G. 1956. *The Idea of History*. Oxford: Oxford University Press.

Coolidge, F.L., and T. Wynn. 2001. "Executive Functions of the Frontal Lobes and the Evolutionary Ascendancy of *Homo sapiens*." *Cambridge Archaeological Journal* 11: 255–60.

Cooper, James Fenimore. [1827]. *The Prairie*. New York: n.p.

Cordain L. 1999. "Cereal Grains: Humanity's Double-Edged Sword." *World Review of Nutrition and Dietetics* 84: 19–73.

Cordain, L., S.B. Eaton, J. Brand Miller, S. Lindeberg, and C. Jensen. 2002. "An Evolutionary Analysis of the Etiology and Pathogenesis of Juvenile-Onset Myopia." *Acta Ophthalmologica Scandinavica* 80: 125–35.

Courtwright, David T. 2001. *Forces of Habit: Drugs and the Making of the Modern World*. Cambridge, MA: Harvard University Press.

Coward, F., and C. Gamble. 2008. "Big Brains, Small Worlds: Material Culture and the Evolution of Mind." *Philosophical Transactions of the Royal Society, Series B*, 363: 1969–79.

Cox, M.P., D.A. Morales, A.E. Woerner, J. Sozanski, J.D. Wall, and M.F. Hammer. 2009. "Autosomal Resequence Data Reveal Late Stone Age Signals of Population Expansion in Sub-Saharan African Foraging and Farming Populations." *PLoS ONE* 4: e6366.

Cronon, William. 1991. *Nature's Metropolis: Chicago and the Great West*. New York: Norton.

Crosby, Alfred W. 2002. *Throwing Fire: Missile Projection through History*. Cambridge: Cambridge University Press.

———. 2003 [1972]. *The Columbian Exchange: Biological and Cultural Consequences of 1492*. Westport, CT: Praeger.

———. 2004. *Ecological Imperialism: The Biological Expansion of Europe, 900–1900*. 2nd ed. Cambridge: Cambridge University Press.

Crützen, P.J., and E.F. Stoermer. 2000. "The Anthropocene." *Global Change Newsletter* 41: 17–18.

Csillery, K., T. Johnson, D. Beraldi, T. Clutton-Brock, D. Coltman, B. Hannson, G. Spong, and J. Pemberton. 2006. "Performance of Marker-Based Relatedness Estimates in Natural Populations of Outbred Vertebrates." *Genetics* 173: 2511–23.

Dalby, A. 1996. *Siren Feasts: A History of Food and Gastronomy in Ancient Greece*. London: Routledge.

D'Altroy, Terence. 2001. "Politics, Resources, and Blood in the Inka Empire." In *Empires: Perspectives from Archaeology and History*, ed. Susan Alcock, Terence D'Altroy, Kathleen Morrison, and Carla Sinopoli, 201–26. Cambridge: Cambridge University Press.

———. 2005. "Remaking the Social Landscape: Colonization in the Inka Empire." In *The Archaeology of Colonial Encounters: Comparative Perspectives*, ed. Gil Stein, 263–96. Santa Fe: School of American Research Press.

Daniel, E. Valentine. 1984. *Fluid Signs: Being a Person the Tamil Way*. Berkeley: University of California Press.

Darling, Linda T. 2007. "Social Cohesion (*'Asabiyya*) and Justice in the Late Medieval Middle East." *Comparative Studies in Society and History* 49: 329–57.

Darwin, Charles. 1839. *Narrative of the Surveying Voyages of His Majesty's Ships* Adventure *and* Beagle *between the Years 1826 and 1836: Journals and Remarks 1832–1836.* Vol. 3. London: Coulburn.

———. 1868. *The Variation of Animals and Plants under Domestication.* London: John Murray.

———. 1871. *The Descent of Man and Selection in Relation to Sex.* London: John Murray.

———. 1964 [1859]. *On the Origin of Species by Means of Natural Selection, or the Preservation of Favoured Species in the Struggle for Life.* Facsimile ed. Cambridge, MA: Harvard University Press.

Darwin, F. 1887. *The Life and Letters of Charles Darwin, Including an Autobiographical Chapter.* 3 vols. 3rd ed. London: Murray.

Dasser, Verena. 1988. "A Social Concept in Java Monkeys." *Animal Behaviour* 36: 225–30.

Davis, Wade, and K. David Harrison, with Catherine Herbert Howell. 2007. *Book of Peoples of the World: A Guide to Cultures.* Washington, DC: National Geographic Society.

Dawkins, Richard, and J.R. Krebs. 1979. "Arms Races between and within Species." *Proceedings of the Royal Society of London, Series B, Biological Sciences* 205: 489–511.

Dawood, N.J., ed. 1973. *Tales from the 1001 Nights.* Harmondsworth, U.K.: Penguin.

de Bussac, E., ed. 1999 [1859]. *Naissance de la Préhistoire, récits des premiers témoins.* Clermont-Ferrand: Éditions Paleo, Préhistoire 3.

Deetz, James. 1996. *In Small Things Forgotten: An Archaeology of Early American Life.* Rev. ed. New York: Anchor Books.

DeMarrais, Elizabeth, L.J. Castillo, and T. Earle. 1996. "Ideology, Materialization and Power Strategies." *Current Anthropology* 37: 15–31.

de Menocal, P.B. 2003. "African Climate and Faunal Evolution during the Pliocene-Pleistocene." *Earth and Planetary Science Letters* 220: 3–4.

Dennell, R. 2009. *The Palaeolithic Settlement of Asia.* Cambridge: Cambridge University Press.

Dennett, Daniel C. 1995. *Darwin's Dangerous Idea: Evolution and the Meanings of Life.* New York: Simon and Schuster.

Derrick, Ronald A. 1957. *A History of Fiji.* 2 vols. Suva, Fiji: Printing and Stationery Department.

Déry, C.A. 1997. "Food and the Roman Army: Travel, Transport and Transmission (with Particular Reference to the Province of Britain)." In *Food on the Move: Proceedings of the Oxford Symposium on Food and Cookery,* ed. Harlan Walker, 84–96. Devon, U.K.: Prospect Books.

Di Pellegrino, G., L. Fadiga, L. Fogassi, V. Gallese, and G. Rizzolatti. 1992. "Understanding Motor Events: A Neurophysiological Study." *Experimental Brain Research* 91: 176–80.

Diamond, Jared M. 1987. "The Worst Mistake in the History of the Human Race." *Discover* 8(5): 64–66.

———. 1989. "Quaternary Megafaunal Extinctions: Variations on a Theme by Paganini." *Journal of Archaeological Science* 16: 167–75.

———. 1994. "Zebras and the Anna Karenina Principle." *Natural History* 103: 4–10.

———. 2002. "Evolution, Consequences and Future of Plant and Animal Domestication." *Nature* 418: 700–707.

Dietler, M., and B. Hayden, eds. 2001. *Feast: Archeological and Ethnographic Perspectives on Food, Politics, and Power.* Washington, DC: Smithsonian Institution.

DiFiore, A. 2003. "Molecular Genetic Approaches to the Study of Primate Behavior, Social Organization, and Reproduction." *Yearbook of Physical Anthropology* 46: 62–99.

Dobney, K., and G. Larson. 2006. "Genetics and Animal Domestication: New Windows on an Elusive Process." *Journal of Zoology* 269: 261–71.

Dobson, A., K.D. Lafferty, A.M. Kuris, R.F. Hechinger, and W. Jetz. 2008. "Homage to Linnaeus: How Many Parasites? How Many Hosts?" *Proceedings of the National Academy of Sciences of the United States* 105: 11482–89.

Douglas, Mary. 1984. *Purity and Danger: An Analysis of Concepts of Pollution and Taboo.* London: Ark Paperbacks.

Douglas, Mary, and Baron Isherwood. 1996. *The World of Goods: Towards an Anthropology of Consumption.* 2nd ed. London: Routledge.

Duffy, Eamon. 2006. *Marking the Hours: English People and Their Prayers, 1240–1570.* New Haven, CT: Yale University Press.

Dunbar, Robin. 1992. "Neocortex Size as a Constraint on Group Size in Primates." *Journal of Human Evolution* 20: 469–93.

———. 1993. "The Coevolution of Neocortical Size, Group Size and Language in Humans." *Behavioral and Brain Sciences* 16: 681–735.

———. 1996. *Grooming, Gossip, and the Evolution of Language.* London: Faber and Faber.

———. 1998. "The Social Brain Hypothesis." *Evolutionary Anthropology* 7: 178–90.

———. 2003. "The Social Brain: Mind, Language, and Society in Evolutionary Perspective." *Annual Review of Anthropology* 32: 163–81.

Durkheim, Émile. 1897. Review of Josef Kohler, *Zur Urgeschichte der Ehe. L'année sociologique* 1: 306–19.

Duruy, Victor. 1873. *Abrégé d'histoire générale.* Paris: Hachette.

Dyen, Isidore, Joseph B. Kruskal, and Paul Black. 1992. "An Indoeuropean Classification: A Lexicostatistical Experiment." *Transactions of the American Philosophical Society* 82: iii–iv, 1–132.

Dyer, Christopher. 1998. "Peasants and Coins: The Uses of Money in the Middle Ages." *British Numismatic Journal* 67: 30–47.

Earle, Timothy. 1987. "Chiefdoms in Archaeological and Ethnohistorical Perspectives." *Annual Review in Anthropology* 16: 279–308.

———. 1997. *How Chiefs Come to Power.* Stanford, CA: Stanford University Press.

———. 2002. *Bronze Age Economics.* Boulder, CO: Westview.

————. 2004. "Culture Matters in the Neolithic Transition and Emergence of Hierarchy in Thy, Denmark." *American Anthropologist* 106: 111–25.

Earle, Timothy, and Kris Kristiansen. 2010. *Organizing Bronze Age Societies: The Mediterranean, Central Europe, and Scandinavia Compared.* Cambridge: Cambridge University Press.

Eaton, S.B., and M. Konner. 1985. "Paleolithic Nutrition: A Consideration of Its Nature and Current Implications." *New England Journal of Medicine* 322: 283–89.

Eberle, M., and P. Kappeler. 2007. "Family Insurance: Kin Selection and Cooperative Breeding in a Solitary Primate (*Microcebus murinus*)." *Behavioral Ecology and Sociobiology* 60: 582–88.

Edwards, David P., and Douglas W. Yu. 2007. "The Roles of Sensory Traps in the Origin, Maintenance, and Breakdown of Mutualism." *Behavioral Ecology and Sociobiology* 61: 1321–27.

Egan, Geoff, and Frances Pritchard. 2002. *Dress Accessories, c. 1150–c. 1450.* Woodbridge, U.K.: Boydell Press.

Ehret, Cristopher. 2008. "Reconstructing Ancient Kinship in Africa." In *Early Human Kinship: From Sex to Social Reproduction,* ed. Nicholas J. Allen, Hilary Callan, Robin Dunbar, and Wendy James, 200–231, 259–69. London: Wiley-Blackwell.

Elias, S.E., ed. 2007. *Encyclopedia of Quaternary Science.* 4 vols. Amsterdam: Elsevier.

Eliot, George. 1871. *Middlemarch: A Study of Provincial Life.* 2 vols. Edinburgh: William Blackwood and Sons.

Erhart, E., A. Coelho, and C. Bramblett. 1997. "Kin Recognition by Paternal Half-Siblings in Captive *Papio cynocephalus.*" *American Journal of Primatology* 43: 147–57.

Ernst, Thomas M. 1999. "Onabasulu Cannibalism and the Moral Agents of Misfortune." In *The Anthropology of Cannibalism,* ed. Laurence R. Goldman, 143–59. Westport, CT: Bergin and Garvey.

Evans-Pritchard, E.E. 1940. *The Nuer: A Description of the Modes of Livelihood and Political Institutions of a Nilotic People.* Oxford: Clarendon Press.

————. 1950. "Kinship and the Local Community among the Nuer." In *African Systems of Kinship and Marriage,* ed. A.R. Radcliffe-Brown and D. Forde, 360–91. London: Oxford University Press.

Féblot-Augustins, J. 1993. "Mobility Strategies in the Late Middle Palaeolithic of Central Europe and Western Europe: Elements of Stability and Variability." *Journal of Anthropological Archaeology* 12: 211–65.

Feeley-Harnik, Gillian. 2004. "The Geography of Descent." *Proceedings of the British Academy* 125: 311–64.

————. 2007. "'An Experiment on a Gigantic Scale': Darwin and the Domestication of Pigeons." In *Where the Wild Things Are Now: Domestication Reconsidered,* ed. Rebecca Cassidy and Molly Mullin, 147–82. Oxford: Berg.

Fernández-Armesto, Felipe. 1996. *The Times Illustrated History of Europe.* London: Times Books.

————. 2000. "The Stranger-Effect in Early-Modern Asia." *Itinerario* 24: 80–123.

———. 2001. *Civilizations: Culture, Ambition, and the Transformation of Nature.* New York: Simon and Schuster.

Fisher, George Park. 1885. *Outlines of Universal History, Designed as a Text-Book and for Private Reading.* New York: Ivison, Blakeman, Taylor, and Co.

Flandrin, J.-L., and M. Montanari. 1996. *Histoire de l'alimentation.* Paris: Fayard.

Flannery, K.V. 1969. "Origins and Ecological Effects of Early Domestication in Iran and the Near East." In *The Domestication and Exploitation of Plants and Animals,* ed. P.J. Ucko and G.W. Dimbleby, 73–100. Chicago: Aldine.

Flatt, T., and W.W. Weisser. 2000. "The Effects of Mutualistic Ants on Aphid Life History Traits." *Ecology* 81: 3522–29.

Foley, J.A., R. DeFries, G.P. Asner, C. Barford, G. Bonan, S.R. Carpenter, F.S. Chapin, et al. 2005. "Global Consequences of Land Use." *Science* 309, no. 5734: 570–74.

Foley, R. 1984. "Putting People into Perspective." In *Hominid Evolution and Community Ecology: Prehistoric Human Adaptation in Biological Perspective,* ed. R. Foley, 1–24. London: Academic Press.

Foley, R., and C. Gamble. 2009. "The Ecology of Social Transitions in Human Evolution." *Philosophical Transactions of the Royal Society of London, Series B,* 364: 3267–79.

Forster, Peter, and Colin Renfrew, eds. 2006. *Phylogenetic Methods and the Prehistory of Languages.* Cambridge: McDonald Institute for Archaeological Research.

Foster, K., T. Wenseleers, and F. Ratnieks. 2006. "Kin Selection Is the Key to Altruism." *Trends in Ecology and Evolution* 21: 57–60.

Foucault, Michel. 1977. "Nietzsche, Genealogy, History." In *Language, Counter-Memory, Practice: Selected Essays and Interviews,* ed. D.F. Bouchard. Ithaca, NY: Cornell University Press.

———. 1978. *The History of Sexuality: An Introduction.* New York: Random House.

Fox, Anthony. 1995. *Linguistic Reconstruction: An Introduction to Theory and Method.* Oxford: Oxford University Press.

Fredrickson, W. Timm, and Gene P. Sackett. 1984. "Kin Preferences in Primates, *Macaca nemestrina:* Relatedness or Familiarity?" *Journal of Comparative Psychology* 98: 29–34.

Frere, John. 1800. "Account of Flint Weapons Discovered at Hoxne in Suffolk." *Archaeologia* 13: 204–5.

Gamble, Clive. 1986a. "The Mesolithic Sandwich: Ecological Approaches and the Archaeological Record of the Early Postglacial." In *Hunters in Transition: Mesolithic Societies of Temperate Eurasia and Their Transition to Farming,* ed. M. Zvelebil, 33–42. Cambridge: Cambridge University Press.

———. 1986b. *The Palaeolithic Settlement of Europe.* Cambridge: Cambridge University Press.

———. 1993. *Timewalkers: The Prehistory of Global Colonization.* Cambridge, MA: Harvard University Press.

———. 1999. *The Palaeolithic Societies of Europe.* Cambridge: Cambridge University Press.

———. 2001. "Modes, Movement and Moderns." *Quaternary International* 75:5–10.

———. 2007. *Origins and Revolutions: Human Identity in Earliest Prehistory.* New York: Cambridge University Press.

———. 2008. "Kinship and Material Culture: Archaeological Implications of the Human Global Diaspora." In *Early Human Kinship: From Sex to Social Reproduction,* ed. Nicholas J. Allen, Hilary Callan, Robin Dunbar, and Wendy James, 27–40. Oxford: Blackwell.

Gamble, C. S., S. W. G. Davies, M. Richards, P. Pettitt, and L. Hazelwood. 2005. "Archaeological and Genetic Foundations of the European Population during the Late Glacial: Implications for 'Agricultural Thinking.'" *Cambridge Archaeological Journal* 15: 55–85.

Gamble, C., and E. K. Gittins. 2004. "Social Archaeology and Origins Research: A Palaeolithic Perspective." In *A Companion to Social Archaeology,* ed. L. Meskell and R. Preucel, 96–118. Oxford: Blackwell.

Gamble, C., and R. Kruszinski. 2009. "John Evans, Joseph Prestwich and the Stone that Shattered the Time Barrier." *Antiquity* 83: 461–75.

Gardner, Don. 1999. "Anthropophagy, Myth and the Subtle Ways of Ethnocentrism." In *The Anthropology of Cannibalism,* ed. Laurence R. Goldman, 27–49. Westport, CT: Bergin and Garvey.

Geary, Patrick J. 1990. *Furta Sacra: Thefts of Relics in the Central Middle Ages.* Princeton, NJ: Princeton University Press.

Gell, A. 1998. *Art and Agency: Towards a New Anthropological Theory.* Oxford: Clarendon Press.

Gerasimov, Mikhail Mikhailovitch. 1971. *The Face Finder.* Translated by Alan Houghton Brodrick. Philadelphia: J. B. Lippincott.

Gibbons, A. 2009. "A New Kind of Ancestor: *Ardipithecus* Unveiled." *Science* 326, no. 5949: 36–40.

Gibson, Jon, and P. Carr. 2004. *The Rise of Cultural Complexity in the Southeast.* Tuscaloosa: University of Alabama Press.

Gill, J., J.W. Williams, S.T. Jackson, K.B. Lininger, and G.S. Robinson. 2009. "Pleistocene Megafaunal Collapse, Novel Plant Communities, and Enhanced Fire Regimes in North America." *Science* 326, no. 5956: 1100–103.

Glennie, Paul, and Nigel Thrift. 2005. "Revolutions in the Times: Clocks and the Temporal Structures of Everyday Life." In *Geography and Revolutions,* ed. D.N. Livingstone and C.W.J. Withers, 160–98. Chicago: University of Chicago Press.

Goldstein, Doris. 2004. "Confronting Time: The Oxford School of History and the Non-Darwinian Revolution." *Storia della Storiografia* 45: 3–27.

Goldthwaite, Richard A. 1995. *Wealth and the Demand for Art in Italy, 1300–1600.* Baltimore, MD: Johns Hopkins University Press.

Gómez, Jean-Carlos. 2007. "Pointing Behaviors in Apes and Human Infants: A Balanced Interpretation." *Child Development* 78: 729–34.

Goodall, Jane. 1977. "Infant Killing and Cannibalism in Free-Living Chimpanzees." *Folia Primatologica* 29: 259–82.

———. 1979. "Life and Death at Gombe." *National Geographic* 155: 592–621.

———. 1986. *The Chimpanzees of Gombe: Patterns of Behavior.* Boston, MA: Belknap Press.

Goody, Jack. 1982. *Cooking, Cuisine and Class: A Study in Comparative Sociology.* Cambridge: Cambridge University Press.

Goren-Inbar, N., N. Alperson, M.E. Kislev, O. Simchoni, Y. Melamed, A. Ben-Nun, and E. Werker. 2004. "Evidence of Hominin Control of Fire at Gesher Benot Ya'aqov, Israel." *Science* 304, no. 5671: 725–27.

Gough, Kathleen. 1971. "Nuer Kinship: A Re-examination." In *The Translation of Culture: Essays to E.E. Evans-Pritchard,* ed. T.O. Beidelman, 79–121. London: Tavistock.

Gould, Stephen Jay. 1982. *The Panda's Thumb: More Reflections in Natural History.* New York: Norton.

———. 1987. *Time's Arrow, Time's Cycle: Myth and Metaphor in the Discovery of Geological Time.* Cambridge, MA: Harvard University Press.

Gowers, E. 1993. *The Loaded Table: Representations of Food in Roman Literature.* Oxford: Oxford University Press.

Graebner, D., 1996. "Beads and Money: Notes toward a Theory of Wealth and Power." *American Ethnologist* 23: 4–24.

Grafen, A., 1990. "Biological Signals as Handicaps." *Journal of Theoretical Biology* 144: 517–46.

Gramsci, Antonio. 1992. *The Prison Notebooks.* Edited and translated by Joseph A. Buttigieg. New York: Columbia University Press.

Gray, Russell, and Quentin Atkinson. 2003. "Language-Tree Divergence Times Support the Anatolian Theory of Indo-European Origin." *Nature* 426: 435–39.

Grayson, D.K., and D. Meltzer. 2003. "A Requiem for North American Overkill." *Journal of Archaeological Science* 30: 585–93.

Greenberg, Joseph. 1955. *Studies in African Linguistic Classification.* Bradford, CT: Compass.

———. 1987. *Language in the Americas.* Stanford, CA: Stanford University Press.

———. 2000. *Indo-European and Its Closest Relations: The Eurasiatic Language Family.* 2 vols. Stanford, CA: Stanford University Press.

———. 2005. *Genetic Linguistics: Essays on Theory and Method.* Oxford: Oxford University Press.

Grierson, Philip. 1991. *The Coins of Medieval Europe.* London: Seaby.

Griffin, A., and S. West. 2003. "Kin Discrimination and the Benefit of Helping in Cooperative Breeding Vertebrates." *Science* 302, no. 5645: 634–36.

Grimm, Jacob. 1819. *Deutsche Grammatik.* Göttingen: Dietrich.

Grimm, David. 2009. "A Cure for Euthanasia?" *Science* 325, no. 5947: 1490–93.

Grove, Richard H. 1996. *Green Imperialism: Colonial Expansion, Tropical Island Edens and the Origins of Environmentalism, 1600–1860.* Cambridge: Cambridge University Press.

Groves, Richard H. 1991. "The Biogeography of Mediterranean Plant Invasions." In *Biogeography of Mediterranean Invasions,* ed. Richard H. Groves and F. di Castri, 427–38. Cambridge: Cambridge University Press.

Gruber, Jacob W. 1965. "Brixham Cave and the Antiquity of Man." In *Context and Meaning in Cultural Anthropology,* ed. Melford E. Spiro, 373–402. New York: Free Press.

Gruter, Margaret, and Paul Bohannan. 1983. *Law, Biology and Culture: The Evolution of Law*. Santa Barbara, CA: Ross-Erikson.

Guo, Qingjun, Harald Strauss, Alan J. Kaufman, Stefan Schröder, Jens Gutzmer, Boswell Wing, Margaret A. Baker, et al. 2009. "Reconstructing Earth's Surface Oxidation across the Archean-Proterozoic Transition." *Geology* 37: 399–402.

Gurven, M. 2004. "To Give and to Give Not: The Behavioral Ecology of Human Food Transfers." *Behavioral and Brain Sciences* 27: 543–59.

Gurven, M., M. Borgerhoff Mulder, P.L. Hooper, H. Kaplan, R. Quinlan, R. Sear, E. Schiter, et al. 2010. "Domestication Alone Does Not Lead to Inequality." *Current Anthropology* 51: 49–64.

Habu, J. 2004. *Ancient Jomon of Japan*. Cambridge: Cambridge University Press.

Haile, J., D.G. Froese, R.D.E. MacPhee, R.G. Roberts, L.J. Arnold, A.V. Reyes, M. Rasmussen, et al. 2009. "Ancient DNA Reveals Late Survival of Mammoth and Horse in Interior Alaska." *Proceedings of the National Academy of Sciences of the United States* 106, no. 52: 22352–57.

Hall, K.D., J. Guo, M. Dore, and C.C. Chow. 2009. "The Progressive Increase of Food Waste in America and Its Environmental Impact." *PLoS ONE* 4: e7940.

Hallam, S.J. 1979. *Fire and Hearth: A Study of Aboriginal Usage and European Usurpation in South-western Australia*. Canberra: Australian Institute of Aboriginal Studies.

Hallowell, A.I. 1960. "Ojibwa Ontology, Behavior, and World View." In *Culture in History: Essays in Honor of Paul Radin*, ed. Stanley Diamond, 19–52. New York: Columbia University Press.

———. 1991. *The Ojibwa of Berens River, Manitoba: Ethnography into History*. Edited by Jennifer S.H. Brown. Fort Worth, TX: Harcourt Brace Jovanovich.

Halsey, R.W. 2005. *Fire, Chaparral, and Survival in Southern California*. San Diego, CA: Sunbelt Publications.

Hames, R. 2007. "The Ecologically Noble Savage Debate." *Annual Review of Anthropology* 36: 177–90.

Hamilton, M.J., B.T. Milne, R.S. Walker, and J.H. Brown. 2007. "Nonlinear Scaling of Space Use in Human Hunter-Gatherers." *Proceedings of the National Academy of Sciences of the United States* 104, no. 11: 4765–69.

Hamilton, William D. 1963. "The Evolution of Altruistic Behavior." *American Naturalist* 97: 354–56.

Hansen, Julie M., 1991. *The Palaeoethnobotany of Franchthi Cave*. Fasc. 7 of *Excavations at Franchthi Cave, Greece*. Bloomington: Indiana University Press.

Harbottle, G. 1982. "Provenience Studies Using Neutron Activation Analysis: The Role of Standardization." In *Archaeological Ceramics,* ed. J.D. Olin and A.D. Franklin, 67–77. Washington, DC: Smithsonian Institution.

Harcourt, A. 1987. "Dominance and Fertility among Female Primates." *Journal of Zoology* 213: 471–97.

Hardin, Garrett. 1968. "Tragedy of the Commons." *Science* 162, no. 3859: 1243–48.

Hardy, B.L. 2010. "Climatic Variability and Plant Food Distribution in Pleistocene Europe: Implications for Neanderthal Diet and Subsistence." *Quaternary Science Reviews* 29: 662–79.

Harpending, H., and Bertram, J. 1975. "Human Population Dynamics in Archaeological Time: Some Simple Models." *American Antiquity* 40: 82–91.

Harris, Marvin. 1985. *Good to Eat: Riddles of Food and Culture*. New York: Simon and Schuster.

Harrison, S.P. 2003. "On the Limits of the Comparative Method." In *The Handbook of Historical Linguistics*, ed. Brian D. Joseph and Richard D. Janda, 213–43. Oxford: Blackwell.

Hayden, Brian. 1995. "Pathways to Power: Principles for Creating Socioeconomic Inequalities." In *Foundations of Social Inequality*, ed. T.D. Price and G. Feinman, 15–85. Plenum: New York.

Hegel, Georg Wilhelm Friedrich. 1970 [1837]. *Vorlesungen über die Philosophie der Geschichte*. Edited by Eva Moldenhauer and Karl Markus Michel. Frankfurt am Main: Suhrkamp.

———. 1975. *Lectures on the Philosophy of World History: Introduction; Reason in History*. Translated by H.B. Nisbet. Cambridge: Cambridge University Press.

Henry, D.O. 1985. "Preagricultural Sedentism: The Natufian Example." In *Prehistoric Hunter-Gatherers: The Emergence of Cultural Complexity*, ed. T.D. Price and J.A. Brown, 365–84. San Diego, CA: Academic Press.

Henshilwood, C.S., F. d'Errico, and I. Watts. 2009. "Engraved Ochres from the Middle Stone Age Levels at Blombos Cave, South Africa." *Journal of Human Evolution* 57: 27–47.

Henshilwood, C., F. d'Errico, M. Vanhaeren, K. van Niekerk, and Z. Jacobs. 2004. "Middle Stone Age Shell Beads from South Africa." *Science* 304, no. 5669: 404.

Hickey, Raymond, ed. 2010. *The Handbook of Language Contact*. Oxford: Blackwell.

Hinsley, F.H., ed. 1976. *New Cambridge Modern History*. Vol. 11. Cambridge: Cambridge University Press.

Hodder, Ian. 1990. *The Domestication of Europe: Structure and Contingency in Neolithic Societies*. Oxford: Blackwell.

Hodgen, Margaret. 1964. *Early Anthropology in the Sixteenth and Seventeenth Centuries*. Philadelphia: University of Pennsylvania Press.

Hogendorn, Jan, and Marion Johnson. 1986. *The Shell Money of the Slave Trade*. Cambridge: Cambridge University Press.

Holdaway, R.N., and C. Jacomb. 2000. "Rapid Extinction of the Moas (Aves: Dinonithiformes): Model, Test and Implications." *Science* 287, no. 5461: 2250–54.

Holden, C. 2009. "Clean Pigs Offer Alternative to Stem Cell Transplants." *Science* 326, no. 5956: 1049.

Horwitz, L.K. 1996. "The Impact of Animal Domestication on Species Richness: A Pilot Study from the Neolithic of the Southern Levant." *Archaeozoologia* 8: 53–70.

———. 1999. "Animal Domestication in the Southern Levant." *Paléorient* 25: 63–80.

Hovers, Erella, and Steven L. Kuhn, eds. 2006. *Transitions before the Transition:*

Evolution and Stability in the Middle Paleolithic and Middle Stone Age. New York: Springer.

Hrdy, Sarah Blaffer. 2009. *Mothers and Others: The Evolutionary Origins of Mutual Understanding.* Cambridge, MA: Harvard University Press.

Hunt, Alan. 1996. *Governance of the Consuming Passions: A History of Sumptuary Law.* New York: St. Martin's Press.

Hurford, James R. 2007. *The Origins of Meaning: Language in the Light of Evolution.* New York: Oxford University Press.

Hutchins, E. 1995. *Cognition in the Wild.* Cambridge, MA: MIT Press.

Hutchinson, Sharon Elaine. 1996. *Nuer Dilemmas: Coping with Money, War, and the State.* Berkeley: University of California Press.

Huxley, Aldous. 2004 [1932]. *Brave New World* and *Brave New World Revisited.* New York: Harper Collins.

Huxley, Thomas Henry. 1895. *Man's Place in Nature and Other Anthropological Essays.* Vol. 7 of *Collected Essays.* London: Macmillan.

Ibn Khaldun. 1958. *The Muqaddimah: An Introduction to History.* 3 vols. Translated by Franz Rosenthal. New York: Pantheon Books.

———. 1967. *The Muqaddimah.* Translated by Franz Rosenthal and edited by N.J. Dawood. Princeton, NJ: Princeton University Press.

Ibn Qutayba. 1925–1930. *Kitab 'uyun al-akhbar* [The Book of Choice Narratives]. 4 vols. Cairo: Dar al-Kutub al-Misriyya.

Ingold, Tim. 2000. *The Perception of the Environment: Essays in Livelihood, Dwelling and Skill.* London: Routledge.

———. 2004. "Culture on the Ground: The World Perceived through the Feet." *Journal of Material Culture* 9: 315–40.

Ingram, Catherine J.E., Charlotte A. Mulcare, Yuval Itan, Mark G. Thomas, and Dallas M. Swallow. 2009. "Lactose Digestion and the Evolutionary Genetics of Lactase Persistence." *Human Genetics* 124: 579–91.

Jackson, J.B.C., M.X. Kirby, W.H. Berger, K.A. Bjorndal, L.W. Botsford, B.J. Bourque, R.H. Bradbury, et al. 2001. "Historical Overfishing and the Recent Collapse of Coastal Ecosystems." *Science* 293, no. 5530: 629–37.

James, Wendy. 2008. "Why 'Kinship'? New Questions on an Old Topic." In *Early Human Kinship,* ed. N.J. Allen et al., 3–20. Oxford: Blackwell.

Janzen, D.H. 1966. "Coevolution of Mutualism between Ants and Acacias in Central America." *Evolution* 20: 249–75.

Jefferson, Thomas. 1995 [1782]. *Notes on the State of Virginia.* Edited by William Peden. Chapel Hill: University of North Carolina Press.

Johnson, Allen, and T. Earle. 2000. *The Evolution of Human Societies,* 2nd ed. Stanford, CA: Stanford University Press.

Johnson, Walter. 1999. *Soul by Soul: Life Inside the Antebellum Slave Market.* Cambridge, MA: Harvard University Press.

Johnston, R.F, and M. Janiga. 1995. *Feral Pigeons.* Oxford: Oxford University Press.

Jones, Doug. 2003. "Kinship and Deep History: Exploring Connections between Culture Areas, Genes, and Languages." *American Anthropologist* 105(3): 501–14.

Jones, Martin. 2007. *Feast: Why Humans Share Food*. Oxford: Oxford University Press.

Jones, William. 1788 [1786]. *The Third Anniversary Discourse (On the Hindus)*. *Asiatic Researches* 1: 415–31.

Joseph, Brian D., and Richard D. Janda, eds. 2003. *The Handbook of Historical Linguistics*. Malden, MA: Blackwell.

Kantorowicz, Ernst H. 1957. *The King's Two Bodies: A Study in Mediaeval Political Theology*. Princeton, NJ: Princeton University Press.

Kaplan, H., K. Hill, J. Lancaster, J., and A.M. Hurtado. 2000. "A Theory of Human Life History Evolution: Diet, Intelligence and Longevity." *Evolutionary Anthropology* 9: 156–85.

Kapsalis, E. 2004. "Matrilineal Kinship and Primate Behavior." In *Kinship and Behavior in Primates,* ed. Bernard Chapais and C. Berman, 153–76. Oxford: Oxford University Press.

Kareiva, P., S. Watts, R. McDonald, and T. Boucher. 2007. "Domesticated Nature: Shaping Landscapes and Ecosystems for Human Welfare." *Science* 316, no. 5833: 1866–69.

Kawai, M. 1958. "On the System of Social Ranks in a Natural Troop of Japanese Monkeys, 1: Basic Rank and Dependent Rank." *Primates* 1: 111–48.

Kawamura, S. 1958. "Matriarchical Social Ranks in the Minoo-B Troop: A Study of the Rank System of Japanese Monkeys." *Primates* 1: 148–56.

Keeley, L.H. 1988. "Hunter-Gatherer Economic Complexity and 'Population Pressure.'" *Journal of Anthropological Archaeology* 7: 373–411.

———. 1995. "Protoagricultural Practices among Hunter-Gatherers: A Cross-Cultural Survey." In *Last Hunters, First Farmers: New Perspectives on the Prehistoric Transition to Agriculture,* ed. T.D. Price and A.B. Gebauer, 243–72. Santa Fe, NM: School of American Research Press.

———. 1996. *War before Civilization*. Oxford: Oxford University Press.

Keith, Arthur. 1931 *New Discoveries Relating to the Antiquity of Man*. New York: Williams and Norgate.

Kelly, R.L. 1995. *The Foraging Spectrum: Diversity in Hunter-Gatherer Lifeways*. Washington, DC: Smithsonian Institution Press.

Kemp, Barry J. 1989. *Ancient Egypt: Anatomy of a Civilization*. London: Routledge.

Killerby, Catherine Kovesi. 2002. *Sumptuary Law in Italy, 1200–1500*. Oxford: Clarendon Press.

Kingdon, Jonathan. 1993. *Self-Made Man and His Undoing*. New York: Simon and Schuster.

Kiple, Kenneth F., and Kriemhild Coneè Ornelas, eds. 2000. *The Cambridge World History of Food*. Cambridge: Cambridge University Press.

Kirby, Simon. 2000. "Syntax without Natural Selection: How Compositionality Emerges from Vocabulary in a Population of Learners." In *The Evolutionary Emergence of Language: Social Function and the Origins of Linguistic Form,* ed. C. Knight, 303–23. Cambridge: Cambridge University Press.

———. 2002. "Natural Language from Artificial Life." *Artificial Life* 8: 185–215.

Kirby, Simon, Hannah Cornish, and Kenny Smith. 2008. "Cumulative Cultural Evolution in the Laboratory: An Experimental Approach to the Origins of

Structure in Human Language." *Proceedings of the National Academy of Sciences of the United States* 105, no. 31: 10681–86.

Kirby, S., M. Dowman, and T. Griffiths. 2007. "Innateness and Culture in the Evolution of Language." *Proceedings of the National Academy of Sciences of the United States* 104, no. 12: 5241–45.

Kirch, Patrick. 1985. *Feathered Gods and Fishhooks*. Honolulu: University of Hawaii Press.

———. 2000. *Road of the Winds*. Berkeley: University of California Press.

Kittler, Ralf, Manfred Kayser, and Mark Stoneking. 2003. "Molecular Evolution of *Pediculus humanus* and the Origin of Clothing." *Current Biology* 13: 1414–17.

Klapisch-Zuber, Christiane. 1987. *Women, Family, and Ritual in Renaissance Italy*. Translated by Lydia Cochrane. Chicago: University of Chicago Press.

Klein, Richard G. 1999. *The Human Career: Human Biological and Cultural Origins*. 3rd ed. Chicago: University of Chicago Press.

———. 2000. "Archaeology and the Evolution of Human Behaviour." *Evolutionary Anthropology* 9: 17–36.

Klein, Richard G., with Blake Edgar. 2002. *The Dawn of Human Culture*. New York: John Wiley.

Knappett, C. 2005. *Thinking through Material Culture: An Interdisciplinary Perspective*. Philadelphia: University of Pennsylvania Press.

Knight, Chris. 2008. "Early Human Kinship was Matrilineal." In *Early Human Kinship: From Sex to Social Reproduction*, ed. Nicholas J. Allen, Hilary Callan, Robin Dunbar, and Wendy James, 61–82. Oxford: Blackwell.

Kolen, Jan. 1999. "Hominids without Homes: On the Nature of Middle Palaeolithic Settlement in Europe." In *The Middle Palaeolithic Occupation of Europe*, ed. Wil Roebroeks and Clive Gamble, 139–75. Leiden: University of Leiden.

Kristiansen, Kristian. 1998. *Europe before History*. Cambridge: Cambridge University Press.

Kselman, Thomas A. 1983. *Miracles and Prophecies in Nineteenth-Century France*. New Brunswick, NJ: Rutgers University Press.

Kuhn, S.L. 1995. *Mousterian Lithic Technology: An Ecological Perspective*. Princeton, NJ: Princeton University Press.

Kuhn, S.L., and M.C. Stiner. 1998. "Middle Paleolithic 'Creativity': Reflections on an Oxymoron?" In *Creativity and Human Evolution and Prehistory*, ed. Steve Mithen, 143–64. London: Routledge.

———. 2001. "The Antiquity of Hunter-Gatherers." In *Hunter-Gatherers: Interdisciplinary Perspectives*, ed. C. Panter-Brick, R.H. Layton, and P.A. Rowley-Conwy, 99–142. Cambridge: Cambridge University Press.

———. 2006. "What's a Mother to Do? A Hypothesis about the Division of Labor and Modern Human Origins." *Current Anthropology* 47: 953–80.

———. 2007. "Body Ornamentation as Information Technology: Towards an Understanding of the Significance of Early Beads." In *Rethinking the Human Revolution: New Behavioral and Biological Perspectives on the Origin and Dispersal of Modern Humans*, ed. Paul Mellars, Katie Boyle, Ofer Bar-Yosef, and Chris Stringer, 45–54. Cambridge: McDonald Institute for Archaeological Research.

Kuhn, S., M.C. Stiner, D. Reese, and E. Güleç. 2001. "Ornaments in the Earliest Upper Palaeolithic: New Perspectives from the Levant." *Proceedings of the National Academy of Sciences of the United States* 98, no. 13: 7641–46.

Kummer, H. 1978. "On the Value of Social Relationships to Nonhuman Primates: A Heuristic Scheme." *Social Science Information* 17: 687–705.

Kvavadze, Eliso, Ofer Bar-Yosef, Anna Belfer-Cohen, Elisabetta Boaretto, Nino Jakeli, Zinovi Matskevich, and Tengiz Meshveliani. 2009. "30,000-Year-Old Wild Flax Fibers." *Science* 325, no. 5946: 1359.

La Boétie, Étienne de. 1971 [1576]. "Discours sur la servitude volontaire." In *La Boétie: Oeuvres politiques,* ed. François Hincker. Paris: Éditions Sociales.

Ladefoged, Peter, and Ian Maddieson. 1996. *The Sounds of the World's Languages.* Oxford: Blackwell.

Lahr, M.M., and R. Foley. 1994. "Multiple Dispersals and Modern Human Origins." *Evolutionary Anthropology* 3: 48–60.

———. 2003. "Demography, Dispersal and Human Evolution in the Last Glacial Period." In *Neandertals and Modern Humans in the European Landscape during the Last Glaciation,* ed. T.H. van Andel and W. Davies, 241–56. Cambridge: Cambridge University Press.

Langergraber, K., J. Mitani, and L. Vigilant. 2007. "The Limited Impact of Kinship on Cooperation in Wild Chimpanzees." *Proceedings of the National Academy of Sciences of the United States* 104, no. 19: 7786–90.

———. 2009. "Kinship and Social Bonds in Female Chimpanzees (*Pan troglodytes*)." *American Journal of Primatology* 71: 840–51.

Langlois, Charles V., and Charles Seignobos. 1898. *Introduction to the Study of History.* Translated by G.G. Berry. New York: Holt.

Larsen, Pier Martin. 2001. "Austronesian Mortuary Ritual in History: Transformations of Secondary Burial (*Famadihana*) in Highland Madagascar." *Ethnohistory* 48: 123–55.

Leach, H.M. 2003. "Human Domestication Reconsidered." *Current Anthropology* 44: 349–68.

———. 2007. "Selection and the Unforeseen Consequences of Domestication." In *Where the Wild Things Are Now: Domestication Reconsidered,* ed. R. Cassidy and M. Mullin, 71–99. Oxford: Berg.

LeDoux, Joseph. 1996. *The Emotional Brain: The Mysterious Underpinnings of Emotional Life.* New York: Simon and Schuster.

Lee, Richard. 1984. *The Dobe !Kung.* New York: Holt, Rinehart and Winston.

Lee, Sandra Soo-Jin, Deborah A. Bolnick, Troy Duster, Pilar Ossorio, and Kimberly TallBear. 2009. "The Illusive Gold Standard in Genetic Ancestry Testing." *Science* 325, no. 5936: 38–39.

Lee-Thorp, J., and M. Sponheimer. 2006. "Contributions of Biogeochemistry to Understanding Hominin Dietary Ecology." *Yearbook of Physical Anthropology* 49: 131–48.

Lehmann, J., and C. Boesch. 2009. "Sociality of the Dispersing Sex: The Nature of Social Bonds in West African Female Chimpanzees, *Pan troglodytes.*" *Animal Behaviour* 77: 377–87.

Leibniz, Gottfried Wilhelm von. 1989 [1718]. "Desiderata circa linguas populorum, ad Dn. Podesta, interpretem Caesareum transmissa." In Gottfried Wilhelm von Leibniz, *Opera Omnia,* vol. 6, part 2 (Collectanea Etymologica), ed. Louis Dutens, 228–31. Hildesheim: G. Olms.

Levenstein, H. 1988. *Revolution at the Table.* New York: Oxford University Press.

Lévi-Strauss, Claude. 1963. *Structural Anthropology.* New York: Basic Books.

———. 1969 [1949]. *The Elementary Structures of Kinship.* Translated by James Harle Bell and John Richard von Sturmer and edited by Rodney Needham. London: Eyre and Spottiswoode.

———. 1970. *The Raw and the Cooked.* Translated by J. Weightman and D. Weightman. New York: Harper and Row.

———. 1982 [1975]. "The Social Organization of the Kwakiutl." In *The Way of the Mask,* trans. Sylvia Modelski, 163–87. Seattle: University of Washington Press.

———. 1987. *Anthropology and Myth: Lectures, 1951–1982.* Oxford: Oxford University Press.

Lieberman, Daniel E. 2011. *The Evolution of the Human Head.* Cambridge, MA: Harvard University Press.

Livingstone, D.N. 2008. *Adam's Ancestors: Race, Religion and the Politics of Human Origins.* Baltimore: Johns Hopkins University Press.

Lizot, Jacques. 1991. *Tales of the Yanomami.* Cambridge: Cambridge University Press.

Lloyd-Smith, J.O., D. George, K.M. Pepin, V.E. Pitzer, J.R.C. Pulliam, A.P. Dobson, P.J. Hudson, and B.T. Grenfell. 2009. "Epidemic Dynamics at the Human-Animal Interface." *Science* 326, no. 5958: 1362–67.

Lordkipanidze, David, Abesalom Vekua, Reid Ferring, G. Philip Rightmire, Jordi Agusti, Gocha Kiladze, Alexander Mouskhelishvili, et al. 2005. "The Earliest Toothless Hominin Skull." *Nature* 434: 717–18.

Lordkipanidze, David, Abesalom Vekua, Reid Ferring, G. Philip Rightmire, Christoph P.E. Zollikofer, Marcia S. Ponce De León, Jordi Agusti, and Gocha Kiladze. 2006. "A Fourth Hominin Skull from Dmanisi, Georgia." *Anatomical Record, Part A: Discoveries in Molecular, Cellular, and Evolutionary Biology* 288: 1146–57.

Lounsbury, Floyd G. 1964a. "The Structural Analysis of Kinship Semantics." In *Proceedings of the Ninth International Congress of Linguists,* ed. Horace G. Lunt, 1073–93. The Hague: Mouton.

———. 1964b. "A Formal Account of Crow- and Omaha-Type Kinship Terminologies." In *Explorations in Cultural Anthropology: Essays in Honor of George Peter Murdock,* ed. Ward H. Goodenough, 351–93. New York: McGraw-Hill.

Lourandos, H. 1997. *Continent of Hunter-Gatherers: New Perspectives in Australian Prehistory.* Cambridge: Cambridge University Press.

Lowe, J.J., S.O. Rasmussen, S. Björck, W.Z. Hoek, J.P. Steffensen, M.J.C. Walker, and Z.C. Yu. 2008. "Synchronisation of Palaeoenvironmental Events in the North Atlantic Region during the Last Termination: A Revised Protocol Recommended by the INTIMATE Group." *Quaternary Science Reviews* 27: 6–17.

Lubbock, John. 1865. *Pre-historic Times, as Illustrated by Ancient Remains and the Manners and Customs of Modern Savages.* London: Williams and Norgate.

Luhrmann, Tanya. 1996. *The Good Parsi: The Fate of a Colonial Elite in a Postcolonial Society.* Cambridge, MA: Harvard University Press.

Lyell, Charles. 1860. "On the Occurrence of Works of Human Art in Post-Pliocene Deposits." In *Report of the Twenty-Ninth Meeting of the British Association for the Advancement of Science, Notices and Abstracts,* 93–95. London: John Murray.

Lyons, Martyn. 2010. *A History of Reading and Writing in the Western World.* New York: Palgrave Macmillan.

Macaulay, V., C. Hill, A. Achilli, C. Rengo, D. Clarke, W. Meehan, J. Blackburn, et al. 2005. "Single, Rapid Coastal Settlement of Asia Revealed by Analysis of Complete Mitochondrial Genomes." *Science* 308, no. 5724: 1034–36.

MacDonald, Betty Bard. 1946. *The Egg and I.* Philadelphia: Lippincott.

Maine, Henry Sumner. 1963 [1861]. *Ancient Law: Its Connection with the Early History of Society and Its Relation to Modern Ideas.* Boston, MA: Beacon Press.

Malinowski, Bronislaw. 1974. *Magic, Science and Religion, and Other Essays.* London: Souvenir Press.

Marquardt, William. 1988. "Politics and Production among the Calusa of South Florida." In *History, Environment, and Social Change among Hunting and Gathering Societies,* ed. D. Richies, T. Ingold, and J. Woodburn, 161–88. London: Berg.

Marsden, William. 1782. "Remarks on the Sumatran languages, by Mr. Marsden. In a letter to Sir Joseph Banks, Bart. President of the Royal Society." *Archaeologia: Or, Miscellaneous Tracts Relating to Antiquity* 7: 154–58.

———. 1785. "Observations on the Language of the People Commonly Called Gypsies. In a letter to Sir Joseph Banks, Bart. P.R.S., from Mr. Marsden, F.S.A." *Archaeologia: Or, Miscellaneous Tracts Relating to Antiquity* 7: 383–86.

Martin, P.A. 1984. "Prehistoric Overkill: The Global Model." In *Quaternary Extinctions: A Prehistoric Revolution,* ed. P.S. Martin and R.G. Klein, 354–403. Tucson: University of Arizona Press.

Martinson, D.G., N.G. Pisias, J.D. Hays, J. Imbrie, T.C. Moore, and N.J. Shackleton. 1987. "Age Dating and the Orbital Theory of the Ice Ages: Development of a High-Resolution 0 to 300,000-year Chronostratigraphy." *Quaternary Research* 27: 1–29.

Marx, Karl. 1970. "A Contribution to the Critique of Hegel's 'Philosophy of Right.'" In *Critique of Hegel's "Philosophy of Right,"* trans. Annette Jolin and Joseph O'Malley. Cambridge: Cambridge University Press.

Matras, Yaron, and Peter Bakker. Forthcoming. *Contact Languages.* Berlin: Mouton de Gruyter.

Mauss, Marcel. 1990 [1950]. *The Gift: The Form and Reason for Exchange in Archaic Societies.* Translated by W.D. Halls. New York: Norton.

McBrearty, Sally, and Alison Brooks. 2000. "The Revolution That Wasn't: A New Interpretation of the Origin of Modern Human Behavior." *Journal of Human Evolution* 39: 453–563.

McCormick, Michael. 2001. *The Origins of the European Economy: Communications and Commerce, A.D. 300–900.* Cambridge: Cambridge University Press.

McDonaugh, C.E. 1990. "Tharu Evaluations of Food." In *Food for Humanity: Cross-Disciplinary Readings,* ed. Malcolm Chapman and Helen Macbeth, 46–48. Oxford: Centre for the Sciences of Food and Nutrition, Oxford Polytechnic.

McKendrick, Neil, John Brewer, and J.H. Plumb. 1982. *The Birth of a Consumer Society: The Commercialization of Eighteenth-Century England.* Bloomington: Indiana University Press.

McKinnon, Susan. 1999. "Domestic Exceptions: Evans-Pritchard and the Creation of Nuer Patrilineality and Equality." *Cultural Anthropology* 15: 35–83.

McLennan, J.F. 1869–70. "The Worship of Animals and Plants." *Fortnightly Review* 6: 407–27, 562–82, 7: 194–216.

McMahon, April, ed. 2005. *Quantitative Methods in Language Comparison.* Special issue of *Transactions of the Philological Society* 103(2).

———. 2010. "Computational Models and Language Contact." In *The Handbook of Language Contact,* ed. Raymond Hickey, 128–47. Oxford: Blackwell.

McMahon, April, and Robert McMahon. 2005. *Language Classification by Numbers.* Oxford: Oxford University Press.

———. 2008. "Genetics, Historical Linguistics and Language Variation." *Language and Linguistics Compass* 2: 264–88.

McMahon, April, Paul Heggarty, Robert McMahon, and Natalia Slaska. 2005. "Swadesh Sublists and the Benefits of Borrowing: An Andean Case Study." In *Quantitative Methods in Language Comparison,* special issue of *Transactions of the Philological Society* 103(2): 147–69.

McMahon, April, Paul Heggarty, Robert McMahon, and Warren Maguire. 2007. "The Sound Patterns of Englishes: Representing Phonetic Similarity." *English Language and Linguistics* 11: 113–43.

McNab, B.K. 1994. "Resource Use and the Survival of Land and Freshwater Vertebrates on Oceanic Islands." *American Naturalist* 144: 643–60.

McNeill, J.R. 2000. *Something New under the Sun: An Environmental History of the Twentieth Century World.* New York: Norton.

Mead, Simon, Michael P.H. Stumpf, Jerome Whitfield, Jonathan A. Beck, Mark Poulter, Tracy Campbell, James B. Uphill, et al. 2003. "Balancing Selection at the Prion Protein Gene Consistent with Prehistoric Kurulike Epidemics." *Science Express* 300: 640–43.

Meigs, Anna. 1988. "Food as a Cultural Construction." *Food and Foodways* 2: 341–59.

Mellars, P. 1989. "Major Issues in the Emergence of Modern Humans." *Current Anthropology* 30: 349–85.

Melville, E.G.K. 1994. *A Plague of Sheep: Environmental Consequences of the Conquest of Mexico.* Cambridge: Cambridge University Press.

Michelet, Jules. 1834. *Introduction à l'histoire universelle, suivi du discours d'ouverture prononcé à la faculté des lettres le 9 janvier 1834.* 2nd ed. Paris: Hachette.

Millar, Robert McColl. 2007. *Trask's Historical Linguistics*. London: Hodder Arnold.

Millennium Ecosystem Assessment. 2005. *Ecosystems and Human Well-Being: Current State and Trends*. Washington, DC: Island Press.

Mintz, Sidney. 1985. *Sweetness and Power: The Place of Sugar in Modern History*. New York: Viking.

Mitani, John C. 2008. "Chimpanzee Behavior: There's No Place like Home." *Current Biology* 18: R166–R167.

———. 2009. "Male Chimpanzees Form Enduring and Equitable Social Bonds." *Animal Behaviour* 77: 633–40.

Mitani, J., and D. Watts. 2001. "Why do Chimpanzees Hunt and Share Meat?" *Animal Behaviour* 61: 915–24.

Mitchell, C. 1994. "Migration Alliances and Coalitions among Adult Male South American Squirrel Monkeys *(Saimiri sciureus)*." *Behaviour* 130: 169–90.

Mithen, Steven. 2003. *After the Ice: A Global Human History, 20,000–5000 BC*. Cambridge, MA: Harvard University Press.

———. 2006. "Ethnobiology and the Evolution of the Human Mind." In *Ethnobiology and the Science of Humankind,* special issue of *Journal of the Royal Anthropological Institute* 12: S45–S62.

Moore, A.M.T., and G.C. Hillman. 1992. "The Pleistocene to Holocene Transition and Human Economy in Southwest Asia: The Impact of the Younger Dryas." *American Antiquity* 75: 482–94.

Moore, F.C.T. 1969. *The Observation of Savage Peoples by Joseph-Marie Degérando (1800)*. London: Routledge and Kegan Paul.

Morgan, Lewis Henry. 1851. *League of the Ho-dé-no-sau-nee, or Iroquois*. Rochester, NY: Sage and Brother.

———. 1871. *Systems of Consanguinity and Affinity of the Human Family*. Washington, DC: Smithsonian Institution.

———. 1881. *Houses and House-Life of the American Aborigines*. Washington, DC: Government Printing Office.

Morin, P., and Goldberg, T. 2004. "Determination of Genealogical Relationships from Genetic Data: A Review of Methods and Applications." In *Kinship and Behavior in Primates,* ed. Bernard Chapais and C. Berman, 15–45. Oxford: Oxford University Press.

Morris, Desmond. 1967. *The Naked Ape: A Zoologist's Study of the Human Animal*. London: Cape.

Moseley, C.W.R.D., ed. and trans. 2005. *The Travels of Sir John Mandeville*. London: Penguin.

Mueggler, Erik. 2001. *The Age of Wild Ghosts: Memory, Violence, and Place in Southwest China*. Berkeley: University of California Press.

Müller, Fritz. 1878. "Über die Vortheile der Mimicry bei Schmetterlingen." *Zoologischer Anzeiger* 1: 54–55.

Muller, M., and Mitani, J. 2005. "Conflict and Cooperation in Wild Chimpanzees." *Advances in the Study of Behavior* 35: 275–331.

Muniz, L., S. Perry, J. Manson, H. Gilkenson, J. Gros-Louis, J., and L. Vigilant. 2006. "Father-Daughter Inbreeding Avoidance in a Wild Primate Population." *Current Biology* 16: R156–R157.

Munro, N. 2004. "Zooarchaeological Measures of Hunting Pressure and Occupation Intensity in the Natufian." *Current Anthropology* 45: S5-S33.

Murray, Carson M., Ian C. Gilby, Sandeep V. Mane, and Anne E. Pusey. 2008. "Adult Male Chimpanzees Inherit Maternal Ranging Patterns." *Current Biology* 18: 20–24.

Nadasdy, P. 2007. "The Gift in the Animal: The Ontology of Hunting and Human-Animal Sociality." *American Ethnologist* 34: 25–43.

Nakhleh, Luay, Don Ringe, and Tandy Warnow. 2005. "Perfect Phylogenetic Networks: A New Methodology for Reconstructing the Evolutionary History of Natural Languages." *Language* 81: 381–420.

Naylor, R., H. Steinfeld, W. Falcon, J. Galloway, V. Smil, E. Bradford, J. Alder, et al. 2005. "Losing the Links between Livestock and Land." *Science* 310, no. 5754: 1621–22.

Neiman, F. 1997. "Conspicuous Consumption as Wasteful Advertising: A Darwinian Perspective on Spatial Patterns in Classic Maya Terminal Monument Dates." In *Rediscovering Darwin: Evolutionary Theory and Archaeological Explanation*, ed. C.M. Barton and G.A. Clark, 267–90. Washington, DC: American Anthropological Association.

Nettle, Daniel, and Suzanne Romaine. 2000. *Vanishing Voices: The Extinction of the World's Languages.* Oxford: Oxford University Press.

Nishida, T., and K. Kawanaka. 1985. "Within-Group Cannibalism by Adult Male Chimpanzees." *Primates* 26: 274–84.

Nishida, T., N. Corp, M. Hamai, T. Hasegawa, M. Hiraiwa-Hasegawa, K. Hosaka, K.D. Hunt, et al. 2003. "Demography, Female Life History, and Reproductive Profiles among the Chimpanzees of Mahale." *American Journal of Primatology* 59: 99–121.

Noonan, J.P., G. Coop, S. Kudaravalli, D. Smith, J. Krause, J. Alessi, F. Chen, et al. 2006. "Sequencing and Analysis of Neanderthal Genomic DNA." *Science* 314, no. 5802: 1113–18.

Novick, Peter. 1988. *That Noble Dream: The "Objectivity Question" and the American Historical Profession.* Cambridge: Cambridge University Press.

Odling-Smee, F.J., K. Laland, and M.W. Feldman. 2003. *Niche Construction: The Neglected Process in Evolution.* Princeton, NJ: Princeton University Press.

Om Prakash. 1961. *Food and Drinks in India from the Earliest Times to c. 1200 A.D.* Delhi: Munshi Ram Manoahar Lal.

Oppenheimer, Stephen. 2006. *The Origins of the British: A Genetic Detective Story.* London: Constable Publishing.

Owen, J. 2008. "A Significant Friendship: Evans, Lubbock and a Darwinian World Order." In *Sir John Evans 1823–1908: Antiquity, Commerce and Natural Science in the Age of Darwin*, ed. A. Macgregor, 206–29. Oxford: Ashmolean.

Owren, M., J. Dieter, R. Seyfarth, and D. Cheney. 1993. "Vocalizations of Rhesus (*Macaca mulatta*) and Japanese (*M. fuscata*) Macaques Cross-Fostered between Species Show Evidence of Only Limited Modification." *Developmental Psychobiology* 26: 389–406.

Özdoğan, M. 1997. "The Beginning of Neolithic Economies in Southeastern Europe: An Anatolian Perspective." *Journal of European Archaeology* 5: 1–33.

Pallas, P.S. 1786–89. *Linguarum Totius Orbis Vocabularia Comparativa*. 2 vols. St. Petersburg: Carl Schnoor.

Palombit, R., R. Seyfarth, and D. Cheney. 1997. "The Adaptive Value of 'Friendship' to Female Baboons: Experimental and Observational Evidence." *Animal Behaviour* 54: 599–614.

Pálsson, Gísli. 2002. "The Life of Family Trees and the Book of Icelanders." *Medical Anthropology* 21, nos. 3–4: 231–46.

Pancorbo, L. 2008. *El banquete humano: Una historia cultural del canibalismo*. Madrid: Siglo XXI.

Parfitt, S., R.W. Barendregt, M. Breda, I. Candy, M.J. Collins, G.R. Coope, P. Durbridge, et al. 2005. "The Earliest Record of Human Activity in Northern Europe." *Nature* 438: 1008–12.

Parkes, Peter. 2003. "Fostering Fealty: A Comparative Analysis of Tributary Allegiances of Adoptive Kinship." *Comparative Studies in Society and History* 45: 741–82.

———. 2004. "Fosterage, Kinship, and Legend: When Milk Was Thicker than Blood?" *Comparative Studies in Society and History* 46: 587–615.

Parkinson, S., A.A.J. Jansen, and A.F.S. Robertson, eds. 1990. *Food and Nutrition in Fiji: A Historical Review*. Suva, Fiji: University of the South Pacific Press.

Partner, Peter. 1976. *Renaissance Rome, 1500–1559: A Portrait of a Society*. Berkeley: University of California Press.

Paulsen, Allison C. 1974. "The Thorny Oyster and the Voice of God: *Spondylus* and *Strombus* in Andean Prehistory." *American Antiquity* 39: 597–607.

Pennington, R. 2001. "Hunter-Gatherer Demography." In *Hunter-Gatherers: Interdisciplinary Perspectives,* ed. C. Panter-Brick, R.H. Layton, and P.A. Rowley-Conwy, 170–204. Cambridge: Cambridge University Press.

Pennisi, E. 2008. "Bacteria Are Picky about Their Homes on Human Skin." *Science* 320, no. 5879: 1001.

Perry, S., J. Manson, L. Muniz, J. Gros-Louis, and L. Vigilant. 2008. "Kin-Biased Social Behaviour in Wild Adult Female White-Faced Capuchins, *Cebus capucinus*." *Animal Behaviour* 76: 187–99.

Pfeiffer, John E. 1982. *The Creative Explosion: An Inquiry into the Origins of Art and Religion*. New York: Harper and Row.

Pianka, E.R. 1988. *Evolutionary Ecology*. 4th ed. New York: Harper and Row.

Pinker, Steven. 1997. *How the Mind Works*. New York: Norton.

Pitte, J.R. 1991. *Gastronomie française: Histoire et géographie d'une passion*. Paris: Fayard.

Pitt-Rivers, Julian. 1977. "Women and Sanctuary in the Mediterranean." In *The Fate of Shechem, or The Politics of Sex: Essays in the Anthropology of the Mediterranean,* 113–25. Cambridge: Cambridge University Press.

Polanyi, Karl. 1944. *The Great Transformation*. New York: Rinehart.

Pope, Theresa. 1990. "The Reproductive Consequences of Male Cooperation in the Red Howler Monkey: Paternity Exclusion in Multi-Male and Single-Male Troops Using Genetic Markers." *Behavioral Ecology and Sociobiology* 27: 439–46.

———. 2000. "Reproductive Success Increases with Degree of Kinship in Cooperative Coalitions of Female Red Howler Monkeys (*Alouatta seniculus*)." *Behavioral Ecology and Sociobiology* 48: 253–67.

Postman, Neil. 1985. *Amusing Ourselves to Death: Public Discourse in the Age of Show Business.* New York: Viking.

Potts, R. 1984. "Home Bases and Early Hominids." *Scientific American* 72: 338–47.

Potts, R., and P. Shipman. 1981. "Cutmarks Made by Stone Tools on Bones from Olduvai George, Tanzania." *Nature* 291: 577–80.

Prestwich, J. 1860. "On the Occurrence of Flint Implements, Associated with the Remains of Animals of Extinct Species in Beds of a Late Geological Period, in France at Amiens and Abbeville, and in England at Hoxne." *Philosophical Transactions of the Royal Society of London* 150: 277–317.

Price, E.O. 1984. "Behavioral Aspects of Animal Domestication." *Quarterly Review of Biology* 59: 1–32.

Price, T.D. 1991. "The Mesolithic of Northern Europe." *Annual Review of Anthropology* 20: 211–33.

Proctor, R.N. 2003. "Three Roots of Human Recency: Molecular Anthropology, the Refigured Acheulean, and the UNESCO Response to Auschwitz." *Current Anthropology* 44: 213–39.

Pyne, S.J., P.L. Andrews, and R.D. Laven. 1996. *Introduction to Wildland Fire,* 2nd ed. New York: John Wiley and Sons.

Radcliffe-Brown, A.R. 1952. *Structure and Function in Primitive Society: Essays and Addresses.* New York: Free Press.

Rajpurohit, L., and V. Sommer. 1993. "Juvenile Male Emigration from Natal One-Male Troops in Hanuman Langurs." In *Juvenile Primates,* ed. M. Pereira and L. Fairbanks, 86–103. New York: Oxford University Press.

Ramachandran, V.S. 2006. "Mirror Neurons and Imitation Learning as the Driving Force behind 'The Great Leap Forward' in Human Evolution." *Edge,* www.edge.org/3rd_culture/ramachandran/ramachandran_p1.html, accessed 12 March 2010.

Ramachandran, V.S., and Sandra Blakeslee. 1998. *Phantoms in the Brain: Probing the Mysteries of the Human Mind.* New York: William Morrow.

Ranke, Leopold von. 1885. *Universal History: The Oldest Historical Group of Nations and the Greeks.* Edited by G.W. Prothero; translated by D.C. Tovey and G.W. Prothero. New York: Scribner.

Redding, R. 1988. "A General Explanation of Subsistence Change: From Hunting and Gathering to Food Production." *Journal of Anthropological Archaeology* 7: 56–97.

Redman, Charles L. 1978. *The Rise of Civilization: From Early Farmers to Urban Society in the Ancient Near East.* San Francisco: W.H. Freeman.

———. 1999. *Human Impact on Ancient Environments.* Tucson: University of Arizona Press.

Rendall, D. 2004. "'Recognizing' Kin: Mechanisms, Media, Minds, Modules, and Muddles." In *Kinship and Behavior in Primates,* ed. Bernard Chapais and C. Berman, 295–316. Oxford: Oxford University Press.

Renfrew, Colin. 2000. "At the Edge of Knowability: Towards a Prehistory of Languages." *Cambridge Archaeological Journal* 10: 7–34.

———. 2007. *Prehistory: The Making of the Human Mind*. London: Weidenfeld and Nicolson.

Renfrew, Colin, April McMahon, and Larry Trask, eds. 2000. *Time-Depth in Historical Linguistics*. 2 vols. Cambridge: McDonald Institute for Archaeological Research.

Richards, Audrey. 1941. "A Problem of Anthropological Approach." *Bantu Studies* 15: 45–52.

Richards, M., K. Harvati, V. Grimes, C.A. Smith, T. Smith, J.-J. Hublin, P. Karkanas, and E. Panagopoulou. 2008. "Strontium Isotope Evidence of Neanderthal Mobility at the Site of Lakonis, Greece, Using Laser-Ablation PIMMS." *Journal of Archaeological Science* 35: 1251–56.

Rick, Torben C., and Jon M. Erlandson. 2009. "Coastal Exploitation." *Science* 325, no. 5943: 952–53.

Rightmire, G. Philip, Adam P. Van Arsdale, and David Lordkipanidze. 2008. "Variation in the Mandibles from Dmanisi, Georgia." *Journal of Human Evolution* 54: 904–8.

Rindos, D. 1984. *The Origins of Agriculture: An Evolutionary Perspective*. Orlando, FL: Academic Press.

Roberts, Gareth. 2008. "Language and the Free-Rider Problem: An Experimental Paradigm." *Biological Theory* 3: 174–83.

Roberts, M.B., and S.A. Parfitt. 1999. *Boxgrove: A Middle Pleistocene Hominid Site at Eartham Quarry, Boxgrove, West Sussex*. London: English Heritage.

Roberts, R.G., and B.W. Brook. 2010. "And Then There Were None?" *Science* 327, no. 5964: 420–22.

Robinson, James Harvey. 1912. *The New History: Essays Illustrating the Modern Historical Outlook*. New York: Macmillan.

Rodseth, Lars, Richard Wrangham, Alisha Harrigan, and Barbara Smuts. 1991. "The Human Community as a Primate Society." *Current Anthropology* 32: 221–54.

Romm, James S. 1992. *The Edges of the Earth in Ancient Thought: Geography, Exploration, and Fiction*. Princeton, NJ: Princeton University Press.

Rossi, Paolo. 1984. *The Dark Abyss of Time: The History of the Earth and the History of Nations from Hooke to Vico*. Translated by Lydia G. Cochrane. Chicago: University of Chicago Press.

Rowlands, M. 2003. *Externalism: Putting Mind and World Back Together Again*. Chesham, U.K.: Acumen.

Rubin, Miri. 1991. *Corpus Christi: The Eucharist in Late Medieval Culture*. Cambridge: Cambridge University Press.

Rudwick, Martin. 2005. *Bursting the Limits of Time: The Reconstruction of Geohistory in the Age of Revolution*. Chicago: University of Chicago Press.

Ruff, C.B., E. Trinkaus, and T.W. Holliday. 1997. "Body Mass and Encephalization in Pleistocene *Homo*." *Nature* 387: 173–76.

Ruhlen, Merritt. 1987. *A Guide to the World's Languages*, vol. 1, *Classification*. Stanford, CA: Stanford University Press.

Sahlins, Marshall. 1958. *Social Stratification in Polynesia*. Seattle: University of Washington Press.

———. 1968. "Notes on the Original Affluent Society." In *Man the Hunter,* ed. Richard B. Lee and Irven DeVore, 85–89. Chicago: Aldine.

———. 1972. *Stone-Age Economics.* Chicago: Aldine.

———. 1976. *The Use and Abuse of Biology: An Anthropological Critique of Sociobiology.* Ann Arbor: University of Michigan Press.

Sakata, H. 1994. "How an Ant Decides to Prey on or to Attend Aphids." *Researches in Population Ecology* 36: 45–51.

Sanday, Peggy Reeves. 1986. *Divine Hunger: Cannibalism as a Cultural System.* Cambridge: Cambridge University Press.

Sangma, Milton S. 1979. *History and Culture of the Garos.* New Delhi: Books Today.

Sankoff, Gillian, and Hélène Blondeau. 2008. "Language Change across the Lifespan: /r/ in Montreal French." *Language* 83: 560–88.

Sapolsky, Robert M. 2004. *Why Zebras Don't Get Ulcers.* 3rd ed. New York: Times Books.

Savard, M., M. Nesbitt, and M.K. Jones. 2006. "The Role of Wild Grasses in Subsistence and Sedentism: New Evidence from the Northern Fertile Crescent." *World Archaeology* 38: 179–96.

Scarre, C., ed. 2005. *The Human Past.* London: Thames and Hudson.

Scarry, C. Margaret, and Elizabeth J. Reitz. 1990. "Herbs, Fish, Scum and Vermin: Subsistence Strategies in Sixteenth-Century Spanish Florida." In *Columbian Consequences,* vol. 2, *Archaeological and Historical Perspectives on the Spanish Borderlands East,* ed. David Hurst Thomas, 343–54. Washington, DC: Smithsonian Institution Press.

Scarry, Elaine. 1985. *The Body in Pain: The Making and Unmaking of the World.* New York: Oxford University Press.

Schedel, Hartmann. 1966 [1493]. *Das Buch der Chroniken und Geschichten (Liber Chronicarum, or the Nuremberg Chronicle).* Facsimile reprint. New York: Brussel and Brussel.

Schmidt, Klaus. 2000. "Göbekli Tepe, Southeastern Turkey: A Preliminary Report on the 1995–1999 Excavations." *Paléorient* 26: 45–54.

Schneider, David. 1984. *A Critique of the Study of Kinship.* Ann Arbor: University of Michigan Press.

Schubert, Glendon A. 1989. *Evolutionary Politics.* Carbondale: Southern Illinois University Press.

Scott, James C. 2009. *The Art of Not Being Governed: An Anarchist History of Upland Southeast Asia.* New Haven, CT: Yale University Press.

Searls, David. 2003. "Trees of Life and of Language." *Nature* 426: 391–92.

Semaw, S., P. Renne, J.W.K. Harris, C.S. Feibel, R.L. Bernor, N. Fesseha, and K. Mowbray. 1997. "2.5-Million-Year-Old Stone Tools from Gona, Ethiopia." *Nature* 385: 333–36.

Shady Solis, Ruth, J. Haas, and W. Creamer. 2001. "Dating Caral: A Prehistoric Site in the Supe Valley on the Central Coast of Peru." *Science* 292, no. 5517: 723–26.

Shennan, S. 2010. "Comparative Anthropology and Human Inequality." *Current Anthropology* 51: 115–16.

Sherratt, Andrew. 1981. "Plough and Pastoralism: Aspects of the Secondary Products Revolution." In *Pattern of the Past: Studies in Honour of David Clarke,* ed. I. Hodder, G. Issac, and N. Hammond, 261–305. Cambridge: Cambridge University Press.

Shipman, P. 2009. "The Woof at the Door." *American Scientist* 97: 286–89.

Silk, J. 2001. "Ties that Bind: The Role of Kinship in Primate Societies." In *New Directions in Anthropological Kinship,* ed. L. Stone, 71–92. Lanham, MD: Rowman and Littlefield.

———. 2002. "Kin Selection in Primate Groups." *International Journal of Primatology* 23: 849–75.

Silk, J.B., S.C. Alberts, and J. Altmann. 2003. "Social Bonds of Female Baboons Enhance Infant Survival." *Science* 302, no. 5648: 1231–34.

———. 2006. "Social Relationships among Adult Female Baboons (*Papio cynocephalus*), II: Variation in the Quality and Stability of Social Bonds." *Behavioral Ecology and Sociobiology* 61: 197–204.

Simpson, A.W. Brian. 1984. *Cannibalism and the Common Law: The Story of the Tragic Last Voyage of the* Mignonette *and the Strange Legal Proceedings to Which It Gave Rise.* Chicago: University of Chicago Press.

Simpson, Bob. 2000. "Imagined Genetic Communities: Ethnicity and Essentialism in the Twenty-first Century." *Anthropology Today* 16: 3–6.

Sims, Lionel. 2009. "Entering, and Returning from, the Underworld: Reconstituting Silbury Hill by Combining a Quantified Landscape Phenomenology with Archaeoastronomy." *Journal of the Royal Anthropological Institute* 15: 386–408.

Smail, Daniel Lord. 2008. *On Deep History and the Brain.* Berkeley: University of California Press.

Smail, Daniel Lord, Clare Haru Crowston, Kristen B. Neuschel, and Carol Symes. 2011. "History and the Telescoping of Time: A Disciplinary Forum." *French Historical Studies* 34: 1–55.

Smith, E.A., K. Hill, F.W. Marlowe, D. Nolin, P. Wiessner, M. Gurven, S. Bowles, M. Borgerhoff Mulder, T. Hertz, and A. Bell. 2010. "Wealth Transmission and Inequality among Hunter-Gatherers." *Current Anthropology* 51: 19–34.

Smith, K., S. Alberts, and J. Altmann. 2003. "Wild Female Baboons Bias Their Social Behaviour towards Paternal Half-Sisters." *Proceedings of the Royal Society of London, Series B* 270: 503–10.

Smuts, B. 1985. *Sex and Friendship in Baboons.* Hawthorne, NY: Aldine de Gruyter.

Soares, P., L. Ermini, N. Thomson, M. Mormina, T. Rito, A. Röhl, A. Salas, S. Oppenheimer, V. Macaulay, and M.B. Richards. 2009. "Correcting for Purifying Selection: An Improved Human Mitochondrial Molecular Clock." *American Journal of Human Genetics* 84: 740–59.

Soffer, O. 1985. "Patterns of Intensification as Seen from the Upper Paleolithic of the Central Russian Plain." In *Prehistoric Hunter-Gatherers: The Emergence of Cultural Complexity,* ed. T.D. Price and J.A. Brown, 235–70. San Diego, CA: Academic Press.

Soffer, O., J.M. Adovasio, and D.C. Hyland. 2000. "The 'Venus' Figurines: Textiles, Basketry and Status in the Upper Palaeolithic." *Current Anthropology* 41: 511–37.

Spencer, Herbert. 1967 [1882]. *The Evolution of Society: Selections from Herbert Spencer's Principles of Sociology.* Edited by R. Carneiro. Chicago: University of Chicago Press.

Speth, J.D. 2006. "Housekeeping, Neandertal-Style: Hearth Placement and Midden Formation in Kebara Cave (Israel)." In *Transitions before the Transition: Evolution and Stability in the Middle Palaeolithic and Middle Stone Age; Interdisciplinary Contributions to Archaeology,* ed. E. Hovers and S.L. Kuhn, 171–88. New York: Springer.

Spiegel, Gabrielle M. 1990. "History, Historicism, and the Social Logic of the Text in the Middle Ages." *Speculum* 65: 59–86.

Spier, Fred. 2010. *Big History and the Future of Humanity.* Malden, MA: Wiley-Blackwell.

Spriggs, Matthew. 1991. "'Preceded by Forest': Changing Interpretations of Landscape Change on Kaho'olawe." *Asian Perspectives* 30: 71–116.

Spufford, Peter. 1988. *Money and Its Use in Medieval Europe.* Cambridge: Cambridge University Press.

Stamenov, Maxim I., and Vittorio Gallese, eds. 2002. *Mirror Neurons and the Evolution of Brain and Language.* Amsterdam: John Benjamins.

Stanford, Craig B., and Henry T. Bunn. 2001. *Meat-Eating and Human Evolution.* Oxford: Oxford University Press.

Stanley, Steven M. 1998. *Children of the Ice Age.* New York: Freeman.

Steadman, D.W. 1989. "Extinction of Birds in Eastern Polynesia: A Review of the Record, and Comparisons with Other Pacific Island Groups." *Journal of Archaeological Science* 16: 177–205.

Stein, Gil. 1999. *Rethinking World-Systems: Diasporas, Colonies, and Interaction in Uruk Mesopotamia.* Tucson: University of Arizona Press.

Stiner, M.C. 1994. *Honor among Thieves: A Zooarchaeological Study of Neandertal Ecology.* Princeton, NJ: Princeton University Press.

———. 1999. "Trends in Palaeolithic Mollusk Exploitation at Riparo Mochi (Balzi Rossi, Italy): Food and Ornaments from the Aurignacian through Epigravettian." *Antiquity* 73: 735–54.

———. 2001. "Thirty Years on the 'Broad Spectrum Revolution' and Paleolithic Demography." *Proceedings of the National Academy of Sciences of the United States* 98, no. 13: 6993–96.

———. 2002. "Carnivory, Coevolution, and the Geographic Spread of the Genus *Homo.*" *Journal of Archaeological Research* 10: 1–63.

———. 2003. "'Standardization' in Upper Paleolithic Ornaments at the Coastal Sites of Riparo Mochi and Üçagizli Cave." In *The Chronology of the Aurignacian and of the Transitional Technocomplexes: Dating, Stratigraphies, Cultural Implications,* ed. J. Zilhão and F. d'Errico, 49–59. Lisbon: Instituto Português de Arqueologia.

Stiner, M.C., and S.L. Kuhn. 2006. "Changes in the 'Connectedness' and Resilience of Paleolithic Societies in Mediterranean Ecosystems." *Human Ecology* 34: 693–712.

———. 2010. "Tracking the Carbon Footprint of Paleolithic Societies in Mediterranean Ecosystems." In *Human Ecology: Contemporary Research and Practice,* ed. D.G. Bates and J. Tucker, 109–26. New York: Springer.

Stiner, M. C., N. D. Munro, and T. A. Surovell. 2000. "The Tortoise and the Hare: Small-Game Use, the Broad Spectrum Revolution, and Palaeolithic Demography." *Current Anthropology* 41: 39–73.

Stiner, M. C., N. D. Munro, T. A. Surovell, E. Tchernov, and O. Bar-Yosef. 1999. "Paleolithic Population Growth Pulses Evidenced by Small Animal Exploitation." *Science* 283, no. 5399: 190–94.

Strasser, Susan. 1999. *Waste and Want: A Social History of Trash*. New York: Metropolitan Books.

Stringer, C. 2006. *Homo Britannicus: The Incredible Story of Human Life in Britain*. London: Penguin.

Stuard, Susan Mosher. 2006. *Gilding the Market: Luxury and Fashion in Fourteenth-Century Italy*. Philadelphia: University of Pennsylvania Press.

Stuart-Smith, Jane, Claire Timmins, and Fiona Tweedie. 2007. "Talkin' Jockney: Variation and Change in Glaswegian Accent." *Journal of Sociolinguistics* 11: 221–60.

Sumption, Jonathan. 1975. *Pilgrimage: An Image of Mediaeval Religion*. London: Faber and Faber.

Swadesh, Morris. 1952. "Lexicostatistic Dating of Prehistoric Ethnic Contacts." *Proceedings of the American Philosophical Society* 96: 452–63.

———. 1972. "What is Glottochronology?" In *The Origin and Diversification of Language*, ed. Joel Sherzer, 271–84. London: Routledge and Kegan Paul.

Taborin, Y., 1993. "Shells of the French Aurignacian and Perigordian." In *Before Lascaux: The Complex Record of the Early Upper Paleolithic*, ed. H. Knecht, A. Pike-Tay, and R. White, 211–29. Boca Raton, FL: CRC Press.

Tainter, J. A. 2000. "Problem Solving: Complexity, History, Sustainability." *Population and Environment* 22: 3–41.

Taylor, S., L. Cousino Klein, B. Lewis, T. Gruenewald, R. Gurung, and J. Updegraff. 2000. "Biobehavioral Responses to Stress in Females: Tend-and-Befriend, Not Fight-or-Flight." *Psychological Review* 107: 411–29.

Tchernov, E. 1984. "Commensal Animals and Human Sedentism in the Middle East." In *Animals and Archaeology*, vol. 3, *Early Herders and Their Flocks*, ed. J. Clutton-Brock and C. Grigson, 91–115. Oxford: B.A.R.

Tchernov, E., and F. F. Valla. 1997. "Two New Dogs, and Other Natufian Dogs, from the Southern Levant." *Journal of Archaeological Science* 24: 65–95.

Thomason, Sarah Grey. 2001. *An Introduction to Language Contact*. Edinburgh: Edinburgh University Press.

———. 2003. "Contact as a Source of Language Change." In *The Handbook of Historical Linguistics*, ed. Brian D. Joseph and Richard D. Janda, 687–712. Oxford: Blackwell.

Thompson, E. P. 1963. *The Making of the English Working Class*. London: V. Gollancz.

Tjon Sie Fat, Franklin E. 1998. "On the Formal Analysis of 'Dravidian,' 'Iroquois,' and 'Generational' Varieties as Nearly Associational Combinations." In *Transformations of Kinship*, ed. M. Godelier, Thomas R. Trautmann, and F. E. Tjon Sie Fat, 59–93. Washington, DC: Smithsonian Institution Press.

Tomasello, Michael, Malinda Carpenter, and Ulf Liszkowski. 2007. "A New Look at Infant Pointing." *Child Development* 78: 705–22.

Toth, Nicholas, and Kathy Schick. 2006. *The Oldowan: Case Studies into the Earliest Stone Age.* Gosport, IN: Stone Age Institute.

Trautmann, Thomas R. 1987. *Lewis Henry Morgan and the Invention of Kinship.* Berkeley: University of California Press.

———. 1992. "The Revolution in Ethnological Time." *Man* n.s. 27: 379–97.

———. 1997. *Aryans and British India.* Berkeley: University of California Press.

———. 2006. *Languages and Nations: The Dravidian Proof in Colonial Madras.* Berkeley: University of California Press.

Trevor-Roper, Hugh R. 1965. *The Rise of Christian Europe.* New York: Harcourt, Brace, Jovanovich.

Trouillot, Michel-Rolf. 1991. "Anthropology and the Savage Slot: The Poetics and Politics of Otherness." In *Recapturing Anthropology: Working in the Present,* ed. Richard G. Fox, 17–44. Santa Fe, NM: School of American Research Press.

Trut, L.N. 1999. "Early Canid Domestication: The Farm-Fox Experiment." *American Scientist* 87: 160–69.

Tsetskhladze, G.R., ed. 2006. *Greek Colonization: An Account of Greek Colonies and Other Settlements Overseas.* Leiden: Brill.

Turney, C.S.M., T.F. Flannery, R.G. Roberts, C. Reid, L.K. Fifield, T.F.G. Higham, Z. Jacobs, et al. 2008. "Late-Surviving Megafauna in Tasmania, Australia, Implicate Human Involvement in Their Extinction." *Proceedings of the National Academy of Sciences of the United States* 105, no. 34: 12150–53.

Tylor, E.B. 1871. *Primitive Culture: Researches into the Development of Mythology, Philosophy, Religion, Art, and Custom,* 2 vols. London: John Murray.

Van Andel, T.H., and N.C. Runnels. 1995. "The Earliest Farmers in Europe." *Antiquity* 69: 481–500.

Vander Wall, S.B. 1990. *Food Hoarding in Animals.* Chicago: University of Chicago Press.

Vanhaeren, M., and F. d'Errico. 2006. "Aurignacian Ethno-linguistic Geography of Europe Revealed by Personal Ornaments." *Journal of Archaeological Science* 33: 1105–28.

Van Horn, R., J. Altmann, and S. Alberts. 2008. "Can't Get There From Here: Inferring Kinship from Pairwise Genetic Relatedness." *Animal Behaviour* 75: 1173–80.

Van Loon, Hendrik W. 1921. *The Story of Mankind.* New York: Boni and Liveright.

Van Valen, Leigh. 1973. "A New Evolutionary Law." *Evolutionary Theory* 1: 1–30.

Van Valkenburgh, B. 2001. "The Dog-Eat-Dog World of Carnivores: A Review of Past and Present Carnivore Community Dynamics." In *The Early Human Diet: The Role of Meat,* ed. C. Stanford and H. Bunn, 101–21. Oxford: Oxford University Press.

Vaughan, Richard. 2002. *Philip the Good: The Apogee of Burgundy,* 2nd ed. Woodbridge, U.K.: Boydell Press.

Veblen, Thorstein. 2007 [1899]. *The Theory of the Leisure Class: An Economic Study in the Evolution of Institutions.* New York: Oxford University Press.

Viveiros de Castro, Eduardo. 1998. "Dravidian and Related Kinship Systems." In *Transformations of Kinship,* ed. M. Godelier, Thomas R. Trautmann, and F.E. Tjon Sie Fat, 332–85. Washington DC: Smithsonian Institution Press.

de Waal, Frans B.M. 2001. *The Ape and the Sushi Master: Cultural Reflections by a Primatologist.* New York: Basic Books.

———. 2007 [1982]. *Chimpanzee Politics: Power and Sex among Apes.* Baltimore, MD: Johns Hopkins University Press.

Waley, Arthur, trans. 1919. *More Translations from the Chinese.* New York: Knopf.

Warde, Paul. 2007. *Energy Consumption in England and Wales, 1560–2001.* Naples: Consiglio Nazionale delle Richerche.

Wasylikowa, K., J. Harlan, R. Evans, F. Wendorf, R. Schild, A.E. Close, H. Krolik, and R.A. Housley. 1993. "Examination of Botanical Remains from Early Neolithic Houses at Nabta Playa, Western Egypt, with Special Reference to Sorghum Grains." In *The Archaeology of Africa: Food, Metal, and Towns,* ed. Thurstan Shaw, Paul Sinclair, Bassey Andah, and Alex Okpoko, 154–64. London: Routledge.

Watts, David P., and John C. Mitani. 2000. "Infanticide and Cannibalism by Male Chimpanzees at Ngogo, Kibale National Park, Uganda." *Primates* 41: 357–65.

———. 2002. "Hunting Behavior of Chimpanzees at Ngogo, Kibale National Park, Uganda." *International Journal of Primatology* 23: 1–28.

Wayne, R.K., J.A. Leonard, and C. Vilà. 2006. "Genetic Analysis of Dog Domestication." In *Documenting Domestication: New Genetic and Archaeological Paradigms,* ed. M.A. Zeder, D.G. Bradley, E. Emshwiller, and B.D. Smith, 279–93. Berkeley: University of California Press.

Weiner, Annette B. 1976. *Women of Value, Men of Renown.* Austin: University of Texas Press.

———. 1978. "Trobriand Kinship from Another View: The Reproductive Power of Women and Men." *Man* 14: 328–48.

———. 1987. *The Trobrianders of Papua New Guinea.* New York: Holt, Rinehart and Winston.

———. 1992. *Inalienable Possessions: The Paradox of Keeping-while-Giving.* Berkeley: University of California Press.

Wheeler, Peter E. 1991. "The Thermoregulatory Advantages of Hominid Bipedalism in Open Equatorial Environments: The Contribution of Increased Convective Heat Loss and Cutaneous Evaporative Cooling." *Journal of Human Evolution* 21: 107–15.

White, Hayden. 1981. "The Value of Narrativity in the Representation of Reality." In *On Narrative,* ed. W.J.T. Mitchell, 1–23. Chicago: University of Chicago Press.

White, R., 1982. "Rethinking the Middle/Upper Paleolithic Transition." *Current Anthropology* 23: 169–92.

———. 1989. "Production Complexity and Standardization of Early Aurignacian Bead and Pendant Manufacture: Evolutionary Implications." In *The Human Revolution: Behavioural and Biological Perspectives on the Origins of Modern Humans,* ed. P. Mellars and C. Stringer, 366–90. Princeton, NJ: Princeton University Press.

———. 1993. "Technological and Social Dimensions of 'Aurignacian-Age' Body

Ornaments across Europe." In *Before Lascaux: The Complex Record of the Early Upper Paleolithic,* ed. H. Knecht, A. Pike-Tay, and R. White, 277–300. Boca Raton, FL: CRC Press.

———. 2003. *Prehistoric Art: The Symbolic Journey of Humankind.* New York: Harry N. Abrams.

———. 2006. "The Women of Brassempouy: A Century of Research and Interpretation." *Journal of Archaeological Method and Theory* 13: 251–304.

White, Richard. 1995. *The Organic Machine.* New York: Hill and Wang.

Whittle, A. 1996. *Europe in the Neolithic: The Creation of New Worlds.* Cambridge: Cambridge University Press.

———. 2003. *The Archaeology of People: Dimensions of Neolithic Life.* London: Routledge.

Wichmann, Søren. 2008. "The Emerging Field of Language Dynamics." *Language and Linguistics Compass* 2: 442–55.

Widdig, A. 2007. "Paternal Kin Discrimination: The Evidence and Likely Mechanisms." *Biological Reviews* 82: 319–34.

Widdig, A., P. Nurnberg, M. Krawczak, W.J. Streich, and F. Bercovitch. 2001. "Paternal Relatedness and Age Proximity Regulate Social Relationships among Adult Female Rhesus Macaques." *Proceedings of the National Academy of Sciences of the United States* 98, no. 24: 13769–73.

Wiessner, P. 1982. "Risk, Reciprocity and Social Influence on !Kung San Economics." In *Politics and History in Band Societies,* ed. E. Leacock and R. Lee, 61–84. Cambridge: Cambridge University Press.

———. 1989. "Style and the Changing Relations between Individual and Society." In *The Meanings of Things: Material Culture and Symbolic Expression,* ed. Ian Hodder, 56–63. London: Unwin Hyman.

Williams, Henry Smith. 1912. *The Conquest of Nature.* New York: Goodhue.

Wilson, Charles. 1976. "Economic Conditions." In *New Cambridge Modern History,* vol. 12, ed. F.H. Hinsley, 49–75. Cambridge: Cambridge University Press.

Wilson, D. 1862. *Prehistoric Man.* London: Macmillan.

Wilson, Edward O. 1975. *Sociobiology: The New Synthesis.* Cambridge, MA: Belknap Press.

Wilson, Peter J. 1988. *The Domestication of the Human Species.* New Haven, CT: Yale University Press.

Wilson, W.H., and A.J. Burks. 1955. *The Chicken and the Egg.* New York: Coward-McCann.

Winter, Denis. 1978. *Death's Men: Soldiers of the Great War.* London: Allen Lane.

Winterhalder, B. 1998. "Social Foraging and the Behavioral Ecology of Intragroup Resource Transfers." *Evolutionary Anthropology* 5: 46–57.

Winterhalder, B., and C. Goland. 1993. "On Population, Foraging Efficiency, and Plant Domestication." *Current Anthropology* 34: 710–15.

Wobst, H.M. 1977. "Stylistic Behavior and Information Exchange." In *Papers for the Director: Research Essays in Honor of James B. Griffin,* ed. C.E. Cleland, 317–42. Ann Arbor: Museum of Anthropology, University of Michigan.

Wolf, Eric R. 1982. *Europe and the People without History.* Berkeley: University of California Press.

Worsaae, J.J.A. 1849. *The Primeval Antiquities of Denmark.* London: Parker.

Wrangham, Richard W. 2009. *Catching Fire: How Cooking Made Us Human.* New York: Basic Books.

Wright, K.I. 1994. "Ground-Stone Tools and Hunter-Gatherer Subsistence in Southwest Asia: Implications for the Transition to Farming." *American Antiquity* 59: 238–63.

Yates, Frances A. 1966. *The Arts of Memory.* Chicago: University of Chicago Press.

Zalasiewicz, Jan, Mark Williams, Alan Smith, Tiffany L. Barry, Angela L. Coe, Paul R. Bown, Patrick Brenchley, et al. 2008. "Are We Now Living in the Anthropocene?" *GSA Today* 8: 4–8.

Zeder, M.A. 2006. "Central Questions in the Domestication of Plants and Animals." *Evolutionary Anthropology* 15: 105–17.

Zeder, M., and B. Hesse. 2000. "The Initial Domestication of Goats (*Capra hircus*) in the Zagros Mountains 10,000 Years Ago." *Science* 287, no. 5461: 2254–57.

Zeder, M.A., D.G. Bradley, E. Emshwiller, and B.D. Smith. 2006. "Documenting Domestication: Bringing Together Plants, Animals, Archaeology, and Genetics." In *Documenting Domestication: New Genetic and Archaeological Paradigms,* ed. Melinda A. Zeder, Daniel G. Bradley, Eve Emshwiller, and Bruce D. Smith, 1–12. Berkeley, CA: University of California Press.

Zohary, D. 1996. "The Mode of Domestication of Founder Crops of Southwest Asian Agriculture." In *The Origins and Spread of Agriculture and Pastoralism in Eurasia,* ed. D.R. Harris, 142–58. Washington, DC: Smithsonian Institution Press.

Zvelebil, Marek, ed. 1986. *Hunters in Transition: Mesolithic Societies of Temperate Eurasia and Their Transition to Farming.* Cambridge: Cambridge University Press.

Contributors

TIMOTHY EARLE is professor and chair of anthropology at Northwestern University. He is an active field archaeologist, having conducted field projects in Hawaii, Peru, Argentina, Denmark, and currently Hungary. His work focuses on the contrasting economic foundations for the political evolution of chiefdoms and states. He is the author of *How Chiefs Come to Power* (1997), *Bronze Age Economics* (2002), and, with Kristian Kristiansen, *Organising Bronze Age Societies* (2010).

GILLIAN FEELEY-HARNIK, professor of anthropology at the University of Michigan, is interested in all aspects of human social-cultural life. Her books combining ethnographic and historical research include *A Green Estate: Restoring Independence in Madagascar* (1991) and *The Lord's Table: The Meaning of Food in Early Judaism and Christianity* (2nd ed., 1994). She is currently working on two related book manuscripts on kinship and ecology in nineteenth-century Great Britain and the United States, based on archival research.

FELIPE FERNÁNDEZ-ARMESTO is the William P. Reynolds Professor in Arts and Letters at the University of Notre Dame. He has won, inter alia, Spain's national prizes for research in geography and gastronomy, the World History Association's Book Prize, and the John Carter Brown and Caird medals for work in colonial and maritime history, respectively. His books have appeared in twenty-five languages.

CLIVE GAMBLE is professor of geography in the Centre for Quaternary Research at Royal Holloway, University of London. He spent many years at the University of Southampton, where he founded the Centre for the Archaeology of Human Origins. He is author of *Timewalkers: The Prehistory of Global Colonisation* (1993); *The Palaeolithic Societies of Europe* (1999), which won the Society for American Archaeology Book Award in 2000; and *Origins and Revolutions:*

Human Identity in Earliest Prehistory (2007). He is a codirector of the British Academy Centenary research project "Lucy to Language: The Archaeology of the Social Brain."

APRIL MCMAHON is Forbes Professor of Linguistics and English Language as well as vice principal for planning, resources, and research policy at the University of Edinburgh. She is coeditor of the journal *English Language and Linguistics*. Her research focuses on the interaction of phonological theory and sound change and methods for the comparison and classification of languages and dialects. Her books include *Lexical Phonology and the History of English* (2000).

JOHN C. MITANI is professor of anthropology at the University of Michigan. For more than thirty years he has conducted fieldwork investigating the behavior of our closest living relatives, the apes. His current research involves studies of cooperation and competition in an extremely large community of wild chimpanzees at Ngogo, Kibale National Park, Uganda.

HENDRIK POINAR, an evolutionary biologist specializing in ancient DNA, is an associate professor in the Department of Anthropology and the Department of Pathology and Molecular Medicine and director of the Ancient DNA Centre at McMaster University, Ontario. He is the author of more than forty publications, including book chapters and articles in journals such as *Nature* and *Science*.

ANDREW SHRYOCK is Arthur F. Thurnau Professor of anthropology at the University of Michigan. He has done ethnographic fieldwork in Yemen and Jordan and among Arab immigrants in Detroit. His books include *Nationalism and the Genealogical Imagination: Oral History and Textual Authority in Tribal Jordan* (1997), *Arab Detroit: From Margin to Mainstream* (2000), and *Islamophobia/ Islamophilia: Beyond the Politics of Enemy and Friend* (2010).

DANIEL LORD SMAIL is professor of history at Harvard University, where he works on deep human history and, at smaller timescales, the history and anthropology of Mediterranean societies from 1200 to 1600. He has special interests in state formation, violence, and material culture. His books include *On Deep History and the Brain* (2008).

MARY C. STINER is professor of archaeology in the School of Anthropology at the University of Arizona. She conducts archaeological research on Paleolithic and early Neolithic sites across the Mediterranean region. Her interests include human evolution and paleoecology, ancient hunting practices, animal domestication, and early ornamental traditions.

THOMAS R. TRAUTMANN is professor emeritus of history and anthropology at the University of Michigan. His fields of interest are the history of ancient India, kinship and marriage in India, the history of anthropology, and the history of Orientalist scholarship in British India. He is the author of *Lewis Henry Morgan and the Invention of Kinship* (1987), *Aryans and British India* (1997), and *Languages and Nations: The Dravidian Proof in Colonial Madras* (2006).

Index

Page numbers in italic indicate illustrations.

COMPOSITOR   BookMatters, Berkeley
ILLUSTRATOR   Bill Nelson
INDEXER   Alexander Trotter
PRINTER/BINDER   Sheridan Books, Inc.